STUDIES IN EARLY ENGLISH HISTORY
Edited by H. P. R. Finberg

VI

THE EARLY CHARTERS OF NORTHERN ENGLAND AND THE NORTH MIDLANDS

STUDIES IN EARLY ENGLISH HISTORY

KING EADWIG TO HIS THEGN ÆTHELNOTH. GRANT OF LAND AT DARLASTON, NEAR STONE, STAFFORDSHIRE. A.D. 956.

Burton Charter No. XVII. William Salt Library, Stafford, MS. 84/1/41.

THE EARLY CHARTERS
OF NORTHERN ENGLAND
AND THE NORTH MIDLANDS

by

C. R. HART

M.A., M.B., D.Litt., F.R.Hist.S.

LEICESTER UNIVERSITY PRESS

1975

First published in 1975 by
Leicester University Press
Distributed in North America by
Humanities Press Inc., New Jersey

Copyright © Leicester University Press 1975

Set in Monotype Perpetua
Printed in Great Britain by
Western Printing Services Ltd, Bristol
Bound by
G. and J. Kitcat Ltd, London

ISBN 0 7185 1131 X

The publication of this book has been assisted
by a grant from the Twenty-Seven Foundation

To

MONICA, NICHOLAS, AND PENELOPE

CONTENTS

INTRODUCTION

THIS BOOK carries to a stage nearer completion an
enterprise begun by Professor H. P. R. Finberg, whose
Early Charters of Devon and Cornwall first appeared in 1953,
and listed for those two counties all the known land charters of
pre-Conquest date. Since then, successive volumes have covered
Essex, the west Midlands, Wessex, and eastern England. The
present hand-list extends the survey to six counties in the
central and north Midlands, and to the whole of England north
of the River Trent. It will be followed by Dr Margaret Gelling's
volume on the Thames Valley, leaving Kent and Sussex alone
of the English counties not covered by the series.

As the survey has proceeded, various conventions have been
developed for summarizing the mass of material, and criteria
have been established for the inclusion of particular entries in
the hand-lists. For our purpose the term 'charter' embraces
all forms of contemporary written records of land transactions,
but only in a few cases does the original document itself
survive; for the most part we have to be content with a post-
Conquest copy, very often defective and occasionally incorporating spurious material. A code of symbols has been
devised to give some indication as to the authenticity of
surviving texts, but this study is still in its infancy, and until a
fresh edition of the whole *corpus* of the charters is produced,
it will often be impossible to reach a final judgement on the
validity of a particular text.

In addition to the many records surviving in charter form,
details of early land transactions are sometimes incorporated in
narrative sources. For Northumbria these are sufficiently numerous to warrant treatment in a separate chapter. A further
chapter has been devoted to a tract reciting the history of
certain estates of the see of Durham in the eleventh century.

THE BURTON CHARTERS

Central to the study of early land tenure in the north
Midlands lies the impressive collection of pre-Conquest

diplomas whose texts were preserved at Burton Abbey throughout the Middle Ages. These much-neglected charters first came to my attention in the early 1960s, as a result of an investigation into the fiscal system within the Five Boroughs and the Northern Danelaw. When Professor Finberg invited me to undertake the present volume in 1966, I determined to include within it a full edition of the entire Burton *corpus*.

Permission to publish was readily granted, photographs and photostats were obtained, and the edition was well under way, when a year later it came to my notice that Mr P. H. (now Professor) Sawyer had recently decided to embark upon the same project. I wrote to him immediately, but he was in America at the time, and it was not until December that year that he was able to visit me to discuss the situation. He then asked me to abandon my edition.

By then I had put in a substantial volume of work on the charters, and because of their importance for the wider study with which my book was concerned, I felt unable to accede fully to his request. After discussion with Professor Finberg, however, I agreed to limit my edition to those texts that were either unpublished or edited from inferior sources. Since we reached agreement on this matter, Professor Sawyer and I have worked quite independently of each other. It will be of interest, and I hope instructive, to compare our treatment of these charters, when Professor Sawyer's edition eventually appears.

HAND-LISTS AND EDITIONS OF ANGLO-SAXON CHARTERS

For nearly a century now, scholars have bemoaned the lack of a satisfactory edition of the Anglo-Saxon charters.[1] The gap is a serious one, affecting the quality of many modern studies in our early language and literature, in archaeology, numismatics, art history, palaeography, topography, and a number of other related disciplines. It is made worse by the circumstance that a growing body of local and national historians are unequipped with ordinary classical Latin, much less medieval

---

[1] Chaplais 1965, pp. 48–9.

Latin and Old English. The number of scholars who can utilize with ease an Anglo-Saxon diploma as part of their source material has never been large, and shows no sign of increasing.

With this in mind, the series in which this volume appears was planned as a pilot survey of the whole *corpus* of the charters, to provide an epitome for those whose main interests lie outside the range of charter diplomatic, and to ease the way for later workers in the field.

The basic classification we have adopted is topographical, enabling a picture to be built up of the charter collections pertaining to particular regions, which can be compared one with the other. Charters are listed by counties as they existed before the reorganization of local government in 1974. This topographical approach is carried further in detailed studies of the charter boundaries – 28 boundaries have been elucidated so far in this series and in subsidiary studies, and the present volume adds a further 12 to the total. There have also been many place-name identifications. The hidage of each estate is quoted. The royal style is recited in full for each charter appearing in the hand-lists. An assessment is attempted of the authenticity of each text. In many cases origins of the formulas appearing in the charters are discussed. Often the witness lists are analysed, and biographical details are supplied – nearly 300 biographies appear in the present volume. The collections of such major repositories as Winchester, Worcester, Thorney, and Burton have received detailed treatment. A large number of texts, some previously unrecorded, have been edited in this series for the first time. Lost texts are listed and discussed.

Meanwhile Professor Sawyer has published an annotated list and bibliography of all the known Anglo-Saxon charters (Royal Historical Society, 1968). The substance of this valuable book lies in its complete listing of the manuscript sources for each charter. To these he has appended references to the printed texts, and a selection, which does not pretend to completeness, of comments and *obiter dicta* by various scholars. In smaller type than the body of the text Professor Sawyer prints a concise summary of each charter, omitting any reference to the royal style, the hidage assessment, and considerations involved in the grant. His book is thus essentially a guide – and one for which editors may well be grateful – to the manuscript sources of Anglo-Saxon charters; but it is not, and does not claim to be, a guide to the charters themselves.

The reader who has followed me to this point is now in a position to decide for himself how far Professor Whitelock was justified in declaring that Professor Sawyer's book has 'superseded' our hand-lists.[1]

A project is now afoot for a complete edition of the charters, sponsored jointly by the British Academy and the Royal Historical Society. It is to be published according to the charter repositories; presumably a volume will be devoted to each major monastic collection. Let no one imagine that this welcome edition, when completed – perhaps thirty years hence – will be definitive. The study of the charters is still in its infancy, and far too much remains to be done for final pronouncements to be possible in the foreseeable future. Moreover, to base an edition on the repositories means that many of the volumes will have to deal with a very mixed bag of texts, for charters issued from each particular scriptorium were soon widely dispersed, and the surviving texts are often distributed over several archive collections. Ultimately, the only system of classification likely to lead to effective and durable coverage of the whole *corpus* is not topographical, nor archival, but chronological, dealing with individual kingdoms up to the time of the Danish settlement, and the country as a whole thereafter.

THE PRINCIPLES OF CHARTER CRITICISM

Before the ultimate can be achieved in the field of Anglo-Saxon charter criticism, an enormous amount of groundwork has still to be covered. The study of charter Latin is still rudimentary, and as yet only the most superficial investigation has been made into questions of diplomatic. There is scope for much more comparative work with Continental material. Palaeography has received more attention, but there are still

---

[1] F. M. Stenton, *Anglo-Saxon England* (3rd edn, 1971), p. 702.

great gaps in our knowledge – little study has been devoted to the evidential value of chrismons and endorsements, to give two simple examples. As yet, no one has examined the significance of the order of appearance in the witness lists of ealdormen, bishops, abbots, and (above all) thegns, even in a particular group of texts, much less the whole *corpus*; yet this can be a fundamental test of authenticity.

In far too many cases, the topography of individual charters has been insufficiently examined. The necessity for placing each charter in its correct topographical setting has been demonstrated over and over again. Until this is achieved, the historical value of the text cannot be properly assessed, nor can its authenticity be fully established. There is still room for detailed place-name studies, and as yet the correlation of archaeological and charter evidence has hardly been attempted.

It will be a long while before we can assign with confidence each individual charter to its particular scribe or scriptorium. We have not even settled beyond dispute the basic question whether or not there was a royal chancery, and between what chronological and geographical limits its activity may have extended.

In all these fields there is plenty of room for everybody for several generations to come, and any attempt by a particular group to monopolize charter studies should be strongly resisted. Indeed, the only issue that appears to be beyond debate is the fundamental value of the charters for our knowledge and appreciation of Anglo-Saxon England.

LAND TENURE IN THE MIDLANDS AND THE NORTHERN DANELAW

No very rewarding study can be undertaken of the early Northern charters without some preliminary reference to the drastic change in land tenure and fiscal administration that was brought about by the Danish settlement of the 870s. Until that settlement, a single cadastre had been applied over nearly the whole of England; almost everywhere land was assessed in hides, and upon this assessment the *bretwalda* or overlord, through his subject kings and princes, made regular levies of tribute.[1] Throughout the country bishops and abbots, ealdormen and thegns held their lands by book-right, their evidence of title being royal diplomas written in the local episcopal or monastic scriptorium and ratified by the witness of the *witan* wherever the court happened to be at the time.[2] Not all land was held by book-right; large tracts of forest and many great agricultural estates were in the direct possession of local kings and princes, and there was in addition an ancient form of tenure known as folk-right, whose tribal origins antedated the era of the landbooks.[3] The precise extent to which folkland had survived into the mid-ninth century is unknown, but there is little doubt that by this time it had been largely supplanted by bookland.[4]

The Scandinavian settlement changed all this. Throughout the half of England lying to the east and north of Watling Street, English landlords were dispossessed of their estates, their landbooks destroyed, and the fiscal system built up over the centuries by the English rulers was swept away.

The Danes had ideas of their own as to the way they should meet their public liabilities, and showed remarkable administrative ability in carrying them out. In place of the old cadastral unit of the hide, based ultimately on the value of the entire agricultural package farmed as a single unit, and including besides arable the woodland, pasture, and meadow appurtenant to each holding, the Danes introduced a unit of assessment called the ploughland, this being nominally the amount of arable capable of being ploughed in a single season by a team of eight oxen.[5] There were considered to be 120 geldable acres in each ploughland.

Like the old hidation, the ploughland assessment (which we

[1] C. Hart, 'The Tribal Hidage', *Transactions of the Royal Historical Society*, 5th series, XXI (1971), pp. 135–57.

[2] CS 432, 453.   [3] OB pp. 64–127.

[4] In what follows, I have chosen to ignore the tenure of land by leasehold. It was, I believe, much less common than bookland, especially for the larger holdings. It seems likely, however, that *laenland* was normally held by charter, in much the same manner as bookland. The nature of such tenure made the long-term preservation of its muniments of little value, and there are few surviving early records.

[5] AHEW pp. 479–80.

shall call the carucation) was imposed centrally, from above
downwards; but whereas the hides had been grouped on a
decimal basis, the ploughlands were arranged duodecimally,
with groups of eight, twelve, and twenty-four ploughlands
predominating. It has been estimated that on average, each
Danish army settler of the ordinary rank and file received as his
share an estate assessed at between eight and twelve ploughlands.[1] Moreover, an intermediate unit of local government
was created, a subdivision of the army settlement area called
the wapentake. This comprised a territory with fixed boundaries, administered by an open-air assembly of army settlers,
meeting at regular intervals and answerable to the earl for a
precise number of ploughland groupings.

Heading this elaborate and highly efficient administrative
structure were a number of earls, each of whose influence was
centred on a fortified *burh* at the hub of his army's settlement
area. Everything points to the early establishment of a system
of taxation based on the carucation, with the proceeds payable
to the local earl at his *burh*. This arrangement held good to a
greater or lesser degree throughout the Danelaw, but in this
book we are concerned chiefly with that part of the territory
known as the Five Boroughs (of Derby, Leicester, Nottingham,
Stamford, and Lincoln), together with the much less stable
and less well organized country further north, centred on
York and Durham.

One has to remember that in spite of their remarkable
administrative and trading ability, the Vikings came here as
illiterate pagans. Runes might serve for divination and the
casting of lots, but they are unsuitable as a means of com-
munication, and throughout the early Danelaw there were no
landbooks or other written evidences of title.

Subject only to meeting their military and fiscal liabilities to
the earl, the Scandinavian army settlers enjoyed the freehold
of such estates as had been allotted to them in the share-out
accompanying the settlement. When a settler died, commonly
his lands were divided among his relatives, and in the course of
time estates became much fragmented. From the early years

[1] See the discussion in my *Hidation of Cambridgeshire* (Leicester 1974),
pp. 11–12.

there was a money economy, and a free market soon sprang up in small parcels of land. As with other forms of trading, dealings in land were carried out orally, before the witness of the wapentake, or the court of the *burh*. Elaborate customary rules governed these transactions, brought with them by the settlers from their Scandinavian homelands. They became so firmly established over here, that among the English the settlement areas were known and respected as 'the Danelaw'.

THE TRANSFORMATION OF THE MIDLANDS

This, then, was the situation facing Edward the Elder when at the turn of the ninth century he inherited from Alfred his father the united but much attenuated kingdom of Wessex and Mercia. Inevitably, the revolutionary changes within the Danelaw had profound repercussions on land tenure and fiscal administration in those parts of England subject to his direct rule. Coincident with, and to some extent consequent upon, the Danish settlement, there had been a disintegration of monastic life and secularization of ecclesiastical endowments. Folkland had disappeared, and with it the old tribal administrative groupings. The need to finance and maintain the fortified *burhs*, newly constructed in the south and west of the country to counter the menace of the Vikings, led to a fundamental revision of the English cadastre, along lines modelled closely upon the Scandinavian pattern.[1]

The new hidation retained its decimal character, but like the ploughland each new hide now became answerable for 120 geld acres, and units of five and ten hides were grouped to form hundreds, in imitation of the wapentakes. North of the upper Thames, the hundreds of the west Midlands were grouped in turn to form new administrative areas, to be known in later years as shires or counties.[2] Each Midland county was administered from a shire town, from which in

[1] D. Hill, 'The Burghal Hidage: the Establishment of a Text', *Medieval Archaeology*, XIII (1969), pp. 84–92; C. A. Ralegh Radford, 'The Later Pre-Conquest Boroughs and their Defences', *Medieval Archaeology*, XIV (1970), pp. 83–103.

[2] C. Hart, 'The County Hidage', *Hid. Northants.*, pp. 15–16, 45–6.

time it was to derive its name. Close correspondence with the Danelaw pattern will again be noted.

In the second decade of the century, when possession of the eastern Danelaw was regained by the English crown, English units of assessment were reimposed there, along the lines that had already been established in the west Midlands.[1] But by the time of the redemption of the Five Boroughs, a quarter of a century later, the Danish cadastre had become too firmly rooted to allow of disruption. The line of demarcation between the carucated and the hidated shires was fixed, therefore, along the course of the River Welland, which with minor exceptions divided the territory of the Five Boroughs from the shires of the County Hidage. The division was to persist until Domesday and later; and with rare exceptions bookland was never to be re-established, nor did the king's writ run, outside the hidated areas.[2]

ENGLISH ROYAL DIPLOMAS IN THE TENTH CENTURY

Against this historical background, we may now examine briefly the production of royal diplomas in tenth-century England. It can be argued that the remarkable hiatus in their flow between the years 904 and 925 is no accident, for it was precisely during this period that the country's cadastral structure was being reorganized. The magnitude of this upheaval could well have led to a temporary suspension of the issue of royal landbooks.

It may be significant that the first three texts with which the run of charters is resumed in 925–6 all concern Mercian estates, and in all probability were composed in the Worcester scriptorium.[3] It is not until the year 928 that we have evidence of similar activity from Winchester.[4]

---

[1] This was true even of East Anglia, see ECEE *passim*.

[2] After the redemption of the Five Boroughs, a number of royal diplomas were issued granting estates in Derbyshire and Yorkshire to prominent laymen, usually of royal descent, who acted as the king's representatives within the newly regained territory. Elsewhere within the carucated Danelaw, bookland was reserved for a few highly placed ecclesiastics.

[3] Nos. 80 and 101 in this hand-list, and CS 658.   [4] CS 663–4.

Ever since the appearance of Drögereit's classic monograph in 1935, it has been recognized that the scribes who drafted the great majority of the royal landbooks issued for Wessex and Mercia in the period 930 to 959 were trained in the Winchester scriptorium. It is unsafe to assume that they always wrote their charters within the curtilage of the Old Minster. Indeed, the early diplomas of Athelstan make it clear that their scribes were peripatetic with the king; his charters were drawn up on the spot, during the meeting at which they were ratified.[1] There is no direct evidence that this practice was continued after 934, but equally there is no evidence of a widespread change in procedure during the next quarter of a century. The presumption is that the routine for issuing royal diplomas remained basically unchanged from Athelstan's time until the Benedictine reformation, which led to the re-establishment of monastic scriptoria.

The rebirth of monasticism could not take place without substantial repercussions on land tenure, but in the early stages the encroachments were localized, and it was several decades before the balance of land ownership was greatly altered over the country as a whole. As each monastery was reformed, the monks and their lay patrons addressed themselves to reconstituting its ancient endowments. Land was obtained by gift, by purchase, by exchange, and (one suspects) some-times by confiscation. The better organized of the new scriptoria were allowed to draft their own title deeds, and sometimes those of neighbouring landowners.

The first monastery to concern itself with the production of royal landbooks was Glastonbury, where Dunstan was installed as abbot in 940. Immediately he established a scriptorium there, at which royal charters were composed to record the endowments of his newly reformed abbey. The earliest surviving example uses an established Winchester formula,[2] but very soon Dunstan developed his own distinctive protocol, an alliterative and poetical text breaking clean away from the

[1] It is difficult to see how else one should interpret the phrase *in villa X nuncupatur . . . perscripta est* that occurs repeatedly in the dating clauses, e.g. CS 669, 677, 689, 691–2, 695 etc.
[2] CS 752.

Winchester tradition, and first encountered in two charters issued late in 940 for the thegn Wulfric, who is probably to be identified with the thegn of that name who was Dunstan's brother, and who had been placed in charge of the abbey's endowments.[1]

For reasons which we shall consider presently, this alliterative formula (which we shall term 'Dunstan A') came to be reserved for a series of charters relating to estates in the Danelaw. Dunstan then proceeded to work out a fresh protocol for the use of the Glastonbury scriptorium, which continued to issue in the name of the king a number of diplomas for estates south of the Thames, mostly in the West Country. Two early examples exhibit a new form of the king's style and title, which was to become the standard for the series: *divina gracia favente* (later *allubescente*) *rex et primicerius totius Albionis*.[2] By 951 all the essential elements of the new protocol had been established. They are found in CS 889, a charter relating to Buckland Dinham, Somerset. The text opens with a dating clause, and goes on to describe the king by the title already discussed. The hidage of the estate is represented by the uncommon Latin *mansiunculae*.[3] The boundary clause is introduced by the phrase *et his limitibus haec telluris prefate pars circumquaque* (in later charters, *particula circumgirari*) *videtur*. The witness list is introduced by the phrase *et huius doni testes* (later, sometimes *constipulatores*) *exstiterunt, quorum inferius nomina subscribuntur* (later, *caraxari videntur*). Early charters in

---

[1] CS 750, 751; DC pp. 128–9. As yet I have been unable to trace Dunstan's sources for this protocol.

[2] CS 816 dated 946, and CS 880 dated 949. The latter is a grant to Christ Church, Canterbury, drawn up by Dunstan at the king's request. It survives in the original, being the earliest dated example of Glastonbury script from the reformed scriptorium. A third charter, CS 817 dated 944 × 946, is more in keeping with Winchester formulas, but betrays its Glastonbury origin with the phrase *vel alicujus gradus vel unius pedis longitudinem*, on which see Chaplais 1966, p. 164. The boundary clause concludes by referring to *wiltshire dorseteschire and hampteschire*, the earliest charter reference known to me for these West Saxon shires.

[3] *mansiunculis* is first found in CS 321, an original Kentish charter dated 805. It next occurs in CS 751, the prototype of the 'Dunstan A' protocol.

the series are not witnessed by the king. This second protocol came to be used extensively in the reformed houses of Dunstan's circle; we shall term it 'Dunstan B'.

Let us now consider the chain of events that led to the 'Dunstan A' protocol being used for Danelaw charters issued between the years 942 and 955. With the redemption of the Five Boroughs in 942, a large portion of the northern Danelaw was brought back under English control. During the next four years, King Edmund's rule was extended to the far north. The chief architect of these victories was Athelstan Half King, ealdorman of East Anglia, who was virtually the regent at this period. He was a close friend of Dunstan, and I have argued elsewhere that he utilized this friendship to secure a Glastonbury scribe for attachment to the king's immediate entourage, to draw up royal diplomas on the 'Dunstan A' model for Danelaw estates.[1] An interesting feature of these charters is the king's title, rex Aengulsaexna ond Nordhymbra imperator, paganorum gubernator, Brittonumque propugnator. This celebrates Edmund's victories, the 'pagans' being the Norsemen from Dublin who controlled the northern Danelaw at the time of the campaigns, and the 'Brittonum' the British inhabitants of southern Cumbria.

The 'Dunstan A' series came to an end with the death of King Eadred late in 955, which brought with it a profound change in the circumstances attending the issue of charters for estates north of the Thames. During the first year of the reign of his successor King Eadwig, Athelstan Half King retired to become a monk at Glastonbury, and Dunstan was banished. Eadwig's position outside Wessex was never very secure, and with the possible exception of CS 937 (copied perhaps at Worcester from a 'Dunstan A' exemplar), the few surviving Mercian charters he issued appear all to have been the work of Winchester scribes; it is evident that the Glastonbury tradition for the production of royal landbooks north of the Thames was discontinued.

[1] DC pp. 125–32. The complete list of charters employing the 'Dunstan A' protocol is as follows: CS 751, 771–3, 815, 876, 882–4, 890, 893, 909, 911, 1346. Of these, CS 751 and probably CS 882 concerned estates in which Glastonbury had a direct interest. Later charters copying the formula

Returning once more to Glastonbury, we find the scriptorium there active in producing charters employing the 'Dunstan B' protocol from 951 right up to the end of King Edgar's reign (975).[1] By 956, if not earlier, the formula had been borrowed by the neighbouring abbey of Bath, which was an important early outpost of the reform movement. 'Dunstan B' charters continued to be issued from the Bath scriptorium up to 972.[2]

Meanwhile, in 957 Eadwig's brother Edgar had revolted, and set himself up as king of Mercia, East Anglia, and Northumbria. In this capacity he issued a number of royal diplomas during the next two years. All the surviving examples appear to have been written at Worcester, where Dunstan had been enthroned after his recall from exile by Edgar.[3] Two of these Worcester charters are modelled on the 'Dunstan B' protocol.[4] The remarkable Westminster charter CS 1048, enacted at Glastonbury after Dunstan's elevation to Canterbury, is a further example of Dunstan's continued adherence to the 'B' protocol. It survives in a contemporary

are CS 937 and ECEE pp. 193–8. For forgeries or heavily modified texts using the same exemplar, see DC pp. 126–7, and the last part of CS 812.

[1] The following 'Dunstan B' charters were issued from Glastonbury: CS 816, 889, 931 (a doubtful text), 903–4, 1188, 1294, and 1315. A small group of Glastonbury charters dated 961 × 965, including two originals, employed different formulas: CS 1072, 1104, and 1165. These are notable for the use of the past tense *haefð gebocod* in the endorsements. CS 887, which also claims to be a Glastonbury charter, is of doubtful authenticity.

[2] The following 'Dunstan B' charters were issued from Bath: CS 1009, 1073, 1164, 1287, and K 643. As with many of the pre-Conquest charters of Bath, the surviving cartulary text of K 643 has been misdated by some stupid revisionist; the correct date is 1006 × 1009. The rest of the text has survived intact; it is modelled on the 'Dunstan B' protocol, and there are no grounds for denouncing this charter as a 'ridiculous forgery' (Encom. Emmae, p. 64 n. 1).

[3] The following charters belong to this group: CS 1023, 1036–7, 1040–4, 1052. Of these, CS 1023 is wrongly ascribed to King Eadred, but was issued by Edgar between 9 May 957 and 2 June 958; it relates to land at Old Swinford, Worcs. (ECWM 279). CS 1040 and 1041 employ similar formulas, found again in CS 1119, a Worcester charter; some of these reappear in CS 1042. CS 1052 has a Worcester proem (cf. CS 665), but utilizes Winchester formulas, as do the paired charters CS 1043–4.

[4] CS 1036–7.

text, which should be dated 959. Later, Dunstan caused the same protocol to be employed to record the grant to him of an estate at Chaldon in Surrey.[1]

Our attention now focuses upon Abingdon, where Dunstan's pupil Æthelwold appears to have been installed as abbot in 953, rather earlier than has been generally accepted. As with Dunstan at Glastonbury, Æthelwold was prompt to institute an effective scriptorium. The texts survive of a series of Abingdon charters employing the 'Dunstan B' protocol, issued between the years 953 and 973.[2] Not all early diplomas from the Abingdon scriptorium follow the 'Dunstan B' protocol; many have formulas almost indistinguishable from those of the Winchester scribes, and only the subtlest indications survive of their Abingdon origin. One good pointer is any reference, either in the dispositive clause or in the OE perambulation, to land 'in communi terra' or 'gemaene land', in which acre strips lay in mixed ownership in common fields.[3]

Abingdon remained under King Eadwig's jurisdiction after Edgar's revolt, and Abbot Æthelwold began to witness Eadwig's charters towards the end of the reign.[4] There is no space here to discuss the reasons for the prolific number of diplomas handed out by Eadwig. Some – perhaps most – of them appear to have been drawn up by Winchester scribes, but one remarkable charter, CS 935 dated 956 and surviving in the original, is attributed by Mr T. A. M. Bishop to Abingdon.[5]

---

[1] CS 1198. This completes the list of charters issued from houses of the Dunstan connection using the 'Dunstan B' protocol, with the exception of CS 1314 dated 975, by which a fresh landbook was issued for a Sussex estate whose earlier charter had been burnt. The verb *rescribere* is used in CS 1314 to describe this transaction, and I would suggest that the replacement diploma used the same formula as its destroyed predecessor. It was preserved at Winchester, but may have been issued from Canterbury under Dunstan's rule.

[2] CS 899, 900, 908, 924, 1209, 1292, and probably CS 987 (dated 957).

[3] The following Abingdon charters of the period 953 × 964 contain such references: CS 900, 925, 975, 1027, 1032, 1034, 1079, 1095, 1120, 1138. Subsequently, the tradition was passed to the Winchester scriptorium, e.g. CS 1145 (972). The agricultural significance of these references is discussed in AHEW pp. 488–94.

[4] CS 1030 and 1045, both to be dated 959.

[5] Bishop p. xix.

Though written by an unskilled scribe, the charter is the earliest dated attempt at caroline minuscule. The introduction of this beautiful script to English scriptoria was one of the chief monuments of Dunstan's abbacy at Glastonbury,[1] and credit would seem to be due to his pupil Æthelwold for its utilization in royal diplomas. It is not yet certain how many of the large number of Berkshire charters issued this year came from the Abingdon scriptorium, but some of the formulas of CS 935 – notably the royal attestation, and the short anathema following the witness list – are to be found elsewhere in cartulary texts, and the originals of these might well have come from the hand of the same scribe.[2]

Eadwig's death on 1 October 959 at the early age of 19 was a momentous event for the Benedictine reform movement. He was succeeded as king of all England by his brother Edgar, then only 16, and still very much under the influence of Dunstan and Æthelwold, his childhood mentors. While Edgar's kingdom was confined to the north of the Thames, Dunstan's guidance had been unchallenged, but now he faded into the background as Æthelwold's more forceful personality impressed itself on Edgar's youthful mind.

By concentrating upon diplomas modelled on the formulas 'Dunstan A' and 'B', we have perhaps produced a rather distorted picture of the production of royal landbooks during the years leading up to Eadwig's death. They can have comprised, however, only a small proportion of the total, and there can be no doubt that the great bulk of Eadwig's charters continued to follow the stereotyped form hitherto characteristic of Winchester scribes.

Once Edgar succeeded to the West Saxon crown, control of the issue of royal landbooks appears to have been taken over by Abbot Æthelwold; from then until Æthelwold's elevation to

---

[1] R. W. Hunt, 'St Dunstan's Classbook from Glastonbury: Cod. Bibl. Bodl. Oxon. Auct. F. 4.32', *Umbrae Codicum Occidentalium*, IV (1961), pp. xiv–xvi.

[2] CS 924, 930, 938, 968 etc. Some of these charters were preserved at Winchester. It is important to recognize that just because a diploma was kept in the archive repository of a particular house, one cannot assume that it was drawn up in that house.

Winchester on 29 November 963 it seems that most of Edgar's charters were written by a scribe or scribes trained at Abingdon. Six charters of the period 960 to 963 survive in the original. They dispose of land in Suffolk, Kent, Middlesex, Berkshire, Sussex, Hampshire, and Wiltshire, and all are in the hand of the same scribe, who came almost certainly from Abingdon.[1]

We must examine one of these further. CS 1066 grants 22 hides at Ringwood, Hampshire, to the abbey of Abingdon in 961. Its formulas, though still elaborate, are far more business-like than the Aldhelmian compositions characteristic of scribes writing the landbooks of Athelstan and his successors. The Latin is good. The membrane itself is of outstanding importance as an example of one process by which a landbook could be drawn up at this period. Mr Bishop points out that after the text had been completed in the main hand (an insular minuscule) as far as the boundary clause, the membrane was folded horizontally (but not vertically).[2] The witness list was added not long afterwards by a second scribe, probably also from Abingdon; he wrote in a competent English caroline minuscule, and his work was corrected at two places by his colleague, who had written the body of the text. Later the charter was folded vertically; there is no contemporary endorsement.

One cannot avoid the supposition that having been drafted as far as the boundary clause, the charter then had to be submitted physically at court for ratification. Notice was taken of who was at court at the time, and from this the witness list was compiled, presumably, back in the abbey scriptorium. In fairness, it must be added that only one other contemporary charter of this period gives such clear-cut evidence of similar processes in its production.[3] But one cannot imagine that the procedures for drawing up these two charters were isolated cases. Clearly, if the charters were not usually folded at the time of their ratification by the *witan*,

[1] Chaplais 1966, p. 60; Drögereit p. 355. The charters are CS 1055, 1066, 1082–3, 1085, and 1101.

[2] Bishop pp. xix, xxi, 9, and pl. IX.

[3] Bu XXIII, dated 968. See pp. 182, 184.

the break in continuity of the writing after the insertion of the boundary clause might well be difficult to detect today.[1]

Moving from palaeography to questions of diplomatic, we are faced immediately with the issue that three original charters dated 962 and 963, all written by the Abingdon scribe who wrote CS 1066, utilize identical formulas and carry similar endorsements.[2] This was destined to become the standard protocol for King Edgar's charters, and altogether the texts of no less than 29 examples issued throughout his reign have been preserved.[3] It would seem probable that this Abingdon scribe moved on to Winchester with Æthelwold when the latter was appointed bishop there late in 963. Æthelwold reformed the Old Minster the following year, and it seems that the scriptorium of the reformed house then resumed the main responsibility for the issue of royal diplomas, utilizing the formulas that had been developed at Abingdon under Æthelwold's abbacy.

This group of 29 charters with identical formulas (the proems vary, but little else), issued throughout Edgar's reign, disposes of land in all the counties of southern England with the exception of Kent, Devon, and Cornwall. North of the Thames, individual charters in the series relate to properties in Oxfordshire, Buckinghamshire, Middlesex, Cambridgeshire, Staffordshire, Lincolnshire, and Yorkshire.

Moreover, if we examine the remaining diplomas of the period, it will be found that many of them contain portions of the same protocol. A simple example must suffice. CS 1257 and

---

[1] One should perhaps include in this discussion OS Facs II, Exeter 11, dated 1031, a Devonshire charter assigned tentatively by Chaplais (1966, pp. 23–4) to the Crediton scriptorium, but written in the same hand as K 744, which Bishop (p. xxiii n. 5) assigns to Canterbury. The dating clause (and hence the witness list) appears to have been written after the charter had been folded in two vertically. When the scribe reached the fold, his writing strayed off the line. On subsequent lines, letters written in the depth of the fold were cramped in form.

[2] CS 1083, 1085, 1101 relating to estates in Wiltshire, Middlesex, and Essex.

[3] CS 1095, 1099, 1100, 1113 (1353), 1114–17, 1120, 1123–5, 1186, 1196, 1199, 1200, 1214–16, 1218, 1230, 1286, 1302, 1305, 1309, 1312, 1316.

1269 are two charters issued on the same date in 970, employing identical formulas, for the abbeys of Bath and Ely respectively, in whose muniment rooms they were preserved.
The first relates to land in Somerset, the second to an estate
far away in Suffolk. Down to the dispositive clause, they
utilize the standard protocol of charters of King Athelstan issued
between 23 March 931 and 26 January 933.[1] From the
exemption clause onwards, however, they follow strictly the
standard formula of the 29 charters of Edgar's reign that we
have been discussing. Mr Eric John, rightly in my opinion,
thinks that probably both were drafted by the same scribe; it
is highly likely that he came from Winchester.[2]

However, it seems probable that a few royal diplomas
continued to be issued from Abingdon after Æthelwold's move
to Winchester. This late Abingdon group is confined to
nearby estates, in Berkshire and in the Thames valley.[3] For the
most part they adhere to the standard protocol, but they can
readily be distinguished from the main Winchester series,
because in 966 the Abingdon scriptorium adopted a more
elaborate form of attestation for the principal witnesses,
borrowed from formulas current in 934–45.

From the closing years of Edgar's reign, royal diplomas
survive at an average rate of five a year; this drops to four a
year for the early part of the reign of Æthelred II. Sandwiched
in between we have the reign of Edward the Martyr, lasting
three years and nine months, for the whole of which period the
texts of only three possibly authentic royal diplomas have
come down to us. Two of these seem to have been written at
Crediton, and were preserved at Exeter,[4] and the solitary

---

[1] CS 674–7, 689, 691–2, 696.   [2] OB p. 202.

[3] CS 1176 (an original charter preserved at Winchester, cf. WCD
p. 63), 1189, 1221–2, 1224–7, 1260.

[4] OS Facs II, Exeter 7 and 14 (dors), cf. Chaplais, *Exeter*, pp. 15–16.
The first of these, in a near-contemporary hand, has no chrismon. It
was endorsed in the main hand before the membrane was folded. The
endorsement runs þis is ðære gyrde boc to hyples eald lande ðe eadþeard cynicg het
gebocian ælfric his ðegne on éce yrue. The membrane is ruled horizontally and
there are two vertical rulings for the left-hand margin, but no prickings
survive. het gebocian is, I think, unique in OE endorsements, but let gebocýan
occurs in the boundary clause of William I's confirmation charter to Bishop

charter remaining came from Winchester.[1] Any explanation of the administrative organization underlying charter production has to take this remarkable gap fully into account, for it can hardly be due to chance.[2]

The charters of Æthelred II are much more difficult to classify than those of King Edgar. Sir Frank Stenton remarked on their tendency to recite the history of the properties with which they are dealing.[3] This air of retrospection shows itself in another characteristic, namely the frequency with which formulas are utilized from diplomas of earlier periods.[4] Such copying sometimes extends to the complete text of the exemplar.[5] As Æthelred's reign proceeds, however, one finds

Leofric of Exeter (Exeter D&C no. 2528), which is also ruled vertically as well as horizontally, and was almost certainly written at Exeter. This charter, however, was endorsed after the membrane had been folded. The charter for *hyples eald lande* resembles that of CS 1056, an original charter dated 960, preserved at Exeter and relating to land in Cornwall. Both are endorsed by the same method, before folding. The unusual spelling *gebocude* in CS 1056 should be noted. The bounds are entered in a microscopic hand at the foot of the membrane. CS 1056 is almost certainly from the same scriptorium as CS 1303, an original charter dated 974, relating to land in Cornwall. This charter also has the spelling *gebocude* in its endorsement, and very probably it was written at Crediton. I think it safe to assume that both charters of Edward the Martyr whose texts were preserved at Exeter were written (like CS 1056 and CS 1303) at Crediton; but I am not satisfied that either of these two charters is authentic in its present form.

[1] K 611, which repeats a chancery formula originating in 941 (CS 767 etc.), but has an impeccable witness list. Two Abingdon charters, K 1276–7, are of very doubtful authenticity.

[2] Over 70 charters survive from the reign of King Eadwig, which lasted only one month longer than that of his nephew Edward the Martyr.

[3] LC p. 74. About one-third of Æthelred's charters show this propensity, throughout his reign.

[4] The earliest examples of this trend, mostly from the Abingdon scriptorium, antedate Æthelred's reign. CS 978 (Bu XIV) dated 956 is modelled on a text of the year 942. Next we find CS 1074 dated 961, based on formulas originating in 932. Similarly, the text of CS 1081 (Bu XIX) dated 962 is close to that of CS 743, dated 939. CS 1142 dated 964 uses formulas of the period 944–6 (CS 799, 818). K 611 dated 977 repeats the formulas of CS 767, dated 941. But such repetition is uncommon before Æthelred's succession.

[5] K 621 dated 979 resembles CS 1291 dated 973; K 632 dated 982 resembles CS 1125 dated 960; K 693 and K 1282, almost identical texts dated 984, are modelled on charters of the years 939 × 940; K 1281 dated

that more often the borrowing is restricted to individual clauses, such as the proem or the anathema.[1] Towards the end of the reign one encounters charters that appear to utilize a whole range of earlier exemplars, with individual passages being drawn from a number of different formularies.[2]

It might be thought that texts of this kind, written at the turn of the century and later and using mixed formulas not found in other charters of the period, could perhaps have come from some provincial scriptorium such as Burton. But the extraordinary fact is that for nearly two decades after King Edgar's death, not a single monastic scriptorium other than the Old Minster at Winchester appears to have been active in producing royal diplomas.[3] There is nothing attributable to Abingdon,[4] to Glastonbury, to Bath, or even to Worcester;

984 copies a text dated 944 × 947; K 1285 dated 990 is based on charters of the period 930 × 934; K 691 dated 995 uses a formula found in Bu XIX dated 962. The list could be extended substantially, but these examples will suffice.

[1] The early part of K 663 dated 988 repeats formulas found in CS 891 dated 951; the forms of subscription of K 686 dated 998 derive from a charter dated 961; the proem of K 1291 dated 996 is found in CS 862 dated 948; the proem of K 691 dated 995 first occurs in CS 743 dated 939; the anathema of K 1283 dated 985 repeats that of CS 663 dated 928.

[2] See the comments to Bu XXXV on p. 243.

[3] This does not preclude the possibility that authentic royal diplomas of Winchester origin may have been *copied* in other monastic scriptoria during this period, but I know of no clear-cut example. The earliest surviving version of K 657, dated 987, is in a near-contemporary hand; it appears to have been preserved in the Rochester archives, and it relates to Bromley in Kent, an estate that came into the possession of Rochester in 998. The late Professor A. Campbell thought that the formulas of this charter were of Rochester origin (Rochester p. xxvii), but in this he was wrong; the text employs strictly Winchester formulas, and the original charter must have been witnessed on the same occasion as K 658, which is undoubtedly a Winchester product. The surviving membrane of K 657 may be a copy of a lost Winchester original, made in 998 when the estate was given to Rochester. Further work on the palaeography is needed before the hand of this copy can be referred with confidence to any particular scriptorium.

[4] The texts of six apparently authentic charters, dated 982 to 985, are entered in the Abingdon cartularies. None of the originals survive (K 1278–83). Of these, four concern land in Berkshire, one in Oxfordshire, and one in Wiltshire. One is a gift directly to the abbey (K 1279). All of these charters closely resemble standard Winchester texts in their general structure and formulas. For example the whole text and witness list of K 1282, a

nor can we find authentic examples from Rochester, Chertsey, Evesham, St Albans, and St Augustines, nor from the four fenland houses.[1]

Thirty charters survive from this period for estates in Hampshire and Wiltshire, but of these only two are made out to West Country religious houses, and both have formulas strongly suggestive of a Winchester origin.[2] The only surviving authentic monastic foundation charter of the period comes from Tavistock, and this too uses Winchester formulas.[3] Further afield, King Æthelred's grant of Wolverhampton to the lady Wulfrun in 985 was almost certainly the work of a Winchester scribe, as was the diploma issued two years later for Æsce, which may have been a north Midland estate.[4]

Evidence that Winchester was the centre of production of Æthelred's royal diplomas during the early years of his reign is very strong. If we examine, for example, the king's subscription to authentic charters of the period from 979 to the first half of 983, we find the same formula repeated in nearly all of them.[5] Three of these diplomas were grants to the Old Minster.

Berkshire charter, is almost identical with that of K 639, a Wiltshire charter issued on the same date, preserved in the *Codex Wintoniensis* and bearing a standard endorsement (CW p. 22 n. 2). The formula is taken piecemeal from a Winchester text of the year 940 (CS 749, 758). Similarly, the text of K 1281 is lifted from a Winchester charter of the period 940 × 949. Four of these Abingdon charters (K 1278–81) refer to common land (see p. 22), but this information could have been supplied to Winchester scribes by reeves or clerics from Abingdon who had perambulated the estate boundaries.

[1] Two charters whose texts were preserved at Malmesbury ought perhaps to be mentioned here. K 632 dated 982 uses Winchester formulas, but it is a very doubtful text and should be dismissed from the present argument. K 654 dated 986 relates to Littleton upon Severn, Gloucestershire. It employs – uniquely for the period – elements of the 'Dunstan B' protocol. Its highly anomalous witness list, in which the order of attestation of bishops, ealdormen, and thegns departs considerably from the norm, precludes this charter from being used as evidence for the composition of an authentic royal diploma at Malmesbury or Worcester in 986.

[2] K 641 dated 984 for Shaftesbury; K 659 dated 987 for Glastonbury.

[3] H. P. R. Finberg, *Tavistock Abbey* (2nd edn, 1969), pp. 278–83.

[4] K 650; Bu xxv.

[5] K 622, 624, 626, 632, 640, 1379. It recurs in K 663, dated 988.

A new form of royal attestation then appears, and is repeated altogether in no less than thirteen surviving texts up to the year 990; it does not occur in charters outside these dates.[1] Most of the estates conveyed lie in Wiltshire and Hampshire, but examples survive from Staffordshire, Oxfordshire, Berkshire, and Kent. There are too many other parallels in the formulas used for these charters to allow of definitive treatment of the diplomatic here, but an examination of four of them written in 987 and early in 988 has shown that almost certainly they were drawn up by the same scribe.[2]

The majority of the charters of Æthelred we have mentioned so far were preserved at the Old Minster. Whenever records of their endorsements have survived, they follow without exception traditional Winchester formulas.[3] The great charter to Abingdon issued by King Æthelred in 993 represents a break away from this tradition.[4] Mr Bishop has shown that it was written at Abingdon.[5] With it, the Winchester monopoly was broken, and increasingly thereafter royal diplomas were drawn up in the scriptoria of other houses. Criticism of the texts becomes correspondingly complicated, and lies outside the scope of this introductory review.

WAS THERE A ROYAL CHANCERY?

The bibliography on this question goes back to the time of George Hickes, and the debate continues. It is important that users of this present hand-list should be aware of the views held, rightly or wrongly, by its editor. For this reason I propose to state them baldly, without attempting to display here the evidence that has prompted me to take up my present position. Much of the evidence is to be found scattered throughout the rest of this volume.

Initially, bookland was reserved for the church; but by the

---

[1] K 639, 648, 650, 652, 657, 659, 664, 673, 1280, 1282–3; Bu xxiv, xxv.

[2] See the notes to Bu xxv on p. 195. The charters concerned are K 657, 659, 664, and Bu xxv. Another diploma by the same scribe is K 658.

[3] CW pp. 20–4.   [4] K 684, on which see OB pp. 172, 181–8.

[5] Bishop p. 13.

early tenth century the bulk of it was in lay hands. The chains of circumstance that could lead up to the issue of a landbook were many and varied. Let us follow the path of one hypothetical Warwickshire thegn of small estate, as he sets out early in 933 to acquire an additional property, protected by a royal title deed.

We may suppose that he has heard of the forfeiture to the royal fisc (on account, say, of some crime that need not concern us) of a ten-hide village lying some 20 miles or so from his own hall. His first task is to seek out a priest with sufficient education and local knowledge, and to ride the bounds of the estate with him, accompanied perhaps by the nearest royal reeve. Each landmark is noted, and as they go round, the priest writes down the perambulation in the vernacular upon some convenient piece of skin. We may pause here, to remark on the fact that although many surviving texts of charters are believed to have been forged in order to secure the title to land fraudulently, in no case do we have evidence of tampering with the bounds marked out in the perambulation.

Next, the thegn must needs mobilize his portable wealth. Land could be handed out as a gift by the king in reward for service, but one suspects that in the great majority of cases bookland had to be purchased with gold (measured by weight in mancuses) and silver pennies. The tariff would vary according to the quality of the land, and its capital investment in terms of equipment, livestock, and slave labour. No doubt the nearest royal reeve would act as assessor, and machinery must have existed for his valuation to be passed on to the royal court.

Armed with his perambulation and his money, our thegn now rides off to seek out the king wherever he may happen to be. In January 933 he was at his royal manor of Chippenham in Wiltshire. The court was continually in progress throughout Wessex, and occasionally north of the Thames. Even in times of peace it could never rest for more than a few days on end, at one of a number of royal palaces, boroughs, cathedrals, abbeys, or large rural estates in royal, episcopal, or lay hands. Its appetite in terms of food and drink, fodder and hunting, was insatiable. The arrival of the royal entourage must have appeared to the native inhabitants like the visitation of a plague of locusts.

Our thegn is fortunate if he can find at court a friend in the form of his local ealdorman, bishop, or royal reeve to ease his path to the king's presence and sponsor his application. Faced with such a request, how is the king to know if the estate in question is properly within his gift at the time, and if so, what is its value? It seems highly likely that there was some primitive form of central registry of bookland, the muniments of which have not survived.

The royal favour granted, our thegn betakes himself first to the chamberlain (or was it one of the discthegns who held responsibility for guarding the royal treasure?) and hands to him the purchase price of the estate. Then on to the Winchester-trained clerk, peripatetic with the king, to whom has been assigned the task of drawing up the royal landbooks. Here it is all a matter of routine, for there is always at court a constant procession of thegns and ealdormen and ecclesiastics in search of bookland.

The scribe reaches for a fresh membrane, and dips his quill in the ink. At the top left-hand corner he inscribes a small cross, for the royal diploma is a sacred instrument. He proceeds to copy out once more from his formulary the well-known proem *Flebilia fortiter detestanda* . . . The task completed (perhaps for the two hundredth time) he enquires the name of the recipient, the purchase price of the estate, its hidage and place-name, and moves on to enter on the membrane the dispositive clause, opening with the sonorous and ceremonial royal style: *Ego Æthelstanus rex Anglorum, per Omnitonantis dexteram totius Bryttaniæ regni solio sublimatus* . . . He pauses. Does the estate include among its appurtenances a river perhaps, or some woodland? Receiving an answer in the affirmative, he continues with the clause setting out the terms by which it is to be held . . . *cum pratis, pascuis, siluis, riuulis, omnibusque ad eam utilitatibus pertinentibus, libenter ac aeternaliter quamdiu verberanti occellorum convolatu auraque spirabili potiatur habeat* . . .

The particular formula here in use is unique in that it makes no provision for reserving the three common dues of bridge and fortress work and army service from the charter's general clause of exemption, but there can be no doubt that such reservation is implied. Next, the scribe copies in the bounds, and reaches back to his formulary for the impressive anathema: *Si autem, quod absit, aliquis diabolico inflatus spiritu hanc meae compositionis vel confirmationis breviculam elidere vel infringere temptauerit, . . .*

Batches of diplomas are submitted at court from time to time (but never on a Sunday) for ratification. The scribe enquires the day on which the next ceremony will be held. It will be the Saturday before Ephiphany 3. He opens up the pages of his *computus* to work it out in laborious detail from the Roman kalendar and lunar tables: *Anno Dominicæ Incarnationis DCCCCXXXIII, regni vero michi commissi IX, Indictione VI, epacta XII, concurrente I, septimis Februarii kalendis, luna XXVI. In villa omnibus notissima quæ CIPPENHAM nominatur, tota optimorum pluralitate sub alis regiæ dapsilitatis perscripta est.*

The witness list (and perhaps the dating clause) will have to wait until the day of the ratification ceremony, at which the name of each Welsh under-king, each bishop, abbot, and ealdorman, and each of the 50-odd thegns at court is scrupulously recorded in the correct order of precedence.

At last it is all complete – or nearly so. Once the ink is dry, the scribe folds the membrane perhaps twice horizontally and three times vertically, so that the written surface faces inwards. On one of the outer panels he enters a summary of the transaction in the vernacular, so that those unskilled in the Latin tongue may know what is recorded inside: *Dis is þara. X. hida boc þe Eþælstan cing ge bocode Wulfricæ his þegne æt Wudetunæ on ece yrfe.* This is the standard endorsement for charters destined to be stored with the king's *haligdom* at Winchester. In the case of wills, two or three copies are sometimes made, one for each interested party, but this custom does not appear to have been followed as a rule for royal diplomas. Presumably, if Wulfric wishes to defend his ownership of the estate in a dispute, reference must be made to the royal archive repository for evidence of title. Perhaps (and I think this is very likely) Wulfric himself had the choice as to where the diploma should be laid up – the royal archives, the local cathedral (later in the century, the local abbey), or his own muniment chest. It would have to be somewhere safe, and somewhere known to him, and if placed in any of the larger repositories, the filing system would have to be sufficiently sophisticated for the ready identification of Wulfric's particular grant, without going to the trouble of opening out innumerable landbooks before the right one was found. Hence the endorsement.

In tracing Wulfric's hypothetical progress, we have described a simple yet efficient organization for the issue of royal diplomas. Just how many such title deeds were produced each year we shall never know, for far more must have perished than have survived. Yet after 929 there are very few years in the tenth century unrepresented by a single surviving diploma, and for the year 956 alone over 50 texts have come down to us – no less than 7 per cent of the total hidage of Berkshire is booked in the surviving charters of that year.

Dangerous though such an exercise may be, we shall now attempt another hypothesis, this time an estimate of the average annual production of royal landbooks during the years 930 to 990. From various sources – in particular Domesday, and the County and Burghal Hidages, we may postulate that in the mid-tenth century, England south of the Thames was rated at 23,000 hides, and the hidated shires north of the Thames accounted for 27,000 hides, giving a total hidage of around 50,000. Let us assume further that 10 per cent of this was permanently assigned to the royal fisc, being shared between the king, his consort, and the aethelings. Another 5 per cent might be allotted to the ealdordoms, and 5 per cent to the church (its share was to increase dramatically with the Benedictine reform). We are left with an estimated 40,000 hides, and for the purpose of our hypothesis we shall assume that all of this was booked to thegns, the average total holding of each thegn being 10 hides.[1] Many, of course, would possess

---

[1] This gives us an estimate of 4,000 thegns spread over the 26 shires of hidated England. Allotting to these shires a population of 600,000 (excluding the towns) in 950, we obtain a ratio of one landed thegn to 150 persons of lower status. These figures are rather lower than those suggested by Domesday Book.

only 5 hides, the minimum holding for thegnly status; but to counterbalance this would be a small number of richer thegns, each with estates totalling as many as 100 hides or more.

We are discussing, then, the title-deeds to 4,000 properties.[1] How often would renewal of the landbooks be necessary? An average thegn might expect to secure the bulk of his landed endowment, whether by purchase or inheritance, by the age of 30; he could certainly expect to die by the age of 45. Individual estates would change hands then, one supposes, about every 15 years; each year, therefore, some 265 estates in hidated England would pass to a new owner. Most of these, we may imagine, would descend by oral or written will, and the original title-deeds would descend with the property, so that fresh ones would not be required. Against this, a proportion of landbooks were constantly being lost by fire, flood, and pillage, or storage in some forgotten repository. We know that on such occasions, new charters were sought from the king. Moreover, properties were continually devolving to the royal fisc by intestacy, gift, and forfeiture. Furthermore, we have confined the discussion so far to estates held by persons of thegnly rank. No account has been taken of diplomas issued to the church.[2]

We emerge from this discussion with an estimated average requirement of 100 new royal landbooks per annum. Such a production would be well within the capacity of a single clerk. One could imagine ratification ceremonies being held perhaps

---

[1] We may check this conclusion in another way. For the four West Saxon shires of Wiltshire, Hampshire, Somerset, and Dorset, records survive of 90 estates totalling 897 hides being booked to thegns between the years 930 and 990. The average assessment approaches very close to 10 hides per landbook. Suppose this to be typical of estates booked to thegns elsewhere in Wessex and Mercia during this period. Then if we accept the same provisional total of 40,000 for the hidage of all the estates under review, we arrive at the identical estimate of 4,000 properties for which title-deeds in the form of royal diplomas are required.

[2] The high proportion of surviving landbooks recording grants to the church rather than to laymen gives a distorted picture of the ratio of their issue. It will be obvious on reflection that since all surviving texts come from ecclesiastical repositories, charters issued to laymen had a relatively poor chance of survival. I believe that the great bulk of tenth-century landbooks fell within this latter class.

six or seven times a year – at the three great ecclesiastical
feasts, and on other convenient occasions such as synods and
the enthronement of bishops. At each gathering, the grants of a
dozen or so estates would be read out to the assembly. If half
of them were deposited eventually in the royal archive
repository at Winchester, in thirty years the collection there
would amount to some 1,500 charters. With them would be
kept perhaps an equal number of wills and law memoranda
recording in the vernacular cases concerning land tenure held
before the shire courts. A dozen or so large chests would
suffice to hold the lot.

The impact on all this of the Benedictine reformation may
now be assessed. From 940 to 975, diplomas were being
drawn up at Glastonbury. Most of them concerned estates
that formed part of the abbey's landed endowment; a few
might have been written for smaller West-Country religious
houses, and perhaps for lay landlords in the vicinity of the
abbey. The scriptorium at Abingdon was similarly occupied
from 953 onwards, and that at Bath, on a smaller scale, from
956. Between 942 and 955 a Glastonbury-trained scribe was
writing a limited number of diplomas for Danelaw estates,
presumably from the royal court.

The total charter production of all these scribes was
negligible compared with that of the Winchester-trained
clerks who seem to have travelled with the reigning monarch
to issue the royal diplomas of Athelstan, Edmund, and Eadred.
In Eadwig's time this activity appears to have become centred
on the Old Minster at Winchester, but Abingdon may have
begun to take over an increasing share of the work at this
period.

North of the Thames, a scriptorium was in operation at
Worcester throughout the tenth century, producing inter alia
episcopal leases. Between 957 and 959 charters were drawn
up there for Edgar while king of the Mercians; subsequently
royal diplomas were constructed there occasionally for
Mercian estates. As soon as Edgar succeeded to the whole
kingdom in 959, the main centre for charter production was
moved to Abingdon, under the supervision of Abbot Æthelwold.
When Æthelwold was appointed to Winchester at the end

of 963, he took the royal charter organization with him.
Glastonbury, Worcester, Abingdon, and Bath remained active
on a local scale, and from about 960 onwards some charters
were perhaps written at Crediton for estates in the Dumnonian
peninsula. Two charters survive (in cartulary texts) which
may have been written at Malmesbury in 974. There is no
reliable evidence that royal diplomas were composed at any
other houses during King Edgar's reign, and Canterbury in
particular seems to have been inactive in this respect throughout the tenth century, except possibly for a few 'Dunstan B'
charters during Dunstan's tenure of the primacy. At court,
direction of the activities of the royal writing office at
Winchester appears to have devolved upon Ealdulf, a layman,
a godson and protégé of Bishop Æthelwold, who acted as
chancellor during the closing years of Edgar's reign.

Upon the death of King Edgar there was a very considerable
reaction against the build-up of monastic endowments which
had characterized his reign. The impact of this revolt upon
land tenure was much greater than has been hitherto suspected
by historians of the period. Were it not for two doubtful
charters from a West-Country scriptorium and a solitary
example from Winchester, we might well have concluded
that during the reign of Edward the Martyr the whole process
of issuing royal landbooks was in abeyance, as it had been in
the time of his namesake Edward the Elder, though for different
reasons. Moreover, when the flow of charters is resumed with
the accession of Æthelred II in 979, we find Glastonbury,
Bath, Abingdon, and Worcester all strangely silent. For the
next fourteen years the issue of royal diplomas seems to have
been reserved strictly for the scriptorium of the Old Minster
at Winchester. Control over the issue of these landbooks was
directed from the royal court, where the three abbots of Ely,
St Augustine's, and Glastonbury each took turns to act as
chancellor for a period of 4 months each year. Of these,
Brihtnoth of Ely certainly, and the other two probably, were
nominees of Bishop Æthelwold. Their precise functions are
not clear, but they may have been supervisory. In 987 a thegn
called Ælfwine was King Æthelred's *scriptor*; he may have been
concerned with the issue of writs as well as charters (see p. 189).

He was rewarded with an Oxfordshire estate which must soon have reverted to the royal fisc, for in 1042–6 part of it was granted by the Confessor to his priest Leofric, who may also have been connected in some way with the royal writing office; Florence of Worcester called him 'the chancellor'.

Those diplomas that survive from the first half of Æthelred's reign are mostly grants to Wessex thegns; charters for monasteries other than the Winchester group are rare. Not until 993, when Æthelred issued his great confirmation charter to Abingdon, do we find any sign of a change in policy.

Any debate as to the existence of an English royal chancery must take all this into account. Apart from a short spell at Abingdon early in Edgar's reign, we find that from 930 to 993 the routine production of royal diplomas was in the hands of Winchester-trained scribes, working in a royal writing office. At first they moved around with the king on his perambulations, but later their activity became centred at the Old Minster in the rapidly growing royal town of Winchester, where the royal archives reposed.

For long periods (930 to 940, 977 to 993) this royal writing office appears to have enjoyed an absolute monopoly in charter production. Outside these dates, it was still responsible for drawing up the great majority of landbooks, although local franchises were exercised by a few religious houses. Even when landbooks were drawn up at these monastic scriptoria however, it appears that they had to be taken before the royal court for ratification, and they depended on information from the royal writing office for their witness lists.

We have argued that the central organization for the issue of landbooks need only have been small, but that it was efficient. From the time of Edgar onwards it seems to have been directed by an official called by later writers the chancellor. It exhibits all the characteristics attributable to a permanent royal establishment – routine attention to such details as the king's style and title, precision in defining the privileges and liabilities conveyed by the grant, painstaking recording of the bounds and hidage assessment, and strict adherence to order of precedence in the witness lists. Above all, it shows continuity – the formulas may vary from period to period, but the substance of the diplomas is unchanging, the series hardly broken from Athelstan to Æthelred. As Professor Bullough recently concluded, whether or not we choose to call this organization a royal chancery is a question of terminology rather than of interpretation of the charter evidence.[1]

When one approaches this issue from the wider viewpoints of the topographer and the institutional historian, rather than those of the more specialized disciplines of palaeography and diplomatic, the case for the existence of a royal chancery is seen to be very strong indeed. The history of tenth-century England is remarkable for the trend one finds, in many different aspects of national administration and economy, towards the build-up of a strong and sophisticated machinery of central government.

In the early years of the century this is evidenced by the fortification of boroughs, the shiring of the Midlands, and the reorganization of the national cadastre. Later, it shows itself again in such diverse ways as the introduction of a standard literary form of English,[2] tight control of the coinage,[3] and the management of the sea-*fyrd*.[4] At the very end of the century we encounter the emergence of a new and peculiarly English administrative phenomenon, the royal writ authenticated by a seal. It is no accident that the introduction of the secular royal writ coincided with the loosening of chancery monopoly over the issue of the sacred royal diploma. The writ was a more effective instrument of royal control, and its evidential value was so much greater as to constitute a revolutionary advance in the science of diplomatic.

The royal writ is a notification to the magnates of a shire of the king's pleasure and command concerning a particular matter at issue. Those of the Anglo-Saxon period were written in the vernacular, and it is clear that they were read out before the shire court, then stored with the archives of the beneficiaries. We are concerned here with those writs dealing with land ownership and jurisdiction. The earliest come from

[1] Bullough p. 494 n.   [2] Helmut Gneuss in ASE 1, pp. 63–83.
[3] R. H. M. Dolley and D. M. Metcalf in *Anglo-Saxon Coins*, ed. R. H. M. Dolley (1961), pp. 136–68.
[4] ASC E, *s.a.* 992.

the middle years of Æthelred's reign. By the time of Edward the Confessor there were very many of these instruments, and it has been argued (and can still be argued) that collectively they put the existence of a royal chancery beyond all reasonable doubt.

Against this it has been urged that two of the surviving writs of the Confessor appear to have been written by the scribes of the beneficiaries, and that writs preserved in the archives of a particular house occasionally have protocols sharing similar phrases, which may have been characteristic of the scriptorium of that house.

This special pleading on behalf of ecclesiastical scriptoria has yet to account for the undoubted fact that the great majority of writs, whoever the beneficiary and wherever the estates they were concerned with might be, adhered strictly to a common diplomatic form which can only have been of central origin. Nor does such special pleading account for the fact that there are very many references to these documents being accompanied by a seal. Now it will be clear to all that if the royal seal matrix was physically attached to a writ, then this instrument must have emanated from a royal chancery. Unfortunately it is not established beyond question that the tongue of any early surviving writ was intended originally to bear a seal; it can be argued that the tongue was used merely to wrap around the document, to hold it in a compact form. The next step in this ingenious if not tortuous argument is to suppose that the seal accompanying the writ was physically separate from it. This enables the further supposition to be advanced, that the royal writ was always written by the beneficiary, and that there was no royal chancery at all.

The fundamental difficulty in accepting this viewpoint lies, I think, in the circumstance we have encountered already in the case of royal diplomas, namely that all surviving examples of writs come from ecclesiastical repositories, whose chief function was to preserve the title-deeds of their particular religious houses. With royal writs issued for the church, as with royal diplomas, it is not unreasonable to assume that sometimes the house in question was granted the privilege of drawing up its own document. It would then be submitted at court for ratification, either (in the case of a diploma) by reading it before the *witan* (in which case the chancery supplied the issuing house with the witness list) or (in the case of a writ) by impressing upon it the king's seal – surely the function and prerogative of the royal chancery, and no other body.

To accept all this for church tenure in no way conflicts with the reasonable assumption that the great majority of royal instruments giving title to land, whether writs or diplomas, were drawn up by chancery scribes for lay beneficiaries. If we open the pages of Domesday Book we shall find plenty of references to these lost texts, in which a thegn is said to have held land of the gift of the Confessor, *et inde habet sigillum ejus*. Still more specifically, we hear of a writ *with the seal of King Edward* which was found in the church of St Mary, Shaftesbury during the Domesday inquest.[1] Unless the *sigillum* was physically attached to the writ, it could not be held to prove anything very specific to the Domesday jurors; to assume otherwise is to strain the interpretation of the evidence beyond credulity. If the seal was attached to the writ, then one has to assume the existence of a royal chancery. And there the case rests.

[1] VCH *Dorset* III, p. 83a.

ACKNOWLEDGEMENTS

MY BEST thanks are due to the Marquess of Anglesey, for permission to publish charters entered in BM Loan MS 30, and to the Trustees of the William Salt Library, for permission to publish Burton Abbey charters in their possession. The custodians of collections at Burton Public Library, the National Library of Wales (Department of Manuscripts and Records), and the British Museum (Department of Western Manuscripts) have all proved unfailingly helpful. The publication of the book has been assisted by a grant from the Twenty-Seven Foundation.

To Mr F. B. Stitt, the Staffordshire County Archivist and Librarian, I am indebted for placing at my disposal his expertise on the county's muniments and topography. Mr D. Pritchard, of the Department of Classics, National University of Wales, Aberystwyth, generously and painstakingly checked my transcripts from the Peniarth Cartulary, eliminating much that was unsound. Dr David Kirby kindly read through the whole book in manuscript (with the exception of the introduction), and it has benefited greatly from his suggestions, especially those stemming from his deep knowledge of early Northumbria. I have sought and received advice on innumerable matters from Professor H. P. R. Finberg, who has monitored the project throughout. Without his constant support it would never have been completed.

To Mrs Norma Corby, who typed the whole book from manuscript, I owe a special debt of gratitude. She has dealt faultlessly with Old English, medieval Latin, and my own scribble, which at times is wellnigh indecipherable. Few could have done it as well, and none better.

These northern charters have taken up much of my spare time over the past decade, in odd moments snatched day and night from the major commitment of running a busy general practice. To my wife and children for their good-humoured toleration of such eccentricities, I owe more than I can ever repay. They are the real heroes of this book, and to them it is gratefully dedicated.
C.J.R.H.

42

POSTSCRIPT

THIS BOOK was in the press when the sad news came of the death of Professor H. P. R. Finberg, the General Editor of *Studies in Early English History*. Besides contributing himself two notable volumes to the series, he has taken a close personal interest in the remainder. His sustained and original work on the early history of this country in general, and on Anglo-Saxon charters in particular, will ensure him an honoured place among the English historians of his generation. My personal indebtedness to him is well known; having first gained my interest in the period, he inspired and directed my studies for more than twenty years. Others of his pupils and colleagues were similarly encouraged, and we are all proud to have known him as a friend.

C.J.R.H.

BIBLIOGRAPHY AND ABBREVIATIONS

Abingdon = Stenton, F. M., *The Early History of the Abbey of Abingdon*. Reading, 1913.

AD = William of Malmesbury, *De antiquitate Glastoniensis ecclesiæ*, in *Adami de Domerham, Historia de rebus gestis Glastoniensibus*, ed. T. Hearne. London, Vol. I, 1727, pp. 1–122.

AHEW = *The Agrarian History of England and Wales*, ed. H. P. R. Finberg. Cambridge, Vol. I, 1972. Part II, A.D. 43–1042, by H. P. R. Finberg, occupies pp. 385–532.

Anglesey Cartulary = BM Loan MS. 30; the manuscript is described on p. 155 below.

Anon., *Historia Abbatum* = *Historia Abbatum auctore Anonymo*, in Plummer, *Bede*.

ASC = Anglo-Saxon Chronicle. The various texts are referred to as A, B, C, D, E, F. The edition used here is *Two of the Saxon Chronicles Parallel*, ed. J. Earle and C. Plummer. 2 vols. Oxford, 1892. Translations used are *The Anglo-Saxon Chronicle*, trans. G. N. Garmonsway. London, 2nd edn, 1955; and *The Anglo-Saxon Chronicle*, trans. D. Whitelock, D. C. Douglas, and S. I. Tucker. London, 1961.

ASE = *Anglo-Saxon England*, ed. P. Clemoes, Cambridge. Vol. I, 1972; Vol. II, 1973.

Asser = *Asser's Life of King Alfred*, ed. W. H. Stevenson. Oxford, 1959 impression.

Æthelweard = *The Chronicle of Æthelweard*, ed. A. Campbell. London, 1962.

Barlow = Barlow, F., *The English Church 1000–1066*. London, 1963.

Barlow, *EC* = Barlow, F., *Edward the Confessor*. London, 1970.

Bede, *Historia Abbatum* = *Historia Abbatum auctore Baeda*, in Plummer, *Bede*.

Bishop = Bishop, T. A. M., *English Caroline Minuscule*. Oxford, 1971.

Bishop and   =Bishop, T. A. M., and Chaplais, P. (ed.),
Chaplais 1957   *Facsimiles of English Royal Writs to A.D. 1100 presented to V. H. Galbraith.* Oxford, 1957.

BM   =British Museum.

BM Facs   =*Facsimiles of Ancient Charters in the British Museum.* 4 parts. London, 1873–8.

Bridgeman   =Bridgeman, C. G. O., 'Staffordshire Preconquest Charters', in W. Salt, 1916, pp. 67–136.

Bu   =(followed by a number) a Burton Abbey charter; numbers listed on pp. 167–71 below.

Bullough   =Bullough, D. A., 'The Educational Tradition in England from Alfred to Ælfric: Teaching *Utriusque Linguæ*', *Settimane di studio del Centro italiano di studi sull' alto mediaevo*, XIX (Spoleto, 1972), pp. 453–94.

Cart Rams   =*Cartularium Monasterii de Rameseia*, ed. W. H. Hart and P. A. Lyons. 3 vols. Rolls Series, 79, 1884–93.

CAS   =Cambridge Antiquarian Society (Proceedings).

Chaplais 1962   =Chaplais, P., 'The Original Charters of Herbert and Gervase Abbots of Westminster (1121–1157)', *A Medieval Miscellany for Doris Mary Stenton*, ed. Patricia M. Barnes and C. F. Slade (Pipe Roll Society, new ser., XXXVI, 1962 for 1960), pp. 89–110.

Chaplais 1965   =Chaplais, P., 'The Origin and Authenticity of the Royal Anglo-Saxon Diploma', *Journal of the Society of Archivists*, III (1965), pp. 48–61.

Chaplais 1966   =Chaplais, P., 'The Anglo-Saxon Chancery: from the Diploma to the Writ', *Journal of the Society of Archivists*, III (1966), pp. 160–76.

Chaplais 1968   =Chaplais, P., 'Some Early Anglo-Saxon Diplomas on Single Sheets: Originals or Copies?', *Journal of the Society of Archivists*, III (1968), pp. 315–36.

Chaplais, *Exeter*   =Chaplais, P., 'The Authenticity of the Royal Anglo-Saxon Diplomas of Exeter', *Bulletin of the Institute of Historical Research*, XXXIX (1966), pp. 1–34.

Chron Abingd = *Chronicon Monasterii de Abingdon*, ed. J. Stevenson. 2 vols. Rolls Series, 2, 1858.

Chron E = *Chronicon Abbatiæ de Evesham*, ed. W. D. Macray. Rolls Series, 29, 1863.

Chron Rams = *Chronicon Abbatiæ Rameseiensis*, ed. W. D. Macray. Rolls Series, 83, 1886.

Clemoes = Clemoes, P. (ed.), *The Anglo-Saxons*. London, 1959.

Cooper = Cooper, Janet, *The Last Four Anglo-Saxon Archbishops of York*. Borthwick Paper no. 38. York, 1970.

Craster 1925 = Craster, H. E., 'Some Anglo-Saxon Records of the See of Durham', *Archaeologia Æliana*, 1 (1925), pp. 189–98.

Craster 1954 = Craster, H. E., 'The Patrimony of St Cuthbert', *EHR* LXIX (1954), pp. 177–99.

Crawf = *The Crawford Collection of Early Charters and Documents*, ed. A. S. Napier and W. H. Stevenson. Oxford, 1895.

Crispin = *Gilbert Crispin, Abbot of Westminster*, ed. J. Armitage Robinson. Cambridge, 1911.

CS = *Cartularium Saxonicum*, ed. W. de G. Birch. 3 vols. London, 1885–93.

CW = Hart, C., 'The *Codex Wintoniensis* and the King's Haligdom', *Agricultural History Review*, Supplement to XVIII (1970), pp. 7–38.

D = Dugdale's list of charters at Worcester in 1643 (Bodleian Library, MS. Dugdale 12, pp. 502–6).

DB = Domesday Book.

DC = Hart, C., 'Danelaw Charters and the Glastonbury Scriptorium', *Downside Review*, 90 (1972), pp. 125–32.

Davis = Davis, G. R. C., *Medieval Cartularies of Great Britain*. London, 1958.

Dugdale = Dugdale, W., *Monasticon Anglicanum*, ed. J. Caley, H. Ellis, and B. Bandinel. 6 vols. in 8. London, 1817–30.

Duignan = Duignan, W. H., *The Charter of Wulfrun to the Monastery of 'Hamtun'*. Wolverhampton, 1888.

Drögereit   =Drögereit, R., 'Gab es eine Angelsächsishe Königskanzlei?', *Archiv für Urkundenforschung*, XIII (1935), pp. 335–436.

ECDC   =Finberg, H. P. R., *The Early Charters of Devon and Cornwall* (2nd edn). Leicester, 1963.

ECEE   =Hart, C., *The Early Charters of Eastern England*. Leicester, 1966.

ECEss   =Hart, C., *The Early Charters of Essex* (2nd edn). Leicester, 1971.

ECW   =Finberg, H. P. R., *The Early Charters of Wessex*. Leicester, 1964.

ECWM   =Finberg, H. P. R., *The Early Charters of the West Midlands* (2nd edn). Leicester, 1972.

Encom. Emmæ   =Campbell, A. (ed.), *Encomium Emmæ Reginæ*. Royal Historical Society, Camden 3rd series, Vol. 72. London, 1949.

Eddius, *Vita Wilfridi*   =Colgrave, B., *The Life of Bishop Wilfrid by Eddius Stephanus*. Cambridge, 1927.

EHD   =*English Historical Documents*, ed. D. C. Douglas. London (Vol. I, ed. D. Whitelock, 1955; Vol. II, ed. D. C. Douglas and G. W. Greenaway, 1959).

EHR   =*English Historical Review*.

EYC   =*Early Yorkshire Charters*, ed. W. Farrer. Edinburgh. Vol. I, 1914.

Finberg 1969   =Finberg, H. P. R., *West-Country Historical Studies*. Newton Abbot, Devon, 1969.

FlWig   =*Florentii Wigorniensis Monachi Chronicon ex Chronicis*, ed. B. Thorpe. 2 vols. London, 1848.

Freeman, NC   =Freeman, E. A., *The History of the Norman Conquest of England*. 5 vols., and index vol. Oxford, 1870–9.

GC   =Dom Aelred Watkin (ed.), *The Great Chartulary of Glastonbury*. Somerset Record Society, 3 vols. LIX, LXIII, LXIV. 1947–56.

H   =Harmer, F. E. (ed.), *Anglo-Saxon Writs*. Manchester, 1952.

Ha   =Harmer, F. E. (ed.), *Select English Historical Documents*. Cambridge, 1914.

Hart 1973   =Hart, C., 'Athelstan Half-King and his Family', *Anglo-Saxon England*, II. Cambridge, 1973, pp. 115–44.

Hart, *History Studies*   =Hart, C., 'The Site of Assandun', *History Studies*, I (1968), pp. 1–12.

HC   =Mellows, W. T. (ed.), *The Chronicle of Hugh Candidus*. Oxford, 1949.

HCY   =*The Historians of the Church of York and its Archbishops*, ed. J. Raine. 3 vols. Rolls Series, 71, 1879–94.

HE   =*Historia Ecclesiastica*, in Plummer, *Bede*.

Hid Northants   =Hart, C., *The Hidation of Northamptonshire*. Leicester, 1970.

JEPN   =*Journal of the English Place-Name Society*.

K   =Kemble, J. M. (ed.), *Codex Diplomaticus Aevi Saxonici*. 6 vols. London, 1839–48.

KBL   =*The Heads of Religious Houses: England and Wales 940–1216*, ed. D. Knowles, C. N. L. Brooke, and Vera C. M. London. Cambridge, 1972.

Ker   =Ker, N. R., *Catalogue of Manuscripts Containing Anglo-Saxon*. Oxford, 1957.

Kirby   =Kirby, D. P., 'Bede and Northumbrian Chronology', EHR LXXVIII (1963), pp. 514–27.

LC   =Stenton, F. M., *The Latin Charters of the Anglo-Saxon Period*. Oxford, 1955.

LE   =Blake, E. O. (ed.), *Liber Eliensis*. Royal Historical Society, Camden 3rd series, Vol. 92. London, 1962.

Levison   =Levison, W., *England and the Continent in the Eighth Century*. Oxford, 1946.

LH   =*Liber Monasterii de Hyda*, ed. E. Edwards. Rolls Series, 45, 1866.

Lucerna   =H. P. R. Finberg, *Lucerna*. London, 1964.

LVH   =*Liber Vitæ: Register and Martyrology of New Minster and Hyde Abbey, Winchester*, ed. W. de Gray Birch. Hampshire Record Society, 1892.

Muchelney   =*Two Cartularies of the Benedictine Abbeys of Muchelney and Athelney*, ed. E. H. Bates. Somerset Record Society, XIV (1899).

OB = John, E., *Orbis Britanniæ and Other Studies*. Leicester, 1966.

O'D = O'Donovan, Mary Anne, 'An interim revision of episcopal dates for the province of Canterbury, 850–950', *Anglo-Saxon England*, I, Cambridge, 1972, pp. 23–44; II, Cambridge, 1973, pp. 91–114.

OE = Old English.

Offler = Offler, H. S. (ed.), *Durham Episcopal Charters, 1071–1152*. Surtees Society, CLXXIX. Gateshead, 1968.

Oleson = Oleson, T. J., *The Witenagemot in the Reign of Edward the Confessor*. Oxford, 1955.

ON = Old Norse.

OS Facs = *Facsimiles of Anglo-Saxon Manuscripts*, ed. W. B. Sanders. 3 parts. Southampton, 1878–84.

Peniarth Cartulary = National Library of Wales, MS. Peniarth 390, ff. 173^r–184^v; the manuscript is described on p. 153 below.

PN = (followed by the name of a county) the publications of the English Place-Name Society.

Plummer, *Bede* = *Venerabilis Bedæ Opera Historica*, ed. C. Plummer. 2 vols. Oxford, 1896.

R = Robertson, A. J. (ed.), *Anglo-Saxon Charters* (2nd edn). Cambridge, 1956.

RBD = Craster, H. E., 'The Red Book of Durham', ERH XL (1925), pp. 504–32.

Richardson and Sayles = Richardson, H. G. and Sayles, G. O. *The Governance of Mediæval England*. Edinburgh, 1963.

Robinson = Robinson, J. A., *The Times of St Dunstan*. Oxford, 1923.

Rochester = *Charters of Rochester*, ed. A. Campbell. London, 1973.

S = Sawyer, P. H., *Anglo-Saxon Charters*. Royal Historical Society. London, 1968.

SBW = Robinson, J. A., *The Saxon Bishops of Wells*,

British Academy Supplementary Paper V. London, 1919.

SD = *Symeonis Monachi Opera Omnia*, ed. T. Arnold. 2 vols. Rolls Series, 75. 1882–5.

Staffs DB = Slade, C. F., 'The Staffordshire Domesday', VCH *Staffs*, IV, 1958.

Stenton = Stenton, F. M., *Anglo-Saxon England* (2nd edn). Oxford, 1946.

Stenton, *Medeshamstede* = Stenton, F. M., 'Medeshamstede and its Colonies', *Historical Essays in Honour of James Tait*. Manchester, 1933, pp. 313–26.

Stenton, *Papers* = *Preparatory to Anglo-Saxon England: The Collected Papers of Frank Merry Stenton*, ed. D. M. Stenton. Oxford, 1970.

Stenton, *Types* = Stenton, F. M., *Types of Manorial Structure in the Northern Danelaw*. Oxford, 1910.

TRE = in the time of King Edward the Confessor.

Th = Thorney charter, edited in ECEE, pp. 146–209.

VCH = (followed by the name of a county) Victoria County History.

Vita Wlsini = Talbot, C. H. (ed.), 'The Life of St Wulsin of Sherborne by Goscelin', *Revue Benedictine*, LXIX (1959), pp. 68–85.

W = Whitelock, D. (ed.), *Anglo-Saxon Wills*, Cambridge, 1930.

W. Salt = William Salt Archaeological Society, *Collections for a History of Staffordshire*.

WCD = Winchester Cathedral Documents (*Documents relating to the History of the Cathedral Church of Winchester*, ed. W. R. W. Stephens and F. T. Madge. Hampshire Record Society, 1897, II, pp. 60–4).

WDB = The Westminster Domesday, an unpublished cartulary written early in the fourteenth century, and preserved in the abbey archives, Muniment Book II; cf. Davis No. 1013.

Widmore, *Westminster* = Widmore, R., *Enquiry into the Time of the first Foundation of Westminster Abbey*. 1743.

WM   =William of Malmesbury, *Gesta Regum*, ed. W. Stubbs. 2 vols., Rolls Series, 90. 1887–9.

YE   =East Riding of Yorkshire.

YN   =North Riding of Yorkshire.

YW   =West Riding of Yorkshire.

CODE OF SYMBOLS

† Original charter, authenticity not in doubt. This symbol is reserved for a text surviving on a single membrane, written in a hand thought to be contemporary with the transaction it records.

* Charter available only in a later copy or copies, authenticity not in doubt. The copy may survive either on a single membrane written in a hand which is thought to be later than the transaction which it records, or as an entry in a gospel-book or cartulary, or as a late manuscript or printed copy of an original charter since lost. This section includes otherwise reliable charters which lack short portions of the original text, such as names in the witness list, and boundary clauses; or having late forms of personal or place-names.

** Charter available only in a later copy or copies, thought to embody the substance of the original, but having some material, spurious or genuine, substituted or interpolated.

*** Charter thought to be fundamentally a fabrication, but which may embody some authentic material or record a genuine transaction.

**** Charter thought to be a complete fabrication.

◆ English translation.

PART I
THE NORTH MIDLANDS

CHAPTER I

THE EARLY CHARTERS OF NORTHAMPTONSHIRE[1]

1. 664   ****WULFHERE, king of the Mercians and Middle and Southern Angles, to the monastery at *Medeshamstede* (Peterborough). Foundation charter. Lands granted include *Wermington* (Warmington), *Undale* (Oundle), *Aiston* (Ashton Wold), *Chirchefelde* (Churchfield), *Stoke* (Stoke), *Benifelde* (Benefield), *Glapthorn* (Glapthorn), *Cotherstoke* (Cotter-stock), *Stanewigge* (Stanwick), *Irtelingburge* (Irthling-borough), *Ketteringge* (Kettering), *Cotingham* (Cottingham), *Carleton* (East Carleton), *Pittelle* (Pytchley), *Norhamtonne* (Northampton), and *Ollanege* (Olney). Lands in Hunts., Kent, Leics., Lincs., Notts., Rutland, Salop, Soke of Peterborough, and Yorks.   CS 22, 22a.

ASC E *s.a.* 656; HC pp. 10–13. A post-Conquest forgery, see ECEE No. 1. See also pp. 67, 111, and 117.

2. 944   †EDMUND, king of the English, to Ælfric, bishop [of Hereford]. 30 'mansas' *æt Baddanbyrig and to Doddanforda and to Eferdune* (Badby, Dodford, and Everdon), free of all but the three common dues.   CS 792.

Birch notes the inclusion of several parenthetic sentences in the boundary clause, and it is possible that the surviving membrane is a contemporary copy of a chancery charter, made for Bishop Ælfric's use. On the subsequent history of this estate, see No. 18. It was acquired by Evesham Abbey some time in the late eleventh or early twelfth century, and the charter was preserved there subsequently. The bounds, which are very detailed, are worked out (probably by F. M. Stenton) in PN *Northants.*, p. 10 n.1, where it is established that the estate comprised Newnham,

---

[1] Rutland and the Soke of Peterborough, which once formed part of Northamptonshire, are dealt with in ECEE.

in addition to Badby, Dodford, and Everdon. On the hidation, see *Hid. Northants.*, pp. 35–7.

3. 946 (after 26 May) *EADRED, king of the Anglo-Saxons and Northumbrians, pagans, and Britons, to his *pedisequus* Wulfric. 7 'manentes' at *Wurcingtune* (Warkton), free of all but the three common dues.   CS 815.

EHD I, pp. 508–9. The surviving text lacks the boundary clause. The grant was made at Kingston-on-Thames, on the occasion of Eadred's coronation. On the king's title, see ECEE pp. 196–7. This charter is one of the 'Dunstan A' alliterative group discussed in DC pp. 125–32 (see p. 19 above).

4. 956 *EADWIG, king of the English and surrounding peoples, to his thegn Eadwig. 8 'mansae' at *Brantestun* (Braunston).   CS 978.

Bu XIV. OS Facs III, Anglesey 1. The surviving text may be a copy made later in the tenth century, but the frequent high 'e' ligatures are more often encountered in mid-tenth-century texts. The membrane measures 376 mm. long by 432 mm. wide. It was folded four times at an early date, so forming 16 panels. On one of the outside panels is entered an early, but probably not contemporary, endorsement in regular form (CW p. 22). The last three letters of the king's name in this endorsement were added at a later date, presumably over an erasure; it is not possible to tell whether the original name was Ead*red* or Ead*gar*; Ead*mund* would take up too much space. Hidage: *Hid. Northants.*, pp. 34–5. Bounds: PN *Northants.*, p. 14 n.1; Stenton, *Types*, p. 72 n.3. The witness list, which is incomplete and has been amended by a different hand, is similar to those in some Abingdon texts, particularly the contemporary CS 965; probably these two charters were issued on the same date, in the autumn of 956. The proem appears to have originated in 940 (CS 761), but the whole charter is modelled on a text of the year 942, exemplified by the Berkshire charter CS 778, preserved in an Abingdon cartulary.

The charter is considered at present to be authentic, but in view of the alterations to the endorsement and the witness list, there must be some reservation concerning this. So far, I have not found any other of the numerous charters of King Eadwig that is modelled so completely on an exemplar some 14 years earlier in date. There is, however, evidence of such a trend commencing early in Edgar's reign; e.g. Bu XIX, dated 962, is modelled on a text similar to that of CS 743, dated 939 (see No. 56). The issue of conservative charters of this type became common in the reign of Æthelred II.

It is quite possible that we have in the text of this charter an early example of a diploma drawn up by an Abingdon scribe; further palaeographical study is needed before any conclusion can be reached as to whether the surviving copy is in a contemporary script, and whether this script can be assigned to the scriptorium at Abingdon or some other major centre.

5. 956   *EADWIG, king of the English and other peoples, to his thegn Ælfsige. 10 'cassati' æt Cytringan (Kettering), free of all but the three common dues.   CS 943.

> Bounds: PN *Northants.*, p. 184 n.1. The recipient, who was given part of Ailsworth in Northants. by King Eadred in 948 (CS 871), and Haddon in Hunts. by King Eadred in 951 (ECEE no. v), owned part of Yaxley in Hunts. towards the end of Eadred's reign (R XLIV). The estates at Yaxley and Ailsworth descended to his son Wulfstan Uccea; he exchanged them for other lands with Bishop Æthelwold of Winchester, who used them for the endowment of Thorney Abbey (ECEE no. VII). Kettering was used to endow Peterborough Abbey, probably also via Wulfstan Uccea and Bishop Æthelwold (No. 7).
>
> This is a typical chancery text of the year 956, with formulas close to those of No. 106, issued on the same day. There is a problem over the hidation of this charter, see *Hid. Northants.*, p. 34.

6. 956   *EADWIG, ruler of the whole island of Albion, to his relative Brihthelm, bishop-elect [of Wells]. 5 'mansæ' æt Stowe (Stowe Nine Churches).   CS 986.

> Bounds: PN *Northants.*, p. 30 n.1. Hidation: *Hid. Northants.*, p. 34. Brihthelm gave this estate to Abingdon (Chron Abingd I, p. 234), a house with which he had other dealings (R XXXI). The charter was preserved at Abingdon.

7. N.D.   (c. 971 × 984)   *Bishop ÆTHELWOLD's gifts to Peterborough Abbey on its restoration. Lands include

Undelum with its berewicks, and *Keteiringan* (Oundle and Kettering). Lands in Hunts. and the Soke of Peterborough.
R xxix.

ECEE No. 13. On the revised date, see p. 326. After the death of King Edgar, Oundle and Kettering were appropriated by a thegn called Leofsige, who was killed by order of Ælfwold, brother of Ealdorman Æthelwine of East Anglia; the estates were restored to Peterborough by the sentence of an assembly at London, confirmed by the shire-court of Northampton. LE pp. xii–xiii.

8. 972   ***Edgar, king of Great Britain, at the petition of Bishop Æthelwold, to the monastery once called *Medesham-stede* and now, being restored, called *Burch* (Peterborough). Confirmation of privileges, and lands including the vill of *Undale* with the whole of the jurisdiction of the adjacent vills, called in English *Eahtahundred* (the eight hundreds of Oundle); also *Wermington* (Warmington), *Æsctun* (Ashton Wold), and *Kyteringas* (Kettering). Lands in Hunts., Lincs., and the Soke of Peterborough.
CS 1258, 1280 (Latin), 1281 (OE).

ECEE 15. For the eight hundreds of Oundle, see H. Cam, *Liberties and Communities in Mediæval England*, 2nd edn, London, 1963, p. 101; also *Hid. Northants.*, pp. 21, 39 n.3. The meeting-place of this group of hundreds in late Saxon times was at Wansford (R p. 76; LE p. 85).

9. (28 Dec. 974) ***King Edgar to Ramsey Abbey. Foundation charter, confirming the gifts of lands by various donors, including *Isham* (Isham) and *Wichentonam* (Whiston), given by Ealdorman Brihtnoth. Lands in Cambs., Hunts., and Norfolk.
CS 1310, 1311.

ECEE 18. Forged by Osbert de Clare, see Chaplais 1962, pp. 92–5. Chron Rams pp. 116–17 has a story that Brihtnoth, leading his army to battle against the Danes (presumably at Maldon), sought unsuccessfully food and hospitality from Abbot Wulfsige of Ramsey. Angered by this refusal, he moved on to Ely where the reception was very different, and his troops were fully provisioned. He transferred his gift, therefore, of Isham

and Whiston from Ramsey to Ely. The account goes on to say
that Brihtnoth, dying on the battlefield, repented of his decision
and gave Ramsey one hide at *Dodintonam*, which must be Denton,
1 mile south of Whiston. DB shows Ramsey holding 3 hides at
Denton and Whiston. Some details of the story are confirmed in
an Ely source (LE p. 135), but the dying bequest at Maldon
sounds very improbable, and there are too many inconsistencies
of chronology for this account to be accepted without reservation
(LE p. 422; E. V. Gordon, *The Battle of Maldon*, 2nd edn,
London, 1949, pp. 8–9).

10. 975 × 979 BYRHTNOTH, abbot of Ely, to Eadnoth,
prior of Ramsey. One hide at *Bottintonia* (Boddington).
Chron Rams pp. 74–5.

This gift formed part of a wider exchange of property between
the two abbeys, cf. ECEE 317, where *Bottintonia* is wrongly
identified with Boughton, Northants.

11. N.D. (983 × 985) *List of sureties for Peterborough
estates, including: *Wyrmingtune* (Warmington), *Beringafelde*
(Benefield), *Esctune* (Ashton Wold), and *Ludingtune*
(Lutton). Lands in the Soke of Peterborough. ◆ R XL.

ECEE 164.

12. N.D. (c. 987) *Record of a transaction concerning
land at *Bernewelle* (Barnwell), *Wiclea* (Weekley), and
Aclea (Oakley), and land in Hunts.
Chron Rams pp. 76–8.

ECEE 23. This is a complicated three-cornered transaction,
which reads like a Latin abstract of one of the OE law memoranda characteristic of the period. The three parties were the
monks of Ramsey (represented by their prior, Eadnoth),
Leofwine son of Ealdorman Æthelwine of East Anglia, and a
priest called Osward who was related to Alfwenna, the youngest
daughter (wrongly called the *wife* in this account) of Athelstan
Mannessune, a prominent thegn of the eastern Danelaw, and a
benefactor to Ramsey Abbey. The transaction took place some
time after Athelstan's death on 14 June 986. By virtue of his relationship with Athelstan, Osward had acquired 10 hides at St Ives,
Hunts., which ought to have descended to Ramsey according to

Athelstan's will (ECEE 21). At the same time, Leofwine had succeeded in a lawsuit against Osward's son, in which he claimed 8 hides at Oakley and 10 at Weekley, although this issue was still being contested. The monks at Ramsey, for their part, had 18 hides in Barnwell, the possession of which had also been in dispute, a shire-court held at Northampton in the reign of Edward the Martyr (975–9) having declared that the estate should descend to the king. (Evidently this dispute arose during the anti-monastic upsurge in Edward's reign.) King Edward, however, had allowed it to stay in the possession of Ramsey. Osward's solution, which was accepted by Eadnoth and agreed to by the king (presumably Æthelred II), was as follows: Ramsey should give 2 hides at Thurning (formerly in Hunts., now in Northants.) to Leofwine, together with the tenancy of its 18 hides at Barnwell; Leofwine should forgo his claim to Oakley and Weekley in favour of Osward's son, and Osward should surrender the 10 hides at St Ives to Ramsey. For Athelstan Mannessune, see CAS LVI–LVII, 1964, pp. 61–7.

13. N.D. (990 × c. 1000) *Will of ÆLFHILD. Land at *Cloptuna* (Clapton) to her chaplain Ælfmær, with reversion to Ramsey Abbey.   CS 1061.

ECEE 26.

14. 993 × 1006 Ealdorman ÆLFHELM [of Deira] to Peterborough Abbey. *Cotingham* (Cottingham), *Middletune* (Middleton), and *Benefeild* (Benefield), with all their appurtenances.   Lost.

HC p. 69. ECEE 347. Peterborough had already acquired an estate at Benefield (No. 11); presumably Ælfhelm's gift added to this.

15. 1013 *ÆTHELRED, ruler and monarch of the Anglo-Saxons and Northumbrians, protector of the heathens, and emperor of the Britons and other provinces, to the thegn Northman. 3½ 'cassatae' at *Twiwelle* (Twywell), free of all but the three common dues.   K 1308.

Edited in ECEE pp. 193–8. Bounds: PN *Northants*, p. 188. Hidation: *Hid. Northants*, p. 34.

16. 1016 × 1034 ÆTHELRIC, bishop of Dorchester, to Ramsey Abbey, for the support of the monks. Lands at *Bernewelle* (Barnwell) and *Hemingtone* (Hemington). Lands in Cambs. and Hunts. *Lost.*

    Chron Rams p. 144. ECEE 320.

17. 1017 × 1035 *Will of MANTAT the Anchorite. *Twywelle* (Twywell) and *Cunintun* (Conington, Hunts.) to Thorney Abbey. ◆ W XXIII.

    Also edited, from an earlier text, in ECEE pp. 204–5.

18. 1020 ****CNUT, king of the English, and his wife Ælfgifu, to the church of the Blessed Virgin Mary and St Ecgwine at *Eouesham* (Evesham), for the benefice of their beloved monk *Euich* (Æfic). 4 'mansae' at *Badebi* (Badby) and *Newæham* (Newnham), free of all but the three common dues. K 1316.

This charter forms one of a small series of texts, ostensibly pre-Conquest, relating to Badby and Newnham, all of them entered in a twelfth-century Evesham cartulary (Nos. 2, 18, 19, 31). In two cases the original (or near-original) charters have been preserved (Nos. 2, 19). By reconstructing, as far as is ascertainable, the highly complex history of the estates concerned, it is possible not only to assess the authenticity of these texts, but also to establish some of the circumstances leading to their composition. That the monk Æfic was a historical personage there can be no doubt. Under the name *Avicius*, he figures in the Evesham Chronicle's account of the abbacy of Ælfweard, who held the abbey in plurality with the bishopric of London. Æfic was prior of Evesham Abbey at this period, and no doubt its effective ruler; he was also the first of a long line of deans of the Vale of Evesham (Chron E pp. 83, 85). We find his death recorded in ASC C *s.a.* 1037. Returning to the abbey's chronicle, we are told that Æfic inherited Badby and Newnham from his father, and gave them to the abbey; from analogy with similar grants to other monasteries at this period, we may suppose that these estates were the price paid by his parents for the reception of Æfic into the monastery as a child oblate, or possibly for his subsequent election as prior. His father may have inherited the estates from Ælfric, bishop of Hereford, to whom they had been granted by King Edmund in 944, by a charter of which an early copy passed into the possession of Evesham (No. 2). The boundary clause of this charter suggests that Badbury may have been a small fortified *burh* (constructed perhaps during Edward the Elder's campaign against the Danish army of Northampton), and that some of the adjacent territory remained in King Edmund's possession after his grant to Ælfric. King Cnut's charter granting Newnham to Æfic in 1021 × 1023, also preserved at the abbey, was perhaps no more than a confirmation of the allocation of this estate to the endowment of Evesham (No. 19). There is some difficulty here, because Evesham also preserved the text of an OE boundary embracing Badby, Newnham, and Dodford, but excluding Everdon (No. 31); the date appears to fall between Nos. 2 and 19, and it is in fact the earliest authentic text to mention Newnham (the 'new ham') by name, but it would be hazardous to speculate on the circumstances attending its composition (see further, *Hid. Northants.*, pp. 35–7). This problem, however, need not detain us; what matters is that according to the Evesham story, which appears to be reliable, Badby and Newnham were given to the abbey by Æfic. Subsequently, for some reason unknown to us, Æfic's parents took back possession of these two estates into their own hands – unjustly, according to the Evesham account; eventually, they are said to have been restored to the abbey by Æfic's brother Wulfsige (Chron E p. 83). Some account of Wulfsige is given elsewhere in the Evesham Chronicle (Chron E p. 322), and in Peter of Blois's continuation of the pseudo-Ingulf (Fulman, *Scriptores*, pp. 121–4), from which it appears that he was a monk of Crowland who came to Evesham at some unspecified date and led an eremetical life there for many years (the Evesham Chronicle says 75 years), dying in 1097–8; he was buried at Evesham, and subsequently became a local saint, whose festival was kept there until the Dissolution. We may think it improbable that Wulfsige spent 75 years as an anchorite, and still more so that he was Æfic's brother; it is tempting to speculate that he was really Æfic's son, and that this inconvenient relationship was suppressed by the chronicler. Whatever the precise kinship, we have here a clue to the DB entry that Crowland owned Badby TRE, and was still the owner in 1086. By 1104 at the latest, Badby and Newnham had been acquired by Evesham (EHR XLVIII

(1933), pp. 195–6), and they remained in Evesham's possession until the Dissolution (Dugdale II, pp. 31, 47–8). It cannot be doubted that the Evesham Chronicle is correct in its claim that they were restored to the abbey by Wulfsige. Armed with this information, we can turn at last to the examination of K 1316, which we find to be a transparent forgery, based on the text of the authentic No. 19. It is best regarded as one of the extensive group of charters manufactured at Evesham during the abbacy of Walter at the end of the eleventh century. Besides this Badby text, the group includes charters for Evenlode, Glos. (ECWM 35, 44, 161), and Wixford and Temple Grafton, Warwicks. (No. 57); all share the common feature that they are modelled on authentic texts. The date of composition of the Badby charter can be pinpointed to the period 1097 × 1104, and it seems likely that the whole series of Evesham forgeries is to be similarly dated.

19. 1021 × 1023 †CNUT, king of the Anglo-Saxons, to the monk Æfic. 5 'cassati' æt Niwanham (Newnham). K 736.

BM Facs IV, 16. For the chrismon prefacing this charter, see the notes to Bu XXXII. The charter was drawn up by Æthelric, the diocesan bishop, see EHR XXIX (1914), p. 693 n. 18; EHD I, p. 342; Chaplais 1966, p. 13. See also the notes to No. 18 above. Wrongly located in Nottinghamshire by Sawyer (No. 977). For the bounds, see PN Northants., p. 26 n.1. According to the Evesham Chronicle, Cnut also gave one hide in Northampton to the abbey (Chron E p. 75).

20. 1041 × 1057 Earl RAULF [of Herefordshire] to Peterborough Abbey. Estun (Easton), Prestegraue (Prestgrave), and Dreitun (Drayton). Lands in Leics. and Rutland.
Lost.

HC p. 69. ECEE 352. See also p. 71.

21. 1042 × 1055 The Lady GODGIT to Peterborough Abbey. Land in Bernuele (Barnwell). Lands in Lincs. and Yorks. *Lost.*

HC p. 70. ECEE 353. Probably she is to be identified with Godgifu, the wife of Earl Siward of Northumbria and Huntingdon. See also p. 129.

22. 1043 ****LEOFRIC, earl of 'Chester', to Coventry Abbey. Foundation charter, naming, among other lands, *Kyldesby* (Kilsby) and *Wynwyke* (Winwick). Lands in Ches., Glos., Leics., Warwicks., and Worcs.   K 939.

ECWM 159. Miss J. Lancaster, 'The Coventry Forged Charters: a Reconsideration', *Bulletin of the Institute of Historical Research*, XXVII (1954), pp. 113–40. See also pp. 71, 87, and 129.

23. 1043 ****EDWARD, king of the English, to Coventry Abbey. General confirmation of lands and privileges, naming, among other lands, *Kildesbig* (Kilsby) and *Winewican* (Winwick). Lands in Ches., Leics., Warwicks., and Worcs.   K 916.

ECWM 160. See No. 22, also pp. 71, 88, and 129.

24. 2 July 1044 Will of ÆLFWEARD, bishop of London. Land at *Hemmingetonam* (Hemington) to Ramsey Abbey. Land in Cambs.   *Lost.*

Chron Rams p. 198. ECEE 337.

25. N.D. (1055 × 1065) *King EDWARD to Bishop Wulfwig, Earl Tostig, the sheriff Northman, and all his thegns in Northamptonshire. Writ declaring that he has confirmed the agreement made between Ælfwine, abbot of Ramsey, and Leofric, abbot of Peterborough, by which nine virgates of land at *Lodintonam* (Lutton) have been given to Ramsey in exchange for land at *Marham* (Marholm, in the Soke of Peterborough); in addition, King Edward confirms an agreement between Ramsey and Peterborough for provision of building stone from Barnack (in the Soke of Peterborough), and a further agreement between Ramsey and Siward, abbot of Thorney, concerning the boundaries of King's Delph in Whittlesey Mere, Cambs.   ◆ H 62.

ECEE 45. The earliest surviving copy of this writ is in a charter of inspeximus now in the possession of Ramsey Abbey School (photo at Cambridge County Archive Office, Huntingdon). Five of the nine virgates at Lutton are named in the writ, the four remaining virgates comprising a hide of land called *Huntinges hide*.

26. 1060   ***Restoration by King EDWARD to Leofric, abbot of Peterborough, of *Astuna* (Ashton Wold), and lands in Lincs. and Hunts., all of which had come into the hands of Queen Edith.   HC p. 40.

ECEE 358. This is a post-Conquest forgery, but there is no reason to disbelieve that the transaction took place. Probably these estates had been assigned to augment the dowry of Queen Edith, which comprised part of Rutland.

27. c. 1060   BURRED and his parents to Peterborough Abbey. *Bartune iuxta ketteringe* (Barton Seagrave).   *Lost*.

HC p. 69. ECEE 356. This sounds like a gift accompanying the presentation of Burred as a novice at the abbey. There is no means of dating it precisely. The entry goes on to say that the estate was held in demesne and at farm, but Geoffrey, bishop of St Lothe (i.e. Coutances), the king's justiciar, stole it from the abbey. DB shows him holding $4\frac{1}{2}$ hides there.

28. (c. 1062)   ***EDWARD, king of all Britain, to Ramsey Abbey. Confirmation of title to lands including *Wichinton* (Whiston), *Ysham* (Isham), *Bernewell* (Barnwell), and *Hemingeton* (Hemington). Lands in Hunts., Lincs., Cambs., Beds., Norfolk, and Suffolk.   K 809.

ECEE 47. A post-Conquest forgery by Osbert de Clare; cf. Chaplais 1962, pp. 92–5.

29. 1065   ***King EDWARD to Westminster Abbey. Confirmation of estates, including *Den* (Deene) and *Suthburhc* (Sudborough). Lands in Middlesex, Herts., Essex, Surrey, Kent, Sussex, Suffolk, Bucks., Berks., Oxon., Rutland, Worcs., Glos., and Staffs.

Widmore, *Westminster*, App. II.

ECEss 69; ECEE 118A; ECWM 184. Forged possibly by Osbert de Clare; cf. Chaplais 1962, pp. 92–4. See also p. 100.

30. 28 Dec. 1065   ***King EDWARD to Westminster Abbey. Confirmation of estates, including *Dene* (Deene), and *Suthburhte* (Sudborough). Lands in Middlesex, Herts., Essex, Surrey, Kent, Sussex, Bucks., Oxon., Rutland, Worcs., Glos., and Staffs.   K 824.

> ECEss 68; ECWM 183. Forged by Osbert de Clare; cf. Chaplais 1962, pp. 92–4. See also pp. 100–1.

31. N.D.   *Bounds of *Baddanbyrig* (Badby).   K 1356.

> The bounds are typical of a late OE perambulation. See further, p. 62.

32. N.D.   *Bounds of *Undelam* (Oundle) and *Beringafeld* (Benefield).   CS 1129.

> PN *Northants.*, p. 213, gives a few identifications, but these bounds have not as yet been fully worked out. The first part of the perambulation, as far as Churchfield (grid ref. 003876), is easy to follow, but afterwards one gets lost, and it is apparent that the ancient bounds of Benefield embraced a much smaller area than the present parish.

ADDENDUM

11a. N.D.   (c. 985 × 1002)   †Will of ÆTHELGIFU. Land at *Þeodune* (Weedon Bec) to Leofsige. Land at *Þadforda* (Watford) to her kinswoman Leofrun, with reversion to Leofrun's daughter Godwif. Land *æt þrope* (Thrupp) to her kinswoman Leofrun, with reversion to Leofrun's own kindred. Lands in Beds. and Herts.

> ◆ D. Whitelock, *The Will of Æthelgifu*. Oxford, The Roxburghe Club, 1968.

CHAPTER II

THE EARLY CHARTERS OF LEICESTERSHIRE

(1) 664 ***WULFHERE, king of the Mercians and Middle and Southern Angles, to the monastery at *Medeshamstede* (Peterborough). Foundation charter. Lands granted include *Bredun* (Breedon on the Hill), *Langeton* (Langton), and *Eston* (Great Easton), with its appurtenant estates at *Brimhurst* (Bringhurst) and *Prestegrave* (Prestgrave, Np). Lands in Hunts., Kent, Lincs., Northants., Notts., Rutland, Salop, Soke of Peterborough, and Yorks. Cs 22, 22a.

See also pp. 55, 111, and 117.

32a. N.D. (675 × 691) FRIDURIC, the most religious of King Æthelred's *principes*, to the *familia* of St Peter's at the monastery of *Medeshamstede* (Peterborough), for his soul's health, and with the consent of Saxulf, bishop [of the Mercians] and Æthelred, king [of the Mercians]. 20 *manentes* at *Bredune* (Breedon on the Hill), to found a monastery there, and to appoint a priest of good repute to minister baptism and teaching to those people assigned to him. *Lost.*

The epitome of this lost charter was published by Birch as CS 841 from the Peterborough *Liber Niger*. The entry goes on to say that the brethren of *Medeshamstede* chose one of their number, the priest Hedda, to be the first abbot at Breedon, on condition that he acknowledged himself as a member of their fraternity. ◆Stenton's *Medeshamstede*, p. 316, the source of the above translation. There is no reason to doubt any of the information in this entry.

33. (680) ***Pope AGATHO to Æthelred, king of the Mercians, Theodore, archbishop of Canterbury, and Saxulf, bishop of the Middle Angles or Mercians. Letter

granting privileges to *Medeshamstede* (Peterborough), with confirmation by King Æthelred of privileges and lands including *Bredune* (Breedon on the Hill). Lands in Salop, Lincs., and Kent.   CS 48 (Latin) and 49 (OE).

See Stenton's *Medeshamstede*, p. 314, Levison p. 201; ECWM p. 427; ECEE 146. The Latin version derives from a translation of the OE in Spelman's *Concilia*, 1, pp. 164–5, and has no early authority.

34. 848   *BEORHTWULF, king of the Mercians, to Abbot Eanmund and the *familia* of the monastery at *Breodune* (Breedon on the Hill). Grant of freedom from those obligations called *feorme* and *eafor* (provision of food and conveyance), including the provisioning of all the royal hawks, huntsmen, horses, and their attendants; except that ambassadors visiting the king from across the sea, or messengers from the West Saxon or Northumbrian peoples, if they arrive at the monastery between tierce (about 9 a.m.) and midday, must be given a meal; or if they arrive after none (about 3 p.m.) they must be provisioned for the night, and fed again before they set out in the morning. For this privilege the monastery gives King Beorhtwulf 180 mancuses of pure gold, and 15 hides in two places, at *Stanlega* and at *Bellanforde*. In addition, Humberht, prince of the *Tomsætan*, releases the monastery from all dues large and small that are owed to him, in return for a gift of money in a valuable drinking vessel of noble origin, beautifully made and partly ornamented with gold. This *scedula* was written at the ancient monastery at *Hrypadune* (Repton, Derbyshire) and subsequently confirmed and ratified by the king in the presence of witnesses.   CS 454.

Stenton, *Medeshamstede*, p. 318 n.3. AHEW p. 459. *Stanlega* may be Stanley, Derbyshire, 8 miles north of Breedon. One of the most important sources for the later history of the Mercian kingdom, this charter has been strangely neglected by historians. The scribe who entered it in the Peterborough Liber Niger misread DCCC.XLVIII as DCCC.XLIIII, but the correct date is preserved by the Indiction, XI. The witness list is wholly compatible with the date, and the formulas are typical of Mercian charters of the period. The long proem is repeated in CS 588, a Wessex charter of 901. Parts of it recur in charters of Edmund (CS 764, 789) and Eadred (CS 862, 864–5, 867, 871), and in later charters modelled on these texts (K 640, 770). In the dispositive clause *magistratuum* recurs in CS 416, dated 836, and *donans donabo* is the normal Mercian form (Chaplais, 1965, p. 59 n. 92). Again, *venerabili abbati . . . et ejus familie . . . libertatis gratiam . . . mihi et omnibus Mercis . . . in elemosinam. . . Id est ut sit liberatum et absolutum illud monasterium ab illis . . .* all recur in CS 434, dated 841. The notable entry which records that the charter was first written, then confirmed by witnesses, is in accord with the evidence of CS 432, which was first written at Cropthorne, Worcs., and subsequently ratified at Tamworth, Staffs., at the Christmas assembly of 841. The charter establishes that Breedon-on-the-Hill was situated in the province of the *Tomsætan*, which included within its bounds King's Norton, south-west of Birmingham (CS 455). The capital was at Tamworth, and it is possible that the *Tomsætan* occupied the whole of the territory of the South Mercians, allotted 5,000 hides by Bede.

35. 1 Nov. 971   Will of Bishop OSCYTEL [of Dorchester]. Land in *Bebui* (Beeby) to Bishop Æthelwold [of Winchester].   *Lost.*

    LE p. 96. ECEE 304.

36. 971 × 975   ÆTHELWOLD, bishop of Winchester, to Thurcytel, abbot of Ramsey [*sic*, for Bedford or Crowland], in exchange for land in Cambs. Land at *Bebui* (Beeby).   *Lost.*

    LE p. 96. ECEE 305.

37. 967 for 974   *EDGAR, ruler of the whole of Britain, to Bishop Æthelwold [of Winchester], for the church of *breodone* (Breedon). 3 'cassati' at *æbredone* (Breedon), 3 at *þifeles Ðorþe* (Wilson), 4 at *digþesþyrþe* (Diseworth), and 3 and *æþeredesdune* (Atterton), free of all but the three common dues.   CS 1283.

    Bu XXII. Stenton, *Types*, p. 78. The bounds are omitted from the surviving text. The date 967 given for this charter is incompatible with the witness list; Oswald, who witnesses as archbishop, did not accede at York until 972. On the other hand, Cyneweard who appears as abbot was appointed from Milton to the see of Wells soon after 15 May 974; and Frithugar, who also witnesses as abbot, was preceded at Evesham by Osweard, who still witnesses as abbot in 974 (†CS 1303).[1]

The charter is modelled on the most common of all the formulas current in Edgar's reign. Individual components such as the exemption clause and the anathema first appear in diplomas of his elder brother Eadwig, but the complete formula (including the king's title, the dispositive clause, passages describing the estate conveyed, naming the recipient, and granting powers of alienation, the exemption and dating clauses, and the anathema) is not encountered until 962, when it is exemplified in two original charters (CS 1083, 1085). From then onwards it occurs in over 25 charters throughout the reign, the latest being CS 1305 and CS 1312, dated 974 and 975 respectively.

Characteristically, the proems of this group of charters differ widely from each other, but apart from this the texts show remarkably little variation. The charter under consideration, however, departs widely from this norm. The unique proem contains a misquotation from Prudentius, *Hamartigena*, l. 257. In the clause naming the recipient, the rarer *vocabulo* replaces the word *onomate* usually employed; similarly, *fidelissimo* appears in place of *fideli*, *constructione* in place of *restauracione*; other unusual words and phrases include *vite sue diebus*; *fastu superius inflatus*; *deputetur*; *satagerit*; *facta est*. It is hard to believe that this charter was drawn up by a chancery scribe; possibly it was written at Æthelwold's foundation at Peterborough, for Breedon was a satellite of Peterborough before the Danish settlement, and Æthelwold is known to have attempted the reconstruction of Peterborough's endowment. Whoever composed this text would appear, however, to have used a contemporary chancery charter for his exemplar.

38. c. 985   FRANE of Rockingham (Northants.) to Peterborough Abbey. *Langtun* (Langton).   *Lost.*

HC p. 70. ECEE 345.

---

[1] Osweard also witnesses as abbot **CS 1304, which claims to be dated 974; but this charter's dating clause appears to depend on the entry for 974 in ASC C, which was not written before the mid-eleventh century.

39. N.D.   (1002 × 1004)   *Will of Wulfric Spot. The estate *æt Twongan* (Tong, Salop) to Æthelric, with reversion to Burton Abbey. *Scenctune* (Shangton), *Wicgestane* (Little Wigston), and one hide at *Scearnforda* (Sharnford) to Burton Abbey. Lands in Glos., Staffs., Lancs., Yorks., Derbys., Lincs., Worcs., Cheshire, and Warwicks.   ◆ W xvii.

   Bu xxviiib. OS Facs iii, Anglesey 2. ECWM 144. ECEE 152. See also pp. 84, 99, 109, and 126.

40. 1004   *Æthelred, king of the English, to Burton Abbey. Exemption from all but the three common dues of lands belonging to the abbey, including *Scenctune* (Shangton), *Witgestane* (Little Wigston), and *Scearnforda* (Sharnford). Lands in Glos., Staffs., Derbys., Salop, Lincs., Warwicks., and Cheshire.   K 710.

   Bu xxviiia. Bridgeman pp. 115–18. Substantial sections of the formulas are identical with those of the Wherwell foundation charter, dated 1002 (K 707). The rest of the diplomatic, and the whole of the witness list, is fully compatible with the date. See also pp. 84, 99, 109, and 126.

(20) 1041 × 1057   Earl Raulf to Peterborough Abbey, *Brinninghurst* (Bringhurst). Lands in Northants. and Rutland.   *Lost.*

   See also p. 63.

(22) 1043   ****Leofric, earl of 'Chester', to Coventry Abbey. Foundation charter, naming, among other lands, *Burbagh* (Burbage), *Barwell* (Barwell), *Scraptofte* (Scraptoft), and *Pakyngton* (Packington). Lands in Warwicks., Northants., Glos., Worcs., and Cheshire.   K 939.

   ECWM 159. See also pp. 64, 87, and 129.

(23) 1043   ***Edward, king of the English, to Coventry Abbey. General confirmation of lands and privileges, naming, among other lands, *Burhbeca* (Burbage), *Barwalle*

(Barwell), *Scrapetoft* (Scraptoft), and *Pakinton* (Packington). Lands in Warwicks., Worcs., Cheshire, and Northants.

K 916.

ECWM 160. See also pp. 64, 88, and 129.

CHAPTER III

THE EARLY CHARTERS OF
WARWICKSHIRE[1]

41. N.D. (?697 × 699) *ÆTHELRED, king [of the Mer-
cians], to Oftfor, bishop [of the Hwicce]. 44 'cassati' at
Fledanburg (Fladbury, Worcs.), in order that monastic
life may be re-established there, as when the place was
first granted. Endorsed with a statement by Oftfor's
successor Ecgwine that he has granted Fladbury to
Æthelheard for life, with a proviso that the rules of
monastic life are still to be kept there, and with reversion
to the bishopric. He has done this in order to recover
from Æthelheard 20 'cassati' at *Strætfordæ* (Stratford-
on-Avon). CS 76.

   ECWM 198. See also No. 45.

42. 699 × 709 **King OFFA to the church of Worcester.
33 'cassati' at *Scottarith* (Shottery). Woodland in Worcs.
CS 123.

   ECWM 200 and p. 182, where it is shown that Offa, called
   mistakenly the king of Mercia in this charter, was in fact king
   of Essex. Bounds: PN *Warwicks.*, p. 239 n.

43. N.D. (704 × 709) *ÆTHELHEARD and ÆTHELWEARD
to Cutsuith, in return for a payment of 600 shillings.
5 'manentes' at *Ingin* (Ingon in Hampton Lucy)
CS 122.

   The five witnesses appear without titles. Coenred, the first,
   was king of Mercia 704–9, whence the dates assigned to the

---

1 Several places in the modern county are surveyed under Worcestershire
in DB, and their charters are to be found in ECWM. These include Tred-
ington, Shipston-on-Stour, King's Norton, Oldberrow, and Little Compton.

charter. The second witness was Ecgwine, bishop of the Hwicce 693 × 717. The names follow of Æthelheard and Æthelweard, the donors. They were brothers, princes of the Hwicce (ECWM p. 177). Cuthbert, the last witness, was probably the *comes Wicciorum* of that name who witnessed CS 116 dated 706, a charter of Æthelweard. Cutswith the recipient of Ingon may have been his relative (?sister); probably she is to be identified with the Abbess Cutswith who received *Penintanham* by CS 85 (ECWM 82; ECW p. 251), on which charter the text at present under discussion was entered as an endorsement (ECWM p. 177 n. 4).

44. 710   ****CEOLRED, king of Mercia, to the church of St Mary, Evesham. 35 'cassati' *in plaga Warewicensi*, namely *Rageleia* (Ragley), *Arue* (Arrow), *Eccleshale* (Exhall), *Wiveleshalle* (unidentified), *Eadrichestone* (Atherstone), *Dorsintone* (Dorsington in Welford-on-Avon), *Brome* (Broom in Bidford), *Mulecote* (Milcote), *Graftone* (Temple Grafton), *Bunintone* (Binton), *Budiford* (Bidford), *Hildeburhwrthe* (Hilborough in Temple Grafton).

CS 127.

Forged at Evesham c. 1097 × 1104, see p. 63. Some of these estates were among those said to have been recovered by Abbot Æthelwig, and usurped again by Bishop Odo of Bayeux (Chron E pp. 95, 97); they appear in a writ to the abbey by William I (Dugdale II, pp. 17–18). Temple Grafton is said to have been given to Evesham by Edward the Confessor in 1055 (Chron E p. 75). On the subsequent history of many of these estates, see R. R. Darlington in EHR XLVIII (1933), pp. 8–9, 10 n.3, 20–1, 189, 195–6.

45. 714   **Statement by ECGWINE, bishop of the Hwicce, for the information of posterity, concerning the lands acquired by him, with full immunities, for the monastery at *Homme* (Evesham): in all, 120 'mansæ'. From King Æthelred, the monastery at *Flendaburch* (Fladbury, Worcs.), which the bishop subsequently exchanged for another monastery at *Streatforda* (Stratford-on-Avon). Other lands include *Withelea* (Weethley), *Samburne* (Sambourne), *Kineuuarton* (Kinwarton), *Saltforde major et minor*

(Salford Priors and Abbots Salford), and *Mapeldosbeordi* (Mappleborough). Lands in Glos. and Worcs.

CS 130, 131.

ECWM 11. CS 131 is an expanded version, giving a fuller account of the Stratford transaction. According to this, King Æthelred gave Stratford to Bishop Ecgwine, and also the monastery at Fladbury which he had inherited from his wife Osthryth; subsequently Stratford was 'unjustly' occupied by Prince Æthelheard of the Hwicce, and in order to get this back Ecgwine gave Æthelheard the monastery at Fladbury. It seems likely that this information is based on No. 41, which has been misinterpreted in some details.

46. 718 × 737 *ÆTHELBALD, king of the Mercians and all of the provinces known as the *Suthengli*, to Æthelric, son of the late King Oshere of the Hwicce. 20 'cassati' at *Uuidutuun* (Wootton Wawen), beside the river *Æluuinnæ* (Alne), in the region of the *Stoppingas*, for a monastery.

CS 157.

ECWM pp. 177–8. OB p. 105. Written at Worcester; cf. Chaplais 1968, p. 333 n. 178.

47. 781 *HEATHURED, bishop of the Hwicce, to Offa, king of the Mercians. Surrender, in a synod at Brentford, of 90 'manentes' belonging to the minster at Bath, with the addition of 30 'cassati' south of the Avon which the bishop has purchased from Cynewulf, king of Wessex. In return, Offa confirms the bishop in possession of certain other lands which had been in dispute between them, the king having claimed them as heir of his kinsman Æthelbald, viz. 30 'cassati' at *Stretforda* (Stratford-on-Avon), 38 at *Sture* (the river Stour in east Worcs. and Warwicks.), 14 'manentes' at *Sture in Usmerum* (the river Stour that joins the Severn at Stourport), 12 at *Breodune* (Bredon, Worcs.), and 17 in *Homtune* (Hampton Lucy); he grants also that they shall be subject to no greater payment than is the episcopal see, and he releases them from payment of provender-rent for three years. CS 241.

◆ EHD I, p. 466; ECWM 228; OB pp. 86–9. See also No. 48.

48. 26 Dec. 781 *OFFA, king of the Mercians, to the church of St Peter, Worcester. Grant of freedom from all royal tribute, and from the duty of provisioning with food, laid upon 12 'manentes' at *Homtune* (Hampton Lucy) and 5 at *Fæhha leage*, which land had been leased for life by Bishop Heathured and the community at Worcester to the king's relative, the abbess Eanburga, with reversion to Worcester. CS 239.

Taking Nos. 47 and 48 together, it is perhaps permissible to infer that Eanburga was abbess of Bath, which had been founded as a double monastery in the late seventh century (CS 43). Professor Finberg has commented on the unusual reference within the foundation charter to separate convents there for men and women (ECWM p. 173). A charter of 757–8 grants an estate to the brethren of Bath (CS 327). The latest clear-cut reference to the nunnery there is a charter dated 681 (CS 57).

Offa's privilege to the church of Worcester was drawn up and witnessed at the royal seat at *Tamuuorthie* (Tamworth, Staffs.) on the festival of St Stephen the first martyr. Heathured did not succeed to Worcester until 781, so it seems probable that the lease to Eanburga was issued on the same occasion as Offa's privilege. It was the custom of the kings of Wessex also to issue charters on the day after Christmas Day, cf. CS 389, 451. The hidation of Hampton Lucy was the same in DB, cf. AHEW p. 414 n. 3. For *Fæhha leage*, see No. 61.

49. 840 × 852 **BEORHTWULF, king of the Mercians, to *Eoveshame* (Evesham). 10 'mansæ' in *Quentone* (Quinton), 5 in *Mepelesbarwe* (Mappleborough in Studley), and 2 in Pebworth, Worcs., free of all but the three common dues. CS 453.

See ECWM 252 for the dating difficulty. The proem of this Evesham charter is unique.

50. 845 *BEORHTWULF, king of the Mercians, to Bishop Heahberht and the community at *Uuergerna cæster* (Worcester) in return for ten pounds of silver. Exemption of the 20 'manentes' of the monastery *bi Eafene* called *Ufera stret ford* (Stratford-on-Avon), from all lawful

secular service, tribute, and taxes; from royal works (i.e. work on royal estates) and provisioning of the king, his princes, and junior retainers; and from entertainment and feeding of royal huntsmen, horses, falcons, hawks, and the servants who lead the (hunting) dogs. Dated in the Christmas festival at *Tomeuuorðig* (Tamworth, Staffs.).
CS 450.

Some of the phraseology, notably . . . *regis et principis vel juniorum eorum*, is repeated in CS 455, another Mercian text. The date *in nativitate domini* does not mean necessarily that the charter was issued on Christmas Day, as Birch assumes; the festival lasted a full week.

51. 872 *WÆRFERTH, bishop of Worcester, to the king's thegn Eanwulf, in return for 20 golden mancuses with which to pay tribute to the barbarians. Lease for four lives of 2 'mansiones' at *Hnuthyrste* (Nuthurst), with reversion to the monastery at *Stretford* (Stratford-on-Avon). CS 533, 534.

◆ EHD i, p. 490. AHEW p. 450. The lease was issued late in the year, after the Danish army (the 'barbarians') had taken up winter quarters in London.

52. 922 *WILFRITH, bishop [of Worcester], to the refectory of the community at Worcester, in return for an annual commemoration of his anniversary. Land at *Clifforda* (Clifford Chambers), with its men and with all profits from fisheries and meadows. ◆ R xxi.

The bounds, of a 2-hide estate, are shown by Miss Robertson to be those of Milcote. ECWM p. 236. See also No. 60.

53. 956 *EADWIG, king of the English and ruler of the surrounding peoples, in the first year of his *imperium*, to Ealdorman Ælfhere. 10 'mansæ' *æt Wilmanlehttune* (Wormleighton), free of all but the three common dues.
CS 946.

Bounds: PN *Warwicks.*, p. 275 n. 1. CS 945 is another charter issued to Ealdorman Ælfhere on the same date (the witness lists are identical) and employing the same chancery formulas, for 20 hides at Cuddesdon, Oxon. Both charters are entered in one of the Abingdon cartularies, but the Oxon. text survives also in a copy made c. 970, in an early English caroline hand. This copy may have been made at Winchester for Abingdon under Bishop Æthelwold's instructions. CS 946 may perhaps have been copied at Winchester at a later date, after Wormleighton came into the abbey's hands (see No. 67).

54. 958   **EADRED, king of the Mercians, and sole monarch of Albion, to his thegn Wulfric. 5 'mansæ' *æt Alduestreow* (Austrey), free of all but the three common dues.

CS 1021.

Bu XVIII. It is clear from the king's title that this was a charter issued by King Edgar during the period May 957 × Oct. 959 when he was in revolt against his brother Eadwig, and was recognized as king by the Mercians and Northumbrians, and in East Anglia (Edgar is given the title *rex Merciorum* in CS 1036–7, dated 958. King Eadred is not given this title in any surviving diploma of his reign). Some later revisionist, suspecting the validity of a diploma issued in these circumstances, sought to authenticate it by the clumsy substitution of King Eadred's name for that of Edgar, and by tampering with the witness list (for similar revisions, see CW p. 14 n. 3). Probably the diplomatic was left intact. The proem is unique. The dispositive clause is close to those of some of King Eadwig's charters of the year 956 (CS 965, 968, 985). Unfortunately the OE bounds have not survived. As with others of King Edgar's charters at this time, it is probable that this was written at Worcester.

Professor Whitelock has suggested (W p. 156) that the Wulfric of this charter was in fact Wulfric Spot, who left the estate to Morcar's wife Ealdgyth in 1002 (No. 39). Subsequently part of it descended to Earl Leofric of Mercia, who gave it to Burton (DB); the gift may have been connected with Wulfric's former ownership of the estate, which accounts no doubt for the survival of this charter in the Burton muniments. It seems to me, however, that the Wulfric who received Austrey in 958 is more likely to have been Wulfric Spot's father, or some other ancestor, than Wulfric Spot himself.

55. 961 × 972   OSWALD, bishop [of Worcester] to —. 1 hide
at Milcote.   *Lost*.

D 20. See also No. 60.

56. 962   ****UUA the Hwede, sheriff of Warwick, to the
church of the Blessed Virgin Mary and of St Ecgwine at
Evesham. 6½ 'mansæ' at *Wihtlachesforde* (Wixford) and
Greftone (Temple Grafton).   CS 1092.

Probably this Evesham forgery was composed 1097 × 1104,
see p. 63. It utilizes the text of a genuine royal diploma of the
year 962 for its exemplar. I have not tracked down Ufa the
Hwede, who may have been a figment of the forger's imagination.
He does occur in Chron E p. 79, but this passage appears to be
based on the present charter. The witness list is compatible
with the date. The proem originated late in Athelstan's reign
(CS 743), and is identical with that of Bu xix (CS 1081) issued
on the same date, relating to land in Wiltshire. The exemption
clause is first found in 956 (CS 946, 948); the anathema is the
same as those of CS 1045, dated 959, and CS 1077, dated 961.
There is no boundary clause in the surviving text of the Wixford
charter, and it is doubtful if one ever existed. The abbey held
5 hides at Wixford in 1086, but DB shows that this was in the
possession of Wigot TRE (see also Chron E p. 79). The present
charter must be related to an alleged writ of William I to Evesham, confirming to the abbey, *inter alia*, *Grafton et Withlakesford*
. . . *in vicecomitatu de Warewic* (Dugdale II, p. 17).

57. 963   *EDGAR, king of the English, to his thegn Wulfgeat.
3 'cassati' *æt Duddestone* (? Duddeston Hall in Aston,
Birmingham) and 3 *æt Ernlege* (Upper Arley, Worcs.),
free of all but the three common dues.   CS 1100.

Bu xx. *Ernlege* was located by Professor Finberg (ECWM 287),
but the location of *Duddestone* is uncertain; the boundary clause
has not survived. *Ernlege* descended to Wulfrun, who gave it to
Wolverhampton (No. 92), so probably Wulfgeat was related
to Wulfric Spot, whence the survival of this charter in the
Burton archives. Two other charters, CS 1099 and 1114, relating to lands in Somerset and Sussex, have identical witness
lists and must have been issued on the same date, some time
before 29 November 963, when Abbot Æthelwold, one of the

signatories, was consecrated bishop of Winchester. The
formulas of the Burton charter are very close to those of CS
1099; see Drögereit, pp. 425–6; only the proem is different,
and this is identical with that of CS 1101. These charters all
appear to be typical chancery texts, written probably at Abingdon.

58. 963   *OSWALD, bishop [of Worcester] to Wulfric, with
the consent of King Edgar and Ealdorman Ælfhere of
Mercia. Lease for three lives of one 'mansa' at *Teodeceslege*
and 3 'mansæ' at *Æpsleage* (Apsley Heath in Ullenhall),
with reversion to Worcester.   CS 1111.

Apsley, a hamlet of Wooton, was formed into an ecclesiastical
parish with Ullenhall. Apsley Heath lies north of Oldberrow.
Teodecesleage, like Apsley, must have bordered on Oldberrow
(now in Warwicks., formerly in Worcs.), for the OE bounds
of both places have points identical with those appearing in the
OE bounds of Oldberrow, which are appended to CS 124
(*oslan mere* and *ulenbeorge* appear in the bounds of *Teodecesleage*
and Oldberrow; *fealamæres broc* in the Oldberrow bounds has
the same element as *fiolomeres forde* in the Apsley bounds).
biotan halh in the bounds of Apsley was perhaps near Botley
Hill in Ullenhall. None of the three sets of bounds have as yet
been worked out in detail.

59. 966   *OSWALD, bishop [of Worcester], to his thegn and
fellow sponsor Eadric, with the consent of King Edgar
and of [Ealdorman] Ælfhere of Mercia. Lease for three
lives of 3 'mansæ' divided between three places: $1\frac{1}{2}$ hides
at *Eanulfestune* (Alveston), every other acre in the divided
hide at *Uferan Strætforda* (Upper Stratford), and every
third acre of open land at *Fachanleah*, and half the wood
on the east side of the road, and that at the earthwork, and
8 acres of meadow on the east side of the Avon, and 12
acres of meadow opposite *Biccenclif*, and 3 acres north of
Avon as a site for a mill, all with reversion to Worcester.
                                        ◆ R XLIII.

The recipients are named in the rubric as Eadric and Wulfrun
(presumably the second life), for whom see Nos. 63, 64. For
Fachanleah, see No. 61.

60. 966   *OSWALD, bishop [of Worcester], to his thegn
Withelm, with the consent of King Edgar and of Ealdorman
Ælfhere of Mercia. Lease for three lives of 2 'mansae'
æt Clifforda (Clifford Chambers) with reversion to
Worcester.   CS 1181.

According to Wanley, the original of this charter was at
Worcester in 1643 (*Catalogue*, p. 300, No. 78). The rubric in
Heming's Cartulary gives Wihtflæde as the second life and
Godhyse as the third life. There are no detailed bounds, but
an OE clause in the lease records that it was made in return for
riding service; of the two hides, 1½ were *ge dal landes*, i.e. land
divided into strips scattered in the common fields, and the
remaining half hide lay *on thaere ege*, i.e. an island formed by
branches of the River Stour (AHEW p. 488). A postscript adds
that the three leases belonged to *strætforda*, i.e. the minster at
Stratford-on-Avon, cf. No. 50. See further, ECWM p. 236.

61. 969   *OSWALD, bishop of the Hwicce [i.e. Worcester],
to his faithful Æthelheard, with the consent of King
Edgar and the community at Worcester. Lease for three
lives of 7 'mansae' *æt Tidinctune* (Tiddington in Alveston),
and at *Faccanlea*, free of all royal and ecclesiastical dues,
with reversion to Worcester.

                                                     CS 1232.

The rubric gives Æthelmær as the second life, and an OE
clause in the lease gives the assessment of Tiddington as 5 hides,
and that of *Faccanlea* as 1½ hides. There is no boundary clause.
Faccanlea is clearly the *Fachan leah* of No. 59 (dated 966) and
the *Fæhha leage* of No. 48 (dated 781). It lay in the vicinity of
Tiddington, Alveston, and Hampton Lucy, all near Stratford-
on-Avon. It is the most plausible site yet suggested for the battle
of *Fethanleag* recorded in ASC *s.a.* 584. The Warwickshire Avon
represented the limit of West Saxon advance against the Britons
at this date, see Map 9 in *Anglo-Saxon Pottery and the Settlement of
England*, by J. N. L. Myres, Oxford, 1969, p. 118.

62. 969   *EDGAR, king of all Britain, to his thegn Ælfwold.
10 'cassati' at *Cyngton* (Kineton), free of all but the three
common dues.   CS 1234.

◆ EHD I, p. 519. Bounds: PN *Warwicks.*, p. 282. This was

one of the Somers charters, the presumed original of which was at Worcester in 1643. CS 1229 is another charter issued to Ælfwold on the same date (with one exception, the witness lists are identical), and employing the same formulas, for 15 hides at Apsley Guise, Beds. The original of this second charter was also preserved at Worcester. Ælfwold, the recipient, was the brother of Ealdorman Æthelwine of East Anglia, the lay patron of Ramsey Abbey (Hart 1973, pp. 131–2). These two charters may have been deposited at Worcester because of the close connection between Bishop Oswald, the founder of Ramsey, and Ælfwold's family. Because of the location of these two charters at Worcester, Bishop (p. 17) has assumed that CS 1229 was written there, and because the scribe of CS 1229 also wrote part of a Virgil now in the Vatican Library, he ascribes this latter MS. also to the Worcester scriptorium (Vatican City, Bibl. Apost. Reg. Lat. 1671). The argument appears to me to be a dangerous one. The fact is that the formulas of CS 1234 and CS 1229 are typical chancery texts; there is no evidence to tell at what scriptorium the scribe who composed them was trained – it could well have been Winchester. The surviving text of CS 1229 could, perhaps, be a copy of the original charter made by a Worcester scribe, but I doubt it. Certainly the drawings of the initials in the Vatican MS. are very close to the Winchester tradition, and a Virgil would be more likely to come from Winchester than from Worcester at this date (compare Bishop, pl. xvii, with the initials of the early Winchester psalter, Bodl. Junius 27 ff. 115v, 121v, plates iiib and ivc in *England before the Conquest*, ed. P. Clemoes and K. Hughes, Cambridge, 1971).

63. 977   *Oswald, archbishop [of York], to his thegn Eadric, with the consent of King Edward [the Martyr] and Ealdorman Ælfhere of Mercia. Lease for three lives of 3 'mansae' at *Tidingctun* (Tiddington), with reversion to the bishopric of Worcester.   K 617.

Kemble wrongly prints the bounds of Teddington, Worcs., as part of this lease (ECWM p. 85). The Worcester entry names Wulfrun as the second life. For Eadric and Wulfrun, see Nos. 59, 64, 65.

64. 985   *Oswald, archbishop [of York], to his thegn

Eadric, with the consent of King Æthelred and Ealdorman Ælfric of Mercia. Lease for three lives of 5 'mansae' at *Tidantune* (Tiddington) and *Eanulfestune* (Alveston), which he formerly had as loan-land, free of all but the three common dues, with reversion to the bishopric of Worcester.   K 651.

Bounds: PN *Warwicks.*, p. 231 n. 1. As with Nos. 59 and 63, the rubric names Wulfrun as the second life. There can be little doubt that she was the Wulfrun who founded Wolverhampton (No. 90). Eadric may have been her brother.

65. 988   *OSWALD, archbishop [of York], to his thegn Eadric, with the consent of the community at Worcester. Lease for three lives of 3½ 'mansæ' at *Cloptun* (Clopton in Stratford-on-Avon), with 6 acres of meadow opposite the mill at *Eanulfestune* (Alveston), and half the mill at *Bluntesige*, free of all worldly service, except the supply and service of the cathedral church, to whose ownership the estate shall revert.   K 666.

Bluntesige was possibly near Blunts Green in Wooton Wawen, a few miles from Clopton.

66. 998   †ÆTHELRED, king of the English and other surrounding peoples, to Ealdorman Leofwine. 7½ 'tributarii' lying in three *villulæ*, namely 3 'mansæ' in *Suþham* (Southam), and 4 'manentes' in *hlodbroce* (Ladbroke) and *hreodburnan* (Radbourne), free of all but the three common dues.   Crawf 8.

Bounds: PN *Warwicks.*, pp. 135, 144–5.

67. N.D.   (?999)   *ÆTHELRED, king of the English, to Abingdon Abbey. Grant of lands at *Wilmaleahtun* (Wormleighton), Farnborough (Berks.), and South Cerney (Glos.), free of all but the three common dues, to make up for the withdrawal of lands in Hants. and Wilts. granted to the abbey by King Edgar.   K 1312.

◆ EHD 1, p. 537. ECW 147. ECWM 142. The charter states that Wormleighton and other estates had descended to a widow

named Eadflæd, but had been taken from her wrongly by
Ælfric Cild. Subsequently Ælfric was found guilty of treason
and the estates were forfeited to King Æthelred, who restored
them to Eadflæd; and she, dying some time later, left them
to the king. See No. 53 for the earlier history of Wormleighton.
Ælfric's interest in the estate arose from his inheritance of the
Mercian ealdordom from Ælfhere.

68. 1001 †ÆTHELRED, king of the whole island, to Clofi
25 'mansi' æt Yceantune (Long Itchington), including a
hide æt earnlege (Arley), together with a haga at wærinc
wicum (Warwick), and half the land at Suðham (Southam),
inner and uttur, free of all but the three common dues.

K 705.

BM Facs IV, 12. Bounds: PN Warwicks., pp. 123, 133–4. It
seems likely that inner and uttur in this context stands for
inland (i.e. demesne), and the peasant holdings, later called
warland. On the unusual structure of this charter, which is
possibly a product of the Evesham scriptorium, see LC p. 74
and n. 3; ECEE p. 193. In the witness list, the names of the
æthelings Æthelstan and Edmund are late additions. See CW
p. 22 n. 4 for the endorsement.

(39) N.D. (1002 × 1004) *Will of Wulfric Spot.
Adulfestreo (Austrey) to Ealdgyth, wife of Morcar; Wibbe-
[to]fte (Wibtoft) to Æthelric; Wædedun (?Weddington),
Westune (Weston in Arden), Burhtun (Burton Hastings),
Hereburgebyrig (Harbury), and Eccleshale (?Exhall), all to
Burton Abbey. Lands in Leics., Glos., Staffs., Lancs.,
Yorks., Derbys., Lincs., Worcs., and Cheshire.

◆ W XVII.

Bu xxVIIIb. See also pp. 71, 99, 109, and 126.

(40) 1004 *ÆTHELRED, king of the English, to Burton
Abbey. Exemption from all but the three common dues
of lands belonging to the abbey, including Hwædedun
(?Weddington), Eccleshæle (?Exhall), Westune (Weston in
Arden), Burhtune (Burton Hastings), and Hereburgebyrig

(Harbury). Lands in Leics., Glos., Staffs., Derbys., Salop., and Lincs.   K 710.

Bu xxviiia. See also pp. 71, 99, 109, and 126.

69. 1005   *ÆTHELRED, king of the English, to Eynsham Abbey. Foundation charter, naming among other lands given to the abbey by its founder Ealdorman Æthelmær, 10 'mansiones' *æt Erdintune* (Yarnton, Oxon.), which he had obtained from his relative Godwine, in exchange for 10 'mansae' *æt Cestertune* (Chesterton, Oxon.), and 5 *æt Stodelege* (Studley). Lands in Cambs., Devon, Essex, Glos., Oxon., Surrey, Sussex, and Worcs.   K 711.

◆ *Eynsham Cartulary*, ed. Salter, Oxford Historical Soc., 1907, I, pp. 19–28. ECEss 39; ECWM 148. The structure and some of the formulas of this charter are based on the foundation charter of Thorney Abbey, Cambs. See ECEE p. 176 n. 2.

70. 1012   *ÆTHELRED, king of the English, to his man Theodulf. 5 'cassatæ' *æt Burtune* (?Burton Hastings), free of all but the three common dues.   Bu xxxv.

Edited on p. 241. The bounds are omitted in the surviving text, and the location is therefore uncertain.

71. 1016   *LEOFSIGE, bishop [of Worcester], to his thegn Godric. Lease for three lives of 1 'mansa' at *Biscopes dun* (Bishopton in Stratford-on-Avon), and separately 15 acres of meadow in the furlong by the river opposite *Tidingtun* (Tiddington), and the ninth half-acre at *Scothomme* (a riverside enclosure at Shottery), and 12 acres of arable between the river and the dyke at the stone quarry, and a *haga* at *Wærincwican* (Warwick), and Ælfric's meadow, and every third acre of beanland at Bishopton, all to be held free of worldly tribute, except the three common burdens and renders to the church, with reversion of the whole to Worcester.   K 724.

Bounds: PN *Warwicks.*, p. 238 n. 1.

72. N.D.   (c. 1016 × 1025)   †Record of an agreement

between the community at Worcester and Fulder. He is to hold the estate at *Ludintune* (Luddington) for three years, in return for three pounds which he lent to the community. The estate is then to revert to Worcester, with all its stock (listed).   ◆ R LXXIX.

73. 1033   *CNUT, king of all Britain, to Abbot Siward and the monks of St Mary, Abingdon. 3 'cassatæ' in *Mytun* (Myton in Warwick St Nicholas), free of all but the three common dues.   K 751.

Bounds: PN *Warwicks.*, p. 265 n. 1. The witness list is compatible with the date. The charter was issued after 19 August 1033, when Bishop Leofsige of Worcester died (ASC), for it is witnessed by his successor. There can be little doubt that this charter was composed and written at Abingdon Abbey. The whole of the diplomatic, with the exception of one sentence, is derived from texts of the period 960–1, most of them from Abingdon. Thus the proem and dispositive clauses first appear in CS 1058, and the exemption clause and anathema in CS 1054; the introduction to the bounds is first encountered in CS 1053, 1058, and the dating clause in CS 1066 (some of these formulas are to be found in CS 680 and 683, but these Abingdon charters are of doubtful authenticity). The remaining sentence is a second anathema based on 1 Cor. xvi, 22, and reserved for those attempting to challenge the grant by using other, false, land-books concerning the estate. The anathema itself is to be found in CS 1227, an Abingdon text of the year 968, and some of the other phraseology of this sentence occurs in CS 581, an Abingdon grant of the late ninth century. See further, No. 74.

74. 1034   **CNUT, king of all Britain, to Abbot Siward, for the monastery of St Mary, Abingdon. 3 'manentes' in *Mytun* (Myton in Warwick St Nicholas), free of all but the three common dues.   Chron Abingd 1, pp. 434–5.

The general structure of this charter, which commences with a dating clause (after a brief invocation), and goes straight on to a dispositive clause without any proem, is similar to that found in some other diplomas of Cnut (e.g. K 739, 749). The basic formulas are modelled on a charter or charters of the period 935 × 957. The uncommon invocation is first seen in

CS 810, dated 945; it reappears in a small group of charters dated 955–7 (CS 909, 949, 956–7, 987, 995), and in K 684, the great diploma of King Æthelred to Abingdon dated 993. The king's title derives from the later charters of Athelstan (CS 707–9, 743 etc., cf. OB p. 54), and the charter repeats the fashion of dating from the year of the king's *imperium* which began early in Edmund's reign (OB p. 55). The rare phrase *populis et tribubus præ electus in regem* is found elsewhere only in a group of charters based on a common formula, which appears to have originated at Winchester in 956 (CS 948, 927, 994, 902, 1032, 1112, 1260; K 687, in chronological order). The formula of the exemption clause first appears in 940 (CS 763), and the passage *sit ipse in profundum chaos igneis nexibus mancipatus, et ejus memoria caliginis mortis obtecta* in the anathema is found in CS 878, dated 949, and in later charters. The elaborate form of this anathema suggests that the charter was necessary because the earlier gift of Myton to Abingdon by Cnut (No. 73) had been challenged. In the surviving version there is no boundary clause, and only the first four witnesses have been preserved; they are the same as the first four in No. 73. It is unlikely that Cnut would issue two charters in successive years concerning the same estate, and it seems probable that this second charter was manufactured at Abingdon to reinforce the abbey's claim to the property.

75. 1038 × 1046   LYFING, bishop [of Worcester], to —.
Land at *Wdeton* (?Wootton Wawen).   *Lost.*

   D 80 (printed as No. 81).

(22) 1043   ****LEOFRIC, earl of 'Chester', to Coventry Abbey. Foundation charter, naming, among other lands, half of the town of *Couentriæ* (Coventry), *Honington* (Honington), *Newenham* (Kings Newnham), *Chaddleshunt* (Chadshunt), *Ichenton* (Long Itchington), *Olufton* (Ufton), *Suðam* (Southam), *Grænesburgh* (Grandborough), *Burting-bury* (Birdingbury), *Merston iuxta Auonam* (Marston in Wolston), *Herdwike* (Priors Hardwick), *Wasperton* (Wasperton), *Chesterton* (Chesterton), *Suðham*, half of *Ruyton* (Ryton in Dunsmore), and *Sow* (Walsgrave on Sowe). Lands in Ches., Glos., Leics., Northants., and Worcs.   K 939.

There is record of only one estate named *Suðham* in Warwickshire, and the second entry of this name in the charter appears to be either a mistaken repetition, or possibly a misspelling of the *Suocham* which had been given by Earl Leofric to Evesham, but was subsequently returned to him by the abbey in exchange for Hampton, Worcs., cf. Chron E pp. 84–5; ECWM 344. See also pp. 64, 71, and 129.

(23) 1043   ***EDWARD, king of the English, to Coventry Abbey. General confirmation of lands and privileges, naming, among other lands, *Souðam* (Southam), *Greneburgan* (Grandborough), *Ickentonam* (Long Itchington), *Hunitonam* (Honington), *Neowenham* (Kings Newnham), *Hulhtune* (Ufton), *Chadeleshunte* (Chadshunt), *Herdewyk* (Priors Hardwick), *Cestretune* (Chesterton), *Waspertune* (Wasperton), *Suohham*, *Byrtingabirig* (Birdingbury), *iuxta Auen*, *Merston* (Marston in Wolston), half the vill of *Ruitune* (Ryton in Dunsmore), and *Sowe* (Walsgrave on Sowe). Lands in Ches., Glos., Leics., Northants., and Worcs.

K 916.

See also pp. 64, 71, and 129. For *Suohham*, see the note to No. 22.

76. N.D.   (1043 × 1053)   *King EDWARD to his bishops, earls, and thegns in the shires in which Abbot Leofwine of Coventry has lands. Writ declaring that Leofwine is to have sake and soke, toll and team, over his lands and men within and without borough, as fully and completely as ever Earl Leofric had.   Latin H 46.

The OE text is edited by Miss Harmer, with commentary and translation, in ◆ Clemoes pp. 89–103.

77. N.D.   (1043 × 1053)   ****King EDWARD to Archbishop Eadsige and all his bishops, abbots, earls, thegns, and sheriffs, and all his lieges. Writ confirming lands, stock, gold, silver, and treasures given by Earl Leofric [of Mercia] and Godgifu to Abbot Leofwine and the brethren and the minster at Coventry. Grant of full freedom, sake and soke, toll and team, hamsocn, foresteall,

blodwite, fihtwite, weardwite, and mundbreach. The monks are to live according to the rule of St Benedict.

◆ H 45.

See No. 76 for King Edward's authentic writ to Coventry.

78. N.D.   (1058 × 1062)   *Declaration by Ealdorman ÆLF-GAR that Ordwig, father of Abbot Æthelwig, gave *Actun* (Acton Beauchamp, Herefordshire) after his lifetime to Evesham '*ad victum fratrum*', and *Dorsitune* (Dorsington) after his wife's death '*ad vestitum fratrum*'.   K 964.

See further ECWM 424.

79. C.1060   HAROLD, earl [of Wessex], to Peterborough Abbey. *Cliftune* (Clifton), and land beside the monastery of St Paul in London, next to the landing place called *Etheredeshythe* (Queenhithe, Middlesex).   *Lost*.

HC p. 70; ECEE 357.

CHAPTER IV

THE EARLY CHARTERS OF STAFFORDSHIRE

80. 925 *ATHELSTAN, king of the English, to his faithful minister Eadric, to replace a charter which had been lost. 7 'manentes' *æt Hwitantune* (?Whittington, near Lichfield), free of all but the three common dues.   CS 642.

> Bu III. ◆ Robinson pp. 42–5. Stenton, *Types*, p. 72 n. 3. LC p. 53. The location is uncertain, as the bounds are omitted in the surviving text. For similar phraseology in other charters replacing lost muniments, see CS 592, 624.
>
> This is the earliest charter of King Athelstan of which the text survives, and much of the formula was repeated in the charters of his successors. Thus the invocation (on which see Bullough p. 469) reappears in CS 743, 817, 1005, 1081, and in K 691; the king's title recurs in CS 877, 878, 888, and 892; the anathema is repeated in CS 743, 754, 778, 978, and 1005. There is nothing specifically Mercian about these formulas, but the only bishops witnessing came from Mercian sees, and the only abbot witnessing was from Evesham. The charter might well have been composed at Worcester, using Winchester formulas.

81. 850 [for 940] ****ATHELSTAN, king of the Anglo-Saxons, emperor of the Northumbrians, ruler of the heathen, and protector of the Britons, to the thegn Brihthelm. 5 'cassati' at *Eatun* (? Church Eaton), free of all but the three common dues.   CS 746.

> Bu II. The location is not certain, as the bounds are omitted in the surviving text. Church Eaton was a 5-hide estate by the time of DB (Nos. 220, 285, 289, and 298 in the Staffs. DB entries), but it was not then held by Burton Abbey, in whose archives the charter was preserved.
>
> The short proem, king's title, and dispositive clauses are all to be found in Mercian texts of the mid-tenth century preserved

in the Burton archives, and the king's title could not have originated before 946 (ECEE p. 197). The remainder of the text is taken from genuine chancery charters of the year 940, with which the indiction and the dating clause correspond. The formulas used to describe the estate conveyed, and the exemption clause, occur in CS 743, 754, and 761, dated 939 × 940. From the anathema onwards the text is virtually identical with that of CS 763, dated 940; the witness list, with the correct forms of attestation, occurs in CS 748, an original of 940 preserved at Winchester. Further anachronisms include the name of the donor, and the date (850) given in the charter for the year of grace. It is difficult to conclude that this charter is other than an outright forgery, manufactured at Burton, possibly after the Conquest, but in the absence of further evidence it would be hazardous to suggest what may have been the forger's motive. I would disagree with Professor Whitelock's view that the charter is 'in itself acceptable', O'D I, p. 42. See also No. 84.

82. 942 *EDMUND, king of the Anglo-Saxons, to Wulfsige Maur'. 40 'hyde' at *Alrewasse* (Alrewas), *Bromleage* (Abbots and Kings Bromley), *Barton* (Barton-under-Needwood), *Tatenhyll* (Tatenhill), *Brontiston* (Branston), *Stretton* (Stretton), *Roðulfeston* (Rolleston), *Clyfton* (Clifton Campville), and *Hagnatun* (Haunton in Clifton Campville). Dated from *Wincelcumbe* (Winchcombe, Glos.).

CS 771.

Bu v. ◆ Bridgeman pp. 82–4, with discussion. The bounds are omitted from the surviving text, as is the exemption clause. See also Nos. 83, 102, and DC pp. 125–32. The lands conveyed run from south to north along the western bank of the River Trent as far as Rolleston; Clifton and Haunton, with which the list concludes, lie further to the south-east, but still in Staffordshire. For topographical reasons, therefore, it would seem likely that *Bromleage* in the charter represents King's rather than Abbot's Bromley, but consideration of Bu xxvii shows that this is not the case, for Wulfsige the Black is mentioned therein as a former owner of Abbot's Bromley (see pp. 159, 206). In fact, it seems likely that *Bromleage* in 942 covered both places. Of the 40 hides conveyed in the charter, 34½ hides can be accounted for in the Staffordshire Domesday

(Staffs. DB nos. 12–13, 21, 30, 33, 88–91, 149, 204, 268), a further 3 in Bu xxvii, and 3 carucates, comprising part of Clifton, lay in Derbyshire.

83. 942 *Edmund, king of the Anglo-Saxons, to Wulfsige Maur'. Lands including *Newanbolde* (Newbold in Barton-under-Needwood). Lands in Derbyshire.   CS 772.

Bu vi. ◆ Bridgeman pp. 84–6, with discussion. DC pp. 125–32. See also Nos. 82, 102, and p. 104.

84. 949 ****Eadred, king of the English, to his faithful thegn Athelstan, in return for 60 gold mancuses. 10 'manentes' at *Eatun* (?Church Eaton), free of all but the three common dues.   CS 885.

Bu x. ◆ Bridgeman pp. 88–9. The OE bounds are omitted (except for the first few words), and the location is therefore uncertain. The hidage corresponds with the DB assessment of Church Eaton + Lapley + High Onn.

The formulas of this grant differ fundamentally from those of any surviving authentic text issued in Eadred's reign. The phrase *omnibus meis notum volo et esse fidelibus quod ego* . . . following the king's title is characteristic of a writ, and one does not find it in authentic pre-Conquest diplomas before the time of Æthelred II.[1] The remainder of the text also has a general structure and formulas commonly encountered in diplomas of the eleventh century, particularly those of the period 1042 × 1046. Thus *dei nutu* following the king's title occurs in K 778 (dated 1045); in the dispositive clause, *cuidam meo fideli*

---

[1] CS 462 has *volo et præcipio*, but this is a Worcester forgery. CS 860, dated 948, has *notum esse volo omnibus*, but the formulas of this diploma are highly abnormal, suggestive of a late forgery. The writ form recurs in the phrase *non solum presentibus sed etiam futuris* in the proem. CS 1185 has *volo*, but this is a late Christ Church forgery. K 1289, dated 995, has *volo notum adesse fidelibus quod ego* . . . , and although this charter has an anomaly in the witness list (EHD i, p. 525) it must be considered basically authentic. K 1305, dated 1005, which has *notum volo adesse omnibus meo subiectis*, claims to have been drawn up under the direction of Wulfgar, abbot of Abingdon; the charter has some doubtful elements, however. ECEE No. ix, dated 1006 × 1011, has *meis notum volo adesse fidelibus*, and appears to be wholly authentic. K 754, dated 1020 × 1038, has *notum volo esse*, but the recipient and some of the witnesses have Norman names.

ministro . . . obsequio occurs in K 764–5, 770, 772 (dated 1042–4); the alienation clause, the grant of exemption, and the anathema appear almost verbatim in CS 767 (dated 1043); the exemption clause is also paralleled in CS 762 (dated 1042), and in CS 772, 774–5 (dated 1044); the formula introducing the bounds is the same as that in CS 783 (dated 1046); use of the present tense in the attestations of the witnesses occurs also in K 762, and the phrase *genetricis eiusdem regis* following the queen's attestation recalls *regina eiusdem regis* in K 778, and *collaterana eiusdem regis* in K 780 (both dated 1045). The dating clause is similar to that of K 770 (dated 1044). Two of the witnessing bishops (Ælfsige, and the second Ælfric) are not encountered elsewhere. Finally, it may be noted that the chrismon prefacing the cartulary text of this charter is of a form that originated later than 949. It resembles those of a group of charters written in the period 962 × 975 (OS Facs II, Westminster 6; BM Facs III, 17, 27, 29, 31) and some later forgeries, so that if the cartulary copyist was reproducing the chrismon in his exemplar accurately (as he nearly always did), then his exemplar was certainly not an original charter of the year 949.

It is of course dangerous to reject an ostensible tenth-century charter on the ground that it contains formulas encountered in charters of the eleventh century, for it is now well known that late Anglo-Saxon diplomas constantly utilize formulas that have originated a century or more previously. Nevertheless, the overwhelming preponderance of parallels from texts of Edward the Confessor's reign, the writ form, and the complete absence of similar formulas in the authentic charters of King Eadred, his predecessors, and his immediate successors, all point to the conclusion that this Burton text is a post-Conquest forgery, modelled perhaps on a genuine charter of 1042 × 1046. The occurrence in the Burton archives of a second forged charter relating to an estate called *Eatun* (No. 81) serves merely to reinforce one's suspicions of the present text.

85. 951   *EADRED, king of the English, to the thegn Wulfhelm. Land *æt Mærcham* (Marchington in Hanbury), free of all but the three common dues.   CS 890.

Bu XI. ◆ Bridgeman pp. 89–91. This charter has formulas, date, and witness list identical with those of CS 893, a Thorney charter edited in ECEE pp. 155–9. It is a typical alliterative

and poetical Danelaw diploma, and much of its phraseology
can be traced in other Danelaw charters of Eadred's reign,
particularly those preserved in the Burton archives (the 'Dunstan
A' series, see p. 19). See further, DC pp. 125–32. For the
recipient, see No. 87.

86. 956   *EADWIG, king of the English and ruler of the whole
of Britain, to his faithful thegn Æthelnoth. Land at
Deorlaueston (Darlaston, near Stone), free of all but the
three common dues.   CS 954.

   Bu XVII. ◆ Bridgeman p. 96. Edited on p. 172.

87. 957   **EADRED, king and *primicherius* of Britain, to his
thegn Wulfhelm. 5 'mansiunculæ' *æt Eastun* (Little Aston
in Shenston) and *æt Bearre* (Great Barr), free of all but the
three common dues.   CS 987.

   Wulfhelm, the recipient, is probably identical with the
recipient of No. 85. The witness list of this charter corresponds
(except in two particulars) with those of charters issued by
King Eadwig in the early months of 957, before the revolt of
his brother Edgar. The indiction agrees with the year of grace,
and one must assume that Eadwig's name in the body of the
charter has been supplanted by that of Eadred by a later copyist,
who was also, presumably, responsible for the suppression of
Edgar's name from the witness list, and the introduction into
the list of a second 'Æðelstan, Dux', intended no doubt for
Athelstan Half King, who retired to Glastonbury in 956. Seen
in this light, CS 987 is a respectable charter of King Eadwig
that has been tampered with (like so many others of this period)
by a later copyist, in order to give the semblance of a more
secure title.
   The text is preserved in the *Codex Wintoniensis*, and the first
part of the charter, down to the witness list, adheres closely to
the 'Dunstan B' protocol (see pp. 19–20). What marks out our
text as being very different from its predecessors in the
'Dunstan B' series, however, is that the bounds are entered
after the witness list; in this the charter resembles those using
the 'Dunstan A' protocol, issued for the Danelaw in the period
942 × 955 (see p. 19). This similarity is strengthened considerably by the remarkable OE anathema with which the

text is concluded; this is identical with the anathema of R xxx, dated 955, and a typical member of the 'Dunstan A' Danelaw series (DC pp. 125–32). It is possible that our text was drawn up by an Abingdon scribe.

88. 975 †EDGAR, ruler of the whole of Britain, to Bishop Æthelwold [of Winchester]. 3 'mansæ' at *Madanlieg* (Madeley), free of all but the three common dues.

CS 1312.

BM Facs III, 31. The original charter was still preserved in the Winchester muniments in 1643 (WCD II, p. 63). The location is established by the occurrence of *wriman forda* in the bounds; the name underlies the early forms of the neighbouring village of Wrinehill. It is possible that Æthelwold acquired this property for the endowment of Breedon, cf. No. 37. The charter has typical chancery formulas, and it was endorsed in the orthodox fashion (CW p. 22 n. 4).

The OE bounds of *Madanlieg* can be followed on OS 2½" sheet SJ 74. With minor variations, they are identical with the modern bounds of Madeley parish. They proceed in a clockwise direction:

1. *on witena leage* Literally, 'the wood of the witan, or counsellors'; the bounds commence at grid ref. 745446, at the south-west corner of Wrinehill Wood, where the three county boundaries of Staffordshire, Shropshire, and Cheshire meet. The bounds run due north along a stream.

2. *in eardele* Reading OE *gyrd-leah*, 'wood where poles are got'. At 744457, just north-east of Checkley Wood, the stream joins the Checkley Brook. The bounds turn north-eastwards here, running upstream along the Checkley Brook, which still forms the Staffordshire-Cheshire boundary at this point.

3. *in wrimanford* Wrinehill Bridge, at 755466, where the road from Madeley to Wrinehill crosses the Checkley Brook. Ekwall (*Dictionary of English Place-Names*) notes *le wrineford* in an inquisition of 1322. The settlement at Wrinehill first appears as *Wrinehull* in the Close Roll for 1225; the spelling *wryme* occurs in a late fourteenth-century source. Unfortunately the forms are too late to allow confident identification of the first element, especially as it is not clear whether the name applied initially to the hill or to the

ford. The hamlet of Wrinehill lies in a valley; there is a choice of several hills in the vicinity for the site of the original Wrinehill. Possible cognates are OE *wreon* 'to cover, conceal', and OE *wrigian* 'to twist, struggle, venture'. The possibility that this first element was Celtic is, however, worth considering.

4. *ondlong broces on hedenan mós*   OE *mōs* 'bog, marsh' developed into *moss* in the dialect of the north-west midlands and northern England, possibly due to the influence of the ON cognate *mosi*. The bounds proceed up Checkley Brook to its source at Craddock Moss, 781480. *hedenan* in the charter should perhaps be read as OE *hǣðenan* 'heathen', i.e. 'the heathen swamp'. Within three miles are Gravenhunger Moss in Woore, Cracow Moss north of Wrinehill, and Moss Farm and cottages to the west of Madeley village.

5. *ymbe heafca bæce . . . on thone hege*   Up the valley south of Hayes Wood to join a hedge to the west of Bates Wood at 796479, where the present parish boundary turns sharply southwards, running up over the hill at Scot Hay.

6. *on wilburge wege*   At 795470 the bounds join a minor road running south through Leycett to Madeley Heath. It is just possible that the road was named after Wilburh, daughter of King Penda of Mercia; I have not found any survival of it in local place-names.

7. *in cærsihtan wyll*   'Stream where watercress grows'. The bounds join the upper reaches of Hazeley Brook at 793455.

8. *in tha dic*   After running upstream to the source of Hazeley Brook, the bounds pass through Dunge Wood down a steep ridge, to join a dyke at 797434, where they turn westwards, running down the dyke.

9. *in tha micle mós*   The dyke joins the River Lea at 783423, turning sharply southwards. The *micle mós* is the wide expanse of marshy ground to the north-east of the site of Old Madeley Manor.

10. *in tha sic in wierdes ford*   Running south-eastwards along a marshy stream, the modern parish boundary joins the A53 from Whitmore to Market Drayton where the road crosses the stream at 795404.

11. *on thone hreoditan more*   'the reedy moor'. Moor is used fairly commonly to describe local patches of rough land, e.g. Whitmore, and Moor Hall just west of Madeley village. The name is perhaps preserved in the first element of

Radwood, where the bounds turn sharply in the rough ground at the foot of Camp Hill, at 774412.

12. *in tha hæthihta leage* Here OE *lēah* is perhaps best rendered as 'meadow'; the bounds join the River Lea (a British name) at 766424, south of Lower Bittern's Wood. OE *haethihta* 'heather' describes the rough scrubby low-lying ground, providing good cover for snipe.

13. *in tha hyrste on tha greatan ac* 'to the great oak in the wood'. The bounds run upstream through a wood to join the Shropshire-Staffordshire county boundary at 752423, a place where oak trees still abound. Here they turn sharply northwards, to follow the county boundary.

14. *in tha sic eft on witena leage* The county boundary joins a stream at Newhouse Farm, 747436, and runs along it northwards to the meeting-place of the three shire boundaries, where the OE bounds of Madeley begin.

89. 985 *ÆTHELRED, king of the English, to the lady Wulfrun. 10 'cassati' in two places, of which 9 are *æt Heantune* (Wolverhampton), and one *æt Treselcotum* (Trescott), free of all but the three common dues.   K 650.

◆ Bridgeman pp. 101–4, with a discussion. For Wulfrun, see No. 90. The bounds have not as yet been worked out. The diplomatic, including the long and turgid proem, is a repetition of that of K 648, a Berkshire charter of the same date and with an identical witness list, entered (as is this one), in the *Codex Wintoniensis* (CW p. 11). The anathema is found also in K 1280, an Abingdon text dated 983; ultimately it derives from charters issued in 940 (CS 763). In the witness list, Ordbriht, Siric, and Leofric are wrongly entitled ealdormen instead of abbots, and Ælfweard is called abbot instead of thegn.

90. 994 *Privilege of SIGERIC, archbishop of Canterbury, for the lady Wulfrun. Confirmation of her land endowment of the monastery of *Hamtune* (Wolverhampton), including 10 'jugera cassatarum' for her soul and that of her husband, 10 more for her kinsman Wulfgeat, and 10 more for her daugher Ælfthryth. The names of the estates are *Earnleie* (Upper Arley, Worcs.), *Eswich* (Ashwood in Kinver Forest), *Bilsetnatun* (Bilston),

Willenhale (Willenhall), *Wodnesfeld* (Wednesfield), *Peole-
shale* (Pelsall), *Ocgintun* (Ogley Hey), *Hiltun* (Hilton in Ogley
Hey), *Hagenthorndun* (Hatherton), *Kinwaldestun* (Kinvas-
ton), *Hyltun* (Hilton, near Featherstone), and *Feotherstan*
(Featherstone). Dugd. VI, pp. 1443–4.

◆ Duignan; Bridgeman pp. 105–15, both with discussions,
and topographical accounts of the OE bounds, which are very
detailed. Written by the king's *scrinarius*, see p. 189.

91. 996 *ÆTHELRED, king of the English, to his faithful
thegn Wulfric. 3 'cassati' *æt Bromleage* (Abbots Bromley),
free of all but the three common dues. Bu XXVII.

Edited on p. 201.

92. 996 ***ÆTHELRED, king of the English and ruler of all
Britain, to his faithful thegn Wulfric. Land at *Bedintun*,
free of all but the three common dues. Bu XXVI.

Edited on p. 196.

(39) N.D. (1002 × 1004) *Will of WULFRIC SPOT.
Rólfestun (Rolleston) and *Héorlfestun* (Harlaston) to [Eal-
dorman] Ælfhelm; *Beorelfestune* (Barlaston) and *Mærcham-
tune* (Marchington) to Wulfheah; *Elleforda* (Elford),
Acclea (Oakley), and land at *Tamwurþin* (Tamworth) to
his daughter, with reversion of the first two to Burton
Abbey; *Baltryðeleage* (Balterley) to his servant Wulfgar,
just as his father had acquired it for him; *Byrtun* (Bur-
ton) on which the monastery stands, *Stræt[tu]n* (Stretton,
near Rolleston), *Bromleage* (Abbots Bromley), *Bedintun*,
Gageleage (Gailey), *Witestan* (Whiston), *Halen* (?Sheriff
Hales), *Deorlafestun* (Darlaston, near Stone), *Rudegeard*
(Rudyard), the little estate at *Cotewaltune* (Cotwalton),
Lege (Leigh), *Acofr[e]* (Oakover), *Hílum* (Ilam), *Celfdun*
(Caldon), *Cætesþyrne* (Castern), and one hide at *Sceon*
(Sheen), all to Burton Abbey. Land at *Langandune* (Long-
don) to the community at *Tom[wy]rðin* (Tamworth),
just as they had leased it to him (Wulfric); and half the
usufruct is to go to Tamworth, and the other half to the

monks at Burton Abbey. Lands in Leics., Warwicks., Glos., Lancs., Yorks., Derbys., Lincs., Worcs., and Cheshire. ◆ W xvii.

Bu xxviiib. See also pp. 71, 84, 109, and 126.

(40) 1004 *Æthelred, king of the English, to Burton Abbey. Exemption from all but the three common dues of lands belonging to the abbey, including *Byrtune* (Burton), where the monastery stands, *Strætun* (Stretton, near Rolleston), *Bromleage* (Abbots Bromley), *Bedintun*, *Gageleage* (Gailey), *Witestan* (Whiston), *Halen* (? Sheriff Hales), *Deorlafestune* (Darlaston), *Lege* (Leigh), *Hilum* (Ilam), and *Acofre* (Oakover). Lands in Leics., Glos., Warwicks., Derbys., Salop, and Lincs. K 710.

Bu xxviiia. See also pp. 71, 84, 109, and 126.

93. 1008 *Æthelred, king of the English, to Wulfgeat, abbot of Burton. $2\frac{1}{2}$ 'mansæ' at *Rolvestun* (Rolleston), free of all but the three common dues, in exchange for *Ælfredintun* (Arlington, Glos.), and *Ealdesworthe* (Aldsworth, Glos.), two estates given to the abbey by Wulfric. Bu xxx.

Edited on p. 211. The bounds are omitted in the surviving text.

94. 1012 *Æthelred, king of the English, to Wulfgeat, abbot of Burton, in return for 70 pounds in gold and silver. $1\frac{1}{2}$ 'mansæ' at *Wiþmere* (Wetmoor), free of all but the three common dues. Bu xxxiv.

Edited on p. 235.

95. N.D. (1053 × 1066) ***King Edward to Bishop *Leuen* and Earl *Leuen* and all his thegns in Staffordshire. Writ informing them that he has granted to his priests at *Hampton* (Wolverhampton) freedom for their minster, and sake and soke as fully as he himself once possessed it. ◆ H 114.

As Dr Harmer points out, if the first *Leuen* stands for Bishop Leofwine of Lichfield (1053 × 1066), then the second *Leuen* cannot be Earl Leofwine, the father of Earl Leofric of Mercia, for he was dead by 1032; possibly it is a mistaken rendering of Leofric (H p. 406).

96. N.D.   (C. 1061)   **Earl ÆLFGAR [of Mercia] to the abbey of St Remigius of Rheims. The vill called *Lappeleya* (Lapley).   Dugdale VI, p. 1042, No. 1.

♦ Bridgeman 1916, pp. 126–9, with comments. The charter is said to have been prepared in two versions, of which one in OE was kept by Earl Ælfgar, and the other in Latin was given to Rheims. The surviving record of Ælfgar's gift appears to be a free rendering of the Latin version; the witness list is convincing, and there seems no need to question the basic authenticity of the record.

97. 28 Dec. 1065   †King EDWARD to Bishop Leofwine, Earl Edwin, and all his thegns in Staffordshire. Writ informing them that he has given to St Peter, Westminster, the land at *Pertune* (Perton in Tettenhall), and everything belonging to it, in woodland and open country, with sake and soke, as fully and completely as he himself possessed it, for the abbot and community.   ♦ H 96.

OS Facs II, Westminster 12. Bishop and Chaplais 1957, pl. 23b. One of the three surviving writs bearing an authentic impression of Edward the Confessor's great seal.

(29) 1065   ***King EDWARD to Westminster Abbey. Confirmation of estates, including *Pertune* (Perton in Tettenhall). Lands in Middlesex, Herts., Essex, Surrey, Kent, Sussex, Suffolk, Bucks., Berks., Oxon., Rutland, Worcs., Glos., and Northants.

Widmore, *Westminster*, App. II.

See also p. 65.

(30) 28 Dec. 1065   ***King EDWARD to Westminster Abbey. Confirmation of estates, including *Pertune* (Perton in Tettenhall). Lands in Middlesex, Herts., Essex, Surrey,

Kent, Sussex, Bucks., Oxon., Rutland, Worcs., Glos., and Northants.   K 824.

See also p. 66.

98. 28 Dec. 1065 ***The Telligraphus of King EDWARD concerning Westminster Abbey.
WBD ff. 43b ff. BM. MS. Cott. Faust. A iii, ff. 113b ff.

Unpublished. Discussion: H p. 290; ECEss 70. Similar to, but not identical with, No. 29. This ascribes the gift of Perton to Hughelin, the king's chamberlain.

CHAPTER V

THE EARLY CHARTERS OF DERBYSHIRE

99. 835 *CYNEUUARA, abbess [of Repton], to Prince Humbert [of the Tomsætan], on condition that he shall pay annually a rent of lead worth 300 *solidi* to Archbishop Ceolnoth and his successors at Christ Church, Canterbury. Land at *Wyrcesuuyrthe* (Wirksworth). CS 414.

Stenton, *Types*, p. 71; *Medeshamstede*, p. 318 n. 3. AHEW p. 422.

100. 800 [? for 900] *ÆTHELFLÆD, lady of the Mercians, to her faithful friend Alchelm, for 60 swine and 300 *solidi*. 2 'manentes' in *Stantune* (? Stanton in the Peak, with its berewick at Birchover). CS 583.

Bu 1. The bounds are omitted in the surviving text, and the location is therefore uncertain, but see the notes to Bu XXIII. Omission of reference to the three common dues occurs in other charters of Æthelflæd and her husband Æthelred. The diplomatic of this charter exhibits characteristic early Mercian forms, e.g. the use of *donabo* in the dispositive clause (as with CS 450, 454, 466, 511, 513, 522 etc.). The phrase *hii sunt vero testes* . . . introducing the witness list seems to have originated in the Worcester scriptorium (CS 490, 540), and the terminal grace and anathema is close to the verse preceding the witness list of CS 587, an original chirograph of Æthelred and Æthelflæd to Wenlock Abbey, also written at Worcester, in all probability. Other passages are to be found in the Mercian texts CS 443, 547, and 557.

Something is wrong with the dating clause, which runs: *Anno dominice incarnationis. DCCC luna Indictione vero iij a.* The indiction is correct for the year DCCCC, which is compatible with the witness list, but the inclusion of the word *luna*, meaningless as it stands, implies either that the charter originally had a fuller date, giving the age of the moon obtained from a kalendar, or else – perhaps more likely – the copyist was unable to decipher fully what was written after the third 'C' of the date in his exemplar, and wrote the word *luna* to fill in the gap. It is known from Irish sources that by 902 Æthelred's ill-health often precluded him from active participation in government. If the present charter be accepted as authentic, it would appear that Æthelflæd had taken over effective control in Mercia as early as 900. Charters of 901 (†CS 587) and 904 (CS 608), however, both show Æthelflæd and her husband acting jointly, and Æthelred appears to have been involved in negotiations with the Danes as late as 906 (CS 102).

101. 926 *ATHELSTAN, king of the Anglo-Saxons, to Uhtred, for 30 mancuses of gold. 60 'manentes' at *Hope* (Hope) and *Æscforda* (Ashford), free of all but the three common dues. The estate had been bought from the heathen (i.e. the Danes) by King Edward and Ealdorman Æthelred [of the Mercians] for 20 pounds in gold and silver.   CS 658.

Bu iv. The formulas are Mercian, possibly from Worcester. Some of the copyist's errors can be amended by comparison with the text of CS 659, a charter with identical formulas, drawn up on the same occasion; this also supplies names omitted in the witness list. Stenton (*Types*, pp. 74–5) suggests that the purchase from 'the heathen' took place probably in 906, and certainly before 911. Uhtred at the time of the grant was not yet an ealdorman. Later, he was given the near-by estate of Bakewell (No. 104). By the time of DB, these two estates, together with Bakewell, were back in royal hands; they were then assessed at 51 carucates (DB p. 272b). Unfortunately, the bounds are omitted from the surviving text.

The invocation *In nomine domini nostri Jhesu Christi* is, as may be imagined, a very common formula, occurring unmodified in over 70 charters edited by Birch and Kemble, and in five of the Burton charters (Nos. iv, xv, xvii, xxvi, and xxxv). It was used in its simplest form throughout the whole Saxon period, the earliest authentic example being a Kentish diploma dated about 675 (CS 40; cf. ECEE p. 120 n. 1). Most of the surviving seventh-century charters, however, add *saluatoris* to the formula, a development retained in many Mercian texts throughout the eighth century, and extended to Wessex charters from 825 onwards (e.g. CS 393). Kentish charters of the first half of the eighth century usually insert *Dei* after *domini*; subsequently *Christi* is replaced by *Salvator Mundi*.

(83)   942   *EDMUND, king of the Anglo-Saxons, to Wulfsige Maur'. Lands including *æt Waletune* (Walton-on-Trent), *suðenne monna Cotnhalfne* (the land of the men of the southern half of Coton-in-the-Elms), *æt Caldewællen* (Cauldwell), *æt Dracan hlæwen* (Drakelow), and *æt Lintone* (Linton). Land in Staffs.   CS 772.

Bu VI. See also p. 92.

102.   942   *EDMUND, king of the Anglo-Saxons, to Wulfsige Maur'. Lands including *Crokeshalle'* (Croxall), *Canton'* (possibly for *Catiton*, i.e. Calton), *Waleton'* (Walton-on-Trent), *Drakel'* (Drakelow), *Stapenh'* (Stapenhill), and *Sulueston'* (? for *Rulueston*, i.e. Rosliston).   CS 773.

Bu VII. ◆ Bridgeman pp. 86–7, with discussion. See also Nos. 83–4, and p. 159. Rosliston is derived from OE 'Hroðlafs tun', from which the form *Rulueston* is a possible development, bearing in mind the confusion that would be generated locally by the existence of Rolleston (either OE 'Hroðwulfs tun', or a Grimston-hybrid '*Hroðulfr's tun') in Staffordshire near by. Rosliston is clearly an integral part of the territories conveyed in Nos. 83 and 102, so that it seems very likely that the copyist misread OE 'R' as 'S' when transcribing this name.

The three charters Nos. 82, 83, and 102 were drawn up for the same recipient on the same occasion. They utilize identical formulas, and are best considered as a group. Evidently the occasion of the grants was immediately after Edmund had redeemed the Five Boroughs (ASC C). The lands conveyed form a large and compact group on either side of the River Trent, giving effective command over the upper Trent valley. The Staffordshire holdings, on the west bank of the river, are granted by No. 83, and the Derbyshire holdings, on the east bank, by Nos. 84 and 102; note that in the former case the hidage is given, but no assessment is recorded for the Derbyshire properties (whereas Staffordshire was hidated, Derbyshire was carucated). Most of this huge block of land descended to Wulfric Spot, and was used by him to endow the abbey of Burton-on-Trent. The three charters are important examples of the alliterative 'Dunstan A' series issued for estates within the Danelaw in the period 942 × 955, see DC p. 125.

103. Easter 949   *EADRED, king of the Anglo-Saxons, emperor of the Northumbrians, ruler of the heathen, and protector of the Britons, to the thegn Ulfketel, in return for 50 mancuses of refined gold. 4 'ruris cassatæ' in *Suþtone* (? Sutton-on-the-Hill), free of all but the three common dues, Ulfketel having purchased from others the royal licence of the fifth ploughland. Dated from *Sumertun* (Somerton, Somerset) at the royal crown-wearing at Easter.   CS 876.

Bu VIII. Easter Day fell on 22 April 949. The bounds are omitted in the surviving text, and the location is therefore uncertain, but the *Suttun* of Wulfric Spot's will may be the same estate. In the witness list, Ældric results from a miscopying of 'Ælfric' (bishop of Hereford); *Ædelflæd consiliarius* was presumably the king's mother, in spite of the masculine termination. This metrical charter is very characteristic of the 'Dunstan A' Danelaw series; large sections of the text are closely paralleled in CS 882–4, dated the same year. The proem derives from the Proverbs of Solomon, ch. viii (cf. CS 750). See further, DC pp. 125–32.

104. 949   *EADRED, king of the English, ruler of the Northumbrians, emperor of the heathen, and protector of the Britons, to Earl Uhtred. Land at *Badecanwelle* (Bakewell), free of all but the three common dues.
                                        CS 884.

Bu IX. The charter refers to Bakewell as a *cœnubium* (monastery); the town had been fortified by King Edward the Elder in 924 (ASC). It seems that Bakewell has to be added to the list of fortified monastic sites first compiled by Stenton (*Papers*, pp. 320–1). The list includes Tetbury and Westbury-on-Trym in Gloucestershire, Fladbury in Worcestershire,

Malmesbury in Wiltshire, and Congresbury in Somerset. See further, Stenton, *Types*, p. 75. The bounds are omitted in the surviving text.

A characteristic alliterative diploma from the Danelaw 'Dunstan A' series. The text is very close indeed to that of CS 882, the original of which was preserved at Evesham; these two charters appear to have been witnessed on the same occasion, as the witnesses of CS 882 signed *'triumphali signaculo'* followed by an αω monogram, and the Burton charter was witnessed in an identical fashion. Another very similar charter is CS 883, of the same year. The anathema and grace concluding the Burton text have phrases that are paralleled in CS 815, 876, and 890, all Danelaw charters from Eadred's reign, see DC pp. 125–32.

105. 955 *EADRED, king of the Anglo-Saxons, emperor of the Northumbrians, ruler of the heathen, protector of the Britons, to the *pedisequus* Uhtred Cild. Land at *Cesterfelda* (Chesterfield), free of all but the three common dues. CS 911.

Bu xiii. The bounds are omitted from the surviving text· An alliterative diploma whose formulas have numerous parallels with other texts in the Burton series. The absence of Wulfstan's signature as archbishop of York is noteworthy; in his place there appears the rare attestation of Ealdred, bishop of Chester-le-Street. See further DC pp. 125–32.

106. 956 *EADWIG, king of the English and surrounding people, to his man Maeglsothen. 3 'mansae' *æt Mortune* (? Morton near Tibshelf). CS 951.

Bu xv. Maeglsothen is a variant of an Irish name (see p. 347). The location is not certain; it rests on the assumption that this was the same estate as the *Mortun* willed to Burton Abbey by No. 39. The bounds are omitted in the surviving text. The formulas are typical of chancery texts. Down to the name of the estate conveyed, the charter is modelled on a formula that first appears in CS 869, dated 948, a contemporary Winchester diploma (Chaplais 1965, pp. 59–70); the same formula recurs in two Wilton charters, CS 879 and 917. The next passage, *ea tenus ut hoc diebus suis possideat tramitibus vite sue,* first appears in CS 1345, dated 946; the whole clause is repeated in K 663. The anathema, with its quotation from Ovid, was one of the new formulas introduced in 956 (CS 952–3, 984), as was the clause introducing the bounds; this last formula is confined strictly to charters of Eadwig's reign (CS 943, 946, 955, 976, 1001, 1004, 1022, 1033–4). The forms of attestation of the witnesses are correct for the period (cf. CS 943). The chrismon, as reproduced by the Burton copyist, is also typical of one in use in 956, being almost identical with that of No. 86 above, which has the same invocation; one suspects that the originals of these two charters were from the hand of the same scribe.

107. 966 *EDGAR, king of the whole of Britain, to his thegn Ælfhelm. 10 'mansae' at *Peuerwich* (Parwich), free of all but the three common dues.   CS 1175.

Bu XXI. Stenton, *Types*, p. 76. At the time of Domesday Parwich was in royal hands, assessed at two carucates, with berewicks at Alsop-le-Dale, Hanson Grange, and Cold Eaton assessed at a further two carucates (VCH *Derbys.* I, p. 331a). Nothing else is known of its earlier history, but it is evident from the assessment of this charter that it was the central holding of a major estate incorporating several more berewicks in 966. Unfortunately the bounds are not given in the surviving text. The chrismon, as copied by the cartulary scribe, is identical with that of CS 1066, 1082–3, three charters all by the same hand, dated 961–2. The prototype of the invocation is discussed above (No. 101). Its elaboration commences in the reign of Athelstan (CS 670–1, 748, 767, 777; later copies include CS 1031, K 611), and the fully developed formula first appears in 940 and is commonly employed in charters of the following decade (CS 761, 774, 782, 787–8, 795–6, 801, 814, 821, 831, 867–8, 870, 878). Its use ceases abruptly in 949, and it is rarely copied thereafter (CS 1145, 1312). The proem, including the text from 1 Timothy vi, 7, is one of those originating in the year 956 (CS 974).[1] The form of the royal title is similar to that in

[1] This text also appears in a second proem which was currently in circulation, but here it is always associated with a quotation from Job i, 21 (CS 1058, 1114, 1149, 1169, 1171–2; K 751, 771, 1277). It appears alone in a third proem, that of CS 1076.

CS 1124, 1169; the word *optinens* recurs in CS 1165. The formula describing the recipient also incorporates words found in contemporary texts, e.g. *dilecto* in CS 1134, 1143; *gnosticis* in CS 1125, 1229, 1240. The phrase *quandam telluris particulam* in the dispositive clause is of common occurrence in charters of the period, e.g. CS 1116, 1125, 1218. Later in the same sentence, *animo libenti concedo* recalls *libenter concedo* in the Worcester charters CS 1040–1, dated 958. The clause describing the place conveyed is rather similar to that appearing in charters of 956–7 (CS 940, 955, 974, 992, 994, 1003–4), but a similar clause occurs also in a charter of 970 (CS 1260). For *voti compos possideat* in the following sentence, see ECEE p. 188. The exemption clause and part of the anathema recur in No. 57. The phrase introducing the bounds is similar to that of CS 1176. The dating clause, except for the verb completing the second sentence, originates in 951 (CS 895). It recurs in a charter of 956 (CS 959), and again in 959 (CS 1052–4); for the rest of Edgar's reign it is very common.

In spite of all these parallels, much of the vocabulary of this charter is unusual. Among the words and phrases unique for the period are the rhyming sentence following the proem, *dei disposicione* in the king's title, *scibili* in the description of the recipient, *sue vite diebus* in the dispositive clause, *istud procingitur* in the clause introducing the bounds, *visuntur* in the dating clause, and *libenter*, *subsigillavi*, *karessi*, and *pretitulavi* in the forms of attestation of the witnesses. The appearance of Edgar's queen as a witness at this early date is unusual; that of his son Edgar is unique. *Orgar* in the list results from a miscopying of *Osgar* (abbot of Abingdon). These idiosyncrasies add up to form a most unusual charter for the period, but there are no grounds for suspecting its authenticity. Possibly it is a product of the Worcester scriptorium.

108. 968   †Edgar, king of the English, and ruler of the other peoples round about, to Bishop Wulfric. 1 'mansa' at *Stantun* (Stanton in the Peak), free of all but the three common dues.   CS 1211.

Bu xxiii. Edited on p. 179 from the original text.

109. 987   *Æthelred, king and ruler of the English

peoples, to his thegn Æthelsige. 12 'mansae' æt Æsce
(? Ashford).   Bu xxv.

Edited on p. 193.

(39) N.D. (1002 × 1004) *Will of Wulfric Spot.
Alewaldestune (Alvaston or Elvaston) to Wulfheah;
Hwitewylle (Whitwell), *Clune* (Clowne), *Barleburh* (Barl-
borough), *Ducemannestune* (Duckmanton), *Moresburh*
(Mosbrough), *Eccingtune* (Eckington), and *Bectune*
(Beighton) to Morcar; *Paltertune* (Palterton) to his
kinsman Ælfhelm; *Wineshylle* (Winshill, then in Derbys.,
later in Staffs.), *oðer Niwantune* (Newton Solney), *Suttun*
(Sutton-on-the-Hill), *Ticenheale* (Ticknall), heriot-land
at *Suðtune* (Sutton-on-the-Hill), *Morlege* (Morley),
Bregdeshale (Breadsall), *Mortun* (Morton), *Pilleslege*
(Pilsley), *Oggodestun* (Ogston), *Wynnefeld* (Wingfield),
and *Snodeswic* (lost, near South Normanton and
Glapwell) to Burton Abbey; *Bubandune* (Bupton) to
revert to the bishop [of Lichfield], except that Burton
Abbey is to have the produce and men; *Strættune*
(Stretton in North Wingfield) to the daughter of Morcar
and Ealdgyth. Lands in Glos., Staffs., Lancs., Yorks.,
Leics., Lincs., Worcs., Cheshire, and Warwicks.

◆ W xvii.

Bu xxviiib. Stenton, *Types*, p. 21 n. 1. See also pp. 71, 84,
99, and 126.

(40) 1004 *Æthelred, king of the English, to Burton
Abbey. Exemption from all but the three common dues
of lands belonging to the abbey, including *Wineshylle*
(Winshill), *oðer Niwantun* (Newton Solney), *Suthtun*
(Sutton-on-the-Hill), *Ticenheale* (Ticknall), *Brægdesheale*
(Breadsall), *Mortun* (Morton), *Pillesleage* (Pilsley),
Snodeswic (lost, near South Normanton and Glapwell),
Wynnefeld (Wingfield), and *Oggedestune* (Ogston). Lands
in Glos., Staffs., Leics., Salop., Lincs., and Warwicks.

K 710.

Bu xxviiia. See also pp. 71, 84, 99, and 126.

110. 1009 †ÆTHELRED, king of the English, to his thegn Morcar. 8 'manentes' in and about *Westun* (Weston), 1 'manens' in *Morleage* (Morley), 1 in *Smælleage* (Smalley) and in *Kidesleage* (Kidsley), 1 in *Cryc* (Crich), and 1 in *Englaby* (Ingleby), free of all but the three common dues. Bounds of Weston.   Bu xxxi.

Edited on p. 219.

111. 1011 *King ÆTHELRED to his thegn Morcar. 5 'mansæ' *æt Ufre* (? Mickleover or Littleover).   Bu xxxiii.

Edited on p. 232. The bounds are omitted from the surviving text.

112. 1011 *ÆTHELRED, king of the whole of Britain, to his thegn Elemod, for 21 pounds of gold. 2 'cassatæ' at *burhhalun* (Hallam), free of all but the three common dues.   Bu xxxi.

Edited on p. 228. The bounds are omitted from the surviving text.

113. 1012 *ÆTHELRED, king of the whole of Britain, to his thegn Morcar. 2 'mansæ' *æt Ecgintune* (Eckington).
                                    Bu xxxvi.

Edited on p. 244. The bounds are omitted from the surviving text.

CHAPTER VI

THE EARLY CHARTERS OF NOTTINGHAMSHIRE

(1) 664 ****WULFHERE, king of the Mercians and Middle and Southern Angles, to the monastery at *Medeshamstede* (Peterborough). Foundation charter. Lands at *Mustam* (Muskham) and *Colingham* (Collingham). Lands in Hunts., Kent, Leics., Lincs., Northants., Rutland, Salop, Soke of Peterborough, and Yorks. CS 22, 22a.

See also pp. 55, 67, and 117.

114. 958 (for 956) **EADWIG, king of the English, to Archbishop Oscytel [of York]. 20 'mansæ' at *Suðpellan* (Southwell), free of all but the three common dues. Bounds of *Suðpellan* (Southwell), *Normantune* (Normanton), *Aptune* (Upton), *Hocerþuda* (Hockerwood), and *Fiscetune* (Fiskerton). The bounds conclude with the following statement in OE: 'These are the *tuns* belonging to Southwell with sake and soke; *Fearnesfeld* (Farnsfield), *Cyrlingtune* (Kirklington), *Nordmantune* (Normanton), *Uptune* (Upton), *Mortune* (Morton), *Fiskertune* (Fiskerton), *Gypesmere* (Gibsmere), *Blisetune* (Bleasby), *Gofertune* (Goverton), *Healhtune* (Halloughton), *Healum* (Halam). At Farnsfield two 'manslots' of land belong to Southwell, at Halam every sixth acre and three 'manslots', at Normanton every third acre, at Fiskerton two-thirds of the whole estate and four 'manslots'.

CS 1029, 1348.

◆ EHD 1, pp. 512–14. Farrer, EYC No. 2. AHEW pp. 491–2. The list of dependent estates is given in topographical order, working clockwise round Southwell. On the term 'manslot', see R p. 441. See also Stenton, *Types*, pp. 79–81; *Papers*, pp. 364–70. The charter is dated 958 but this is undoubtedly an error, as Eadwig had lost control of York and Nottinghamshire by this time. The indiction corresponds to the year 956. The witness list is notable for the subscription of earls from the northern Danelaw. The formulas are typical of chancery texts.

115. 958 *EDGAR, king of the English, to Bishop Oscytel. 10 'cassatæ' æt Suttone (Sutton, north of East Retford), free of all but the three common dues. Bounds of Sutton, Scroppenþorpe (Scrooby), and Þuresby (lost).

CS 1044, 1349.

Farrer, EYC No. 3. Stenton, Types, p. 81. AHEW p. 402 n. 5. Errors in the witness list can be corrected from CS 1043, a Huntingdonshire charter with identical formulas, drawn up on the same occasion, cf. ECEE p. 24. The formulas are typical of chancery texts issued in 956, and it must be due to copying from an exemplar of this date that Edgar is given the title 'king of the English'. There is no evidence that he claimed such a title before the death of his brother Eadwig.

116. 978 × 1016 *ÆRNKETEL and his wife WULFRUN to Ramsey Abbey. Bequest of estates at Hikelinge (Hickling) and Kinildetune (Kinoulton), and at Lochantona (Lockington, East Riding of Yorks.), after their deaths.   K 971.

Chron Rams pp. 66–7; cf. Stenton, Types, pp. 37–8. See also p. 124. Ærnketel and Wulfrun were the parents of Athelstan, fourth abbot of Ramsey. They died in 1019, and were buried in the abbey (Cart Rams III, p. 167). Their bequest took the form of a chirograph in OE, of which only a Latin translation survives. It runs: 'I Ærnketel, and Wulfrun my wife, make known to our lord King Æthelred [II] and all his [men] of York and Nottingham,[1] that we concede and confirm by this present chirograph, to God and St Mary and St Benedict of Ramsey, after our day, our land at Hickling and Kinoulton, with produce and men,[2] just as we now hold it. And we desire moreover that after our day our bodies shall rest there, God willing; and wheresoever the survivor of us

[1] This seems to imply that notification of the grant was to be laid before the shire-courts of these two towns, after the fashion of a royal writ.

[2] Here the Latin 'cum firma et servitio' may be a rather poor translation of the common OE formula 'mid mete and mid mannum'.

dies, the brothers of Ramsey shall come, as is their custom and that of our friends, and bear the body to be entombed at Ramsey. And I Ærnketel desire that for the price of my sepulchre and the salvation of my soul, the church of Ramsey shall have 15 pounds in silver and gold, and such chattels as I possess at the time of my death. And for the salvation of my wife aforesaid, and for the price of her sepulchre, the land at Lockington[1] shall go to the same church, together with all her chattels. And I Wulfrun bequeath to the church [of Ramsey] on the summer feast of St Benedict (11 July), annually for as long as I live, 10 *mittæ* of malt, 5 of groats, 5 of threshed wheat flour, 8 hams, 16 cheeses, and 2 fat cows from my land at Hickling, in anticipation of their inheritance; and for the brothers during Lent, 8 salmon.'[2] There follows an anathema, and an injunction that neither bishop nor monk is to surrender the property for silver or gold, but it is to remain the perpetual possession of the church.

117. **N.D.** (1055 × 1057) *****Pope VICTOR (II)** to Godgifu, wife of Earl Leofric [of Mercia]. Confirmation of her endowment of Stow St Mary, Lincs., with *Flatburche* (Fledborough) and *Newercha* (Newark), and estates in Lincs.   K 818.

   ECEE 156.

118. Christmas 1060 × 1065 ***King EDWARD** to Earl Tostig and to all his (i.e. the king's) thegns in Yorkshire and Nottinghamshire. Writ confirming the right of Archbishop Ealdred [of York] to sake and soke and to toll and team over his men within the king's own soke, as fully and completely as the archbishop has them in his own lands.   ◆ H 119.

See also p. 130. The lands of the archbishopric in Nottinghamshire became the Liberty of Southwell and Scrooby.

---

[1] There is a Lockington in Leicestershire, only ten miles west of Hickling, but the reference to York early in the grant suggests that Lockington in the East Riding of Yorkshire is the correct location.

[2] Presumably the salmon came from the River Smite at the head of the Vale of Belvoir, which formed the border of both Hickling and Kinoulton. The road journey to Ramsey was 55 miles.

PART II
NORTHERN ENGLAND

CHAPTER VII

THE EARLY CHARTERS
OF THE NORTHERN COUNTIES

(1) 664 ****WULFHERE, king of the Mercians and Middle and Southern Angles, to the monastery at *Medeshamstede* (Peterborough). Foundation charter. Lands granted include *Hoveden* (Howden YE), *Binnington* (Binnington YE), and *Cuningesburge* (Conisbrough YW). Lands in Hunts., Kent, Leics., Northants., Lincs., Notts., Rutland, Salop, and the Soke of Peterborough. CS 22, 22a.

See also pp. 55, 67, and 111.

119. 7 June 934 **ATHELSTAN, king of the English, elevated to the throne of the whole kingdom of Britain, to the church of St Peter, York. Land which he had purchased at *Aghemundesnes* (Amounderness, Lancs.), free of all service. Written at Nottingham. CS 703, 1344.

EYC No. 1. ◆ EHD I, pp. 505–8. On the Hisperic Latinity, see Bullough p. 472 n. 39. The territory conveyed by this charter is probably the largest of all the surviving Anglo-Saxon royal grants, measuring some 15 miles from north to south, and 25 miles from east to west. It was surveyed in the Yorkshire folios of DB; later it became one of the four historic divisions of Lancashire. At the time of this charter, it was bounded to the west by the sea, north by the River Cocker, east by the River Hodder below Dunsop Bridge (which still forms the boundary between Lancashire and Yorkshire), and south by the River Ribble. This was no ordinary landbook, as is emphasized by the inclusion of the three common dues in the exemption clause. Probably the grant should be regarded more as one of jurisdiction than actual ownership of the individual vills within the territory; in later ages it would have been the equivalent to the creation of a palatinate.

This is the last of Athelstan's charters to be witnessed by Osferth, ealdorman of Wessex, by Ælfstan, ealdorman of part of Mercia, and by the Danish earls Thurferth of Northampton-shire, Regenwold of Northumbria, and Haddr of East Anglia. It seems very likely that some if not all of them perished in the Scottish campaign launched by Athelstan that summer.

120. June 934 *King ATHELSTAN to St Cuthbert [at Chester-le-Street]. *Wiremuthe australem* (Bishops Wear-mouth, Durham), with its appendages, namely: *Weston* (Westoe), *Uffertun* (Offerton), *Sylceswurthe* (Silksworth), *duas Reofhoppas* (the two Ryhopes), *Byrdene* (Burdon), *Seham* (Seaham), *Setun* (Seaton), *Daltun* (Dalton-le-Dale), *Daldene* (Dawdon), and *Heseldene* (Cold Hesleden).

RBD p. 525; SD I, pp. 75–211.

Craster 1925, pp. 193–4; 1954, p. 191; SBW pp. 12–13. The gift was recorded in the form of a *testamentum* written in a Gospel Book (thought to have been MS. Cott. Otho B ix, destroyed in the fire of 1731), which was placed by the head of St Cuthbert, in his oratory. The estates belonging to Bishops Wearmouth are listed in topographical order, pro-ceeding southwards along the coast from Wearmouth. RBD has *Westou* in place of SD *Weston*, so confirming the identi-fication here given. Dalton-le-Dale had been given to the abbey of Wearmouth in 704 × 716 (No. 151), and this *testamentum* of King Athelstan should probably be regarded as a reconstruction of Wearmouth's early endowment, which would have been broken up at the time of the Danish settle-ment.

120a. 938 King ATHELSTAN to the church of St John of Beverley. Confirmation of immunities, liberties, and right of sanctuary.   *Lost.*

Dugdale II, p. 129, quoting Leland's *Collectanea*, III, p. 153. The charter was in OE (*Saxonice scripta*) and is therefore unlikely to have been authentic, but it may have preserved authentic traditions. Athelstan is said to have given in addition lands in Brandesburton and Lockington (both in YE), with his right of *hestraffia*, that is the annual provender payable to him for his horses from all the East Riding of Yorkshire. Ripon is said to have been granted similar privileges by Athelstan (Dugdale II, p. 132).

121. (858 for) 958 *EDGAR, king of the Mercians, to the *familia* of St Werburgh at *Leiacestria* (Chester), for his soul and for the souls of his predecessors, Kings Edmund and Athelstan. 17 'manentes' in divers places, namely *Hodeshlið* (Hosely, Flint), *Ceofanlea* (Cheveley, near Chester), *Huntingdun* (Huntington, near Chester), *Huptun* (Upton, near Chester), *Easton* (?Aston Sutton, Cheshire), and *Barue* (Great Barrow, near Chester), free of all but the three common dues. Enacted at *Pencric* (Penkridge, Staffs.). CS 1041.

J. Tait, *The Cartulary or Register of the Abbey of St Werburgh, Chester*, I, Chetham Soc., N.S., LXXIX, 1920, pp. xvii–xviii, 10–13. The boundary clause is omitted in the surviving texts. The charter contains formulas found in other Mercian charters of Edgar, e.g. CS 1040, 1042 (958), CS 1119 (963), and it is probably a product of the Worcester scriptorium. *Ewangelicum paradigma* in the proem is found in the Danelaw series of 942 × 955 (DC p. 126). Ultimately it is Hisperic; it occurs in Aldhelm's prose *De Virginitate*, p. 249 (cf. Bullough 1972, p. 470). The reference to Edmund and Athelstan suggests that they had made earlier grants to St Werburgh.

122. 959 (before 1 Oct.) *EDGAR, king of the whole province of Mercia and the surrounding peoples, to the matron Quen . . . 'cassati' *æt Heaffuddæne* (Howden, YE) and *æt Ealdredrege* (Drax, YW), free of all but the three common dues. List of dependencies of Howden, with sake and soke; *Cnyllingatun* (Knedlington), *Beornhyll* (Barnhill Hall, west of Howden), *Cafeld* (Caville, in Eastrington), *Thorp* (Thorpe Lidget), *Hyðe* (Hive), *Eastringatun* (Eastrington), *Belleby* (Belby, in Howden), and *Celpene* (Kilpin). Bounds of Howden and Drax. CS 1052.

Farrer, EYC No. 4. ◆ *Yorkshire Archaeological Journal*, XI (1891), pp. 363–5. Stenton, *Types*, pp. 80–1. Issued before the death of King Eadwig, and probably therefore the work of a Mercian scribe, possibly from Worcester, since the proem, including the quotation from Luke xxi, 10, originated there (CS 665).

The bounds of Howden can be traced on 2½" O.S. sheets SE 92–3, 82–3, 72–3. They run clockwise through flat, marshy ground:

1. from *Usan*. The River Ouse.
2. up *Wilbaldes fleote*. 'Fleet' is a common name for local dykes draining the marshland, e.g. Yokefleet, Bromfleet. Probably this dyke ran from Asselby to join the River Ouse at a point near grid ref. 725260.
3. to the *dic*. A second dyke.
4. along the dyke to *Deorwentan*. The River Derwent, joined at about 700300.
5. right on to *Cærholm*. Holme upon Spalding Moor, 805385.
6. along the dyke all round the wood to *fulanea*. The River Foulness, joined perhaps at 775345.
7. to *ealdan Deorwentan*. The Old Derwent River.
8. back to *Usan*. The River Ouse, joined at Brough, 930260.

The bounds of Drax can be traced on 2½" O.S. sheets SE 72, 62. They run clockwise through flat, marshy ground:

1. from *Yr*. The River Aire, which joins the River Ouse at 720260.
2. to *Hrodlafesholm*. This name must underlie Rawcliffe (DB *Roudeclif*), 685228.
3. to the boundary mark at Sighere's oak. Perhaps at 650270.
4. to *Usan*. The River Ouse, reached at about 665295.
5. back up *Yr*. The River Aire.

123. 963 (after 29 Nov.) *EDGAR, king of the English and all the peoples round about, to Æslac. 20 'cassati' at *Sireburnan* (Sherburn-in-Elmet, YW), free of all but the three common dues. Bounds of the 20 hides of *inland* at Sherburn, and a list of its dependencies, comprising: ½ hide at *Hibaldes tofte* (unidentified), 1 hide at *fryþetune* (Monk Fryston); 2 oxgangs at *hillum* (Hillam); 2 oxgangs at *Lundby* (Lumby); 7½ hides at *mysenforda* (South Milford) and *stiuetuna* (Steeton, near Bolton Percy); 2 hides at *miclanfelda* (Micklefield); all of *luttringtun* (Lotherton), except 1 hide; 1½ hides at

fentune (Church Fenton); 1½ hides at *kapuda* (Cawood), and all the district[1] that belongs to it along the *usan* (the River Ouse), between *peorf* (the River Wharfe, a tributary of the Ouse) and *ðacy* (unidentified; presumably the name of another tributary of the Ouse), in wood, in water, and in field. CS 1112, 1352.

EYC No. 6. Stenton, *Types*, pp. 82–4. The bounds of the *inland* of Sherburn have not as yet been worked out. The charter is said to have been drawn up by Æthulf, bishop of Elmham, on the king's instructions, cf. Chaplais 1966, p. 13; he used chancery formulas of the period 956 × 958 (CS 927, 948, 994, 902, 1032). It was witnessed, *inter alia*, by the northern earls Gunnar and Thored, and by Æthelwold, bishop of Winchester, who was not appointed to that see until 29 November 963. On the occurrence of units called 'hides' in this charter, see pp. 185–6.

124. 963 (after 29 Nov.) *EDGAR, ruler of the whole of Britain, to Earl Gunnar. 30 'cassati' at *Niubotle* (North and South Newbald, YE), free of all but the three common dues. CS 1113, 1352.

EYC No. 5. Stenton, *Types*, pp. 81, 86. Drögereit pp. 394–400. Later, this estate appears to have been sold by King Edgar to Archbishop Oscytel, see No. 125. The text survives in a York cartulary, but the formulas are typical of chancery texts of the period. For the proem, see Chaplais, *Exeter*, p. 13. Unfortunately, the cartulary text is a poor one. Among the *duces* witnessing, for *Ælfstan* read 'Ælfheah', for *Æstan* read 'Æthelstan', for *Apeline* read 'Æthelwine'. The boundary is particularly corrupt, requiring considerable editing before it can be utilized. PN *East Riding of Yorkshire* is helpful, and fortunately the compass points are often given. The bounds can be traced on O.S. 2½" sheets SE 83, 93, 94. They embrace the modern parishes of North and South Newbald, together with a large expanse of moorland to the north and east, proceeding in a clockwise direction:

1. *ærest suðpeard peg ðe gemære to seristre*. Note the form *særistre* in landmark no. 19 below. Assuming the northern dialect form *trē* (as in the Northumbrian Gospels), we obtain for

1 Reading *lid* in the charter as ON *hlið*.

seristre the reading *sēares trē* = 'withered tree'. The road to Eastrington leaves the road running southwards from Newbald to Welton at grid ref. 914341, a little to the south of the modern boundary of South Newbald.

2. *ðonan pest pid anes þornes*. Westwards to a thorn at about 902338, at Hillside Plantation.

3. *þonan norð to þan broce*. North to Mill Beck, joined just east of Hotham Field at 904356.

4. *ꝗ ilc oder acra be fastan hode*. OE *hōd*, for 'hood-shaped hill', was the early form underlying Hotham (*PNER Yorks*. p. 225). Reading *eastan* for *fastan*, we can interpret this passage to mean that every other acre in Hotham Field (east of Hotham) is to be included within the estate. On this, see AHEW p. 491.

5. *of þan broce pest to þan dice*. West to Twin Beck, joined at 895362.

6. *ꝗlang dices to Elfredes bricge*. North along Twin Beck to the point where it is crossed by the road from North Newbald to North Cliffe, at 895366. An alternative would be 896371, a little to the north, where Alfred's bridge would perhaps have carried a Roman road (now vanished) across the beck. The charter bounds run to the east of the modern parish boundary here.

7. *þonne norð to Ylemere*. The name recurs as *Illemere* in a Yorkshire inquisition of 1282. Probably the pool at 895377, near where the charter bounds join the modern parish bounds.

8. *ꝗ þonan to Saxferdes lape*. Saxferth's *hlaw* or burial mound was perhaps at 895385, where the bounds turn eastwards.

9. *norð on þa dic, ꝗ lang dices on þene sic*. The bounds run along a dyke to Newbald Sike (*ibid.*, p. 227).

10. *ꝗlang sices be þere acera anheafda on þa strete*. Moving along the sike draining the headlands, to the Roman road running north to Sancton. This was crossed by the sike at 903386.

11. *Of þere strete east onan up one yalde be nordan farþis dal*. The etymology of *farþis dale* is obscure; possibly there is a corruption. For *yalde* read *palde*. The wold lies to the north of a dale which runs north-eastwards from Newbald Sike to Hessleskew Gare.

12. *on þa ealdan dic*. Gare gate joins the dyke at 928396.

13. *ꝗlang dices to brusan lapa*. Reading *hruȝan lapa*, 'rough

hill', we have the early name of Rowley (*ibid.* p. 203), but it is clear from the assessment of Newbald that *hruʒan lapa* in this charter comprised the great expanse of wold stretching from Cherry Burton Wold southwards to Hunsley Beacon. This high land forms a watershed between dales draining westwards towards Newbald, and those running eastwards towards Bishop Burton. The bounds are noticeably vague at this point. The whole area is wild and beautiful, with great clusters of tumuli.

14. *ʒlang þes grene peges þaet hit cymð to fif lapan.* A road joined at Monkton Walk, 362952. There are so many tumuli, it is difficult to decide which five are referred to in the charter, without knowing the precise course of the boundary.

15. *ʒ þonne suð ʒlang peges Deoppendale.* Along Whin Lane to the head of Deepdale at 348932.

16. *suð andlang denes.* Along Rudstone Dale, to the south of South Wold.

17. *up to þan pege.* The Roman road from Newbald to South Cave, joined at 913345.

18. *andlang peges to þins housum.* ? possibly the house belonging to the *þing* – an assembly building.

19. *þon spa forð ʒlang peges þest to særistre.* Back to the starting point.

125. c. 972   *Declaration by Archbishop Oswald [of York], concerning church lands in Northumbria.   ◆ R LIV.

The memorandum is in several parts, as follows:

(1) List of *tuns* which have been taken away from *Ottanleage* (Otley, YW), comprising *Haddincham* (Addingham), *Hyllicleg* (Ilkley), *Mensinctun* (Menston), half of *Burhleg* (Burley in Wharfedale), *Gislicleh* (Guisely), *Scefinc* (Chevin), *Middeltun* (Middleton), half of *Dentun* (Denton), *Timmel* (Timble), *Lindeleh* (Lindley), *Stanburne* (Stainburn), *Becwudu* (Beckwith), and half of *Byllinctun*.

The list proceeds from west to east along the southern slopes of Wharfedale, then from west to east along the northern slopes. *Byllinctun*, therefore, is probably Bilton, north-east of Harrogate.

(2) List of *tuns* which have been taken away from *Rypum* (Ripon, YW), comprising *Heawic*, the other

Heawic (Bridge and Copt Hewick, YW), *Ansætleh* (possibly Sawley, YW), one hide at *Stanley* (Stainley, YW), *Helperby* (Helperby, YN), *Myðtune* (Myton-on-Swale, YN), and two hides from *Popeltune* (Poppleton).

(3) List of what has been taken from *Scireburnan* (Sherburn-in-Elmet, YW), comprising half of *Ceoredesholm* (unidentified), half of *Cawudu* (Cawood, YW), and half of the soke belonging to Sherburn; memorandum that *Gisferþesdæll* (unidentified) has always belonged to Sherburn.

(4) List of estates in Northumbria purchased by or granted to Archbishop Oscytel, namely: *Æffeltune* (? one of the Yorkshire Appletons), bought from Deorwulf for 24 pounds; *Yferingaham* (Everingham, YE), bought from Osulf's father for 44 pounds; land at *Neoweboldan* (Newbald, YE) bought from King Edgar for 120 mancuses of red gold; *Heolperbi* (Helperby, YN), forfeited to him because two brothers had one wife; and estates belonging to Helperby, comprising two parts of *Mytun* (Myton-on-Swale, YN), the soke of *Wisbustan* (Wide Open Farm in Skelton, YN), and *Þurulfestun* (Tholthorpe, YN), *Ioletun* (Youlton, YN), *Þorp* (unlocated), *Scyteby* (Skidby, YE), bought for 20 pounds; and 3 hides at *Bracenan* (Bracken, YE), bought from King Edgar, who granted it by a charter for St John's [Beverley].

(5) Declaration by Archbishop Oswald concerning all the estates in Northumbria obtained by Archbishop Oscytel, and granted to Oswald for St Peter's [York Minster] when he was at *Snotingaham* (Nottingham) together with the other estates aforementioned; all these estates had been held by Oswald, but were afterwards robbed from St Peter's.   ◆ R LIV.

◆ EHD I, pp. 521–2. Stenton, *Types*, pp. 84–6. Cf. Ker p. 302 for the last line.

(116) 978 × 1016   *ÆRNKETEL and his wife WULFRUN to Ramsey Abbey. Bequest of *Lochantona* (Lockington, YE) and estates in Nottinghamshire, after their deaths.

K 971.
See p. 112.

126. 979 × 992 †Record of a grant by Earl THORED to St Cuthbert [at Chester-le-Street]. 2 hides at *Smiþatune* (Great Smeaton, YN), 2 hides at *Creic* (Crayke, YN), and 1 hide at *Suþtune* (Sutton-in-the-Forest, YN).

◆ R LX.

Facsimile: *Liber Vitæ Ecclesiæ Dunelmensis*, Surtees Society, CXXXVI, 1923. See also Ker p. 186; Craster 1954, pp. 183, 194.

127. c.994 *Earl NORTHMAN to St Cuthbert [at Durham]. *Ediscum* (Escombe, Durham), and the fourth acre at *Feregenne* (Ferryhill, Durham). ◆ R LXVIII.

Craster 1954, p. 194.

128. c.994 *ULFKETEL, son of Osulf, to St Cuthbert [at Durham]. *Norðtun* (Norton, Durham), with sake and soke. ◆ R LXVIII.

Craster 1954, p. 193. The gift included the vill of Stockton.

129. 995 × 1006 Bishop EALDHUN to the three earls Northman, Æth(el)red, and Uhtred. Lease of lands belonging to St Cuthbert, including *Gegenford* (Gainford), *Queorningtun* (Quarrington), *Sliddewesse* (Sledwitch, near Gainford), *Bereford* (Barforth in Cleveland, YN), *Stretford* (unlocated), *Lyrtingtun* (Lartington, YN), *Marawuda* (Marwood), *Stantun* (Staunton, near Barnard Castle), *Stretlea* (Streatlam), *Cletlinga* (Cleatham), *Langadun* (Langton near Staindrop), *Mortun* (Morton Tinmouth), *Persebrigce* (Piercebridge near Darlington), *Alclit II* (Bishop and West Auckland), *Copland* (Copeland, near Bishop Auckland), *Weardseatle* (Warsull, near Yarm in Teesdale), *Bynceastre* (Binchester), *Cuthbertestun* (Cotherstone in Teesdale), *Thiccelea* (Thickley, near Bishop Auckland), *Ediscum* (Escombe, YN), *Wudutun* (Witton-le-Wear), *Hunewic* (Hunwick), *Neowatun* (Newton Cap), and *Healme* (Helmington). *Lost.*

RBD p. 527. SD I, pp. 83–4, 213. Craster 1925, p. 195; 1954, pp. 182, 194–5. These lands, all in Durham unless

otherwise stated, were all subsequently lost to the see. The
transaction may be dated before Uhtred took over the earldom
of all Northumbria in 1006. Craster regards it as a compressed
account of three separate leases, one to each earl.

(39) N.D. (1002 × 1004) *Will of WULFRIC SPOT. Lands
between *Ribbel* and *Mærse* (the Rivers Ribble and
Mersey) to Ælfhelm and Wulfheah. The estate at
Cunugesburh (Conisbrough, YW), to Ælfhelm. The
estate *æt Doneceastre* (Doncaster, YW) to Morcar. The
estate at *Niwantun æt þære wi[c]* (Newton, near Middlewich, Cheshire) to Burton Abbey. Lands in Glos.,
Staffs., Leics., Derbys., Lincs., Worcs., and Warwicks.
◆ W XVII.

Bu xxviiib. See also pp. 71, 84, 99, and 109.

(40) 1004 *ÆTHELRED, king of the English, to Burton
Abbey. Exemption from all but the three common dues
of lands belonging to the abbey, including *Niwantun æt
ðære wic* (Newton, near Middlewich, Cheshire). Lands
in Glos., Leics., Staffs., Derbys., Salop, Lincs., and Warwicks.   K 710.

Bu xxviiia. See also pp. 71, 84, 99, and 109.

130. 1003 × 1016 *STYR, son of Ulf, to St Cuthbert [at
Durham]. *Dearningtun* (Darlington) with its appendages,
with sake and soke; and he gives the following territory,
all of which he has purchased: 4 carucates at *Cingescliffe*
(High Coniscliffe), 4 in *Cocertune* (Cockerton), 4 in
Halhtune (Haughton le Skerne), 3 in *Northmannabi*
(Normanby, near Middlesbrough, YN), 2 in *Ceattune*
(unlocated) with sake and soke, and 2 in *Lummalea*
(Lumley).   *Lost.*

RBD p. 526; SD I, pp. 83, 212–13. The gift, recorded in
charter form, was made at York with King Æthelred II's
permission, and in his presence, and in that of Archbishop
Wulfstan (RBD says Ælfric, wrongly) of York, Bishop Ealdhun

of Durham, Abbot Ælfwold (who was 'under' Bishop Ealdhun), and other magnates. Note the references to *carucates* in Durham, in a pre-Conquest source. It implies that County Durham (not surveyed in DB) was carucated like the rest of the northern Danelaw. See further, Craster 1954, p. 193.

131. 1003 × 1016 SNACULF, son of Cytel, to St Cuthbert [at Durham]. *Brydbyrig* (Bradbury), *Mordun* (Mordon, near Sedgefield), *Socceburg* (Sockburn, near Darlington), and *Grisebi* (Girsby YN, on the Tees opposite Sockburn), with sake and soke.   *Lost*.

   RBD p. 526; SD I, pp. 83, 213. Sockburn had been the site of a monastery in the late eighth century, and was used for the consecration of a bishop of Lindisfarne and an archbishop of York (ASC D, *s.a.* 780; SD II, p. 58). Snaculf's gift was made soon after that of Styr (No. 130). See further, Craster 1954, pp. 193–4.

132. 1031 King CNUT to St Cuthbert [at Durham]. *Standropa* (Staindrop, Durham), with sake and soke, just as he himself had held it, with its appendages, namely: *Cnapatun* (unidentified), *Scottun* (West Shotton), *Raby* (Raby), *Wacarfeld* (Wackerfield), *Efenwuda* (Evenwood), *Alclit* (Bishop Auckland), *Luteringtun* (Lartington, YN), *Elledun* (Eldon), *Ingeltun* (Ingleton), *Thiccelea* (Thickley), and *Middeltun* (Middleton, near Auckland). Also *Bromtun* (Brompton YN, near Northallerton), with sake and soke. Confirmation of the territories held by St Cuthbert in Yorkshire (YN), by the ancient gifts of kings and princes: *Segger* (Sessay, with its sokeland in Hutton Sessay); *Horbodyby* (Hornby in Great Smeaton); *Hoton, Hograve, Norton, Suthton, Hulme, Throp* (Hutton Conyers, with its sokeland in Howgrave, Norton Conyers, Sutton Howgrave, Holme, and Thorpe); *Eueneton, Foxton* (Knayton, with its sokeland of Foxton); *Cryssiby* (Girsby), *Dicton* (Deighton), *Neowiton* (Winton), *Osmunderle* (Osmotherley), *Herleseie* (West Harlsey), *Alrebeck* (Ellerbeck), *Siggeston* (Sigston), the church of *Cucewald* with the land adjacent (Coxwold); the church

of *Smittona* with two carucates of land (Great Smeaton); the church of *Gressiby* (Girsby), with 24 carucates of land at *Bromtune* (Brompton, near Northallerton).

Lost.

RBD p. 527; SD I, pp. 90, 213. See also EYC II, p. 270; Craster 1954, pp. 195–6. The gift was made in the time of Edmund, bishop of Durham.

133. 1033 *CNUT, king of all the English peoples, to Ælfric, archbishop of York. 43 'cassati' *æt Partingtune* (Patrington, YE), free of all but the three common dues.

K 749.

The edition in EYC No. 8 includes the boundary clause, omitted by Kemble.

134. N.D. (c. 1041 × 1064) *GOSPATRIC to all his *wassenas* and to all dwelling in the lands that were Cumbrian. Writ informing them that Thorfynn mac Thore shall be free of all things that are Gospatric's in *Alnerdall* (Allerdale), from *Shauk* (Chalk Beck) to *Wafyr* (the River Waver), to *poll Waðoen* (Wampool), *bek Troyte* (Wiza Beck), and the plain at *Caldebeck* (Caldbeck). Men dwelling with Thorfynn at *Carðeu* and *Combeðeyfoch* (Cumdivock) shall be as free as Melmor and Thore and Sigulf were in the days of Eadred. The peace granted him by Gospatric and Earl Siward shall not be broken. Whoever dwells there is to be exempt from the geld as is Gospatric, and Willann, Waltheof, Wigand, Wiberht, Gamell, Kunyth, and all Gospatrick's kindred and *wassenas*. Thorfynn shall have sake and soke, toll and team, over all the lands in Cardew and Cumdivock that were given to Thore in the days of Moryn, free from the obligation of providing messengers and witnesses.

◆ H 121.

The Gospatric who issued this writ was probably the son of Earl Uhtred of Northumbria. This part of Cumberland, a border district which had only recently been detached from the kingdom of Strathclyde and annexed to Northumbria, may be roughly defined by the Derwent, the Eamont, the lakeland mountains, and the marshes at the head of the Solway (Stenton, *Papers*, p. 217 n. 1).

(21) 1042 × 1055 The lady GODGIT to Peterborough Abbey. *Binitun* (Binnington, YE) and *Cunninggesburch* (Conisbrough, YW). Lands in Lincs. and Northants.
Lost.

HC p. 70. ECEE 353. See also p. 63.

135. 1042 × 1056 Earl COPSI to St Cuthbert [at Durham], in perpetuity. The church of St Germain in *Merscum* (Marske in Cleveland, near Redcar), with its endowment, comprising 10½ carucates in Marske, 2 carucates in *Thorntun* (Thornton Fields, near Upleatham), 10 bovates in *Theostcota* (Tocketts, YN), ½ carucate in *Readeclive* (?Redcar in Cleveland), and 1 carucate in *Gisburham* (Guisborough, YN).
Lost.

SD I, p. 97. Craster 1954, p. 196.

(22) 1043 ****LEOFRIC, earl 'of Chester', to Coventry Abbey. Foundation charter, naming, among other lands, *Eaton iuxta aquam quæ dicitur Dee in Cestriæ prouincia* (Eaton, Cheshire). Lands in Warwicks., Glos., Worcs., Leics., and Northants.
K 939.

ECWM 159. See also pp. 64, 71, and 87.

(23) 1043 ***EDWARD, king of the English, to Coventry Abbey. General confirmation of lands and privileges, naming, among other lands, *Eatuna iuxta fluuium Dee* (Eaton, Cheshire). Lands in Warwicks., Worcs., Northants., and Leics.
K 916.

ECWM 160. See also pp. 64, 71, and 87.

136. Christmas 1060 × 1065 *King EDWARD to his bishops, earls, and thegns in the shires in which Archbishop Ealdred [of York] has land. Writ confirming the

I

archbishop's rights to sake and soke over all his lands and men, and to toll and team within town and without.

◆ H 118.

(118) Christmas 1060 × 1065 *King EDWARD to Earl Tostig and to all his (i.e. the king's) thegns in Yorkshire and Nottinghamshire. Writ confirming the right of Archbishop Ealdred [of York] to sake and soke and to toll and team over his men within the king's own soke, as fully and completely as the archbishop has them in his own lands.   ◆ H 119.

See also p. 113.

137. Christmas 1060 × 1065 *King EDWARD to Earl Tostig and all his thegns in Yorkshire. Archbishop Ealdred has his permission to draw up a 'privilegium' for the lands belonging to St John's minster æt Beferlicc (Beverley, YE). The minster is to be free in all things as is any other minster; it is to be subject to the bishop, who is to be its guardian. No one but the bishop may take anything from it. And the life of the community there is to continue for ever.   ◆ H 7.

According to tradition preserved at Beverley, King Edward gave the church there dominium in Leven (YE) at Archbishop Ealdred's request (Dugdale II, p. 129). Possibly dominium in this context should be translated as 'soke'.

CHAPTER VIII

EARLY NORTHUMBRIAN MONASTIC ENDOWMENTS

138. 647 × 652   AIDAN, bishop of Lindisfarne, to Hilda. The place of one 'familia' on the north bank of the River Wear, for a monastery.   HE IV, c. 23.

> On the second date, see Kirby p. 519.

139. c. 651   OSWINE, king of Deira, to St Cuthbert. Land beside the River *Bolbenda* (Bowmont, Northumb.), with the vills of *Suggariple* (?Saughtree, south of Hobkirk, Roxb.), *Hesterhoh* (Hesterheugh, Roxb.), *Gistatadun* (?Gateshaws, near Morebattle, Roxb.), *Waquirtun* (?Whitton, Roxb.), *Cliftun* (Clifton, Roxb.), *Scerbedle* (Morebattle, Roxb.), *Colwela* (?Colwell, near Hexham, Northumb.), *Eltherburna* (?Halterburn, Roxb.), *Thornburnum* (?Thorneyburn, north-west of Bellingham, Northumb.), *Scotadun* (Shotton in Glendale, Northumb.), *Gathan al. Getham* (Yetholm, Roxb.), *Minethrum* (Mindrum, near Coldstream, Northumb.).   SD I, p. 197.

> Arnold, in a note, points out that the transaction is unhistorical; several of the identifications are tentative, but it is probable that the account is based on some early record of the endowment of Melrose with lands along the Northumbrian border. Craster 1954, p. 180 mistakenly ascribes this gift to King Oswiu.

140. c. 654 × 656   ŒDELWALD, king of Deira, to Cedd, bishop of the East Saxons. Land to endow a monastery at *Læstingaeu* (Lastingham, YN).   HE III, c. 23.

> On the date, see Kirby p. 519, and Plummer, *Bede*, II, p. 179.

141. 656   OSWIU, king of Northumbria, on the occasion of

the dedication of his daughter, Ælfflæd, to the religious life, grants six estates each of 10 'familiæ' in Deira, and six similar estates in Bernicia, for the needs of monks.

HE III, c. 24.

This gift by Oswiu was in thanks for his victory at *Winwæd*. On the date, see Kirby p. 519. Two years later Ælfflæd obtained (presumably from her father) 10 'familiæ' at *Stræonæshealh* (Whitby), where she founded the famous abbey.

142. c. 658 × 661   ALHFRITH, sub-king of Deira, to Wilfrid. 10 'familiæ' at *Stanford* (unlocated) and (soon afterwards) 30 'familiæ' at *Inhyrpum* (Ripon, YW), for the foundation endowment of a monastery there.

Eddius, *Vita Wilfridi*, c. 8; HE v, c. 19.

Plummer, *Bede*, I, p. 325. B. Colgrave and R. A. B. Mynors, *Bede's Ecclesiastical History*, Oxford, 1969, p. 615, index the first gift at Stamford, Lincs.; but this identification cannot be regarded as being established conclusively. See also Stenton, *Types*, p. 85. For further gifts to Wilfrid, see the *Vita Wilfridi*, c.17.

143. 674   ECGFRITH, king of Northumbria, to Cuthbert, prior of Lindisfarne. *Carrum* (Carham, Northumb.), with all that belonged to it.   SD I, p. 200.

This donation was made after a battle there, in which Ecgfrith defeated Wulfhere, king of Mercia. The church of Carham was dedicated to St Cuthbert. See further, Craster 1954, p. 184.

144. 674   ECGFRITH, king of Northumbria, to Benedict Biscop. The land of 50 'familiæ' for the foundation endowment of a monastery at *Uuiræmuda* (Wearmouth, Durham).   Anon., *Historia Abbatum*, c. 7.

Plummer, *Bede*, I, p. 390; ◆ EHD I, p. 699. According to Bede, *Historia Abbatum*, c.4, the foundation endowment was the land of 70 'familiæ'. According to the anonymous *Historia*, c. 33, Ecgfrith and his successors increased the endowment, so that by 716, when Abbot Ceolfrith died, the combined endowment of Wearmouth and Jarrow comprised about 150 'familiæ' by the English computation. See also No. 145.

145. 682 ECGFRITH, king of Northumbria, to Benedict Biscop. The land of 40 'familiæ' for the foundation endowment of a monastery *in Gyruum* (Jarrow, Durham).

Anon., *Historia Abbatum*, c. 11;

Bede, *Historia Abbatum*, c. 7.

Plummer, *Bede*, I, p. 391; ◆EHD I, p. 700. See also No. 144.

146. Easter 685 ECGFRITH, king of Northumbria, and THEODORE, archbishop of Canterbury, to Cuthbert, bishop of Lindisfarne. All the lands from the wall of the church of St Peter, York, to the great gate to the west, and from the church wall to the city wall to the south. The vill of *Crecam* (Crayke, 12 miles north of York) and 3 miles round about it, for a lodging for Cuthbert when visiting York. Also *Lugubalia*, known as *Luel* (Carlisle), with 15 miles round about it.

SD I, pp. 31–2, 199.

This gift, if genuine, was made immediately after Cuthbert's election to the see of Lindisfarne, and presumably during a vacancy at York, after the explusion of Bosa and before the restitution of the bishopric of York to Wilfrid, for the grant appears to give to Cuthbert some of the temporalities of the see of York. King Ecgfrith was killed on 20 May 685 at *Nechtansmere*. The anonymous *Life of St Cuthbert* says that the saint was at Carlisle when the king died. The land at Carlisle has been identified as the parish of St Cuthbert Without (Craster 1954, pp. 180–3). Crayke became the site of a monastery, and Carlisle a nunnery. Haddan and Stubbs (*Councils and Ecclesiastical Documents*, III, p. 166 n.) considered this record as 'spurious', but it seems authentic to me. See further, W. Bright, *Chapters on Early English Church History*, 3rd edn, Oxford, 1897, p. 374 n.7.

147. 685 ECGFRITH, king of Northumbria, to Cuthbert, bishop of Lindisfarne. Land called *Cartmel* (Cartmel, Lancs.) with all the Britons belonging to it, and the vill called *Suth gedluit al. Suth-gedling* (Gilling, near Richmond, YN) with its appurtenances. SD I, p. 200.

148. 686 ALDFRITH, king of Northumbria, and his counsellors, to Abbot Benedict Biscop (founder of Wearmouth
and Jarrow), in return for two beautifully worked silk
altar-cloths which Benedict had obtained in Rome. The
land of 3 'familæ' lying to the south of the estuary of the
River Wear.   Bede, *Historia Abbatum*, c.9.

This record establishes that Sunderland formed part of the
early endowment of Jarrow. It is noteworthy that the OE
Bede says that Bede was born in the *sundurlond* of the abbey of
Jarrow. Bede himself says he was born '*in territorio eiusdem
monasterii*' (HE v, c.24). Wearmouth was not founded until he
was about a year old; Bede was given to Wearmouth at the age
of seven, and Jarrow was founded two years later.

149. 689 ALDFRITH, king of Northumbria, to Abbot Benedict Biscop, in exchange for a cosmographical manuscript
which Benedict had obtained in Rome. The land of 8
'familiæ' beside the River *Fresca* (unlocated), for the
monastery of St Paul [at Jarrow].
                           Bede, *Historia Abbatum*, c. 15.

Bede states that Benedict settled the terms of this purchase,
but died before it could be completed; his successor Abbot
Ceolfrith gave the manuscript to King Aldfrith. Subsequently
Ceolfrith exchanged this estate, together with a sum of
money, with King Osred (705 × 716) for the land of 20
'familiæ' *ad villam Sambuce* (? Cambois, Northumb.), which
was nearer to the monastery.

150. 704 × 716 WIHTMÆR to Ceolfrith, abbot of St
Peter's [Wearmouth]. The land of 10 'familiæ' at *Daltun*
(Dalton-le-Dale, Du), which he had been given by King
Aldfrith.   Bede, *Historia Abbatum*, c. 15.

150a. 705 × 716 OSRED, king of Northumbria, to the see
of York (for the church of Beverley). The church of South
Dalton (YE).   Dugdale II, p. 129.

Recorded in the anonymous *Vita S. Johannis*, see No. 150b.

150b. 705 × 718 PUCH, a *gesith*, to the church of Beverley, when his daughter Yolfrida became a nun there. The manor of Walkington (YE).

Dugdale II, p. 128.

John of Beverley, bishop of York 705 × 718, cured Puch's wife of an illness (HE v, c.4). The post-Conquest *Vita S. Johannis* by Folcard of St Bertin's says the miracle occurred at Puch's villa 'quae Australis Burtun dicitur'; this is located by Raine at Bishop Burton, 3 miles west of Beverley (HCY I, p. 249). Walkington lies 2 miles south of Bishop Burton. Details of Puch's gift appear in a later, anonymous *Vita S. Johannis* cited in Leland's *Collectanea*, III, p. 153, the source of Dugdale's account. The anonymous *Vita* says Yolfrida died on 13 March 742, and was buried at Beverley. Possibly Bede, Folcard, and the anonymous writer all drew on a series of early collections of miracle stories of John of Beverley since lost, and the traditions of all the donations recorded in the anonymous *Vita S. Johannis* may be authentic. See also Nos. 150a, c, d.

150c. 705 × 718   ADDI, a *gesith*, to the church of Beverley. Cherry Burton (YE) with its church.

Dugdale II, pp. 128–9.

John of Beverley cured Addi's servant of an illness (HE v, c. 5). The gift of Cherry Burton is recorded in the anonymous *Vita S. Johannis* cited by Leland, see No. 150b.

150d. 705 × 721   JOHN, bishop of York, to the church of Beverley. Lands which he has purchased in Middleton in the Wolds, Welwick, Bilton, and Patrington (all in YE).

Dugdale II, p. 129.

Recorded in the anonymous *Vita S. Johannis*, see No. 150b.

151.   (737)   CEOLWULF, king of Northumbria, on the occasion of his receiving the tonsure, to St Cuthbert [at Lindisfarne]. *Bregesne* (Brainshaugh) and *Werecworðe* (Warkworth) with their appendages, and the church built there; *Wudecestre* (? Woodhorn), *Hwittingaham* (Whittingham), *Eadulfingham* (Edlingham), and *Ecgwulfingham* (Eglingham).

SD I, pp. 47, 201–2; RBD p. 523.

Craster 1954, pp. 185–6. All these territories lay in Northumberland. The gift of the four places last mentioned is said in one account to have been made jointly by Ceolwulf and a bishop named Esred, who consecrated churches in each of the four vills. No other references to a bishop of this name survive, and there is no room for him in the succession at Lindisfarne. It is probable that the name is a corruption of Ecgred; a man of this name was bishop of Lindisfarne 830 × 845, and a benefactor to St Cuthbert of various estates, upon some of which he had built churches (No. 154). Ecgred venerated King Ceolwulf, whose body he translated to Norham, the new resting-place of St Cuthbert (SD 1, p. 52).

One entry referring to this donation quotes the bounds of Warkworth; the estate with its appendages covered a long stretch of coastline with its hinterland, from the River Lyne to the River Aln, including Hauxley (*Hafodscelf* in the bounds), and reaching as far inland as Brinkburn (*Brincewelæ* in the bounds).

152. N.D. (c. 756 × 875) Bounds of *Lindisfarnensis terræ* (lands belonging to Lindisfarne). From the River *Tweoda* (Tweed) to *Warnamuthe* (Warren Beck, near Holy Isle), thence upwards to the source of this river called *Warned* (south-west of Warenford, Northumb.), by the hill called *Hybberndune* (the hill of Hepburn, Northumb., known as Ros Castle), thence to the river called *Bromic* (Breamish), then to the river called *Till* (Till); and all the land lying to either side of the River Breamish, right up to its source; also the land beyond the River Tweed, from the source of the River *Edræ* (White Adder, Berwicks.) to the north, down to where it joins the River Tweed, and all the land lying between the River Adder and another river called *Leder* (Leader Water, Berwicks.) to the west, and all the lands lying on the east side of Leader Water, as far as the place where it runs into the River Tweed towards the south; and all the land belonging to the monastery of St Balthere (an anchorite), called *Tinningaham* (Tynningham in East Lothian), from *Lombormore* (Lammermore Hills, East Lothian) to *Escemuthe* (the mouth of the River Esk).

SD 1, p. 199.

It is difficult to regard this archaic description of the bounds of Lindisfarne territory as being other than authentic; it has important implications for early Northumbrian history. The bounds demarcate (1) the northern quarter of the modern county of Northumberland, (2) the whole of the modern shire of Berwick, and (3) the whole of the modern shire of East Lothian. These shire boundaries appear, therefore, to have originated in the eighth century, if not earlier. See Craster 1954, pp. 178–9, for the later history of this territory.

Symeon of Durham has inserted into his *Historia Regum*, under the year 854, a number of additional estates which are said to have been owned by Lindisfarne. These are *Mailros* (Melrose, on the Tweed), *Tigbrethingham* (unidentified), *Eoriercorn ad occidentalem partem Edwinesburch* (Abercorn, to the west of Edinburgh), *Pefferham* and *Aldham* (both in Tynningham parish), *Coldingaham*, *Tillemuthe*, and *Northam* (Coldingham in East Lothian, Tillmouth at the junction of the Rivers Till and Tweed, Norham on the east bank of the River Tweed). Of these, Melrose, Abercorn, Coldingham, Norham, and Tynningham, and probably Tillmouth, were all early Anglian monasteries; Sir Edmund Craster suggested that all became colonies of Lindisfarne, which held in the Bernician diocese the same position of predominance that the monastery of Iona did in the Celtic church (Craster 1954, p. 179). It might be added that Peterborough, further south, in Mercian territory, had similarly a large number of dependent colonies (see Stenton's *Medeshamstede*).

153. **757 × 758** *Letter of Pope PAUL (I) to Ecgberht, archbishop [of York] and Eadberht, king [of Northumbria], urging the restoration of monasteries at *Staningagrave* (Stonegrave, YN), *Cuhapalda* (Coxwold, YN), and *Doncæmuþe*, which had been granted by a certain abbess to Abbot *Forþreth*, and stolen from the abbot by the king, and given by the king to his brother, a patrician named Moll. CS 184.

◆ EHD 1, pp. 764–5. This papal letter, which shows every sign of being genuine, has received very little attention in the past. In a note to her translation, Professor Whitelock records Sir Frank Stenton's suggestion that *Doncæmuþe* was an otherwise unrecorded monastery at the mouth of the Yorkshire River

Don. Nothing is known of Forthred, who is most unlikely to be identifiable with the abbot of that name who witnessed a number of Mercian charters in the late eighth century, and whose death is recorded in ASC *s.a.* 805 (for 803). Presumably Moll is to be identified with the Æthelwold, named also Moll, who seized power in Northumbria after the slaying of Eadberht's son Osulf in 759.

154. 830 × 845 ECGRED, bishop of Lindisfarne, to the church of St Cuthbert, in perpetuity. *Northam* (Norham, Northumb.); *Gedwearde* (Jedburgh, Roxb.), and *altera Gedwearde* (Old Jeddart), with all that pertains to it, from *Duna* (Dunian Hill, south-west of Jedburgh), to *Tefegdemuthe* (the junction of the River Teviot and Rule Water), and from there to *Wiltuna* (Wilton, near Hawick), and thence to the hill further towards the south (?Berry Fell Hill, south-west of Hobkirk); *Geinforde* (Gainford, Durham) with the church he had built there, and all that pertains to it, from the River Tees to the River Wear, and from the road called *Deorestrete* (the Roman road running north from Scotch Corner, B 6275) to the hill towards the west (the high land about Butter Knowle), and the land on the other side of the River Tees (i.e. south of Gainford), 3 miles towards the south, and 6 miles towards the west; the two vills *Ileclif* (Cliffe on Tees, Durham) and *Wigeclif* (Wycliffe, Durham); also *Billingham* (Billingham on Tees, Durham) in *Heorternesse* (the district around Hart and Hartlepool, Durham).

SD I, pp. 52–3, 201.

Craster 1954, pp. 180, 182, 186–8. Wycliffe and Cliffe were both sokeland of the manor of Gilling (see No. 147) by the time of DB. For Gainford, see No. 163. Craster notes that there were already churches at Billingham and Gainford in the seventh or eighth centuries. Norham became for a while the resting-place of St Cuthbert.

155. c. 883 GUTHFRITH, king of Northumbria, to St Cuthbert [at Chester-le-Street], in perpetuity. All the land

between the River Tyne and the River Wear, from *Deorestrete* (the Roman road from Chester-le-Street to Gateshead) to the sea, with right of sanctuary, and with all customs, including sake and soke, and *infangentheof*.

RBD p. 524; SD I, pp. 69–70, 203–4.

The gift is said to have been confirmed by King Alfred. Craster noted that this grant would have included the properties of the destroyed monasteries of Jarrow and Wearmouth (Craster 1954, p. 189).

156. c. 883   EADRED, abbot of Carlisle, to St Cuthbert [at Chester-le-Street]. Estates at *Seletun* (Monk Hesleden), *Horetun* (Horden), *duas Geodene* (Castle and Little Eden), *Holum* (Hulam), *Hotun* (Hutton Henry), and *Twilingatun*, which he had bought from King Guthfrith and the Danish army. SD I, p. 207.

For *Twilingatun*, see No. 157. All the other estates are in the parishes of Easington and Hesleden, near Hartlepool (Craster 1954, p. 189).

157. 900 × 915   BERRARD, a priest, to St Cuthbert [at Chester-le-Street], for the confraternity of the abbey there. His vill of *Twilingatun*. SD I, p. 208.

This gift, and that of No. 158, restored to Chester-le-Street properties which had been given to it by Abbot Eadred in 883 (No. 156), and which were subsequently alientaed. *Twilingatun* is possibly Willington near Wallsend on the left bank of the Tyne, cf. Craster 1954, pp. 189–90, but there are etymological objections to this; see further, p. 141.

158. 900 × 915   TILRED, abbot of Heversham (Westmorland) purchases *Iodene australem* (Little Eden, Durham). He grants half of it to St Cuthbert [at Chester-le-Street], in return for the confraternity of the monastery there, and half to *Northam* (Norham, Northumb.), in return for his election as abbot there. SD I, p. 209.

See No. 157. On Norham, see No. 152. Craster 1954, pp. 188–9.

159. 901 × 915 CUTHEARD, bishop of Chester-le-Street, purchases with the money of St Cuthbert the vill called *Ceddesfeld* (Sedgefield, Durham), with its appurtenances, except for the lands of Aculf, Æthelbriht, and Frithlaf, over whom, however, he had sake and soke.

SD I, p. 208.

Craster noted that this purchase would have included Bishop Middleham (Craster 1954, pp. 189, 192).

160. 901 × 915 CUTHEARD, bishop of Chester-le-Street, purchases with the money of St Cuthbert the vill called *Bedlingtun* (Bedlington, Northumb.), with its appendages, *Nedertun* (Netherton), *Grubba* (?Gubeon), *Twisle* (Twizle), *Cebbingtun* (Choppington), *Sliceburne* (Sleckburn), and *Commer* (?Cambois).   SD I, p. 209.

Craster 1954, p. 189.

161. 901 × 915 WULFHEARD, son of Hwætred, to St Cuthbert [at Chester-le-Street]. The vill called *Bynnewalle* (Benwell, Northumb.).   SD I, p. 210.

Craster 1954, p. 190. In SD I, pp. 208–10, we have mention of *Elfred filius Birihtulfinci*, *Wulfheardus filius Hwetreddinci*, and *Edred filius Rixinci*; it seems likely that the names in the author's source were Alfred Brihtwulfing (i.e. the son of Brihtwulf), Wulfheard Hwætreding, and Eadred Ricsiging.

162. 901 × 915 CUTHEARD, bishop of Chester-le-Street, to Alfred, son of Brihtwulf, in return for his homage and service. Lease of vills called *Esington* (Easington, near Durham), *Seletun* (Monk Hesleden, near Hartlepool), *Thorep* (Thorpe, near Castle Eden), *Horedene* (Horden, Durham), *Iodene* (Castle Eden), *duas Sceottun* (the two Shottons, near Castle Eden), *Iodene australem* (Little Eden), *Holum* (Hulam, near Hartlepool), *Hotun* (Hutton Henry, Durham), *Twinlingtun*, *Billingham* (Billingham, Durham), with its appendages, and *Scurufatun* (Sheraton, near Hartlepool).   SD I, p. 208.

Craster 1925, p. 195; 1954, pp. 186, 190. For the name of the recipient, see the note to No. 161, and for his earlier activities, see No. 163. He was killed in 918 at the second battle of Corbridge. *Twinlingtun* may perhaps be located near the Twin Beck, Newbald YE.

163. 901 × 915 CUTHEARD, bishop, and the confraternity of Chester-le-Street, to Eadred, son of Ricsige. Lease of land with the following bounds: from *Cuncaceastre* (Chester-le-Street) to the River *Dyrwente* (Derwent), then southwards to *Werram* (the River Wear), then to the road called *Deorestrete* (the Roman road running south from Chester-le-Street) to the west and south; and the vill called *Geagenforda super Tese* (Gainford on Tees), with all that belongs to it. SD I, p. 210.

Craster 1925, p. 195; 1954, pp. 186–7, 189–90. Eadred's father has been identified with the former Northumbrian King Ricsige, who reigned 873 × 876, see E. W. Robertson, *Scotland and her Early Kings*, I, 1882, p. 58. Craster (1954, p. 190) conjectured that Eadred and Alfred (No. 162) had fled eastward over the Pennines from the Norsemen, who settled at this time on the Cumberland coast. The lands leased to Eadred comprised the western properties of the see. Their rather vague bounds appear to have enclosed the land lying to the south and west of Chester-le-Street, bounded westwards approximately by the A68 road (for another opinion, see SD II, p. xxix). The line of *Deorstrete* south of Chester-le-Street is not yet fully established. For Eadred's name, see No. 161. The account in the *Historia de Sancto Cuthberto* goes on to say that Eadred was killed at the second battle of Corbridge (918), and his lands were given by Rægnald, the victor, to Esbriht the son of Eadred, and to his brother Earl Ælfstan, both of whom had fought for him.

164. 913 × 915 RÆGNALD, a Viking, shares out the eastern lands of St Cuthbert, which he has won by conquest. The southern half, between *Iodene* (Castle Eden) and *Billingham* (Billingham on Tees), is given to Scule, and the other half, between Castle Eden and the River Wear, to Onlafball. SD I, pp. 73, 209, 238.

Stenton, *Papers*, p. 137 n. 1; SD II, pp. xxvi–xxix. Scule gave his name to School Aycliffe.

165. c. 930   SCOTT, son of Alstan, to St Cuthbert [at Chester-
le-Street]. *Aclea* (Great Aycliffe), together with its
dependencies.   *Liber Vitæ Dunelm*, p. 75.

   Craster (1954, p. 191) surmised that Scott's father was
the Earl Ælfstan of No. 163.

CHAPTER IX

THE TRACT
DE OBSESSIONE DUNELMI

HIS CURIOUS piece survives only in ff. 50r–51v of MS.
Corpus Christi College, Cambridge, No. 139, which
contains also the unique copy of the *Historia Regum*
usually attributed to Symeon of Durham. The two works were
written c. 1165–70 in the same hand, in the scriptorium of
Sawley Abbey in the West Riding of Yorkshire.[1] The most
satisfactory edition of the *De Obsessione* is that by Thomas
Arnold in *Symeonis Monachi Opera Omnia*, Rolls Series No. 75,
I, 1882, pp. 215–20.

The tract deals with Northumbrian history in the eleventh
century, and it seems to have been compiled at Durham some
time after the unsuccessful rebellion of Earl Waltheof II in
1075;[2] there is no evidence to support the attribution to
Symeon of a sixteenth-century addition to the *incipit*. In spite
of the title, the siege of Durham receives only passing reference
in the opening paragraph, and it is clear that the main purpose
of the tract was to record the descent of certain lands of the
see of Durham which Bishop Ealdhun gave as dowry to his
daughter Ecgfrida, upon her marriage to Earl Uhtred some
time before 1006. Subsequently, Uhtred abandoned her, and
she married Kilvert son of Ligulf, a Yorkshire thegn. At the
time the tract was compiled, possession of the remnants of
this property (which had been devastated after Earl Waltheof's
disgrace) was being disputed between Waltheof, Ecgfrida's
great-great-grandson by her first marriage (to Earl Uhtred),
and Cospatrick, her great-grandson by her second marriage
(to Kilvert). In seeking to explain the background to this

---

[1] P. Hunter Blair in *Celt and Saxon*, ed. N. Chadwick, Cambridge, 1963,
p. 116.

[2] F. S. Scott, 'Earl Waltheof of Northumbria', *Archaeologia Æliana*, 4th
series, xxx (1952), p. 150.

THE LATER EARLS OF NORTHUMBRIA: their pedigree as given in the tract *De Obsessione Dunelmi*. Earls of Northumbria in capitals; the dates are those of their tenure of the earldom. Names underlined are of persons claiming estates given by Bishop Ealdhun to Ecgfrida.

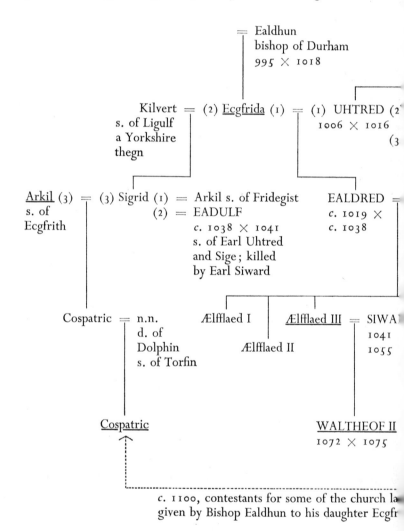

c. 1100, contestants for some of the church la▪
given by Bishop Ealdhun to his daughter Ecgfr▪

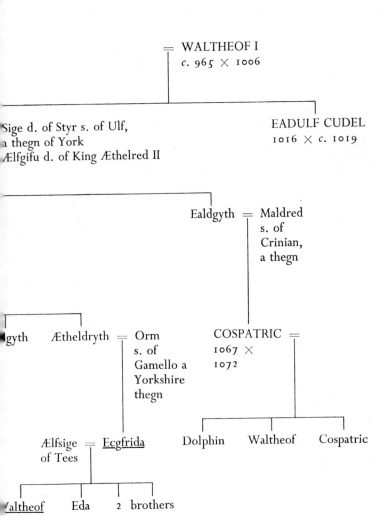

= WALTHEOF I
c. 965 × 1006

Sige d. of Styr s. of Ulf,
a thegn of York
Ælfgifu d. of King Æthelred II

EADULF CUDEL
1016 × c. 1019

Ealdgyth = Maldred
s. of
Crinian,
a thegn

gyth   Ætheldryth = Orm
s. of
Gamello a
Yorkshire
thegn

COSPATRIC =
1067 ×
1072

Ælfsige = Ecgfrida
of Tees

Dolphin   Waltheof   Cospatric

Waltheof   Eda   2 brothers

quarrel, the tract draws extensively on an account of the earls of Northumbria which has since been lost.[1] The genealogical and topographical information contained in this account was evidently detailed and accurate, but on matters of chronology the compiler of the tract was less well informed, and this led him to several historical assumptions which more reliable sources prove to be erroneous.

The tract is not well put together, and it ends abruptly without offering any clue as to the reason for its compilation. It is too diffuse for it to have been prepared as a law memorandum in a case for the restitution of those church lands remaining in lay possession. The free translation which follows omits some of the repetitive material, while seeking to retain every useful scrap of historical information. The pedigree shown on pp. 144–5 has been compiled entirely from the contents of the tract, and is designed to illustrate the descent of the church lands. A few dates have been supplied, to give some indication of the chronological framework.

Concerning the siege of Durham, the honesty of Earl Uhtred, and of the earls who succeeded him.

In the year of our Lord 969,[2] during the reign of King Æthelred of the English, Malcolm king of Scots (the son of King Kenneth), having with the whole of the Scottish army devastated Northumbria by fire and slaughter, laid siege to Durham, whose bishop at that time was Ealdhun. Earl Waltheof of Northumbria, being too old to lead an army, shut himself up in Bamburgh. Now Bishop Ealdhun had given his daughter Ecgfrida in marriage to Waltheof's son Uhtred, a youth of great vigour and a gifted soldier. For her dowry he gave the following estates of the church of St Cuthbert:

[1] Some of it may have been utilized by the early twelfth-century compiler of the historical sketch of the earls of Northumbria which is inserted in the *Historia Regum* (SD II, pp. 196–9).

[2] The correct date for this siege of Durham is probably 1006, as given in the Annals of Ulster; Professor Whitelock notes that the account in *De Obsessione* resembles that of the siege of 1040 (Clemoes p. 86 n. 1), but there would seem to be nothing suspicious about this: Durham would be the natural objective for a Scottish army raiding across the border.

Bermetun, *Skirningheim*, *Eltun*, *Carltun*, *Heaclif*, and *Heseldene* (Barmpton, Skirningham, Elton, and Carleton near Stockton on Tees; School Aycliffe near Darlington; and Monk Heselden, all in Durham), for Uhtred to hold as long as he remained honourably married to Ecgfrida.

Seeing these estates laid waste by the Scottish host, Durham besieged, and his father powerless to intervene, Uhtred gathered together a large force of Northumbrians and men from York, and slew almost the whole of the Scottish army, whose king was one of the few to escape by flight. As was then the custom, the heads of the victims were transported to Durham, where they were washed by four women in preparation for their exhibition on poles around the town walls; each woman received the gift of a cow for performing this task. Upon hearing of this victory, King Æthelred rewarded Uhtred's valour by giving him his father's earldom,[1] adding to it the earldom of York.

Upon his return home, Uhtred ejected his wife Ecgfrida, thus breaking the terms of his tenancy of the church lands, which were returned to the bishop. Uhtred then married Sigen, the daughter of a rich citizen[2] named Styr the son of Ulf, promising as part of the marriage settlement that he would kill Styr's enemy, Thurbrand. Subsequently Uhtred, encouraged by further military triumphs, aspired to greater things, and took to wife Ælfgifu the daughter of King Æthelred, by whom he had a daughter Ealdgyth, whom Uhtred gave in marriage to the thegn Maldred the son of Crinan; from this union was born Cospatric, the father of Dolphin, Waltheof, and Cospatric.

Meanwhile Bishop Ealdhun's daughter Ecgfrida, after her ejection by Earl Uhtred, had married a Yorkshire thegn named Kilvert, son of Ligulf; their daughter Sigrid married Arkil the son of Ecgfrith,[3] and this union produced a son

[1] Professor Whitelock (*op. cit.*, p. 82) points out that in all probability Uhtred ruled northern Northumbria, under his father, as early as 995. Southern Northumbria (Deira) was ruled by Ealdorman Ælfhelm at this time.

[2] Of York, cf. Whitelock, *op. cit.*, p. 82 n. 5; SD I, pp. 212–13.

[3] In the text, he appears as *Arkil filius Ecgfridæ*, but it is evident that the termination should be corrected to *Ecgfridi*; later in the text he appears as *Arkil filius Ecgfrith*.

named Cospatric, who married the daughter of Dolphin the
son of Torfin; they in turn had a son named Cospatric who
recently was fated to fight against Waltheof, the son of
Ælfsige.[1] Kilvert, the son of Ligulf, repudiated his wife
Ecgfrida, who was ordered by her father Bishop Ealdhun to
return forthwith to Durham. In obedience to her father's
command, Ecgfrida surrendered Brampton, Skirningham, and
Elton to the church and bishop; subsequently she took the
veil, and served God well to the end of her days, and was
buried in Durham cemetery, where she awaits the day of
judgement.

A small addition must be made to the above account of what
befell Earl Uhtred before his death. Swegn, the king of
Denmark, having put King Æthelred to flight into Normandy,
invaded his kingdom. But a short time afterwards Swegn died,
and Æthelred returned to rule his own country, having taken
to wife Emma, the daughter of Richard, duke of Normandy.[2]
After another brief interval, Cnut the son of the aforesaid
King Swegn of Denmark, on arriving in England with a large
army, besought the aid of Earl Uhtred, and all whom he
could command, against King Æthelred, promising him great
honour and power should he agree. Uhtred however had
power enough already, in that he held the earldoms of York
and Northumbria, and he refused to do anything to harm his
lord and kindred. 'No reward could persuade me', he said,
'to do what I ought not to do. As long as King Æthelred lives,
I shall serve him faithfully. He is my lord and also my father-
in-law, by whose gift I have sufficient honour and riches. I will
not betray him.' And so Cnut received no help from Uhtred.

Upon the death of King Æthelred, when Cnut had seized the
whole kingdom of England, he sent to the aforesaid earl,
commanding him to hasten to his new lord. Having obtained
a promise of safe conduct and return, Uhtred obeyed. On the
day commanded, as he made his way to the king's presence at

[1] From the pedigree it will be seen that probably this dispute arose over
the succession to the church lands after Earl Waltheof's disgrace.

[2] Arnold (SD 1, p. 217 n.) points out that King Æthelred had in fact
married Emma eleven years before his flight to Normandy in 1013. Swegn
died in 1014.

Wighill, he and forty companions were killed by a certain powerful king's thegn called Thurbrand the Hold, who hid behind the entrance curtain to the royal chamber.[1]

After his death, his brother Eadulf Cudel, a very idle and cowardly man, succeeded to the earldom. For fear that the Scots should kill him because of his relationship with Uhtred, he ceded to them the whole of Lothian, which by this deed became subject to the Scottish crown.

Before long Eadulf died, and Ealdred the son of Uhtred by Ecgfrida, Bishop Ealdhun's daughter, of whom we have spoken above, succeeded to the whole of Northumbria, and killed Thurbrand, his father's murderer. Carl the son of Thurbrand was greatly incensed by Ealdred's deed, and for some time each sought the opportunity to ambush the other, but at length their friends persuaded them to reach agreement; each pledged his peace to the other, and their bond of friendship grew so great that they planned to journey to Rome together as brothers. But for a long while storms at sea prevented them, and eventually they returned to their own homes.

Then Carl entertained the earl in his house with befitting magnificence, and while Ealdred had no suspicion of evil because of the honour and hospitality he received, Carl killed him in the forest called Risewood,[2] where to this day the place of his murder is marked by a small stone cross. Some time later Earl Waltheof, the son of Ealdred's daughter, who owed much to his grandfather, wished to avenge his death; the sons of Carl were caught unawares and killed while feasting at their elder brother's house at Settrington not far from York. The only ones spared were Cnut, whose life was saved because of his innate goodness, and Sumerled, who had not gone to the feast and who survives to this day. After this massacre, the perpetrators returned home carrying booty of all kinds.

[1] Arnold (SD 1, p. 218 n. 2) points out that Uhtred's death occurred before that of King Æthelred. He had been raiding with Edmund Ironside in the midland shires when he was compelled to return to defend his earldom against Cnut, who had established himself in York. He was unable to dislodge Cnut, however, and it seems likely that he was killed during peace negotiations.

[2] At Rise, in the East Riding of Yorkshire. The murder took place c. 1038.

But our pen must return to the main story. Earl Ealdred had five daughters, three of them having the same name Ælfflæd, the fourth being called Ealdgyth, and the fifth Ætheldryth. From one of these Ælfflæds, Earl Siward produced Earl Waltheof. While this Ælfflæd was the countess, because she was the daughter of Earl Ealdred, who himself was the son of Earl Uhtred and of (Ecgfrida) Bishop Ealdhun's daughter, she claimed as her right of inheritance the aforesaid lands, Barmpton, Skirningham, Elton, Carleton, Aycliffe, and Heselden, which her husband Earl Siward gave her;[1] he gave also to their son Waltheof the earldom of Northumbria, just as his (Waltheof's) grandfather Earl Ealdred had held it.

Upon the deaths of Siward and Ælfflæd, war sprang up and the territories (i.e. the church lands in dispute) were devastated. A long while later Arkil the son of Ecgfrith, who has been mentioned above and who had married Sigrid, the daughter of Kilvert and of Ecgfrida the daughter of Bishop Ealdhun, occupied these territories for himself, and lived in them. After the death of Sigrid, he gave to St Cuthbert Heselden, Aycliffe, and Carleton, which the church still possesses. Sigrid had three husbands: Arkil the son of Fridegist, Earl Eadulf, and Arkil the son of Ecgfrith. After King William came to England, Arkil had to flee into exile, and the remaining territories were again devastated. Later, a Yorkshire thegn named Orm, son of Gamello, married Ætheldryth, one of the five daughters of Earl Eadred, from which union sprang a daughter named Ecgfrida, who married Ælfsige of Tees. They had a son named Waltheof, a daughter named Eda, and two other sons. This Ecgfrida seized Barmpton and Skirningham, claiming them by hereditary right.

[1] Evidently the church lands were still in the possession of Ecgfrida's descendants, in spite of Bishop Ealdhun's effort to reclaim them after she took the veil.

PART III
BURTON ABBEY

CHAPTER X

INTRODUCTION TO THE BURTON CHARTERS

T HE BENEDICTINE ABBEY of Burton on Trent in Stafford-shire preserved within its archives at the time of the Dissolution the texts of 37 supposedly pre-Conquest royal diplomas, together with the will of Wulfric Spot, who founded the abbey in 1004. It is my purpose in this chapter to discuss the circumstances underlying the formation of the Burton collection, and the fate of its various charters, their copies, and editions. Some account will also be given of the historical significance of individual charters, and of the collection as a whole.

THE TEXTS AND THEIR TRANSMISSION

Some time in the mid-thirteenth century, all the known pre-Conquest charters of Burton Abbey were copied into a volume of miscellaneous historical texts, now preserved in the National Library of Wales at Aberystwyth, where it is catalogued as MS. Peniarth 390.[1] The entries are all in the same hand, and occupy ff. 173^r–184^v of the manuscript (this modern foliation, dated April 1972, supplants the older page numbering); we shall refer to this section as the Peniarth Cartulary.

We may suppose that the scribe of the Peniarth Cartulary was a monk of Burton, working in the abbey scriptorium. He

[1] The manuscript was first described by Mr William Maurice of Llansilin in 1658; his account is printed in *Archaeologia Cambrensis*, 3rd series, xv, p. 361, and reprinted in W. Salt 1916, p. 71. A comprehensive analysis by A. J. Horwood appears in *Historical Manuscripts Commission, Second Report*, 1871, Appendix 105. The most detailed description is in a typescript catalogue kept in the National Library of Wales; this was made in April 1972, and refers to all items by the new foliation. This description establishes the date of compilation of the cartulary as c. 1240–64. The Burton Annals (by the same scribe) cease in 1263.

was also the scribe of the Burton Annals, and his hand can be examined in facsimile in the Rolls Series edition of this text.[1] He wrote in a small, neat anglicana with a slight backward slope and a characteristic, easily recognizable 'g'. The Peniarth Cartulary texts are entered chronologically, according to the date assigned to each charter by the copyist. Sometimes he was mistaken about the dates, either because they were wrongly given in the texts before him (Nos. I, II, XXII),[2] or, rarely, because he misread the figures in his source (Nos. XXVI, XXVII). Generally, however, he was a competent, conscientious, and even slavishly accurate copyist; where we are able to compare his transcripts with the documents that lay before him, very few mistakes can be found. He reproduced the chrismons heading each charter with remarkable fidelity, and in transcribing personal and place-names he kept closely to his sources. It is a matter of great misfortune, therefore, that (as was the custom with cartulary copyists in his day) he habitually abbreviated the witness lists, and omitted the bounds and the endorsements. That he was capable of producing accurate copies of texts in OE as well as Latin, is shown by his transcript of Wulfric Spot's will (XXVIIIb) and of the OE section of the Burton foundation charter (XXVIIIa); but by a strange stroke of fate, the only charter whose OE bounds he transcribed has itself come down to us intact, so that the Peniarth Cartulary version is of only minor interest (XXVII).

A brief account of the descent of the Peniarth Cartulary (or rather its parent manuscript, MS. Peniarth 390) will now be given. Presumably it was kept with the rest of the abbey muniments until the Dissolution of the monasteries. Henry VIII founded a collegiate church at Burton, upon which he bestowed the properties of the former abbey, but after only four years this too was dissolved, and early in 1545 the abbey's endowment was granted by the king to his secretary, Sir William Paget (subsequently the first baron), of whom more later. From Sir William the estates have descended, together with the bulk of their muniments, through successive genera-

---

[1] *Annales Monastici*, ed. H. R. Luard, R.S. No. 36; I, 1864.

[2] For the Roman numerals assigned to Burton charters in this chapter, see the table on p. 167–71.

tions of the Pagets to the present Marquess of Anglesey. Not so MS. Peniarth 390, which was separated from the rest of the Burton muniments at an early date; by 1658 it was in the possession of Robert Vaughan of Hengwrt, the Welsh antiquary, being then numbered 150 in the Hengwrt collection.

Vaughan was a friend and correspondent of Archbishop Ussher and of John Selden, both of whom were interested in monastic records, but it is not known from what source he acquired this Burton manuscript. He died in 1667, but his collection remained in his family until 1859, when Sir Robert Williams Vaughan of Nannan left it by will to his distant kinsman William Watkin Edward Wynne of Peniarth. Mr Wynne died in 1880, leaving the Hengwrt-Peniarth collection to his son Mr R. M. Wynne of Peniarth, Lord Lieutenant of Merioneth, from whom it was bought in reversion in 1904 by Sir John Williams, Bart., who presented it to the National Library of Wales upon R. M. Wynne's death in 1909. There it is still preserved, being now entitled the Peniarth collection, of which our manuscript has been numbered 390.[1]

There is extant an earlier cartulary of Burton, written between 1230 and 1241, which descended with the abbey estates after the Dissolution to the Paget family. It was deposited on loan in the British Museum by the sixth Marquess of Anglesey on 2 September 1947.[2] We shall refer to this as the Anglesey Cartulary. Entered within it are four items from the Burton Abbey collection of pre-Conquest texts, namely the foundation charter of the abbey (xxviiia), Wulfric Spot's will (xxviiib), and royal diplomas relating to Rolleston (xxx)

[1] This account is based on Dugdale III, p. 35; on C. G. O. Bridgeman's review in W. Salt 1916, pp. 70–1; and on information kindly supplied by the Keeper and Assistant Keeper of the Department of Manuscripts and Records, National Library of Wales, in letters dated 21 June 1972 and 26 June 1972. A more extensive history of all the Hengwyrt-Peniarth MSS may be seen in the National Library's *Handlist of Manuscripts*, pp. iii–xxiii.

[2] BM. Loan MS. 30; Davis no. 91. Thanks are due to Mr A. F. Borrie for supplying the date of deposition of this manuscript at the British Museum. A third Burton cartulary, deposited by the sixth marquess at Burton on Trent Public Library on permanent loan in June 1947, has been searched by me for pre-Conquest texts, without result (Davis no. 92).

and Wetmore (xxxiv). Our interest in these copies is concentrated on the Rolleston and Wetmore charters, which
include boundary clauses, and enable us to speculate on the
organization of the Burton muniments in the period before the
Peniarth Cartulary was drawn up. This topic is discussed later
in this chapter (see p. 164).

Just how many of the supposedly original membranes of the
pre-Conquest Burton charters survived the Dissolution, it is
hard to say. No. xii was in the hands of W. Burton (the surname
is a coincidence) in 1622, when he published a poor version of
it on pp. 209–10 of his *Description of Leicestershire*. Burton does
not reveal where he obtained his charter, but he printed the
following note in the margin of his edition: 'The Originall
heereof I gave to the right honorable, the Lord *Coke*, in whose
custody it now is.' It has not been recorded since. Nos. xiv
and xxviiiab appear to have descended with the abbey estates;
they were in the family archives of the Marquess of Anglesey
in 1884, when they were reproduced in facsimile for the
Ordnance Survey series, and in June 1947 they were deposited
by the sixth marquess on permanent loan at Burton Public
Library and Museum, where they are still preserved.[1]

Five more pre-Conquest charters from the Burton Abbey
archives were discovered quite unexpectedly in 1941, when
the effects of Mr R. H. Landor, a solicitor in Rugeley, Staffordshire, were being examined after his death (xvii, xxiii, xxvi,
xxvii, xxxi). Together with some later deeds relating to
estates of the Paget family, they were found in a safe in his
room (or perhaps in a drawer in his desk; the tradition of the
discovery is not quite secure on this point). His widow
presented them to the William Salt Library at Stafford, where
they are still preserved, being catalogued 84/1/41–84/5/41.
This was certainly the most important and spectacular find of
Anglo-Saxon charters in the present century, and it is desirable
to establish as precisely as possible the provenance of the
documents concerned. Mr F. B. Stitt, the County Archivist
and Librarian, has kindly supplied the following note:

'At one period last century it would seem that the Landors

[1] Information kindly supplied by Mr K. F. Stanesby, F.L.A., Borough
Librarian of Burton, in a letter dated 23 June 1972.

acted as agents, stewards, or solicitors for the Pagets, Marquesses of Anglesey. We are still cataloguing the nineteenth century papers of this estate and the position in the estate administration occupied by Landor is not at present known; possibly he was in charge of the Staffordshire affairs of the estate in one capacity or one sector or another. Later on the Landors became associated as solicitors with a family called Gardner, and eventually when the practices were separated the Paget business passed to the Gardners. Among the records of this firm were very considerable quantities of documents relating to the Paget estates, but one must suspect that the little group of Anglo-Saxon deeds together with six later deeds which were found with them must have come to light before the dissolution of the partnership, and found their way into the desk or safe of one of the partners.'[1]

A letter by John Bale, dated 30 July 1560, names William Paget, the first baron (1505 × 1563), as one of those who had collected many documents after the Dissolution of the monasteries.[2] As the king's secretary he was of course in a key position, and as the recipient from Henry VIII of the estates of Burton Abbey he would naturally wish to preserve such early muniments as he could find. It is to this fortunate circumstance that we owe the survival of so much precious information concerning a corner of England for which early materials are scarce and enigmatical.

EDITIONS OF THE BURTON CHARTERS

Of the documents now under discussion, we have noted already that the earliest to be published was No. xii, in Burton's *Leicestershire* in 1622. No. xxviiiab, the abbey's foundation charter and Wulfric Spot's will, both entered on the same membrane early in the twelfth century, first appeared in Dugdale's *Monasticon* in 1655–73; he quoted his source as a

---

[1] Letter dated 22 June 1972.

[2] *Trans. Cambridge Antiquarian Soc.*, III, 1865–78, p. 173. Professor Finberg has shown that William Paget was responsible for the survival of at least one other Anglo-Saxon charter, unconnected in any way with the series here under discussion. – *West-Country Historical Studies*, 1969, p. 41 n. 2.

transcript to the Anglesey Cartulary made in 1650, when it was still in the hands of the Paget family; textually, however, his edition is close to MS. Harley 358, ff 40–41v, now preserved in the British Museum. The text of this sixteenth-century copy varies a little from that of the surviving twelfth-century membrane, but I suspect that this is due to the vagaries of the copyist.

Separately or together, the will and foundation charter have been edited and translated many times since, notably by Kemble in his *Codex Diplomaticus* in 1845 (K 710), in the six-volume edition of Dugdale in 1846, in the *Midland Antiquary* by Duignan and Carter in 1886, by Bridgeman in 1916 (W. Salt), and by Whitelock in 1930 (W xvii).[1] S. Shaw published Nos. xxx and xxxiv from the Anglesey Cartulary in 1798 in Volume 1 of his *History and Antiquities of Staffordshire*. In 1885–9, W. de Gray Birch, who had access to the Peniarth Cartulary, printed from it in his *Cartularium Saxonicum* all the Burton charters I to xxiii, but no text dated later than 974. Of these later charters Kemble, who knew nothing of the Peniarth Cartulary, printed only xxviiiab (above); and apart from xxxii and xxxvii, which were edited by F. Barlow in 1970 in his *Edward the Confessor*, they have remained unpublished until this present edition.

Most of the Burton texts appearing in *Cartularium Saxonicum* were edited with a reasonable degree of accuracy, and in selecting charters for this present edition I have confined myself almost exclusively to previously unpublished texts, or to those printed hitherto from inferior sources. Fifteen charters have been included in the edition, and in various other places in this book I have commented on all the remainder, in varying degrees of detail.

THE FORMATION OF THE BURTON COLLECTION

Having traced the later history of the charters, from the time of their entry into the Peniarth Cartulary, we may now

---

[1] The texts of this charter appearing on the single skin, and in the Anglesey cartulary, together with the editions in Dugdale and Kemble, are collated by Bridgeman in W. Salt 1916, pp. 60–1.

venture into much more uncertain territory, and speculate as to how the collection came to be assembled in the first place. The cardinal date is 1004, when the abbey of Burton was founded, and we have first to find an explanation for the undoubted fact that of the 37 supposedly pre-Conquest diplomas preserved at Burton in 1264, no less than 27 claim to be dated earlier than the abbey's foundation.

We may dispose (temporarily) of three of these 27 charters straight away, by labelling them post-Conquest forgeries (II, X, XXVI). Of the remainder, several concern estates that were eventually to descend to Wulfric Spot, and were distributed in his will, although only a few of them were given by him to Burton. First in importance are the three diplomas, issued on the same date and utilizing identical formulas, by which Wulfsige the Black was granted a large block of territory in the upper Trent valley (V, VI, VII). The significance of this transaction has hitherto escaped notice by historians of the period. The grants were made by King Edmund immediately after his redemption of the Five Boroughs in 942, and placed a vulnerable and highly strategic area under the control of a single thegn, who must have been a high-ranking royal official. Among the estates conveyed, Rolleston in Staffordshire descended to Wulfric's mother Wulfrun, the foundress of Wolverhampton, and subsequently by royal charter to Wulfric Spot himself (XXVII). It seems reasonable to conclude that Wulfsige the Black was his ancestor.

Other properties mentioned in Wulfric's will that were granted to his predecessors (some of them ancestors) by earlier charters preserved in the Burton collection, include Marchington and Darlaston near Stone, Staffordshire (XI, XVII), Austrey in Warwickshire (XVIII), and two estates, *Suptone* and *Mortune*, which are probably to be located at Sutton on the Hill and at Morton near Tibshelf, both in Derbyshire (VIII, XV). Abbots Bromley in Staffordshire was granted by King Æthelred II to Wulfric himself (XXVII).

Often when an estate changed hands, its earlier landbooks were handed over to the recipient as evidence of title. It is likely, therefore, that all the authentic diplomas we have mentioned so far were in Wulfric Spot's possession when he founded Burton. Tradition has it that he became a monk there, and it seems a reasonable assumption that he deposited his charters at the abbey for safe keeping. Other members of his family may also have used the abbey as a repository. Wulfgeat, the recipient of Upper Arley in Worcestershire and Duddeston Hall in Warwickshire, was Wulfric's kinsman; although these estates did not descend to Wulfric himself, the presumption is that they were inherited by a near relative, for their landbook survived in the Burton archives (xx).

It is less easy to account for the remaining pre-1004 diplomas coming into the abbey's possession. A few of them had been held by incumbents of Mercian ealdordoms, or by their families. In this category we must place charters relating to *Stantun*, held by Ealdorman Alhhelm (I); Hope, Ashford, and Bakewell in Derbyshire, all held by Ealdorman Uhtred (IV, IX); and Chesterfield near by, given to Uhtred Cild, possibly the ealdorman's son (XIII). It might reasonably be expected that their descendants, once Burton had been founded, should lay up their muniments in the abbey.

The two Burton diplomas that had been granted to Bishop Æthelwold of Winchester (XXII) and Bishop Wulfric of Dorchester (XXIII) both relate to Mercian estates. It seems likely that the former was intended for the endowment of Peterborough Abbey, and it is hazardous to try to reconstruct the chain of events that led to the charter's deposition at Burton. In the case of Bishop Wulfric's diploma, the land conveyed may have been identical with that given earlier to Ealdorman Alhhelm (I), on which see above. Early diplomas relating to two other Mercian estates (XIV, XXI) are also to be found in the Burton collection, but the means by which they came into the abbey's possession are unknown.

Because the boundary clauses are omitted in the surviving texts, it is not now possible to locate *Norðtune* (XII) and *Niþantune* (XVI) with certainty; nevertheless, it is worth while to spend a little more time and space on the diplomas relating to these two estates. The *Norðtune* diploma, by which an eight-hide property is transferred to the thegn Ælfheah, is a typical chancery charter.[1] It repeats many of the formulas of

[1] Drögereit pp. 391–4.

CS 870, an earlier grant to Ælfheah dated 948; it introduces a fresh proem, and this combination provided a popular exemplar for later scribes, e.g. CS 1138 (964) and K 663 (998). All these charters relate to lands south of the Thames, and it should be noted that in 951, when XII was issued, lands in the northern Danelaw were conveyed only by diplomas employing special alliterative formulas, forming a recognizable series (see p. 20). Almost certainly, therefore, *Norðtune* lay further south.

No. XVI, by which an estate of five hides at *Nipantune* is conveyed to the thegn Æthelgeard, is also a typical chancery charter. Its formulas are very closely paralleled in other texts of the same year, 956, notably CS 944. It was issued on the same day, and witnessed by the same signatories, as CS 944, which concerns land in Northamptonshire (No. 5 in the hand-list); another charter issued on the same occasion was XV in the Burton series, relating in all probability to Morton in Derbyshire. This alone may account for the inclusion of XVI in the Burton archives; but probably *Nipantune* was near the rest of Æthelgeard's holdings, and these were concentrated round Wallingford in the Thames valley, at Winchester, and in the Meon valley in East Hampshire.[1] Possible locations are Newton in Berkshire, near Sotwell, another of Æthelgeard's estates, and Newington near Chalgrove in Oxfordshire.

The suggestion that both *Norðtune* and *Nipantune* may be located in Wessex may cause some surprise, but there is really no justification for assuming that just because these charters survive in the Burton archives, the estates conveyed must lie in Mercia. Within the Burton collection one finds texts relating to Hilmarton and Littlecote in Wiltshire (XIX),[2] and to Brighthampton, Aston Bampton, and Lew in Oxfordshire (XXIV). In view of this, the tentative location of *Hwitantune* (III) in Staffordshire, and *Æsce* (XXV) in Derbyshire must be regarded as hardly more than a guess.

Half a century was to elapse between the issue of the

[1] CW p. 15.
[2] The text of XIX (which was probably composed at Abingdon) is derived from an exemplar originating late in Athelstan's reign, which gave rise to CS 743, dated 939.

Norðtune and *Niþantune* charters and the foundation of Burton Abbey, and it is not possible to establish the reasons for their eventual deposition in the Burton archives. Presumably the estates, or their diplomas, descended to some person having close connections with the abbey. If this is the case, one must assume that these diplomas were kept for half a century in lay hands, before their deposition. The same assumption holds good, for longer or shorter periods, for nearly all the pre-1004 texts preserved at Burton. We are so used to dealing with the landbooks preserved at abbeys or cathedrals from a date soon after they were drawn up – almost all the texts known to us owe their survival to such preservation – that we tend to overlook that very many diplomas issued to laymen must have been stored in some way in lay hands, and survived such storage through several decades, even centuries. Many, if not all, of the larger landowning families must have kept their own muniment chests, handed down with their contents from generation to generation.

THE BURTON SCRIPTORIUM

Soon after Burton Abbey was founded, a scriptorium was established there. We have secure evidence of its early activity in composing and copying royal diplomas. Two charters have survived which in all probability were written at the abbey within a few years of its foundation: xxvii, copied from an earlier membrane, and xxxi, which appears to have been composed as well as written at Burton. It is possible, but I think unlikely, that these two diplomas were written by the same scribe; certainly they represent the tradition of the scriptorium. Moreover, we have cartulary texts of two further charters written at Burton at this period, and one of these names its scribe as the monk Wynsige (xxix, xxx).

One cannot assign with certainty the four remaining early eleventh-century charters in the Peniarth Cartulary to any particular sciptorium, but the probability is that all were composed and written at Burton (xxxii–xxxv). All are concerned with Mercian estates, and two were issued to Morcar, Wulfric Spot's close relative (xxxiii, xxxvi). A third charter to Morcar, which survives in the original, has been discussed already (XXXI).

Apart from a solitary diploma of the Confessor which somehow strayed into the collection (XXXVII, dated 1048), the Burton series of charters comes to an abrupt end in 1012, just eight years after the abbey's foundation. It seems very unlikely that the scriptorium was used either for composition or as a repository of royal landbooks issued after the death of Æthelred II. Wulfric Spot's family suffered cruelly in the chaos and anarchy that marked the closing years of Æthelred's reign. Ealdorman Ælfhelm and the brothers Sigeferth and Morcar were all murdered. This is not the place for a detailed review of the abbey's early endowment, but there is no doubt that it suffered appreciably at this period, and the abbey's importance waned considerably during the last half-century of the Old English state.

Production of 'royal charters' within the scriptorium was revived temporarily during or soon after the Domesday Inquest, when a series of forgeries were manufactured to buttress the abbey's title to disputed portions of its endowment. The texts of some of these have survived (II, X, XXVI, XXXIV). Copies of Wulfric Spot's will and the foundation charter of Æthelred II were also made at this time, probably in connection with the same litigation (XXVIIIab).

THE ARCHIVE REPOSITORY AT BURTON

There is good reason to believe that the mid-thirteenth-century scribe of the Peniarth manuscript had before him as separate membranes all the surviving charters of his house of supposedly pre-Conquest date. Evidently they were all jumbled up, and his first task was to sort them out chronologically; this chronological approach was in keeping with his activity as compiler of the Burton Annals. We can watch him at work on the charters by studying his endorsements to the membranes that have survived. His hand is recognizable in several of them (XVII, XXIII, XXVI). He was concerned first of all with establishing the date and the indiction; later, when he came to enter the charters in his cartulary, this information was incorporated into his rubrics. Having dated the charters, he shuffled them into chronological order, and proceeded to number them. Every surviving membrane bears a numbered endorsement in roman capitals, and this number corresponds in every instance with the order in which the text of the charter was entered in the cartulary. Thus No. xvii appears as seventeenth of the charters entered, No. xxiii as twenty-third, and so on. No. xxviii has two texts written on the membrane – the foundation charter and Wulfric Spot's will – so that subsequent charters are numbered one less than might be supposed from their position in the cartulary; thus No. xxxi is the thirty-second text entered.

In listing the Burton charters for reference in this book, I have assigned to each the number that the cartulary copyist must have entered on the membrane when he made his transcript in the mid-thirteenth century; in the case of No. xxviii, I have distinguished the two texts as 'a' and 'b'. The charters are tabulated according to this scheme on pp. 167–71.

It is difficult to establish with any confidence what was the state of affairs with the Burton muniments of allegedly pre-Conquest date before they were rearranged for entry into the Peniarth manuscript. It seems very likely that the earlier arrangement of the charters was not chronological, because the two diplomas xxx and xxxiv, entered next to each other in the early thirteenth-century Anglesey Cartulary (BM. Loan MS. 30), are related to each other textually, in that the text of xxxiv is derived from xxx (see the editions on pp. 211 and 235). The two estates concerned were also adjacent to each other topographically, and there was in addition a tenurial relationship between them. The early thirteenth-century 'filing system' of the Burton charters would appear therefore to have depended (if there was any order at all) on the circumstances underlying the production of the texts in the first instance. This conclusion ties in with the fact that the text of xxviiiab was copied on to the surviving membrane only a little more than a century before its entry into the Anglesey Cartulary.

In spite of all the difficulties, it is important to attempt an estimate of the number of Anglo-Saxon diplomas surviving at Burton at the time of the Norman Conquest. We know that by the mid-thirteenth century there were only 37 (33 if we exclude the post-Conquest forgeries). Is there any reason to suppose that these were merely the rump of a much larger collection, preserved at the abbey up to 1066 or later?

I think the answer could well be in the affirmative. Apart from references in Wulfric Spot's will and the foundation charter, most of the estates listed in DB as being in the possession of Burton in 1066 are unrepresented in the surviving series of pre-Conquest charters (the only estates in this category for which texts of diplomas survive are Abbots Bromley and Darlaston near Stone, if we except the *Bedintun* forgery). Similarly, for estates left by Wulfric to other beneficiaries, very few early charter texts remain in the Burton collection (exceptions include diplomas for Marchington and Rolleston). Conversely, we have the texts of a number of Anglo-Saxon diplomas laid up at the abbey for properties which appear never to have been in the possession of the house; some of these were in places far removed from the rest of the Burton estates.

It seems very likely that in these cases, the few texts that have come down to us can be but chance survivals from a much more comprehensive collection, which would have been particularly rich for Staffordshire and Derbyshire (where bookland seems to have been the normal mode of tenure), but probably was much weaker for the remaining portions of the northern Danelaw, which were carucated in the eleventh century (where bookland was rare). After a careful review of all the evidence, estate by estate, the best estimate one can offer for the number of texts of Anglo-Saxon royal diplomas likely to have been preserved in the Burton archives at the time of the Norman Conquest, is between 150 and 250. To this should probably be added large quantities of wills, law memoranda, writs, and other estate documents written in OE; there is no reason to believe that these classes of muniments were more poorly represented at Burton than at Bury St Edmunds (cf. ECEE p. 11).

If one takes this view, then as a corollary one must postulate that there were very substantial losses of documents of all kinds during the century and a half following the Norman Conquest. I believe this was the case, and I would suggest further that to a large extent this was due to Domesday Book supplanting earlier records as evidence of title in the twelfth and thirteenth centuries. This use of Domesday does not, however, antedate the Angevins; the immediate effect of the Survey was a flurry of litigation that sent the monks everywhere scuttling to their scriptoria, to manufacture title-deeds concerning estates for which their muniment collections were deficient in authentic pre-Conquest evidence.

INTRODUCTION TO THE BURTON CHARTERS

APPENDIX

TABLE OF THE EARLY CHARTERS OF BURTON ABBEY

| Number of Charter | | Edition | Date | Donor | Recipient | Lands conveyed |
In Peniarth cartulary	In hand-list					
I	100	*CS 583	?900	Æthelflæd	Alchelm	? Stanton in the Peak, Db
II	81	****CS 746	940	K. Athelstan	Brihthelm	? Church Eaton, St
III	80	*CS 642	925	K. Athelstan	Eadric	? Whittington, near Lichfield, St
IV	101	*CS 658	926	K. Athelstan	Uhtred	Hope and Ashford, Db
V	82	*CS 771	942	K. Edmund	Wulfsige Maur'	Alrewas, Abbots and King's Bromley, Barton under Needwood, Tatenhill, Branston, Stretton, Rolleston, Clifton Campville, Haunton, all in St

| Number of Charter | | Edition | Date | Donor | Recipient | Lands conveyed |
In Peniarth cartulary	In hand-list					
VI	83	*CS 772	942	K. Edmund	Wulfsige Maur'	Newbold in Barton under Needwood, St; Walton on Trent, Cauldwell, Coton in the Elms, Linton, Drakelow, all in Db
VII	102	*CS 773	942	K. Edmund	Wulfsige Maur'	Croxall, Croxton, Walton on Trent, Drakelow, Stapenhill, ? Rosliston, all in Db
VIII	103	*CS 876	949	K. Eadred	Ulfketel	? Sutton on the Hill, Db
IX	104	*CS 884	949	K. Eadred	Earl Uhtred	Bakewell, Db
X	84	****CS 885	949	K. Eadred	Athelstan	? Church Eaton, St
XI	85	*CS 890	951	K. Eadred	Wulfhelm	Marchington, St
XII	—	*CS 891	951	K. Eadred	Ælfheah	Norðtune, unlocated

XIII	105	*CS 911	955	K. Eadred	Uhtred Cild	Chesterfield, Db
XIV	4	*CS 978	956	K. Eadwig	Eadwig	Braunston, Np
XV	106	*CS 951	956	K. Eadwig	Mæglesothen	? Morton near Tibshelf, Db
XVI	—	*CS 944	956	K. Eadwig	Æthelgeard	Nipantune, unlocated
XVII	86	*p. 172	956	K. Eadwig	Æthelnoth	Darlaston near Stone, St
XVIII	54	**CS 1021	958	(K. Eadred)	Wulfric	Austrey, Wa
XIX	—	*CS 1081	962	K. Edgar	Wulfmær	Hilmarton and Littlecote, W
XX	57	*CS 1100	963	K. Edgar	Wulfgeat	Upper Arley, Wo, and ?Duddeston Hall in Aston, Wa
XXI	107	*CS 1175	966	K. Edgar	Ælfhelm	Parwich, Db
XXII	37	*CS 1283	974	K. Edgar	Bp Æthelwold	Breedon, Wilson, Diseworth, and Atterton, all in Le
XXIII	108	* p. 179	968	K. Edgar	Bp Wulfric	Stanton in the Peak, Db
XXIV	—	* p. 187	984	K. Æthelred	Ælfwine	Brighthampton, Aston Bampton, and Lew, all in O

In Peniarth cartulary	In hand-list	Edition	Date	Donor	Recipient	Lands conveyed
XXV	109	* p. 193	987	K. Æthelred	Æthelsige	*Æsce*, unlocated
XXVI	92	*** p. 196	996	K. Æthelred	Wulfric	*Bedintun*, St
XXVII	91	* p. 201	996	K. Æthelred	Wulfric	Abbots Bromley, St
XXVIIIa	40	* K 710	1004	K. Æthelred	Burton Abbey	Foundation Charter
XXVIIb	39	*W XVII	1004	Wulfric Spot	—	Will
XXIX	—	*** p. 208	1007	K. Æthelred	a thegn	land unspecified
XXX	93	* p. 211	1008	K. Æthelred	Abbot Wulfgeat	Rolleston, St
XXXI	110	† p. 219	1009	K. Æthelred	Morcar	Weston upon Trent, Morley, Smalley, Crich, Kidsley, Ingleby, all in Db
XXXII	112	* p. 228	1011	K. Æthelred	Elemod	Hallam, Db

Number of Charter

XXXIII	111	* p. 232	1011	K. Æthelred	Morcar	? Mickleover, Db
XXXIV	94	*** p. 235	1012	K. Æthelred	Abbot Wulfgeat	Wetmore, St
XXXV	70	* p. 241	1012	K. Æthelred	Theodulf	? Burton Hastings, Wa
XXXVI	113	* p. 244	1012	K. Æthelred	Morcar	Eckington, Db
XXXVII	—	* p. 248	1048	K. Edward	Earl Tofig	*Berghe*, unlocated

CHAPTER XI

THE EARLY CHARTERS OF
BURTON ABBEY

XVII. King Eadwig to his thegn Æthelnoth.
Land at Darlaston, near Stone,
Staffordshire. a.d. 956

Carta Eadþig Regis de Derlaueston. dcccc.lvj. Ind[ictione]. xiiij.

P IN NOMINE D[OMI]NI N[OST]RI IH[ES]U CHR[IST]I.
Omnib[us] quib[us] Chr[ist]ianitatis censura[m] a d[e]i
arcipotentis poli per suam largifluam m[isericord]iam
concessum est. q[uo]d huius Instantis labentis que vitæ
prosperitas totis nisibus restaurare perditos ac nefandos.
per illius auxiliu[m] possumus Ceu psalmi graphus Ita
fando dixit. Initium[1] sapientiæ timor d[omi]ni. Qua propter.
ego eadpig. rex anglorum ac totius bryttannicæ telluris
gubernator et rector. Cuidam meo fideli ministro quem
nonnulli uocitant noto uocamine. Æðelnoðe. Aliqua[m]
partem terrę In loco qui dicitur. deorlauestun. Vt habeat ac
possideat quandi[2] uiuat. et post sé cuicu[m]que uoluerit heredi
derelinquat in æternam hereditate[m]. Sit autem predictu[m]
rús liberu[m] ab omni mundiali obstaculo cu[m] omnib[us]
ad se rite pertinentibus. Campis. pascuis. pratis. Siluis. sine
expeditione. et pontis. arcisue Instructione. Si quis [autem][3]
Infringere temptauerit q[uo]d absit. Sciat sé ratione[m]
reddituru[m] cora[m] d[e]o et angelis eius. Nisi prius híc digna
satis factione emendare maluerit. Istis terminis ambitur
prędicta tellus.

Þis synd þa landgemæra to deorlafestune ærest hit fehð on
trentan þær fulan bróc scýt on trentan. Þonne andlang broces
ongean stream on fulan ford. of ðæm forda on bradan ford. of

---

[1] Psalm xci. 10.   [2] *Sic*, without abbreviation mark, for *quamdiu.*
[3] The insular abbreviation *ħ* is used.

bradan forda pest andlang stræte on hpæte croft of ðæm crofte on grenan hylle. of ðære hýlle andlang slædes ꝥ hit cýmð on þa stræt to þæm ðrym landgemæran. Þonne andlang peges on ðære dic ende. of ðære díc on gerihtna to sceortan stane. of ðæm stane on ðone pylle. of þæm pylle on færdene. of ðære dene þæt eft on trentan.

Hæc carta Scripta est. Anno d[omin]icę Incarnationis. dccccLvi. INdictione. XIIII.

✠ Ego eadpig rex anglorum Indeclinabiliter concessi.

✠ Ego eadgar elusdem[1] regis fr[ater] celeriter consensi.

✠ Ego oda archi ep[iscopu]s cu[m] signo S[an]c[t]ę crucis ✠ roboraui.

✠ Ego ælfsinus pręsul sigillum agię crucis ✠ Impressi.

✠ Ego býrhthelm ep[iscopu]s consignaui. ✠EGO osulf ep[iscopu]s.

✠ Ego cenpald ep[iscopu]s adquieui. ✠EGO býhthelm[2] ep[iscopu]s.

✠ Ego oscytel ep[iscopu]s subscripsi. ✠EGO aþulf ep[iscopu]s.

✠ [3]æðelstan dux.

✠ ælfhere dux.

✠ æðelsige dux.

✠ aþelpold dux.

✠ byrhtnoþ dux.

✠ ælfheah mi[ni]s[ter].

✠ ælfsige mi[ni]s[ter].

✠ [4]ælfric mi[ni]s[ter].

✠ ælfred mi[ni]s[ter].

✠ ælfsige mi[ni]s[ter].

✠ ælfnoþ mi[ni]s[ter].

✠ ælfpig mi[ni]s[ter].

✠ eadric mi[ni]s[ter].

✠ byrnric mi[ni]s[ter].

---

[1] *Sic*, for *eiusdem*.   [2] *Sic*, for *byrhthelm*.
[3] The second column of witnesses begins here.
[4] The third column of witnesses begins here.

ENDORSEMENTS

In the main hand:

✠ deorlafestunæs boc :– an hid æ[t] þan hame. oðer æt stapulforda.

In the Peniarth Cartulary hand:

Anno ab incarnatione domini Dcccclvi regnavit Ædwig.
XVII.

In a thirteenth-century hand:

dccclvj (*sic*).

TEXTS

A. William Salt Library, Stafford, MS. 84/1/41, mid-tenth century or a little later. A reduced facsimile forms the frontispiece to this book.

B. National Library of Wales, Aberystwyth, Peniarth MS. 390, (cited here as the Peniarth Cartulary), f.176ᵛ (old numbering p. 352), c. 1240 × 1264. An accurate copy of MS. A, with the witness list abbreviated. The chrismon of MS. A is reproduced fairly accurately.

EDITIONS

1. CS 954, from B.
2. This edition is from A, with abbreviations extended between square brackets. The punctuation and spelling are retained, but occasionally it is not clear whether an individual letter is intended to be minuscule or majuscule. The rubric heading this edition is taken from the Peniarth Cartulary text.

TRANSLATION

Bridgeman p. 96.

PALAEOGRAPHY

The membrane is 38 cm. wide × 21·6 cm. long, and has been folded three times horizontally and twice vertically, the size of the folded membrane being approximately 12·7 cm. × 5·4 cm. It is in good condition, all words being legible. The hand is that of a practised scribe, with few detectable errors, and may be contemporary with the date claimed for the charter (956), or a little later. Sawyer (S p. 211) is certainly wrong in dating it a century later. The rather elaborate chrismon is absolutely right for a Winchester charter of the mid-tenth century (it is very close to OS Facs II, Winchester II, a contemporary text dated 957), except that one of the curls at the ends of the cross is turned the wrong way. The general format suggests that the charter is a copy, but that the copyist followed his exemplar faithfully. He retained the West Saxon spelling *wylle* in the bounds. The position of the crosses in the attestation clauses of the archbishop of Canterbury and the bishop of Winchester is similar to those in the original charter CS 926, written early in 956 by the scribe of annal 971 in the Parker Chronicle. It may be that the exemplar of the Burton charter was by the same scribe, who worked in the Winchester scriptorium.

The scribe of the surviving copy wrote in a good insular hand, uninfluenced by caroline minuscule. He has used round 'a' throughout the Latin and OE text. Horned 'a' occurs only at the end of the third line and throughout the fourth line; possibly at this point the copyist was reproducing the script of his exemplar. Straight-backed 'c' does not occur. Both the round-backed and the more upright forms of 'd' occur in the Latin, but in the OE the more upright form is the rule. 'e' is very variable in the Latin text; usually it is round-backed, with or without a tongue, but the tall form occurs frequently. In the OE text, however, tall 'e' occurs only once. 'ę' is used for 'æ'. Insular 'f' is identical in Latin and OE and is unremarkable. Insular 'g' has an open tail throughout. 'i' is a descender only after 't'. All three forms of 's' occur. The curve of final 't' is curled up in Latin and in OE. 'y' is straight-limbed, and usually dotted. 'þ' is used initially in words, 'ð' medially and finally. All ascenders are tagged to the left at the top. Descenders are straight throughout. '⁊' does not occur, nor does the ampersand. 'e' is commonly ligatured. Punctuation is by medial dot. Hyphens and '⁚' do not occur. ';' appears only for abbreviations. Insular 'ħ' is used once for *autem*. Vowels are stressed occasionally.

The left-hand border of the copy is irregular, due to lack of vertical ruling. The names of the last three bishops have been crowded into spare space at the end of earlier subscriptions. Spacing between letters is irregular. Commonly prepositions *ac, qui, ab, ad, si* are joined to the following words in the Latin text; similarly with *of, to, on* in OE.

DATE AND WITNESSES

The indiction is compatible with the year of grace, as is the entire witness list, which includes the archbishop of Canterbury, the bishops of Winchester, London, Worcester, Wells, Ramsbury, Dorchester, and Hereford, and the ealdormen of south-east Mercia, central Mercia, Wessex, East Anglia, and Essex. The charter was witnessed late in 956, after the accession of Byrhthelm to Wells, the death of Ealdorman Byrhtferth, the retirement of Æthelstan Half-King, and the appointments of Æthelstan Rota, Ælfhere, Æthelwold, and Byrhtnoth to their respective ealdordoms. The witness list is close to those of CS 927 and 966, the latter being dated 29 November.

FORMULAS

The invocation appears in CS 879, 910, 951, and 955. The quotation from Psalm cxi occurs in CS 892, but the rest of the proem is unique. The king's title occurs also in CS 940, 960, 984, and 988. The phrase *quem nonnulli vocitant noto*, introducing the name of the recipient, appears in CS 926, 974, 976, and 992. The phrase *in loco qui dicitur*, introducing the name of the place conveyed, is very common in charters from the seventh century onwards; *inter alia* it occurs in CS 903–4, 908, 923, 931, 964–5, and 978. The clause granting power of alienation occurs in CS 902, and the exemption clause is of normal form for the period. The anathema, which originated in 949 (CS 879), is repeated in CS 926 and 972. The phrase *istis terminis ambitur predicta tellus* introducing the bounds originated in 951 (CS 891), and occurs commonly in charters of the year 956, e.g. CS 902, 926, 932, 953, 958, 960, 962, and 986. The dating clause recurs in CS 932, 940, 943, 995–6, 961, 976, and 982. The forms of attestation of the witnesses are repeated in CS 926, 943, and 945. Nearly all these quoted parallels are from charters of the year 956, and the exemplar used for the text of this diploma is a typical chancery product for that year. The endorsement in the main hand on the surviving membrane is not typical of those entered on chancery charters of the sixth decade of the tenth century (cf. CW pp. 20–4), and one must assume that it was the creation of the copyist. It was made by someone with access to local knowledge; the copy was therefore perhaps the work of a Mercian scribe, possibly from Worcester. It is shown below (p. 200) that this charter was used as the exemplar for Bu xxvi.

HISTORY

The tenth-century endorsement in the main hand of the surviving copy of the charter records that the land conveyed comprised one hide at the *ham*, i.e. the village of Darlaston, and one at *Stapulforda*, evidently a detached portion of the estate having its own separate bounds, which are not given in the charter. This may be located with confidence at Stableford, some five miles north-west of Darlaston, where the A51 road from Darlaston to Woore crosses the Meece Brook at grid reference 815387. Stableford is not mentioned in Domesday, nor in the Burton surveys, and it seems likely that the holding there was disposed of after its acquisition by Burton Abbey, since it was right out on the periphery of the abbey's landed interests. It may be surmised further that *Stapulforda* comprised the modern parishes of Chapel and Hill Chorlton, recorded as waste in DB, when they were members of the great manor of Eccleshall which belonged to the bishopric of Chester. The name 'Chorlton' derives from *ceorla tun*, the settlement of a group of *ceorls*; it 'denotes a village on an estate which includes more than one unit of settlement. It is not the principal unit, being situated a mile or more away from the seat of the lordship, but it is subject to the same lord . . .' (*Lucerna* p. 159). *Stapulforda*, in other words, was the original *ceorla tun* of the *ham* at *Deorlaf's tun* or Darlaston. After the Danish settlement, the ceorls may well have achieved some degree of independence, and *Stapulforda* may then have become either the sokeland or a berewick of Darlaston; when the monks of Burton obtained Darlaston from Wulfric Spot in 1004, it seems that they sold off this distant appendage. It is noteworthy that the endorsement to the text now under consideration quotes one hide as the assessment for Darlaston; by the time of DB it had been reduced to three virgates, a rating maintained in the early twelfth century when the estate was described in the Burton Abbey surveys. The reduction in hidation was the result of a general relief from geld applied (probably at its foundation) to all the demesne lands of the abbey. The endorsement, therefore, describes a state of affairs that considerably antedates Domesday, and it supplies historical backing for our palaeographical judgement that the surviving membrane was copied soon after the charter had been issued. Apart from this endorsement, there is nothing in the form or content of the surviving version to lead one to suspect that the text of the charter of 956 was tampered with in any way when this transcript was made.

BOUNDS

It is assumed that these relate to Darlaston only, and do not include Stableford. Unfortunately, no early estate maps of Darlaston Hall survive, and it is clear that its OE bounds do not always coincide with the modern parochial and administrative boundaries. The eastern boundary was evidently the River Trent; for the rest, I have assumed that the OE estate was limited by the bounds of the Domesday manors of Walton, Coldmeece, Millmeece, Cotes, Swynnerton, and Tittensor, none of which were the property of Burton Abbey at the time of Domesday. The bounds can be followed on $2\frac{1}{2}''$ OS sheet SJ 83. They run in a clockwise direction:

1. Along the Trent until it reaches the place where the *fulan broc* flows *on trentan*. The foul brook, now Fillybrooks, joins the River Trent at grid ref. 897337. The present boundary leaves the Trent about 300 yards north-west of this point.

2. Upstream along the brook to *fulan ford*. The foul ford would be where the A34 from Darlaston to Aston crosses the Fillybrook at 896336.

3. From the ford to *bradan ford*. Up Fillybrook and along a tributary to 890325, where it is crossed by the A520 from Stone to Eccleshall. One would expect a broad shallow ford at this point from the flat nature of the ground.

4. Westwards along the *stræte* to *hwæte croft*, then to *grenan hylle*. Westwards along the A520 road to the small hillock at 885324, where a cutting now carries the M4 motorway under the road. This appears to be the only possible location for the green hill, and the wheat croft was presumably a small enclosure beside the A520, which I cannot now locate.

5. From the hill along the *slæd* until it comes to the *stræt*. The modern boundary is joined at this point. It runs for two miles northwards along a valley now occupied by the M4 motorway, to join the A51 road from Darlaston to Woore at 866362. Here the boundary turns westwards along the A51.

6. To the three *landegemæran*. Evidently the three boundaries of Tittensor, Swynnerton, and Darlaston met at Sandyford, 862365.

7. Along the *weg* to the *dic ende*. The modern boundary now turns north-eastwards along the lane from Sandyford to Waggersley. The ditch end would have abutted on this somewhere near Greenbirch, 865367.

8. From the ditch, on to *sceortan stane*. The small stone may have been sited at about 867371, in Cumberstone Wood. OE *cumbra* = 'British'. Could the stone have borne Celtic carvings? The second element of Cumberstone is more likely, however, to derive from OE *tun*. The hill fort of Bury Bank (*Wulferecester*) lay within the bounds of Darlaston, just a mile south-east of Cumberstone Wood. Unfortunately, no detailed study of local place-names has as yet been published.

9. From the stone to the *wylle*. Note the West Saxon spelling here, introduced, presumably, by the chancery scribe of the exemplar, and preserved by the Burton copyist. Probably 'spring' or 'well' is meant, rather than 'stream', for the boundary goes to the *wylle* and not along it. There are two wells at 874371 on Tittensor Chase.

10. From the *wylle* to *færdene*, then back to the River Trent. A

footpath from Tittensor Chase leads down through a woodland valley, still beautiful, to the A34 road beside the River Trent at 876374. Evidently the OE bounds then ran south, downstream along the Trent to the starting-point.

XXIII. KING EDGAR TO BISHOP WULFRIC. ONE HIDE AT STANTON IN THE PEAK, DERBYSHIRE. A.D. 968

Carta Eadgari Regis de Stantun dcccc.lxviij. Ind[ictione]. xi.

In nomine d[e]i summi Cunctaque in hoc s[e]c[u]lo temporaliter uersantur. Sine ullo respectus articulo omnib[us] horis atq[ue] momentis p[ro]peranter ad finem festinant. Et tunc sine fine inreuocabilia p[er]manebunt. Quap[ro]pter ego Eadgar rex angloru[m] ceteraru[m]q[ue] gentiu[m] incircuitu p[er]sistentiu[m] gubernator et rector. dedi cuidam uni meo[1] episcopo nuncupato uocamine Þulfric unum[2] mansas[3] agelluli in illo loco ubi uulgari[4] nom[en] inposuerunt Stántun. Quatenus habeat ac perpetualiter possideat quamdiu uiuat. Et post se cuicumq[ue] uoluerit iste exeniu[m] derelinquat in æterna[m] hereditate[m]. Sit [autem][5] predictum rús lib[erum] ab om[n]i mundiali obstaculo cu[m] om[n]ibus ad se rite pertinentib[us] campis. pascuis. pratis. siluis. excepto co[m]muni labore expeditione pontis. arcisuæ coedificatione. Hæc kartula karaxata e[st]. Anno ab Incarnatione d[omi]ni n[ost]ri ih[es]u chr[ist]i dcccĉ lx̂ v̂iii. indict[ione] u[ero] xî.

✠ Ego eadgar rex hanc meam donat[ionem] sabulo[6] glorioso roboraui

✠ Ego dunstan archiepis[copus] c[on]signaui

✠ Ego oscetel archiepis[copus] inp[res]si

✠ Ego æðelpald epis[copus] c[on]sensi

---

[1] After *meo* the scribe commenced to write a word beginning with 'm', probably *ministro*. He erased the 'm' and continued with *episcopo*, without writing over the erasure.

[2] CS 1211 has *viiii*, from misreading of *unū* in the cartulary version.

[3] *Sic*, for 'mansam'; see the OE passage immediately before the anathema.

[4] *Sic*, for 'uulgares'.   [5] Insular *h* is used for 'autem'.

[6] *Sic*, for 'gabulo', see p. 184.

✠ Ego osulf epis[copus] c[on]firmaui
✠ Ego pulfric epis[copus] c[on]clusi
✠ Ego ospald epis[copus] subscripsi
✠ Ego ælfstan epis[copus] roboraui
✠ Ego pynsige epis[copus] inp[res]si
✠ [1]ælfere dux
✠ æþelstan dux
✠ ælfheah dux
✠ æðelpine dux
✠ berhtnoð dux
✠ eanulf discifer
✠ ælfpine discifer
✠ pulfstan discifer
✠ [2]æðelsige pedisec[us]
✠ pulfric min[is]t[er]
✠ æðelm min[is]t[er]
✠ pulfgar min[is]t[er]
✠ pulfsige min[is]t[er]
✠ ælfhelm min[is]t[er]
✠ pulfmar[3] min[is]t[er]
✠ [4]

Ia[m] sequitur istius ruris teminatione ærest of alde píc
þ spa[5] on[6] myra hoh. of myra hoh in ðæt ðæl þ spa on æðeredes.
hoh. of æðeredes hoh[7] in þ dæl. of ðæm dæle in spines hoh þ
spa ꝺlong dæles þ in ðone stanegan fórd. of þæm fórda ꝺlong
broces þ eft in þ alde píc. ðis send ðara tpegra hide gemæro ðe
þulfric biscop hafað ane hide. oðer hafað ælfnað.

Si quis uero filargyrie sp[irit]u inflatus hanc meam munificentia[m] p[ro] d[e]o datam infringere ausus fuerit. sit
anathema ab om[n]ipotenti d[e]o et a congregatione om[n]ium
s[an]c[t]or[um]. nisi hic cum satis factione digne d[e]o et.
hominib[us] emendauerit. Pax perpetue p[ro]speritas augeatur
coram chr[ist]o. s[an]c[t]or[um]. patrocinio patrocinante.

---

[1] The second column of witnesses begins here.
[2] The third column of witnesses begins here.
[3] A fold makes this word difficult to read. Possibly it was spelt þulfmær.
[4] Sic MS., with space unfilled.
[5], [6], [7] Owing to a tear in the membrane, some letters in the words are restored.

ENDORSEMENTS

In the main hand:
pulfrices boc bisc[eop] æt stantune ā on ece erfe.
In the Peniarth Cartulary hand:
Dcccc.lxviij. Indictione xj. Santoñ (*sic*).
In the same hand:
Stantoñ. XXIII.
In a later hand:
XXa.
In a seventeenth-century hand:
Stanton A boundrye.

TEXTS

A. William Salt Library, Stafford, MS. 84/2/41, contemporary. There is no published facsimile.

B. National Library of Wales, Aberystwyth, Peniarth MS. 390 (cited here as the Peniarth Cartulary), f. 178 (old numbering, p. 355), c. 1240 × 1264, a good copy of A, with the witness list abbreviated, and bounds and anathema omitted. The chrismon of MS. A is reproduced accurately.

EDITIONS

1. CS 1211 from B.
2. This edition is from A, with abbreviations extended between square brackets. The punctuation and spelling are retained. The rubric heading this edition is taken from the Peniarth Cartulary text.

PALAEOGRAPHY

The membrane is 25·2 cm. wide × 31·8 cm. long, and has been folded three times vertically and twice horizontally; the folded size is approximately 6·3 cm. × 10·6 cm. It is in fair condition, with only a few letters lost through tears. The scribe wrote in an insular hand using frequent abbreviations and uninfluenced by caroline forms; there is no differentiation in the hand between Latin and OE. The hand is large, practised, but hurried; there has been no ruling. Punctuation is by medial dot only; the comma is used sparingly for terminal abbreviations. 'd' is round-backed. Insular 'g' has an open tail. 'i' does not descend after 't' or 'l'. 'l' is written regularly partly below the line. The bow of 'p' is closed throughout. Insular 'r' has a tail and is characteristic. Long 's' occurs only as the first letter of

OE words. 'y' is straight-limbed in Latin, and 'f'-shaped in OE; neither form is dotted. 'þ' does not occur, except once in the witness list.

The text is written in the same hand throughout, but not all at one time; space was left for the witness list, which was added later (but before folding), as the crowding of the last few episcopal entries shows. This establishes that the hand is contemporary. The roughly drawn chrismon is also contemporary, and probably by the same scribe, though in a paler ink. Its form is unique. Presumably the 'S' intertwining the downstroke of the 'P' stands for 'salvator'. The only other chrismon resembling this that I have encountered in the charters is the very large one heading OS Facs II, Bodleian, a fourteenth-century copy of an apparently authentic charter of King Burghred of Mercia to the church of St Peter, Gloucester, dated 862 (CS 535; ECWM pp. 153–7). Presumably the copyist of this Mercian text has reproduced the chrismon of his exemplar with some degree of accuracy. If so, we may perhaps assume that the Burton text was written in a Mercian scriptorium, possibly Worcester. The entry of the witness list before the anathema and bounds is also suggestive of a Worcester provenance. Unfortunately we have few firmly dated and located Worcester MSS of this period with which to compare it.

DATE AND WITNESSES

The indiction is compatible with the year of grace, as is the entire witness list, which includes the archbishops of Canterbury and York, the bishops of Winchester, Ramsbury, Worcester, London, and Lichfield, and Wulfric of Dorchester, the recipient; the ealdormen are from central and south-east Mercia, Wessex, East Anglia, and Essex. The list is unusual for the period, in that no abbots are represented. Moreover, the thegns are divided into three *disciferi*, one *pedisequus*,[1] and six *ministri*, of whom one at least held land in Mercia.[2] Only one other surviving charter of Edgar (also relating to a Mercian property) distinguishes between the *disciferi* and the *ministri* in this manner.[3] The only surviving charter of Æthelred II to make a similar distinction is Bu XXIV (see p. 189).

[1] Presumably he is the official called by the king 'camerario meo' in CS 1121, dated 963.

[2] Probably the witness Ælfhelm is identical with the recipient of land conveyed in CS 1230, dated 969.

[3] CS 1270, dated 971, in which the title *disc* after four of the witnesses is wrongly extended to *discipulus* by the copyist; see ECEE p. 172 n. 5.

THE RECIPIENT

Stanton was situated within the diocese of Lichfield, but Wulfric the recipient could not have held that see, which was in the possession of Wynsige. Wulfric witnesses from 958 to 970. It seems likely that he was the bishop of Dorchester.

FORMULAS

This is a very unusual charter. The invocation does not occur elsewhere in texts originating after the reign of King Eadred. The earliest surviving examples are from a Hwiccean diploma of 704–9 (CS 122), and a charter of Æthelbert, king of the South Saxons, which appears to be a little later in date.[1] The invocation recurs in a more elaborate form in two eighth-century Mercian diplomas,[2] but after this there is a gap of more than half a century before it appears again, this time reverting to its original simplicity, in a Mercian text of 849 (CS 455); it recurs later in the ninth century in some West Saxon charters.[3] In the tenth century it was elaborated again,[4] but two charters of King Eadred retain the original form (CS 830, 866).

The proem recalls *omnis horis et momentis solor[um]* (? for *seculorum*) in an Exeter diploma of 1044.[5] The king's title is one of the few formulas of this charter that appear commonly elsewhere (e.g. CS 785, 1043, 1118, 1138, 1142, 1145; K 1281). *Uni meo* in the title of the recipient occurs in CS 1002, and again in CS 1197 which uses a similar exemplar; but probably more significant is its appearance in a series of Worcester leases over the period 969–77 (CS 1235, 1237–8; K 613–17). The addition of *agelluli* after the hidage assessment is characteristic of charters issued in the period 938–47 (CS 728, 730, 734, 740, 743, 763, 768, 770, 776–8, 780, 786, 793, 795, 798, 802, 818, 821–2), and in a few later charters utilizing these formulas (e.g. CS 1023; K 611).

The exact form of the clause introducing the place-name appears to be unique. In the clause granting powers of alienation, I have not

[1] CS 211. Several of the personal names of this charter (which has a late confirmation by King Offa and his queen) occur in CS 145, to be dated c. 725. A thorough survey of these early Sussex charters is badly needed.

[2] CS 245, 253; the latter form is repeated in CS 855, a West Saxon text.

[3] CS 544, 549. It occurs in a more elaborate form in CS 463 and 527, professions of bishops of the mid-ninth century. It appears also in CS 244, but this is a spurious charter, cf. ECWM 44.

[4] See the notes to No. XXI, p. 107.

[5] OS Facs II, Exeter xii; cf. Chaplais, *Exeter*, 1966, p. 27.

encountered the word *exenium* (= gift) elsewhere in the charters; according to the *Medieval Latin Word-List* it occurs in literary sources from 1044 onwards. The exemption clause is a modification of a fairly common formula (e.g. CS 1138), but *coedificatione* is uncommon (it occurs however in CS 1068, 1092, 1138). The spellings *kartula*, *karaxata* in the dating clause are much less common than those beginning with 'c', but the 'k' form does appear sporadically throughout the ninth, tenth, and eleventh centuries (e.g. CS 442, 454, 518, 534, 548, 588, 603, 1026, 1043, 1047, 1112, 1136, 1282, 1285), in Mercian, West Saxon, and Kentish texts. The formula *hec carta caraxata est* appears in CS 1092, dated 962; although this is spurious, it is based on an authentic text. The words *sabulo glorioso* after the king's subscription make no sense. Professor Finberg pointed out to me that the scribe has misread his exemplar here, and has been followed by the Peniarth Cartulary copyist, and by Birch in his edition. The correct word is *gabulo*, for the gibbet of the cross. CS 905 (A.D. 955) has *gabulo summo*, and CS 1112 (963) *gabulo glorioso*. In both cases it occurs in attestations by Cynesige, bishop of Lichfield. See also *salutiferi gabuli* in CS 1301 (974), and *gabulo sanctæ crucis* in K 746 (1032).

The arrangement by which the bounds and anathema appear after the witness list is uncommon, but not unique, especially in Mercian charters. I have found only one other example of a similar formula introducing the boundary clause: CS 245, a rather doubtful Westminster text which claims to be dated 785: *Iam sequitur istius ruris cirgyrata terminatio.* The anathema is unique, but individual phrases are echoed elsewhere, e.g. *spiritu inflatus* in CS 1143, *inflatus philargyrie* in CS 887, *philargyrie seductus* in K 629, 686. The grace concluding the charter is also unique; *perpetua maneat pax* occurs in CS 567, *perpetue prosperitas* in the Worcester charter CS 883; and the phrase *sanctorum patrocinio patrocinante* recalls *dominio dominorum dominante* in CS 992, 1022, Bu XII, and elsewhere.

It can hardly be doubted that this is an authentic text. Probably the scribe was using a similar charter for his exemplar, by which an estate was made out to a thegn instead of a bishop (whence the erasure of the letter 'm' after *uni meo* in the dispositive clause). Once it was written, the charter had to be presented before the court for ratification, after which the witness list was added. Only then was the charter folded, and the endorsement added. Such an individualistic diploma could not be the product of a chancery scribe. From the chrismon with which it is prefaced, to the unusual contemporary endorsement, the whole structure is alien to chancery conventions. Several of its peculiarities of style and format point to a Mercian scriptorium as the place of origin, and Worcester is perhaps the most likely location. It is doubtful if any other ecclesiastical centre north of the Thames was capable of producing royal diplomas at this date. Seen in this light, the charter assumes immediately a considerable importance, being the earliest surviving example of a non-chancery royal diploma issued north of the Thames in the tenth century. A search should be made for the hand in MSS. from Worcester and from other Mercian centres at this period.

HISTORY AND BOUNDS

The OE bounds of the two hides at Stanton are difficult to define, because none of the place-names appear to have survived into modern times; moreover, they cannot be completely identical with the present-day bounds of Stanton parish, for whereas the OE bounds cross three hill-spurs (*mỹra hoh*, *æðeredes hoh*, and *swines hoh*), those of the modern parish cross only two (Pilhough and Stanton Moor). It seems very unlikely, however, that the original boundary ever crossed north of the River Wye, or east of the River Derwent; once this is appreciated, the simple solution presents itself almost as a corollary that originally Stanton incorporated Birchover, which lies about a mile to the south on the same escarpment. Certainly the OE bounds of Stanton fit those of the combined modern parishes of Stanton and Birchover as a hand fits a glove; the correspondence is so striking that anyone attempting the perambulation will soon be convinced of the identity. The solution has the added attraction that it accounts for the OE passage following the bounds, which states that Bishop Wulfric held one of the two 'hides' of Stanton, and Ælfnoth the other; it would be natural for these to develop into the two Domesday vills of Stanton and Birchover. The names themselves suggest that the *tun* at Stanton was the primary settlement; the 'birch-covered ridge' to the south would have been cleared and colonized later.

All the above was written before I had opportunity to examine the DB account of Stanton and Birchover (VCH *Derbys.*, I, 343b), which provides most satisfying confirmation of the general thesis. TRE Stanton in the Peak was a manor of one carucate, with land for one plough; it was the freehold of two thegns named Godric and Raven. Birchover was its sole berewick, also assessed at one carucate, with land for one plough; evidently one thegn held the manor and the other the berewick, as had been the case with the ownership a century earlier. One cannot doubt that the word *hid* in the charter was an Anglicization by the scribe of ON *plogsland* (see p. 121). The probability is that Bu 1, concerning 2 'manentes' at *Stantune* in 900, relates to the same estate.

The OE bounds can be traced on the 2½″ OS sheet SK 26. They proceed in a clockwise direction:

1. *of aldewic* Wye farm at grid ref. 252656, where the bounds of Stanton leave the River Wye, striking steeply uphill in a southerly direction.

2. *in mӯra hoh* The first element could be OE *myrig* 'pleasant, agreeable', or possibly OE *mere* 'mare'. The second element, *hoh* 'hill-spur' survives in Pilhough 250650, which is traversed by Stanton Hall lane, along which the modern boundary runs.

3. *in ðæt dæl* The Stanton boundary descends to join the River Derwent at 259644; it then proceeds downstream along the Derwent valley to 265625, where it strikes eastwards towards Cowley Hall; here the OE bounds turn south again, along the modern Birchover parish boundary.

4. *on æðeredes hoh* Æthelred's hill-spur is now called Cowley Knowl, 256618.

5. *in tha dæl* The bounds descend into the dale between Wensley and Birchover, and run up the stream at the bottom of the dale to 251611.

6. *in swines hoh* At the head of the dale the bounds strike northwards, up the steep ridge to Great Close, then westwards along the ridge to Ivy House, 242617. *Swines hoh* is therefore the hill-spur to the south of Clough Lane.

7. *andlong dæles* The boundary now drops down into the dale between Birchover and Harthill Moor, which it reaches at 228618; it proceeds down the dale along Ivy Bar Brook to Eagle Tor, where the Birchover boundary meets that of Stanton. Stanton boundary continues northwards down the brook, through Stoneyhey Wood.

8. *in thone Stanegan ford* The stony ford now called Fillyford, at the bottom of the dale, 242658.

9. *andlang broces eft in tha aldewic* Back down the River Wye to the starting-point.

XXIV. King Æthelred II to his writer Ælfwine. 3 hides at Brighthampton, 2 at Aston Bampton, and 1 at Lew, Oxfordshire. A.D. 984

Carta Æþelredi regis toci[us] albionis de bẏrhtelmingtun dcccc.Lxxxiiij

Regnante d[omi]no n[ost]ro Ih[e]su Chr[ist]o imp[er]pet-uu[m]. Qui ante mu[n]di co[n]stituc[i]o[n]em decem ang[e]lor[um] agmina mirifice collocauit. decemaq[ue] post p[er] sup[er]biam cu[m] suo lucifero in barathrum boraginis elapsis. nouem in sua stabilitate misericorditer co[n]seruauit. quique decimam adimplere cupiens postquam celum terramque conderet. ho[m]i[n]em ex limo terre formauit. formatu[m]q[ue] p[ro]thoplastum serpentin[us] liuor ad mortem usq[ue] p[er]duxit. omneq[ue] humanu[m] gen[us] post illum. Et qu[a]ndo dei inmensa mis[erico]rdia hoc pe[r]spexit. condoluit. unicu[m]q[ue] filiu[m] suu[m] mittens satu[m] de intemerata uirgine Maria p[er] crucis mortem om[n]e humanu[m] genus piissime redemit. Qui assidue nos sacro precio mercatos admonet ut iugiter intenta mente meditemus qualiter in h[a]nc erumpnosam uitam deuenim[us]. vel quali fine iteru[m] hinc redire op[or]teat. Quia ut beatus Iob ait. nudi[1] eg[re]ssi sumus de utero mat[ri]s. nudi iteru[m] in t[er]ram m[at]rem om[n]ium ire debem[us]. Ideo p[er] necessariu[m] est unicuique ut ex caducis [et] deficientib[us] istius mundi diuiciis et[er]nas indeficientesq[ue] diui[c]ias lucretur. Hiis [et] aliis qu[a]mpl[ur]ib[us] exemplis roboratus Ego EÐelred diuina concedente gra[tia] rex [et] monarchus tocius Albionis aliqu[am] portionc[u]lam ruris. uideli[cet]. sex Cassatos in com[m]uni tellure diremtis .iij. scil[ice]t ubi gnostici uocitant Bẏrhtelmingtum[2].ij. ubi a ruricolis nu[n]cup-atur æt Eastun .i. uero situm in loco q[u]i dicitur æt hlæpe cuidam m[ih]i oppido dilecto fideliq[u]e ministro videl[ice]t meo scriptori qui a notis noto Elfþine nu[n]cupatur uocabulo p[ro] ei[us] amabili humiliq[ue] obseq[u]io quo iugit[er] instanter deseruit in sempit[er]n[um] condono. Ut uita comite

1 Job i. 21.   2 *Sic.*

teneat et[er]namq[ue] in hereditatem possideat cu[m] om[n]i-
b[us] que ad se rite p[er]tinent. uidel[ice]t campis. pratis.
pascuis. Cum uero dei p[ro]uidente gra[tia] de hoc uolubili
mu[n]do mig[ra]uerit. cuicu[m]q[ue] sibi placuerit cleronomi
in mun[er]e p[er] om[n]ia derelinq[ua]t. Hoc u[er]o meu[m]
donu[m] firmu[m] p[er]seueret. [et] ab om[n]i seculari
seruic[i]o firma libertas p[er]maneat. trib[us] exceptis causis
que ab om[n]ib[us] notissime constant. Si quis h[a]nc meam
donac[i]o[ne]m amplificare uoluerit ꞉ hic p[re]sente[m] vitam
illi augeat d[omi]n[us]. et in futuro perpetuam in terra
uiuentiu[m]. Quod si aliq[u]is aliter q[uo]d absit inflat[us]
diabolica temeritate aliq[ui]d in hoc dono minuere u[e]l
mutare satagere nisus fuerit ꞉ sciat se a s[an]ctor[um] om[n]ium
co[n]sortio esse exortem. nisi p[ri]us fauente dei gra[tia]
emendauerit. Hec aut[em] scedula carraxata est anno d[omi]nice
Incarn[ationis]. Dcccc.lxxxiiij. Indict[i]o[ne] .xij. Hiis testibus
co[n]sentientib[us] subscribentib[us]q[ue] quor[um] uocabula
inferius scripta cernu[n]tur.

✠ Ego Eðelræd rex Anglor[um] hui[us] donac[i]on[is]
     lib[er]tatem regni toci[us] fastig[iu]m tene[n]s libent[er]
     [con]cessi.

✠ Ego Dunstan Archiep[iscopu]s Doruernensis eccl[es]ie
     cu[m] signo s[an]c[te] semp[er]q[ue] adorande Crucis
     roboraui.

✠ Ego Ospald[us] Eborace[n]sis Ciuitatis Archipresul crucis
     taumate confirmaui.

✠ Ego Ælfstan[us] Ep[i]s[copus] consignaui.
✠ Ego Æðelgar Ep[i]s[copus] consolidaui.
✠ Ego Æscpig Ep[i]s[copus] adquieui.
✠ Ego Æðelsige Ep[i]s[copus] adnotaui.
✠ Ego Þulfgar Ep[i]s[copus] corroboraui.
✠ Ego Sigegar Ep[i]s[copus] faui.
✠ Ego Ælfric Ep[i]s[copus] inp[re]ssi.
✠ Ego Ælfeah Ep[i]s[copus] subsc[ri]psi.
✠ Ego Æðulf Ep[i]s[copus] co[n]clusi.

Et ceteri.[1] Duces sex. Abbates iiij[or]. Disciferi iiij[or]. pincern[æ]
iiij[or]. Ministri. undecim.

---

[1] 'Et ceteri' scored through in MS.

National Library of Wales, Aberystwyth, Peniarth MS. 390 (cited here as the Peniarth Cartulary), f. 178rv (old numbering pp. 355–6). According to the cartulary scribe, the text of his exemplar was prefaced by a cross and an elaborate chrismon.[1] There is no boundary clause in the surviving text, and the witness list is abbreviated.

EDITION

The charter is hitherto unpublished. In this edition, abbreviations are extended between square brackets and the cartulary punctuation is retained. The rubric is that of the cartulary copyist.

DATE AND WITNESSES

The indiction is compatible with the year of grace, as is the surviving portion of the witness list, comprising the archbishops of Canterbury and York, and the bishops of London, Selsey, Dorchester, Sherborne, Ramsbury, Wells, Crediton, Lichfield, and Hereford. The charter was witnessed after 1 August, when Bishop Æthelwold of Winchester died, and before 28 October, when Ælfheah was enthroned at Winchester (ASC A). The separation of the witnessing thegns into *disciferi*, *pincernæ*, and *ministri* is unique among the surviving charters of Æthelred, and carries one stage further the division into *disciferi* and *ministri* appearing in two charters of Edgar (see p. 182). It reveals that there was an elaborate hierarchy among the thegns in Æthelred's court.

THE RECIPIENT

This is the only reference to a *scriptor* in an Anglo-Saxon diploma. Presumably Ælfwine was a layman; his alternative title *minister* indicates that he was of thegnly rank. He could hardly have been a mere copyist; one imagines that he filled the role of a secretary at court. In this capacity, he might well have been directly concerned with drawing up royal diplomas. An almost contemporary gloss gives OE *burthe(g)n* for *cancellarius vel scrinarius*.[2] Archbishop Sigeric's confirmation charter to Wolverhampton was written by King Ethelred's *notarius vel scrinarius* in 994 (No. 90, see p. 98). At the turn of the century, the position may have been held by the Kentish thegn Siward (see p. 359).

[1] A cross and a chrismon appear side by side in K 705, dated 1001, possibly from Evesham.

[2] *Anglo-Saxon and Old English Vocabularies*, ed. T. Wright and R. P. Wülckur, London, 1884, I, p. 190.

ESTATE HISTORY

Some time between 1042 and 1046, Edward the Confessor gave 6 hides at Aston Bampton and the near-by villages of Bampton and Chimney to his clerk Leofric, who according to Florence of Worcester was the Confessor's *cancellarius*. Bampton was the site of a bridge across the upper Thames, to carry the road from Witney to Faringdon. The importance of this route is shown by the fact that whereas the first bridge was of wood (whence OE *bēam tun* = Bampton), by the time of the Norman Conquest it had already been replaced by a stone one, which appears in the OE perambulation of the estate recited in the great Exeter confirmation charter of William I (see below). With the Confessor's gift would have gone jurisdiction over the royal double hundred of Bampton (DB). Leofric became bishop of Devon and Cornwall, and passed on his estate as an endowment for his foundation of canons at Exeter, where he had established his episcopal seat in 1050. Most of the Cathedral property was alienated at an early date, but Aston Bampton stayed in the possession of Exeter until the fifteenth century (Exeter D and C archives, nos. 2526 and 3501, fol. 1a). See further, *The Exeter Book of Old English Poetry*, facsimile edition, Exeter, 1933, p. 20 n. 36; and F. Barlow in *Leofric of Exeter*, University of Exeter, 1972, p. 2 n. 1.

FORMULAS

These repay close study, as a number of phrases recur in K 647, a charter issued in 985 for Æthelred's 'faithful priest' Wulfric; the text survives in the cartulary of Christ Church, Southampton, but unfortunately the places conveyed have not yet been located for certain; they may be Knole and Borstal in Kent. Professor Finberg surmised that Wulfric was a royal clerk or chaplain (*West-Country Historical Studies*, 1969, p. 42 n. 2). The phrases shared between the two charters include the clause granting permanent possession – *ut vita comite . . . in æternam hereditatem*, the power of testamentary disposition *quando de hoc volubili mundo migrauerit*, parts of the anathema including *inflatus diabolica temeritate, aliquid in hoc dono minuere uel mutare (temptauerit), . . . nisi prius deo fauente . . . emendauerit*, the dating clause *hec autem scedula carraxata est . . .*, and the description of Oswald's see as *Eboracensis ciuitatis*. Some of these formulas do not appear elsewhere; there are no similarly extensive parallels between Bu XXIV and other diplomas of Æthelred's reign, and we have to postulate that the Burton charter and K 647 were by the same scribe, or by scribes trained in the same scriptorium.

Turning now to a more general review of the charter's formulas, one finds that the invocation is one of the commonest, appearing (on a quick count, excluding obvious forgeries) no less than 93 times in the charters edited by Birch and Kemble. It is not found in genuine early texts; it seems to have made its début at the Council of Clovesho in 742.[1] It appears in 13 charters of the second half of the eighth century, and in 12 more of the period 800–50, usually from the kingdom of Wessex, but also from Mercia, Kent, and Sussex. It was the form adopted for the charters of King Æthelwulf's second decimation in 854,[2] and this led to a great increase in its popularity, so that it was the commonest form for the remainder of the century (over 30 texts incorporating the invocation survive for this period). It continued in sporadic use throughout the tenth century, from which we have more than 40 examples, five being dated A.D. 940. By the date of the charter under discussion its popularity was waning considerably, and it is rare in eleventh-century texts. The form given in our charter, with *imperpetuum* at the end of the sentence, is most uncommon; I can find it in only three other charters, dated 793 × 854.[3]

The proem is unique. The fall of Lucifer seldom figures in pre-Conquest English diplomas, but it does appear in the proem of K 686, an original dated 994.[4] This Bodmin charter enlarges on an Abingdon proem;[5] the reference to Lucifer forms part of the elaboration, so it seems likely that it was a contemporary theme. The quotation from Job occurs in one apparently authentic eighth-century charter;[6] it recurs in a group of three charters from the *Codex Wintoniensis*,[7] and in another group of no less than eleven charters from the Abingdon cartularies.[8] Not all of the charters in

---

[1] CS 162; it also heads the records of councils held at *Clovesho* in 747, 798, and 824 (CS 174, 291, and 379).

[2] ECW pp. 209–13; CW p. 21.   [3] CS 261, 451, and 473.

[4] Chaplais, *Exeter*, 1966, pp. 19–20. The proem is repeated in two dubious Exeter diplomas (OS Facs II, Exeter X; K 729), ostensibly dated 1018 and 1019 respectively. The nine orders of angels appear in two seventh-century anathemas, cf. ECEE p. 140.

[5] Charters of the 'Orthodoxorum' group, discussed by E. John in *Revue Bénédictine*, 1960, pp. 333–7.

[6] CS 164 from Worcester. Its formula is copied in CS 216, from the same cartulary (Heming's), but this second charter is spurious; cf. F. M. Stenton in EHR 1918, p. 499 n. 67.

[7] CS 1114 and 1230, with similar formulas; CS 1149.

[8] CS 680, 1058, 1169, 1171–2; K 751, 792, 796, 1277, all having identical formulas; CS 1080; K 1295.

these two groups are authentic, but their texts derive from formulas characteristic of the Benedictine reform; probably the prototypes come from the sixth decade of the tenth century. I cannot find the quotation used elsewhere in English diplomas. It is important to note that unlike all the other examples, the quotation in Bu xxiv does not repeat the Vulgate text; the paraphrase varies so widely that it may have been lifted from a commentary on Job, rather than from Job itself.

The introduction to the king's title is unique. In the royal style itself, the replacement by *concedente* of the common *favente* (which appears in K 654, 659, 700, 1309) is not encountered elsewhere, but *rex et monarchus* appears in K 659, 1309, and *totius Albionis* is the regular form.[1] The land conveyed lay *in communi tellure diremtis*, an unusual reference to common fields. Such references occur in charters written by Abingdon scribes in the sixth decade of the century, and the tradition was continued when the chancery settled at Winchester in the seventh decade, see p. 22. In the clause introducing the name of the recipient, *cuidam mihi oppido fideli* occurs in CS 1123, 1218, 1230, 1309–12; K 655; *a notis noto* is found in K 657–8, 664. Finally, in the witness list, the form of the king's subscription, and those of the archbishops and bishops, are characteristic of charters issued in the period 983 × 990,[2] and do not occur elsewhere.

There can be little doubt that the original text of this Burton charter and K 647 were both drawn up at Winchester. The fact that both recipients were in the personal service of the king is certainly relevant. Moreover, it is noteworthy that Aston Bampton was given first to Ælfwine, the royal *scriptor* in 987, then to Leofric, the royal clerk in 1042–6. Florence of Worcester (1, p. 199) called Leofric the *cancellarius*, and there may be more truth in this title than some modern historians would allow.

Probably the original text of this Burton charter incorporated one or more boundary clauses, which were omitted (as with other charters) by the Peniarth Cartulary copyist. The copyist was responsible also for abbreviating the witness list, and for omitting to transcribe any endorsements on the charter before him. One cannot doubt that the surviving text is an incomplete copy of an authentic charter.

---

[1] CS 632, 636, 662, 686, 692, 696, 701, 709, 712, 1279, 1304, 1306, 1309, ECEE No. viii.

[2] K 639, 648, 650, 1280, 1282–3, 652, 657, 659, 664, 673; Bu xxv.

XXV. King Æthelred II to his thegn Æthelsige. 12 mansæ at Æsce. a.d. 987

Carta Æþelredi regis toci[us] Angligene gentis de Æsce. dcccc.Lxxxvij. Ind[ictione]. xv.

Annuente d[e]i pat[ri]s ineffabili humane p[ro]li cleme[n]tia qua adnullata p[ri]mi terrigene piac[u]lo[1] noue restaurac[i]o[n]is admirabile quoddam mu[n]do decus et[er]ne consortem maiestatis filium su[u]m misitare[2] dignat[us] est. qui t[er]rene[3] fragilitate custodite p[er] u[ir]ginei pudicitiam flosculi affatu angeli virginis claustra subint[ra]ns noue Incarnac[i]o[n]is misteriu[m] se ostentando dedicauit. ostendens se dictis u[er]bor[um] factisq[ue] miraculor[um] quib[us] deifice pollebat d[omi]n[u]m. curans om[n]ium imp[er]anti sermone egrotac[i]onum pondus. tandem quadrati p[ro] nob[is] ferens supplicia ligni iugu[m] hereditarie mortis absumens. diu longeq[ue] int[er]dicte reserauit limina porte. p[ro] cuius inenerrab[i]lis gl[or]ie recordacione ego Æðelred[us] gra[tia] d[e]i sublimat[us] rex [et] gubernator tocius Angliene gentis. *aliaru[m]q[ue] gentiu[m] in c[ir]cuitu p[er]sistenti[um] cuidam meo fideli[4] ministro* vocitato no[m]i[n]e Æðelsige *p[ro] sua humilima deuoc[i]one q[ua]ndam telluris p[ar]tic[u]lam* .xij. *videl[ice]t mansas largiendo libent[er] concedens p[er]donabo. illic ubi* Colones[5] *antiqui ita nu[n]cupando nomen indideru[n]t æt æsce. ut habeat ac p[er]hennit[er] possideat q[ua]mdiu viuat in et[er]nam hereditatem. Et p[ost] se cuicu[m]q[ue] sibi placuerit[6] inmunem derelinq[ua]t ceu sup[ra]dixim[us] in eternam possessione[m]. Si quis igit[ur] h[a]nc n[ost]ram donac[i]o[n]em in aliud* [et] c[etera].[7] *Sit aut[em] p[re]dic[tu]m rus.*[8]

---

[1] No abbreviation mark in MS.   [2] Collation with K 664: mittere.
[3] K 664: 'condolens' inserted.   [4] K 664: 'oppido' inserted.
[5] Sic, for 'coloni'.   [6] K 664: 'haeredi' inserted.

[7] K 664: 'quam constituimus transferre uoluerit, priuatus consortio sanctæ dei aecclesiae, aeternis barathri incendiis lugubris iugiter cum Iuda Christi proditore eiusque complicibus puniatur, si non satisfactione emendauerit quod contra nostrum deliquit decretum' inserted.

[8] K 664: 'liberum ab omni mundiali obstaculo cum omnibus ad se rite pertinentibus, campis, pascuis, pratis, siluis, exceptis istis tribus, expeditione, uidelicet, pontis arcisue restauratione' inserted. In K 664, this sentence precedes the anathema.

Istis t[er]m[inis] [et] c[etera].[1] *Ann*[o] *ab Incarn*[atione] d[omi]ni n[ostri] ih[esu] Ch[risti]. dcccc.lxxxvij. Indict[ione]. xv. sc[ri]pta est h[ec] *cartula*[2] [et] c[etera] ut sup[ra].[3]

✠ *Ego Æðelred rex Anglor*[um] h[uius] donac[i]o[n]is lib[er]tatem regni toci[us] fastigiu[m] tene[n]s libenter concessi.

✠ *Ego Dunstan Arch*[iepiscopus] doruern[ensis] eccl[es]ie cu[m] signo s[an]c[t]e crucis *confirmaui.*

✠ *Ego Ospold Arch*[ipræsul] *eborace* Ciuitatis crucis taumate adnotaui.[4]

✠ Ego Ælfpold ep[i]s[copus] c[on]clusi.

✠ *Ego Ælfstan Ep*[i]s[copus] c[on]sensi.[5]

✠ *Ego Æðelgar Ep*[i]s[copus] c[on]solidaui.

✠ Ego Æðelsige ep[i]s[copus] roboraui.

✠ *Ego Ælfheh Ep*[i]s[copus] adq[ui]eui.[6]

✠ Ego Ærcpẏ[7] ep[i]s[copus] inpressi.

✠ *Ego Sigeric ep*[i]s[copus] no[n] renui.[8]

Et ceteri[9] duces. abbates. [et] ministri. viginti [et] un[us].[10]

TEXT

National Library of Wales, Aberystwyth, Peniarth MS. 390 (cited here as the Peniarth Cartulary), ff. 178ᵛ–179ʳ (old numbering pp. 356–7), written c. 1240 × 1264. According to the cartulary scribe, the text was prefaced by a chrismon. There is no boundary clause in the surviving text, and several other clauses are abbreviated, as is the witness list.

EDITION

The charter is hitherto unpublished. In this edition, formulas shared with K 664 are given in italic, and abbreviated clauses are

[1] K 664: 'praedicta terra circumcincta clarescit' inserted. The bounds are omitted in our MS.

[2] There is an unnecessary abbreviation mark over the first 'a'.

[3] K 664: 'his testibus consentientibus quorum nomina infra carraxata sunt' inserted.

[4] 'consensi' in K 664.

[5] 'adquieui' in K 664, where the order of subscriptions differs slightly.

[6] 'adnotaui' in K 664.   [7] *Sic*, for 'Æscwig'.

[8] 'conclusi' in K 664.   [9] 'et ceteri' scored through in MS.

[10] The list in K 664 names 4 *duces*, 6 abbots, and 15 *ministri*, a total of 25 non-episcopal witnesses.

restored in footnotes by collation with K 664. Abbreviations of individual words are extended between square brackets. The cartulary punctuation is retained, and the text is prefaced by the Peniarth Cartulary rubric.

DATE AND WITNESS LIST

This is one of the five surviving charters of the year 987, the others being K 657–9 and *Liber de Hyda* p. 231. The indiction is compatible with the year of grace, as is the whole of the surviving witness list, comprising the archbishops of Canterbury and York, and the bishops of Crediton, Selsey, Winchester, Ramsbury, London, Sherborne, and Dorchester. The charter is the earliest evidence for the accession of Ælfwold to the see of Crediton; probably it was issued later than the other four texts surviving from 987.

HISTORY

A thegn named Æðelsige received 10 sulungs in Bromley in Kent in 987 (K 657). It is uncertain if he can be identified with the recipient of *Æsce*.

FORMULAS

These are practically identical with those appearing in K 664, a diploma from the *Codex Wintoniensis* concerning land in Wiltshire, issued early in 988. Of the other charters issued in 987, K 658 repeats the first line of the proem, and together with K 657 parts of the dispositive clause, most of the anathema, the introduction to the bounds, and the dating clause; K 659 has the entire proem, the anathema, and parts of the king's title. The proem appears only once elsewhere (K 1304, a derived text dated 1014), so that it seems reasonable to assume that K 657–9, 664, and Bu xxv are all chancery texts drawn up by the same scribe.

Apart from the proem, most of the formulas of Bu xxv originate in diplomas of the mid-tenth century. For example, the introduction to the bounds is a modification of that appearing only in charters of the period 956 × 962 (CS 948, 974, 983, 992, 997, 1026, 1028, 1045, 1093), and the anathema, first encountered in 931 (CS 683), recurs in 959 (CS 1045) and is very common for the next twenty years, after which it is seen only in derived texts (e.g. K 725, from an exemplar dated 931, and K 711, which copies the formulas of CS 1268). *Angliene* in the king's title is a slip for *Angligene* (cf. 641, 707, 715, 1301, 1303; Muchelney IV, Crispin p. 167); the latter form appears in the rubric. The letter 'g' is similarly omitted in some words in several Crediton charters of the period, cf. Chaplais, *Exeter*, p. 12. The chrismon, as reproduced by the cartulary scribe, is similar to one current in the period 961 × 966 (see No. xxi). It could well be that the composer of this Burton charter and of K 664 was using a Chancery charter of the period 961 × 962 for his exemplar.

LOCATION

Æsce was a common name, and there can be no certainty as to the location, in the absence of detailed bounds. The duodecimal unit of assessment suggests (but in no way proves) that we are dealing with an estate in the carucated portion of the Danelaw. Ash in Derbyshire might be considered, but the high assessment of 12 *mansae* is against this; in the carucated parts of the Danelaw, *mansae* in a tenth-century royal diploma would stand for carucates, but the DB assessment of Ash was only 16 bovates. It is however quite near to Burton Abbey. But in my opinion a rather more likely possibility is that the *Æsce* of this charter represents the original uncompounded name of Ashford in Derbyshire, for which we have already an earlier charter in the Burton series (Bu IV). By the time of the Confessor, this royal manor together with its twelve berewicks gelded for 22 carucates; Ashford itself might well have accounted for 12 of these (VCH *Derbys.* I, p. 332b).

XXVI. KING ÆTHELRED II TO HIS THEGN WULFRIC. LAND AT BEDINTUN, STAFFORDSHIRE. A.D. 996

Carta. Æþelredi regis de Bedintun. dcccc. xcuj. Ind[ictione]. ix. f[ac]ta Þulfrico.

IN NOMINE D[OMI]NI N[OST]RI IH[ESU] CHR[IST]I. Omnib[us] quib[us] Chr[ist]ianitatis censuram a[1] d[e]i arcipotentis poli p[er] suam largifluum[2] m[isericord]iam concessum est. Q[uo]d huiu(s ins)tantis[3] labentisque vitæ prosperitas totis nisib[us] restaurare p[er]ditos ac nefandos. p[er] illius auxilium possumus. Ceu spalmigr(a)phus[4] ita fando dixit. Initium[5]

---

[1] 'a' inserted above the line by the same hand.

[2] *Sic*, for 'largifluam'.

[3] The cartulary copyist supplied 'presantis' for this lacuna, but Bu XVII shows that the correct word is 'instantis'.

[4] *Sic*, for 'psalmigraphus'.   [5] Psalm cxi. 10.

sapientiæ timor (D)[OMI]NI. Quapropter. Ego Æðelred. rex
anglor[um] ac totius brittanicę telluris gubernator et rector.
Cuida[m] meo fideli ministro quem nonnulli uocitant noto
uocamine. Þulfrici. A(li)quam partem t[er]re. In loco qui dicitur bediNTUN.¹ Vt habeat ac possideat. quand(iu) uiuat. Et
post sé cuicumq[ue] uoluerit heredi derelinquat. In æternam
hereditatem. Sit aute(m p)rædictum rus liberu[m] ab omni
mundiali obstaculo (cu)m omnibus ad sé ríte p[er]tinentib(u)s.
Campis. pascuis. pratis. siluis. sine expeditione. Et pontis.
arcisue Instructione. Siquis aute(m) infringere temptauerit
q[uo]d absit. Sciat se ration(em) redditurum coram d[e]o et
angelis eius. Nisi prius hic digna satisfactione emendare maluc-
rit. Istis terminis a(mbitu)r prædicta (tell)us. Her sutelat þa
landgemæru into bedintun. Þ is ærest to berhtelmes treo. ⁊ spa
forð to mearðes (le)age ⁊ spa forð ofer þa blacelege² to sproges
forda of sproges forda andlang þær broces to gate brẏcge. of gate
brẏcge into spompes næpe. ⁊ of spompes hnæpe. into sceddern
þorn. of sceadder þorn ofer þæne mor into þa[m] sur æppeltreo
æt þære nearapan sætan. ⁊ fra[m] þære nearapan sætan in
þæne holgan broc æt pulfgares more. ⁊ spa forð andlanges³
þæs broces forð Þ hit cẏmð to þam scaman forda. and of
þa[m] scaman forda andlang þæs sices Þ hit cymð to þam
smæle æcels. ⁊ þanon to þam blacan hale. ⁊ þanon in þone
broc. ⁊ spa forð andlangas þæs broces forð Þ hit cẏmð to
brẏxies mæne peig. ⁊ þanone oð Þ hit cẏmð to godrices lea.
⁊ of godrices lea to pulfstanes forda. ⁊ þanone oð Þ hit cẏmð
under þære blacan ecge to þære srtæte⁴ ⁊ ofer þa stræte. eft
in(to ber)htelmes treo:– Hic bellus⁵ caraxatus est anno
incarnationis d[omi]nicę. d. cccc. xc. ui. indictione. ix. his
testibus consentientibus quorum nomina inferius annotantur ∴

✠ Ego æðelred rex anglor[um] hoc n[ost]r[u]m donu[m]
f(irm)a ratione roborare curaui. Ego ælfric dorouernensis
æcclesiæ archie[piscopu]s. Signum s[an]c[t]e crucis imposui.
Ego eald(ul)f eboracensis æccl[esi]ę archiep[iscopu]s consensi.

---

¹ 'i', initially omitted, inserted by the same hand.
² 'le', initially omitted, inserted by the same hand.
³ 'n', initially omitted, inserted by the same hand.
⁴ *Sic*, for 'stræte'.
⁵ *Sic*. The cartulary copyist renders this 'libellus', no doubt correctly.

Ego ælfheah Þintoniensis ep[iscopu]s. iussu d[omi]ni (mei annotaui). Ego Þ(ulf)stan lundoniensis æccl[esi]ę ęp[iscopu]s¹ assensu[m] prebui. Ego ælfheah licetfeldnensis² æccl[esi]ę ep[iscopu]s adquieui. Ego æscpig dorcensis æccl[esi]ę ep[iscopu]s subscripsi. Ego ordbriht australiu[m] saxonu[m] æccl[esi]e ep[iscopu]s titulaui. Ego Goduuine ep[iscopu]s. Ego ælfðrȳð mater regis. Ego æþestan filius regis. Ego ecgbriht filius regis. Ego eadred filius regis. Ego ælfsige abba[as]. Ego ælfþeard abb[as]. Ego Þulgar abb[as]. Ego bȳrhælm³ abb[as]. Ego leofric abb[as]. Ego bȳrhtnoð abb[as]. Ego kenulf abb[as]. Ego Æðelpard. dux. Ego ælfric dux. Ego leafpine.⁴ dux. Ego leofsige. dux. Ego æðelm(æ)r minister. Ego ordulf min[ister]. Ego æðelmær min[ister]. Ego brȳhtpold. min[ister]. Ego æðelric. min[ister]. Ego æðelpard. mi(nister). Ego leofpine. min[ister]. Ego Goduuine minister.

ENDORSEMENTS

In the main hand:
✠ Bedintunes boc.
In the Peniarth Cartulary hand:
Ethelredus regnauit anno ab incarnatione domini Dccccxciij. Bedentones boc. XXVI.

TEXTS

A. William Salt Library, Stafford, MS. 84/3/41. Late eleventh century. There is no published facsimile.

B. National Library of Wales, Aberystwyth, Peniarth MS. 390 (cited as the Peniarth Cartulary), f. 179 (old numbering p. 357), a mid-thirteenth-century copy of A with some clauses, including the witness list, abbreviated, and with the bounds omitted. A chrismon has been supplied by the copyist, either from Bu xxiv or from Bu xxvii.

EDITION

The charter is here edited for the first time, from A, with the original punctuation retained, and extensions of individual words in square brackets. Occasional lacunae due to tears are supplied between curved brackets, using the exemplars Bu xvii and xxvii, collated with B. The rubric is that supplied by the Peniarth Cartulary copyist.

¹ *Sic*, with 'ę' for 'e'.   ² *Sic*, for 'licetfeldensis'.
³ *Sic*, for 'byrhtelm'.   ⁴ *Sic*, for 'leofpine'.

PALAEOGRAPHY

The membrane is 54·6 cm. wide × 14·1 cm. long, and has been folded twice horizontally and four times vertically; the size of the folded membrane is approximately 14·7 cm. × 5·4 cm. There are a number of wide tears, producing several lacunae in the text; these do not appear to have been present when the charter was copied into B. The surviving text is evidently a late copy, for the names of the witness list are entered in continuous lines extending the full width of the membrane, instead of being arranged in columns. Moreover, except for the first witness, the names are not prefaced by crosses, as is the rule with original texts. A space was left for a chrismon in the top left-hand corner of the charter, but this has not been filled in. The whole text is in the hand of a single scribe, writing in the second half of the eleventh century, and probably late in this period. His script is insular, with a few scattered caroline elements; there is little differentiation between Latin and OE. There are occasional slips of spelling, and twice there is inversion of individual letters of words (*spalmigraphus, srtæte*). The scribe undertook some revision upon completion of his text, inserting above the line a number of letters that had been inadvertently omitted. It is instructive to compare the arrangement of the text with that of Bu xxxi, an original membrane of similar dimensions, but of very different format.

In the Latin text 'a' is caroline for the first two letters, and rounded thereafter. Latin 'd' is usually round-backed, but the straight-backed form occurs three times. Latin 'e' is usually horned, but the round-backed form does occur occasionally; in OE the 'e' is commonly horned. Insular 'g' has a closed tail; the second limb of OE 'h' is turned inwards regularly in the Latin text. Round, long, and low 's' are used in OE and Latin in all positions. The long form hardly descends below the line. 'r' is usually insular, but the caroline form does occur once in the Latin text. 'y' is straight-limbed and dotted throughout. 'ę' is often (but not invariably) used for terminal 'æ'. The 'ra' ligature is unusual. 'þ' is used initially, 'ð' medially and finally; the upstroke of 'ð' is long, and tagged to the left at the top. Punctuation is solely by dot, but a semicolon is used once as a mark of abbreviation, and the end of the clause introducing the witnesses is marked by a triangle of dots. The lines are ruled, and spacing between words is regular. There are no divided words at the ends of lines, but there is some variation in the size of the hand.

FORMULAS

Down to the commencement of the bounds, the whole text is derived from Bu XVII (with substitution of personal and place-names) and direct comparison of the membranes leaves one with no doubt that this very charter was used as the exemplar. Moreover, from the end of the bounds onwards, the whole text is derived from Bu XXVII (with omission of the names of a few witnesses), and here again it is clear that the scribe of Bu XXVI was working directly from Bu XXVII for his exemplar. For example, Ælfweard of Glastonbury appears second of the abbots in these two charters only; his normal position is first at this period.

One concludes that the charter was composed by a Burton scribe in the second half of the eleventh century, and probably after the Norman Conquest, and that he used for his exemplars two charters from the abbey's muniment collection. The intention, evidently, was to create a title-deed 'proving' that *Bedintun* had been booked to Wulfric Spot, the abbey's founder.

BOUNDARY

In spite of a diligent search, I have been unable to locate this. The occurrence of 'mor' in the bounds suggests a Staffordshire location.

HISTORY

Bedintun was given to Burton in Wulfric Spot's will. It does not appear in DB, but the twelfth-century Burton surveys show that it was held with Pillatonhall, near Penkridge, Staffordshire (W. Salt 1916, p. 31). It was certainly not identical with Pillaton, as assumed by Sawyer (S pp. 270, 430, 491). The bounds do not fit Pillaton, and the late Burton surveys show that *Bedintun* and Pillaton were two distinct estates. *Bedintun* does not recur in records after the twelfth century.

XXVII. King Æthelred II to his thegn Wulfric. 3 hides at Abbots Bromley, Staffordshire. a.d. 996

Carta Æþelredi regis facta Þulfrico de Bromleg[e]. dcccc.xcuj.

Pollente perp[et]ualiter d[omi]ni n[ost]ri Ih[es]u Chr[ist]i regno. huius instabilitas uitae fortuiti(s at)teritur Casibus. ac uariis uilescendo meroribus. Terminum sue Commutabilitatis iam iamq[ue] praesignat affuturum ꞉ Ut ueritatis praesagio prędicta (eiu)s multiformia malorum iacula. electorum corda non ad desperationem seu tedium diuini amoris p[er]uer(t)ant ꞉ uerum [et]iam ad desideria regni celestis. [et] ad piae deuotionis famulatum magis magisq[ue] acuant ꞉ iuxta illud dominicum. His autem fieri incipientib[us] Respi(c)ite et leuate capita u[est]ra ꞉ quoniam appropinquat redemptio u[estr]a. Huiusmodi diuini documenti oraculis pręmonitus EGO AEÐELRED rex anglorum. Cuida[m] meo fideli ministro a populis Þulfric apellato. quanda[m] ruris trium scilic[et] cassatoru[m] in loco que[m] accolę uicini æt bromleage cognominant partem impendo ꞉ ut ipse dum sospitate[m] uitae habuerit illa[m] sibi in usu[m] necessari[um] sicut mater ei largita est uoti compos optineat ꞉ et post uitae suae terminu[m] Cuicumq[ue] sibi placuerit relinquat superstiti. Consistat autem suprascripta tellus ab omni seruitute secura. Tribus exceptis. Expeditione. Arcis. pontisue Constructione. Qui uero n[ost]r[u]m hoc donum euertere laborauerit ꞉ Timeat se in profundo auerni inmersum a[et]ernaliter torqueri ꞉ Nisi quantotius a sua peruersitate discedat. Attamen siquislib[et] antiquum siue nouum protraxerit libellum. [et] hanc N[ostr]am titulationem superare nisus fuerit, binis mort(i)s periculis obiurgetur obnoxius. quia aut rapina. aut furto illum subdole adeptus est. Huiusmodi terminis prędicta tellus circumducitur.

Of ðam lýtlan hlapan to þan longan snapan on ða strǽte forþ ǽfter strete oð cume to þan rea(d)an ácon ⁊ ðǽr ðþers ofer ða puda þǽt cýme in pire broces heafde ⁊ ǽfter pire broc ðǽt hit gǽþ in bliðe up ǽfter bliþe oð hit cýme in ceabbe broc

æfter broce þæt cume in ðan forde from ðam forde æfter þære
strete þe ligeð cumb þelle léa oð cume on þa grene þege ⁊ forð
æfter grene þege oð hit cȳmeþ eft to ðan lȳtlan laupan. ðus hit
hæfde eadelm ⁊ ælfred ⁊ æþelpold spa sp(a hit) þulfsige ðé
blaca ⁊ æscbrȳht hit ge ærdeden heom. Hic libellus caraxatus est
anno Incarnationis d[omi]nicę. dccc̄. x̄c̄. ui. indict(io)ne ix. his
testibus consentientibus quorum nomi(na) inferius annotantur.

✠ EGO Æþelred rex anglor[um] hoc n[ost]r[u]m donum
    (f)irma ratione roborare curaui.

✠ EGO Ælfric dorno(u)ernensis ęccl[es]ię archi(episcopus
    sig)num s[an]c[t]æ crucis imposui.

✠ EGO Ealdulf eboracensis ecclesię archiep[iscopus] Con-
    sensi.

✠ EGO Ælfæh þintoniensis cccl[esi]e ep[iscopu]s iussu
    d[omi]ni mei Annotaui.

✠ EGO Ulfstan lundoniensis eccl[esi]e ep[iscopu]s Assen-
    sum prebui.

✠ EGO Ælfheah licetfeldensis eccl[esi]e ep[iscopu]s Adqui-
    eui.

✠ EGO Æscpig dorcensis eccl[esi]e ep[iscopu]s Subscripsi.

✠ EGO Ordbrȳht australium saxonum eccl[esi]e ep[iscopu]s
    Titulaui.

✠ EGO Godþine hrofensis eccl[esi]e ep[iscopu]s Non res-
    titi.

✠ EGO Alfþold Cridiensis eccl[esi]e ep[iscopu]s Co(n)-
    fi(r)maui.

✠ EGO Uulfsige Scireburnensis eccl[esi]e (episcopus In-
    pressi).

✠ EGO Sigar Uuȳllensis eccl[esi]e ep[iscopu]s Nil (oppo)-
    sui.[1]

✠ EGO Ealdred Cornubiensis eccl[esi]e ep[iscopu]s Corro-
    (bor)aui.

✠ EGO Sigeferð [   ]² ep[iscopu]s Dig(num i)udicaui.

✠ EGO (A)ðulf Herefordensis eccl[esi]e ep[iscopu]s Con-
    sol(id)aui.

[1] Supplied conjecturally; see the witness list to K 698. There is room for
only four letters.
[2] Space left in the MS., not filled subsequently.

✠ EGO[1] AELFÐRYÐ (mater regi)s.

✠ EGO Æþestan fil(ius re)gis.[2]

✠ EGO Ecgbẏrht filiu(s) regis.

✠ EGO Eadmund filiu(s) regis.

✠ EGO Eadred filius regis.

✠ EGO Ælfsige ABBAS.

✠ EGO Ælfþeard abbas.

✠ EGO Wulfgar abbas.

✠ EGO Bẏrhtelm abbas.

✠ EGO Leofric abbas.

✠ EGO Bẏrht(noð a)bbas.

✠ EGO Keanulf abbas.

✠ EGO Æþelric (a)bbas.

✠ EGO ÆÞELUUEARD (DU)X.

✠ EGO Ælfric (D)ux.

✠ EGO[3] LEOFÞINE DUX.

✠ EGO LEofsige DUX.

✠ EGO Æþelmær Minister.

✠ EGO Ordulf MIN[ISTER].

✠ EGO Æþelmær mIN[ISTER].

✠ EGO Bẏrhtþold Min[ister].

✠ EGO Æþelric Min[ister].

✠ EGO Æþelþeard Min[ister].

✠ EGO Þulfþeard Min[ister].

✠ EGO Leofþine Min[ister].

✠ EGO Leofþine R[4] Min[ister].

✠ EGO Siþerd Min[ister].

✠ EGO SIRED Min[ister].

✠ EGO GODÞINE Min[ister].

✠ [5]

ENDORSEMENTS

In a thirteenth-century hand:
Ethelredus Rex Wulfrico Bromlēg.

[1] Commencement of second column of witnesses.

[2] From here onwards, supplied letters are all from Bu xxvi.

[3] Commencement of third column of witnesses.

[4] This 'R' appears to have been an abbreviation, possibly of a by-name, introduced to distinguish between the two Leofwines.

[5] *Sic* MS.

In the Peniarth Cartulary hand:
XXVII.

TEXTS

A. William Salt Library, Stafford, MS. 84/4/41, in a hand perhaps
a little later than the date claimed for the charter. There is no
published facsimile.

B. National Library of Wales, Aberystwyth, Peniarth MS. 390
(cited here as the Peniarth Cartulary), f. 179ʳᵛ (old numbering
pp. 357–8), a copy of A with the witness list abbreviated. The
chrismon of MS. A is reproduced fairly accurately, except that the
copyist has added a tail to the 'P'.

EDITION

The charter is hitherto unpublished. In this edition of A, abbreviations are extended silently between square brackets, but the original
punctuation is retained. Letters now lost in A through tears are
supplied from B, between curved brackets. The rubric and chrismon
are from B.

PALAEOGRAPHY

The membrane is 46 cm. wide × 29 cm. long, and has been
folded three times horizontally and three times vertically; the size
when folded is approximately 12·6 cm. × 7·2 cm. The whole
charter is in a single hand, a good caroline minuscule (with insular
script for OE), probably of the early eleventh century; it is possible
therefore that it is a copy made at Burton soon after that abbey's
foundation. That the surviving text is a copy is further suggested by
the lack of a contemporary endorsement, and by the inability of the
scribe to enter the correct see after the name of Bishop Sigeferð; he
also wrote one too many crosses for the number of witnesses appearing
in the last column. The chrismon originated in 956 (Bu XVI), but it
was current also in the early eleventh century (OS Facs II, Winchester
College IV; Bu XXIX, XXX, XXXIV, XXXV).

The scribe distinguishes carefully between Latin and OE script;
insular 'd', 'f', 'h', and 'r' are used regularly in OE, caroline in
Latin. Both rounded and caroline 'a' occur in the Latin text. The
ampersand is used regularly for the letters 'et' in all places in Latin
words. Tall 'e' is used only in ligatures. The tail of insular 'g' is
closed. 'ẏ' is invariably rounded and dotted. 'þ' and 'ð' are used
indifferently; the upstroke of 'ð' is prominent. Descenders are
straight in OE, not curved to the left. 'æ' ligatures occur. A dot is
used very sparingly for punctuation in OE; in Latin, punctuation is

usually with the sign ' : '. The lines are ruled, the layout is competent, the spelling is good. The hand is very close to, but perhaps not identical with, that of Bu xxxi. The script resembles that of plate 3(b) in Bishop's *English Caroline Minuscule*, perhaps from Peterborough.

RECIPIENT

The thegn Wulfric to whom Abbots Bromley is given by this charter was presumably Wulfric Spot, who willed the estate to Burton Abbey in 1002 × 1004 (No. 39). The charter says Wulfric is to hold the estate as his mother held it; she was Wulfrun, the foundress of Wolverhampton.

DATE AND WITNESSES

Sawyer (S p. 270) wrongly dates this charter 993. The correct date is 996, given both in the charter and in the rubric to the Peniarth Cartulary version. The indiction is compatible with the year of grace, as is the whole of the witness list. It is possible that all the surviving authentic charters of the year 996 were witnessed on the same date, at a synod at Chelsea (K 696; cf. K 1291–2; *Liber de Hyda* pp. 242–53).

The sees of all the witnessing bishops are named in the charter, with the exception of Sigeferð, who was bishop of Lindsey (K 698). The identification of sees of witnessing bishops is a feature of a number of charters issued during the period 993 × 1001. The names follow of Ælfðryð, the king's mother (who shares with the king the distinction of having her name in capitals), and four of the æthelings. These all appear in K 684, dated 993, and in K 698, dated 997, after which Ælfðryð ceases to witness. It seems likely that the æthelings were included in the witness lists of King Æthelred's charters as soon as they were born. Thus Eadwig first appears in 997 (K 698), Edgar in 1001 (K 706), Edward (the later king) in 1005 (K 714), and Alfred in 1013 (K 1308; ECEE pp. 193–4).

The houses of the abbots, who witness next, may be identified from the lists in K 684 and 698. They are New Minster, Glastonbury, Abingdon, Exeter, Muchelney, Ely, Peterborough, and Athelney, in that order. The four ealdormen were from the Western Shires, Hampshire and Wiltshire, the Hwicce, and the East Saxons. The witnessing thegns all occur elsewhere in charters of the period. There seems no particular reason why the names of two of them should have been entered in capitals.

HISTORY

Our reconstruction of the pre-Conquest history of Abbots Bromley hinges on the identification of *Wulfsige ðe blaca*, named as a former owner in the boundary clause of this charter, with the Wulfsige Maur' who was given by King Edmund 40 hides in Staffordshire, including an estate named *Bromleage*, in 942 (No. 82). There is good reason to believe that *Bromleage* at this period still comprised a large tract of woodland and broom-covered scrubland, which had been cleared and cultivated sufficiently for only a low level of hidage assessment to be imposed upon it. As late as 1086, it was one of the most sparsely settled areas of the county. The two settlements known later as Abbots and Kings Bromley were each assessed at three hides. After Abbots Bromley had been used by Wulfric Spot for the endowment of Burton in 1004, its demesne was relieved of its geld liability, and the reduced assessment of $\frac{1}{2}$ hide was laid upon the estate and its unnamed appendages.

Wulfsige the Black appears to have held Abbots Bromley jointly with one Æscbyrht, who is otherwise unknown to us; possibly he was Wulfsige's tenant. The estate then passed into the hands of three men named Eadhelm, Alfred, and Æthelwold, who may have been co-parceners. Next we find Wulfrun, Wulfric Spot's mother, in possession of the estate. She may have been dead by 996 when it was granted to Wulfric by Æthelred II.

FORMULAS

Much of the diplomatic of this charter is unique; unlike many of Æthelred's charters, it does not appear to be based on the formulas of earlier reigns. The dating clause and forms of attestation are also unique. Some of the phrases, however, are echoed in other royal diplomas of the period; in the anathema, for example, *qui vero evertere* occurs in K 706–7, 714, *hoc nostrum donum* in ECEE p. 187, *libellum* in K 1289, 1303, 1305, and *antiquum vel novum* in K 1296, 1303.

There is no reason to doubt the charter's authenticity, but the location of the scriptorium where the missing original was drawn up remains doubtful; it is unlikely to be a chancery charter. The latter part of the charter was used for the concluding sections of Bu xxvi, see p. 200.

BOUNDS

The bounds of the three hides at Abbots Bromley can be shown to follow, with little variation, the bounds of the present-day parish, which is limited to the east by the Pur Brook, to the south by the Little Blythe, and to the west by the Tad Brook. They may be traced on OS 2½" sheets 02, 12. The perambulation proceeds in a clockwise direction:

1. from the small *hlaw*. A hillock (or more probably a burial mound) at or near grid ref. 076295. I have been unable to locate it, but Scounslow Green, 1 mile eastwards, is probably the site of a second *hlaw*.

2. to the long *snape*. Probably OE **snæp*, 'a boggy piece of ground', is intended here. Big Snape lies 2 miles to the south, in a poorly drained part of Bagot's Wood. The charter bounds run eastwards through marshy ground, along a footpath leading to New Thorntree Farm.

3. on to the *stræte*. Crossing Hobb Lane at 090292.

4. to the *readan ácon*. Presumably a copper variety of *Quercus robur*, the native species. The Red Oak, *Quercus rubra*, is a North American species of recent introduction. The bounds turn sharply southwards at 103283.

5. across the wood to *pire broces heafde*. Up Dixon's Hill and through Birch Coppice in Bagot's Wood to Hen Pool, 104275, the source of the Pur Brook. The brook probably takes its name from OE *pur*, 'bittern, snipe', rather than from OE *pirige* 'pear tree'.

6. along Pur Brook until it runs into the *bliðe*. The present boundary runs down the Pur Brook for about 5 miles, leaving it to join the Little Blithe at 097207.

7. up the (Little) Blithe until it reaches *ceabbe broc*. This is a patronymic, cf. *ceabban sol* in CS 282; *Ceabba may have been a pet form of Ceadda. Later there was confusion with OE *tadda*, 'toad', and the modern name is Tad Brook. The valleys of Tad Brook and the Little Blithe now form two arms of the Blithefield Reservoir. Tad Brook once joined the Blithe at 060236, which still forms the parish boundary.

8. along the brook until it reaches the ford. Of the three possible sites for fords across Tad Brook, the one furthest upstream at 067292 appears the most likely. Here the brook is crossed by a footpath leading from Broomfield to Kingston.

9. to the street at *cumb welle léa*. Cuckold's Haven, on the B5013 road from Abbots Bromley to Uttoxeter, 073295.

10. along the greenway to the little *hlaw*. Along a field boundary back to the starting-point.

XXIX. King Æthelred to his thegn.
Land unspecified. a.d. 1007

Carta Æþelredi Regis de terra. annis et cetera. dcccc.xc. bisque
quinis none septenis.

Cum eni[m] mos liquide in ext[re]ma decrepitac[i]one hui[us] senescentis mu[n]di viteq[ue] mom[en]tanée tamq[ua]m ultime p[ro]sapie abortiuos filios p[ro]creatos nouerim[us]꞉ op[us] om[n]imodis h[ab]em[us] ut tanto in hoc laborioso spatiolo sim[us] cautiores꞉ quanto patulo scim[us] illecebrosas nu[n]c antiq[ui] hostis plus p[ri]scor[um] temp[or]e patru[m] augme[n]tatas fore temptac[i]onu[m] suadelas. quib[us] animo acrit[er] q[ua]timur iunctis ima simul mortuis calamitatu[m] informac[i]onib[us] q[ua]s in corpusculo clematis n[ost]ri cordisq[ue] iugi scrutinio g[ra]ui macerac[i]one sustinem[us]. ut pote uelut pauidi sub vigiliaru[m] excubiis mancipii bellis attriti. clade multati ext[re]me p[re]stolantes clangore[m] buccine quo gen[us] omne hominu[m] quod fuit. q[uo]d est. [et] quod erit futuru[m] ad vni[us] aggregabitur verissimi arbit[ri]s sub attonito pauore examen scunta[1] sine cunctatione cunctoru[m] secreta p[er]spicaci intuitu enucleantis ac condigna tu[n]c meritis rependentis. Hec ego Æþelredus regali infula Anglor[um] pop[u]lis Chr[ist]o allubescente subthonizat[us][2] condono cuida[m] meo minist[ro] talem t[er]ram. [et] c[etera]. Scripta est h[ec] cartula decursis annis ab Incarn[atione] Chr[ist]i .dcccc.xc. bisq[ue] q[ui]nis n[o]ne septenis. Indict[ione].v. hiis fauentib[us] q[uo]r[um] hic subt[us] onomata [et] dignitatu[m] vides officia.

Ego Æþelred regia munifice[n]tia fret[us] hoc datu[m] q[uo]d dedi agye. crucis signamine p[er]petualit[er] c[on]f[i]rmo.
Ego Ælfeh Arch[i]ep[iscopu]s co[n]cessi.
Ego Þulfstan Arch[iepiscopus] co[n]sensi.
Ego Aþulf Ep[iscopu]s co[n]faui.
Ego lyuing Ep[iscopu]s coniuui.
Ego Godpine ep[iscopu]s co[n]pinxi.

[1] *Sic,* ? for 'cuncta'.   [2] *Sic,* for 'subthronizatus'.

Ego Alfpold ep[iscopu]s consc[ri]psi.

Ego Æþelric ep[iscopu]s co[n]sculpsi.

Ego Ælfhun. ep[iscopu]s concaui.

Ego Ælfhelm ep[iscopu]s c[on]signaui.

Ego býrhtpold ep[iscopu]s c[on]firmaui.

Ego Æþelpold ep[iscopu]s co[n]carraxaui.

Et cet[er]i. Clitones.vj. Abb[at]es iiij or. Comites iij. patricius un[us]. Ministri sexdecim.

Ego Þinsye monachus qui hoc testamentu[m] dictitaui atq[ue] p[er]scripsi.

TEXT

National Library of Wales, Aberystwyth, Peniarth MS. 390 (cited here as the Peniarth Cartulary), ff. 181ᵛ–182ʳ (old numbering pp. 362–3), written c. 1240 × 1264.

EDITION

The charter is hitherto unpublished. In this edition, abbreviations are extended between square brackets. The original punctuation is left unchanged.

DATE AND WITNESSES

The date, 1007, is given in an agonizingly complicated form. One encounters such circumlocutions commonly in MSS. of the tenth and early eleventh centuries, but I have not noticed such an elaborate arrangement in other charters of the period. The indiction is correct for the date, as is the surviving portion of the witness list, which includes the archbishops of Canterbury and York, and the bishops of Rochester, Crediton, Dorchester, Hereford, Sherborne, Ramsbury, Wells, London, and Winchester. The high position given in the list to Bishop Æthulf of Hereford is characteristic of the period. The sees of Selsey, Elmham, and Lichfield are unrepresented. The six *clitones* would be the æthelings Athelstan, Edmund, Eadred, Eadwig, Edgar, and Edward, as in K 1303 and 1304, both issued in 1007. The three *comites* would be Ealdormen Ælfric of Hampshire, Eadric of Mercia, and Leofwine of the Hwicce, as in K 1303. The occurrence of a person having the title of *patricius* is unique among the witness lists of the period. The charter was witnessed by 16 thegns, compared with 19 witnessing K 1303, and 15 witnessing K 1304. The list concludes with the name of the monk Wynsige (presumably from Burton), who is said to have composed (*dictitavi*) and written (*perscripsi*) the charter (*testamentum*). He is otherwise unknown.

FORMULAS

The formulas are unique. Some of the Latinity is Hisperic, especially in the elaborate proem, and individual words and phrases are encountered occasionally in charters of Athelstan and his successors, e.g. *subthronizatus* in CS 898, 924; *munificentia* in CS 663, 709; *codono* in CS 708, 714 (and see Chaplais, *Exeter*, p. 14); *regalium infularum* in CS 707; *allubuscente* in CS 924, 949.

AUTHENTICITY

It has been postulated elsewhere (pp. 24, 33) that the texts of non-chancery charters of this period were usually completed as far as the bounds, then submitted to the king's council for ratification, after which the text was completed by the addition of the witness list. Accepting for the moment this sequence of events, then there are some really puzzling features about the text now being considered. It must have been written at first on a separate membrane, or it would not have been entered in the cartulary. Moreover, the charter was first drawn up at or near the date claimed in its dating clause; not only is the witness list wholly compatible, but the text is prefaced (in the cartulary version, and therefore probably in its predecessor) by a chrismon of a form contemporary with this date (it resembles those of Bu xxx, and OS Facs II, Winchester College IV).

If the monk Wynsige (presumably from Burton) who composed the original charter was recording a specific grant of land, surely he would have entered in his text the names of the recipient and of the estate conveyed. Similarly, if these names had been present in the text lying before the cartulary copyist, we can be sure he would have transcribed them, as with others in the Burton series; the copyist might abbreviate the witness list, and perhaps he would omit part or the whole of the dispositive clause, the clause dealing with the obligations of the recipient, the anathema, and the bounds; but to omit the names of the estate and its recipient is to destroy all the evidentiary value of the charter – there is no sense in it and the cartulary copyist did not deal in this way with any other of the 37 texts lying before him.

We must assume, then, that these names were missing in the text composed by Wynsige. Why was this so? Wynsige's composition could not have been intended as an exemplar for recording a genuine transaction, for in such a case there would be no point in completing his charter by adding to it a witness list copied (presumably) from some authentic contemporary instrument. The presence of this list in the cartulary version, and the absence of the names of the estate and its recipient, and also the boundary clause, lead one to consider seriously the hypothesis that Wynsige's composition was intended as an exemplar for a forgery. Such an explanation, however, can only be tentative; we have insufficient information to reconstruct with any degree of certainty the succession of events that brought this text into being.

XXX. King Æthelred II to Abbot Wulfgeat. Grant of 2½ hides at Rolleston, Staffordshire, in exchange for Arlington (in Bibury) and Aldsworth, both in Gloucestershire. a.d. 1008

Carta Æþelredi Regis de Roluestone pro Ealdesþyrðe et Alfredetone. Anno M.º viij.[1]

℘ *Uniu[er]sor[um] conditor [et] creator d[omi]n[u]s n[oste]r Ih[esu]s Chr[istu]s seruili forma semetip[su]m p[ro] n[ost]ra redempcione circu[m]tegens. [et] int[er] ho[m]i[n]es deus homoq[ue] verus conu[er]satus cunctos fideles salutarib[us] instruit documentis [et]*[2] *ad celestia gaudia toto mentis conamine q[ua]mtoci[us] p[ro]p[er]emus talit[er] om[n]ib[us] p[ro]clamat dicens. Thesaurizate*[3] *uob[is] thesauros in celo. ubi nec erugo n[ec] tinea ext[er]minat. [et] ubi fures no[n] effodi[u]nt n[ec] furantur. Hinc co[m]pu[n]ctus*[4] *ego ethelred*[5] *rex anglor[um] [et] cu[m] substa[n]cia*[6] *m[ichi] ab ip[s]o d[omi]no ubertim donata celestia mercari cupiens cuidam meo fideli abbati*[7] *Þulfgeto cognominato q[ua]ndam t[er]re p[ar]tic[u]lam cu[m] eo mutuaui. Ille m[ichi] dedit duas villas. vna vocat[ur] Ealdesworthe*[8] *alia uero Ælfredintun. q[uia] ualde longe erant a monasterio suo. Ideo rogauit obnixis p[re]cib[us] vt aliq[ua]m terram ei co[n]cederem iuxta monasteriu[m] in co[n]gruu[m] locu[m]. [Et] ego dedi ei in loco que[m] solicole vicini æt Roluestun*[9] *appellant. idest duos*

1 This rubric is from B. The rubric in A is 'mutatio duarum villarum pro villa de Rolueston'.

2 *Sic*, for *ut*, as in Bu xxxiv, p. 235. 3 Matt. vi. 20.

4 B *co[m]puctus*. 5 B *Æþelred*.

6 B *cum consubstancia* (omitting '*et*'). Comparison with No. xxxiv shows the A version to be the correct reading.

7 B *abbate*. 8 B *Ealdesþyrðe*. 9 B *Rolfeston*.

cassatos [et] dimidiu[m]. libent[er] inpendo ad monasteriu[m] beati
b[e]n[e]dicti om[n]iumq[ue] s[an]c[t]or[um] q[uo]d est in villula
Bўrtuniensis situm. ad usum dei seruor[um] eidem loco famulantiu[m]
in p[er]petuo confirmo hereditatem. q[ua]tin[us] victum vestitutu[m]-
q[ue] atq[ue] omne[m]¹ utilitate[m] eis administ[ra]ndu[m] q[ua]mdiu
hui[us] volubilis orbis vergit[ur] rota. Si aut[em] contigerit tempore
aliq[uo]² que[m]piam hominu[m] alique[m] antiq[ui]ore[m] libru[m]
cont[ra] isti[us] libri lib[er]tatem p[ro]ducere : p[ro]nichilo co[m]-
putatur :³ Isto p[er] om[n]ia in sua stabilitate p[er]mane[n]te atq[ue]
vigente. Sit aut[em] hec p[re]scripta tellus ab om[n]ib[us] lib[er]a
s[e]c[u]laribus negociis. cu[m] om[n]ib[us] ad illam rite p[er]tinenti.
b[us] In campis. pascuis. p[ra]tis. siluis. aq[ua]rum⁴ cursib[us]-
trib[us] tantu[m] reb[us] exceptis que legaliter seruant[ur]. Hacten[us].
(idest expedic[i]o[n]e pontis. arcisue. co[n]struct[i]o[n]e.)⁵ Si q[ui]s
aut[em] quod no[n] optam[us] hoc n[ost]re munificencie donum
p[er]u[er]tere conamine stolido studuerit : collegio p[ri]uat[us] p[er]petue
felicitatis eru[m]pnam hauriat atrocissime calamitatis mortis n[isi]
ante t[er]minu[m] p[re]sumpc[i]one[m] hanc temeraria[m] legali
satisfactione emendare studuerit. Hiis metis (rus hoc giratur.

✠ Þis syndan þa langemera to Roluestune. Ærest of dufan
on hæcce of hæcce on þone greatan þorn of þan þorne to ðan
hæg stope æfter hæg stope to dottes hlape of dotdes hlape to
þere strete þær on ansidelege. of ansidelege on þa dic. of ðan
dice on ðan fulan sich of ðan fulan siche on pattiches æces of
pattices æces on þan holangrўfe þær ða ealdan broc holan
sўndan of ðan holan on þan ufer ende balcan of balcan to middel
lege. of middel lege to ðan scid hæge æfter scid hæge þpers ofer
bracan hўrste þ̃ on mæran broce dune mid broce to þan
stanigan forde þe ligeð to eadgares lege of ðan forde to
pulffeghes hæge and land⁶ hæges on þa ofesan æfter ofesan to
ðan fulan sўce þ̃ on þan broce of ðan broce on stoc legan ford
of ðan forde abiðan ofesan þ̃ on ðone dic hæge leofnaðes of ðan

---

¹ B omnium. Comparison with No. xxxiv shows the A version to be the
correct reading.
² B alico, omitting 'tempore'. A is preferable, see No. xxxiv.
³ Sic, for computetur. The same slip occurs in No. xxxiv.
⁴ B aquarumque, agreeing with No. xxxiv.
⁵ B omits this passage, substituting 'et cetera'.
⁶ Sic, for 'andlang'.

dice on þan fulan sẏce. æfter sice on pilebroc dun æfter broce
on þan fulan sic þe scot betux[1] tpam lundan æfter sice to
cnapan hẏlle of cnapan hẏlle to ðan hæg stope of ðan hæg stope
on þa deopan dæle of ðan dæle on dufan. on þa bradan strete
æt burtone. an lang stræte to pinstanes gemæra ut ðorh ðone
pudu to ðan þorne þer ða þeofes licgan æfter þære mæd
eafdan on ꝥ þuda aæfter[2] ofesan ꝥ eft on ðan bradan stræte.)[3]

Acta est (aut[em])[4] hec mutac[i]o anno d[omi]nice ap-
paric[i]onis M⁰.viij.⁰ indictio[n]e. vj.ᵃ Co[n]sentientib[us] hiis
testibus.[5]

✠ Ego Ethelred[6] rex angloru[m] hoc donu[m] p[er]petua
ditaui lib[er]tate.

✠ Ego Ethelstan[7] fili[us] regis.

✠ Ego Edmu[n]d[8] fili[us] regis.

✠ Ego Edred[9] fili[us] regis.

✠ Ego Edwig[10] fili[us] reg[is].

✠ Ego Edgar[11] f[ilius] reg[is].[12]

✠ Ego Ælfheah archiep[iscopu]s co[m]posui.

✠ Ego Þulstan archiep[iscopu]s conclusi.

✠ Ego Leofincg ep[iscopu]s co[n]signaui.

✠ Ego[13] Ælfhun ep[iscopu]s co[n]sensi.

✠ Ego Æþelric ep[iscopu]s co[n]dixi.

✠ Ego Æþelpold ep[iscopu]s c[on]f[ir]maui.

✠ Ego[14] Godpine ep[iscopu]s adquieui.

✠ Ego Ælfgar ep[iscopu]s adunaui.

Et cet[er]i Abb[at]es decem. Duces tres. [et] Ministri septem.

TEXTS

A. BM Loan MS. 30 (Marquess of Anglesey) (cited here as the
Anglesey Cartulary), ff. 10ʳᵛ (cf. Davis No. 91), dated c. 1230–41.
B. National Library of Wales, Aberystwyth, Peniarth MS. 390

[1] *Sic*, for 'betþux'.   [2] *Sic*, for 'æfter'.   [3] B omits the bounds.
[4] B omits 'autem'.   [5] B has 'Hiis testib[us] consentientibus'.
[6] B Æþelred.   [7] B Æþelstan.   [8] B Eadmund.
[9] B Eadred.   [10] Eadþig.   [11] B Eadgar.
[12] A ends here, with 'et cetera Archiepiscopi et episcopi'. The remainder
of the witness list is from B.
[13] The second column of witnesses begins here.
[14] The third column of witnesses begins here.

(cited here as the Peniarth Cartulary), f. 182^{rv} (old numbering pp. 363–4), dated c. 1240–64.

EDITIONS

1. S. Shaw, *The History and Antiquities of Staffordshire*, London, 2 vols., 1798–1801; I, p. 28, from MS. A.

2. This edition is from MS. A, collated with MS. B. Extensions of individual words appear between square brackets. Portions of the text surviving only in A are enclosed between round brackets. Those parts of the text appearing also in Bu xxxiv are printed in italic. The original punctuation is retained.

TRANSLATION

Bridgeman pp. 121–3.

DATE AND WITNESS LIST

The indiction is correct for the year of grace, and the whole of the witness list is compatible with the date. The sees represented are Canterbury, York, Wells, London, Sherborne, Winchester, Rochester, and Elmham. The numbers of abbots and ealdormen witnessing are normal for charters of the period, but usually more than seven thegns subscribe. The texts have survived of only two other royal diplomas issued in 1008. These are K 725 from Ely, utilizing for its exemplar a charter of King Athelstan dated 931, and K 1305 from Abingdon, notable for its use of the writ form in the dispositive clause. Of these, the witness list of K 725 is missing.

HISTORY

Ealdeswyrðe was located at Aldsworth in Gloucestershire by Bridgeman in 1916 (Bridgeman p. 123), and *Ælfredintun* was located at Arlington in Bibury, next to Aldsworth, by Finberg in 1964 (ECW p. 249). Both were given by Wulfric Spot to Burton Abbey in 1004, as part of its foundation endowment (K 710). Rolleston first occurs in Bu v, by which King Edmund gave it to Wulfric Spot's predecessor, Wulfsige the Black, in 942. Subsequently, Rolleston was bequeathed by Wulfric to his brother Ælfhelm, ealdorman of Deira, who was murdered in 1006. Evidently the estate came into the king's hands, and was used by him in the exchange recorded by the present charter. It was still rated at 2$\frac{1}{2}$ hides in 1086, but by then it was no longer the property of Burton; at the time of the Norman Conquest it was owned by Earl Morcar (Staffs DB no. 149). Rolleston is the only recorded Staffordshire possession of Morcar, and one is led to speculate that he held it as part of the lands of the Northumbrian earldom, rather than as a personal possession; in the same way, Conisbrough in Yorkshire WR, also given by Wulfric to Ælfhelm, appears to have remained a property held by the earls of Northumbria until the mid-eleventh century (ECEE p. 246). If so, the probability is that the exchange recorded in the present charter did not leave Rolleston in the possession of Burton Abbey for any great length of time, for it would appear to have been restored to the Northumbrian earldom before the tradition of its former connection with that earldom had been forgotten. Finally, it should be mentioned that this charter, if authentic, is the earliest evidence we have for the dedication of Burton Abbey to St Benedict and All Saints.

FORMULAS

The greater part of the charter is couched in a unique phraseology; one does not find such passages as *hinc compunctus, quamdiu huius volubilis orbis vergitur rota, ab omnibus libera secularibus negociis, collegio privatus perpetue felicitatis erumpnam hauriat atrocissime calamitatis*, or *anno dominice apparicionis* elsewhere in the diplomas of Æthelred or his predecessors, with the single exception of Bu xxxiv, a derived text whose formulas are considered later. The only traditional elements in the proem are the opening passage, paralleled in CS 1227 (968) and K 706 (1001), and the quotation from Matthew vi. 20 which appears in a few charters of 953 × 956 (CS 887, 934, 942, 965). The passage revoking earlier landbooks includes a phrase *aliquem antiquiorem librum*, which varies from the *alium antiquum librum* of orthodox Winchester texts of the period 941 × 943 (CS 768, 770, 787, 789). A little later in the charter, the phrase *aquarumque cursibus* repeats a Winchester formula of 983-5 (K 635, 650), which was also utilized at Abingdon in 999 (K 703). In the dispositive clause, the king's title is common enough, and *celestia . . . mercari* first appears in two charters of 956 and 959 (CS 984, 1035). The introduction to the bounds *his metis rus hoc giratur* begins in 960 (CS 1054) and is repeated fairly often in the following decade (CS 1082, Bu xx, CS 1101, 1176, 1307). The phrase *hoc nostre munificiente donum* in the anathema is rare, but it does occur in K 1278 dated 982 from Abingdon, and in K 1299 dated 1003 from Evesham. The most revealing comparison of formulas, however, comes from the witness list. The phrase *hoc donum perpetua ditaui libertate* occurs elsewhere only in K 710, the Burton foundation charter, and the same is true of the order of appearance of the verbs following the episcopal subscriptions: *composui, conclusi, consignaui, consensi,*

condixi, confirmaui, adquieui, adunaui. This concordance points to the
conclusion that whatever its date of composition, the terminal
section of the Rolleston charter was drawn up by a Burton scribe,
who had his abbey's foundation charter before him. Later, he or his
successor copied the Rolleston text almost verbatim when drawing
up the Wetmore charter, Bu XXXIV.

<h2 style="text-align:center">AUTHENTICITY</h2>

It seems very likely that the Rolleston charter was composed
entirely in the Burton scriptorium; for if the witness list was entered
there, it is improbable that the rest of the text was drawn up at some
other centre. It might be argued that the charter could have been
faked in 1086 or later, so that Burton Abbey could lay false claim to
Rolleston. If so, the claim was unsuccessful, for Rolleston was not a
Burton possession at the time of the Abbey Surveys, made early in
the twelfth century. In my opinion, the text is far too close to those
of genuine diplomas of Æthelred's reign for it to be a post-Conquest
forgery. Evidently the Burton scribe had at his disposal a genuine
witness list of the year 1008, for without it he would not have placed
the bishop of Wells so high on the list of his charter. It is quite true
that we have no means of establishing beyond all doubt that the charter
was not manufactured fraudulently some time before the death of
Edward the Confessor. Such a circumstance would, however, appear
very unlikely, in view of the known history of the estate. There is
no good reason known to me for supposing this charter to be
anything other than it claims to be, namely a record of an exchange
of estates made between the king and the abbot in 1008, and
witnessed by the king's council in that year. The chrismon, as
copied by the cartulary scribe, is of contemporary form (OS Facs II,
Winchester College IV). We know that royal diplomas concerning
monastic properties were commonly drawn up in the scriptorium of
the recipient abbey at this period, and our charter, if genuine,
supports other evidence for the existence of an active and competent
scriptorium at Burton within four years of the abbey's foundation.

Faced with a cartulary text of this kind, which withstands every
form of analysis that modern ingenuity can devise, it seems to me to
be good practice for present-day historians to accept it in good faith
as an authentic document, and to utilize it accordingly.

<h2 style="text-align:center">BOUNDS</h2>

The bounds of the $2\frac{1}{2}$ hides at Rolleston can be shown to follow,
with little variation, the bounds of the present-day parish. In addition

they take in a portion of pasture lying beside the River Dove to the south-east of Ryknild Street. They can be traced on OS 2½″ sheet SK 22. The perambulation proceeds in a clockwise direction:

1. from *dufan* to the *hæcce*. A flood-gate controlling a small tributary of the River Dove at grid ref. 257276, at Dove Cliffe, now the site of a weir.

2. to the great thorn. Craythorne, 246269.

3. to the *hæg stowe*. A fenced enclosure, possibly for sheep. The boundary takes three right-angled bends at 245265.

4. to *dottes hlawe*. The ON personal name Dot, Dotus occurs in DB. The name recurs as *Dodeslawe* in Wetmore in the twelfth-century Burton Abbey Survey A (W. Salt 1916, p. 221). One must assume that the tumulus was erected over the burial of a Viking during the pagan period, c. 870 × 900. Now called Horninglow Cross, at 238266, but no tumulus survives there.

5. to the *strete*. The bounds reach the A50 road from Burton to Tutbury at 234264.

6. to *ansideleage*. Stenton (*Papers* p. 321) locates this at Anslow, and remarks that the first element is Eanswith, a woman's name. The Rolleston and Anslow bounds meet at 230267. See also the Wetmore bounds, p. 240.

7. to the dyke running to the foul ditch. The stream, now widened by ornamental lakes, running from Rolleston to Bushton Bridge. The bounds join this at 229270.

8. to *Wattiches æces*. This may represent the OE personal name Hwithyse. The oak trees were perhaps sited at the wooded part of The Lawn at Rolleston, 229272.

9. to the *holan gryffe* where there are old badger setts. OE *griff*, 'a small deep valley'. Probably at 220269, where the bounds take a sharp turn to the north.

10. to the upper end of the balk. Perhaps at 213278.

11. to *middel lege*. The middle grove or clearing, now occupied by Falling Pit Plantation, 222279.

12. to the *scid hæge*. A fence formed by split trunks or branches?

13. crossing over *bracen hyrste*. Shotwood Hill, 226284.

14. to *mæran broc*. Mill Fleam, which forms the county boundary here, 226286. The mill was there in 1086; Staffs. DB no. 149.

15. down midstream to the stone ford leading to Eadgar's *lege*. The ford of the road from Rolleston to Marshton-on-Dove, at 236284. This *Eadgares lege* must be a different place from the holding at Agardsley Park in Hanbury, Staffs. DB no. 150.

16. to Wulfheah's enclosure. The bounds turn at 238285.

17. along the *hæge* to the *ofesan*. The river bank of the Dove at 238285. From this point onwards, the bounds are rather doubtful, owing to changes in the course of the river and its tributaries.

18. to the *fulan syce*. A stream leaving the Dove at 252283.

19. to the *broce*. Joining a brook at 249282.

20. to *stoc legan ford*. A ford by the farmstead meadow, possibly at 250279. I have been unable to locate the Stockley mentioned in W. Salt 1916, p. 123. Certainly this could not be Stockley Park, 201258.

21. along the *ofesan*. The river bank of the Dove, joined at 255279.

22. to *Leofnað's dic hæge*. A ditched enclosure? The bounds enclose a portion of meadow south-west of the river here.

23. to the *fulan syce*. 254277.

24. to *pile broc*; down along the brook to the foul dyke that runs between two groves.

25. to *cnapan hylle*. Reading OE *cnæpp*, 'a short sharp ascent', rather than OE *cnapa* 'boy, young man'. The bottom of the hill at 252274, at Dove Cliff.

26. to the *hæg stowe*. Possibly a cattle pound.

27. to the *deopan dæle*. A deep pit, possibly at the foot of the weir at Dove Cliff.

28. from the *dæle* to *dufan*. Back to the River Dove.

29. to the broad street *æt burtune*. Ryknild Street, which crosses the Dove at 268270.

30. along the street to Winstan's *gemæra*. ? Clay Mills, 263267.

31. out through the wood to the thorn where the thieves lie. A gallows, possibly at 265265, near the bank of the River Trent. Note that the bounds of Wetmoor include a similar gallows for thieves, a mile upstream (pp. 239–40).

32. to the meadow. ?267266.

33. to the wood. ?276260.

34. to the *ofesan*. The river bank of the Dove at 277261.

35. back to the broad street, 273270.

XXXI. King Æthelred II to his thegn Morcar.
Eight 'Manentes' at Weston-upon-Trent,
one each at Morley, Smalley and Kidsley,
Crich, and Ingleby, all in Derbyshire.
A.D. 1009

Carta Æþelredi regis de Þeston. f[ac]ta Morkare ann[o] d[omi]ni
M⁰.ix⁰. Kẏdesleg[e] [et] Cruch.

Omnia que uidentur temporalia sunt [et] que non
uidentur æt[er]na sunt.[1] Idcirco terrenis et caducis
ȩterna [et] iugiter mansura mercanda sunt. ut hís
uisibilib[us] lucris inuisibilia bona que fine carent d[omi]no
d[e]o auxiliante feliciter adquirantur. Quapropter. ego
Æþelredus. diuina mihi arridente munificentia. inperiali
regiminis gentis anglor[um] sceptro p[ot]itus.[2] aliqua[m] terre
partem qua[m] mihi aeternus cȩli creator [et] omniu[m]
reru[m] conditor sua bonitate largiendo indulsit. confero
hon(or)abili meo ministro. MORKARE. id [est].viiiᵗᵒ.
manentes in loco [et] circa locu[m] ubi d[icitu]r antiquo
vo(c)abulo. pestun. [et] .i. man[en]s in morleage. [et] .i. in
smælleage. [et] In kidesleage. [et] .i. in crẏc. [et] .i. In
englabẏ. Cum omnib[us] ad se rite p[er]tinentib(us pr)atis.
pascuis. campis. Siluis(que). ut habeat [et] possideat. [et] post
(se) cuicumq[ue] uoluerit in æternam hereditate[m] derelinquat. Sint quoq[ue] prenominati agelluli absoluti [et] liberi.
Nullisq[ue] humanis seruitiis subiciantur. Exceptis ip(sis
ser)uitiis quib[us] insistere quo(s)q[ue] mon[et] com[m]unis
utilitas regni. id [est] expeditio. [et] arcis pontisq[ue]
restauratio. Qui aute[m] hanc n[ost]ri decreti xanctione[m]
prauo molimi(ne mu)tilare conatus fuerit. certum teneat
portionem poenaru(m c)um ang[e]lis apostaticis se[m]p[er]
(p[er]p)[et]ualiter p[er]pessuru[m] non modic(am); q[ui] uero
benigniter fidelit[er]q[ue] huius ass(criti)oni cẏrografi. fide[m]
ácco[m]modauerit: S[an]c[t]or[um] om[n]iu[m] coetui copulet-
[ur] calce tenus. Hís itaq[ue] confiniis prescripta rura

[1] 2 Cor. iv. 18.
[2] The cartulary copyist left a space here. There is a tear in the membrane.

cinguntur.✠ Ðis sýndan þa landgemæru þe lic(g)eð into pestune. Þ is ærest of siðriðe forda on mæres ford. ꝸ of mæres forda pestan (p)ið ða rugan dic. ꝸ spa on hina hoh. ꝸ spa of ðan ho pestan pið ðæne holan mære forð into ceoleardes beorge ꝸ of ðam beorhge in mæresdic. ꝸ of mæres dice in pulfeardes þorn. ꝸ of pulfeardes þorne in þa grenan díc. andlang þære dice in þone pýtt. ꝸ of þa[m] pýtte in deorpentan in þa mýðan. ꝸ of ðam ge(m)ýðan upp æft[er] treontan eft on siðriðe ford. Ann[o] dominice incarnationis. Mill. ix. scripta [est] uius[1] munificentię singrapha his testib[us] consentientib[us] quor[um] inferius nomina caraxantur.

✠ Ego æþelræd rex anglor[um] hoc donu[m] libenti anim(o con)cessi.

✠ Ego æþelstan filius regis huic donationi consensi.

✠ Ego eadmund fr[ater] predicti clitonis adiuui.

✠ Ego eadred libens annui.

✠ Ego ælfheah archiep[iscopu]s dorobernie non abnui.

✠ Ego pulfstanus eboracensis archipresul n[on] rennui.

✠ Ego godpine ep[iscopu]s ad libitum regis p[ro]p[ri]a manu conscrip(s)i.

✠ Ego liuincg ep[iscopu]s roboraui.

✠ Ego æþelpold ep[iscopu]s adquieui.

✠ Ego aþulf ep[iscopu]s subscripsi.

✠ Ego[2] brih(tp)ald ep[iscopu]s

✠ Ego eadnoð ep[iscopu]s

✠ Ego alfun ep[iscopu]s

✠ Ego æþelric ep[iscopu]s

✠ Ego æþelsig ep[iscopu]s

✠ Ego alfpald ep[iscopu]s

✠ Ego godpine ep[iscopu]s

✠ Ego ælfgær ep[iscopu]s

✠ Ego ælfstan[3] ep[iscopu]s

✠ Ego aldun ep[iscopu]s

✠ Ego[4] germanus abb[as]

✠ Ego ælfsig[5] abb[as]

[1] *Sic.* for 'huius'.   [2] The second column of witnesses begins here.
[3] 's' inserted after initial omission.
[4] The third column of witnesses begins here.
[5] 's' inserted after initial omission.

✠ Ego þulgar abb[as]
✠ Ego ælfsig abb[as]
✠ Ego brihtræd abb[as]
✠ Ego leofgar (a)bb[as]
✠ Ego æluere (ab)b[as]
✠ Ego ælfric DUX
✠ Ego leofþine DUX
✠ Ego eadric DUX
✠ Ego[1] uhtr(ed) DUX
✠ Ego æþelmær[2] MINISTER
✠ Ego æþelric M[inister]
✠ Ego ægelgær M[inister]
✠ Ego ælfþine M[inister]
✠ Ego ulfketel M[inister]
✠ Ego godþine M[inister]
✠ Ego SIFERÐ M[inister]
✠ Ego þiðer M[inister]
✠ Ego æþelþine M[inister]
✠ Ego[3] godþ(ine) M[inister]
✠ Ego fredgist M[inister]
✠ Ego ulf M[inister]
✠ Ego ælfe(h) M[inister]
✠ Ego þulf(r)ic M[inister]
✠ Ego ulfk(e)tel M[inister]
✠ Ego þurferð M[inister]
✠ Ego aske(t)el M[inister]
✠ Ego þulfsig M[inister]
✠ Ego kata M[inister]
✠ Ego[4] þulfstan M[inister]
✠ Ego asketel M[inister]
✠ Ego þulfgeat M[inister]
✠ Ego aþelpold M[inister]
✠ Ego ælfeh M[inister]
✠ Ego stýr M[inister]
✠ Ego þurbrand M[inister]

[1] The fourth column of witnesses begins here.
[2] 'l' inserted after initial omission.
[3] The fifth column of witnesses begins here.
[4] The sixth column of witnesses begins here.

✠ Ego pulfstan M[inister]
✠ Ego Spaue M[inister]
✠ Ego æþelric M[inister]

ENDORSEMENTS

In the main hand:
✠ WESTUNES LANDBÓC.
In a later hand:
Ethelredus Rex. Morkare.
In the Peniarth Cartulary hand:
XXXI.
Further endorsements are illegible.

TEXTS

A. William Salt Library, Stafford, MS. 84/5/41, in a contemporary hand. There is no published facsimile.

B. National Library of Wales, Aberystwyth, Peniarth MS. 390 (here cited as the Peniarth Cartulary), f. 182ᵛ (old numbering p. 364), a copy of MS. A¹ written c. 1240 × 1264, with bounds and witness list abbreviated. The chrismon is reproduced fairly accurately.

EDITION

This edition is from A, with some letters (rendered illegible by rubbing and tearing of the membrane) supplied from B; these are between curved brackets. Abbreviations are extended between square brackets. The original punctuation is retained. The rubric is from B.

PALAEOGRAPHY

The membrane is 51·3 cm. wide × 15·6 cm. long, and has been folded three times horizontally and seven times vertically; the size of the folded membrane is approximately 7·0 cm. × 4·2 cm. The hand, which is perhaps contemporary with the date claimed for the charter, is very close to that of Bu xxvii but there is a difference between insular 'd' and caroline 'g' in the two manuscripts, and I am inclined to think that they are in fact by different scribes.

The chrismon heading the charter is particularly interesting. The

---

¹ The word p[ot]itus in the king's title, partly illegible because of a tear in the membrane, was omitted by the Peniarth Cartulary scribe, a blank space being left for it in his text. It seems probable therefore that the existing tears were already present in the mid-thirteenth century.

custom of carrying the two lower limbs of the cross down to a level with the bottom stroke of the 'P' is first encountered in BM Stowe Ch. 35 (OS Facs III, 36), an original dated 1002. The form of decoration of the angles of the cross is best seen on the obverse dies of the 'Short Helmet' coins of Cnut, but this tendency was already being developed in the later coins of Æthelred's reign. The chrismon is therefore of a strictly contemporary design.

In the text, 'a' is insular for OE, caroline for Latin. Horned 'a' occurs regularly in the caroline 'ra' ligature. Insular 'd' has a sloping back, but this is not so marked as in Bu XXVII. High 'e' does not occur, either alone or in ligatures. The tail of insular 'g' is closed, as is the bow of 'p' in OE and Latin; the end of the bow is curved slightly upwards. Insular long 's' occurs initially and medially, and low 's' initially, medially, and finally. In Latin, minuscule 's' is invariably long. Round 's' occurs in Latin and OE only initially as a majuscule, for proper names and beginning of sentences. Quite often, the tail of long 's' in Latin does not fall below the line. Rounded 'y' is always dotted. Straight-limbed 'y' occurs only once – also dotted. 'þ' occurs initially and medially, and 'ð' initially, medially, and finally. In OE, descenders of 'þ' and 'p', and sometimes 'f', curve to the left; other descenders are straight. 'e' occurs occasionally for 'æ'. '⁊' occurs regularly in OE, '&' in Latin, the latter being used quite often in place of 'et' in the middle of words. '÷' occurs once for 'est'. Very few vowels are stressed. Punctuation is by midline dot throughout. The membrane has been ruled, and spacing both of words and of lines is good; the witness list is nicely balanced across the membrane, the scribe has inserted missing letters in three of the witnesses' names, and the whole product gives the impression of care and competence.

DATE AND WITNESSES

The witness list is right for the date, the sees represented being Canterbury, York, Rochester, Wells, Winchester, Hereford, Ramsbury, Dorchester, London, Sherborne (followed by the Sherborne *chorepiscopus*, Æthelsige), Crediton, Lichfield, Elmham, and Durham. The name of the penultimate bishop, Ælfstan, is perhaps a mistake for Ælfmær of Selsey, the only see (apart from Cornwall) not represented in the list. However, a Bishop Ælfstan also witnesses Bu XXXIII, in the same position in the list, and it is quite possible that, like Æthelsige, he too was a *chorepiscopus*. The presence of all the Danelaw bishops is particularly noteworthy. The ealdormen witnessing are from Wessex, the Hwicce, Mercia, and Northumbria (this is one of the earliest charters to be witnessed by Earl Uhtred). Many of the thegns have Scandinavian names, suggesting that the charter was witnessed somewhere in the Danelaw. It is noteworthy that the only two names written in majuscules are those of Morcar the recipient, and the thegn Siferth in the witness list. This reinforces one's assumption, reasonable on other grounds, that these were the two sons of Earngrim whose murder by Eadric Streona is reported in the ASC annal for 1015. This charter was issued after K 1306, also dated 1009, for Ælfweard had been succeeded by Brihtræd as abbot of Glastonbury.

FORMULAS

The proem, with its quotation from 2 Cor. iv. 18, occurs with precisely the same wording in CS 525, dated 869; slight variations occur in CS 873 (c. 865–75) and in CS 1331 (739); the two first are basically authentic texts, the third is a post-Conquest forgery. The formula was elaborated in a group of charters dating from Athelstan's reign (CS 728, 730, 734, 740, 752), and in a few derived texts (CS 798, 814, 1068), but the proem of the charter now under consideration is modelled either on an exemplar of the late ninth century, or upon a later diploma using a ninth-century formula. The imperial title of Æthelrcd, said to be held by God's bounty, is in keeping with similar claims made in other royal diplomas of the period, but the precise formula cannot be paralleled; *munificentia* does occur, e.g. in K 1295, 672, 655, Bu xxx, etc., but not in relation to the deity; instead, *gratia* is the standard form throughout the century (K 734, 741, 752, 756, 767, OS Facs III, 35, Bu xxxiv, etc.). Similarly, for *inperiali regiminis gentis anglorum sceptro potitus* in the charter, we can quote as parallels only shorter phrases such as *sceptra imperii* in K 687. The next phrase in the text, . . . *quam mihi æternus cęli creator et omnium rerum conditor sua bonitate largiendo indulsit*, is unique, as far as I can discover; so too is the adjective *honorabili* in the title of the recipient, and the phrase *in loco et circa locum ubi dicitur antiquo vocabulo* introducing the name of the estate. *Cum omnibus ad se rite pertinentibus* is standard form (e.g. K 621), but the components *pratis, pascuis, campis, siluisque* are quoted in an order different from the norm (compare K 652, 657, 1281). The clause granting powers of alienation is identical with that in K 657–8 (987) and some other texts of the period. The clause granting freedom of the property is unique as far as I can discover; so too is the clause excluding the three common dues, and almost the whole of the anathema, with the exception of *hanc nostri decreti*, which occurs also in K 1309, and (in the singular case) in K 654, charters dated 1014 and 986 respectively; *cyrografi* occurs sporadically in contemporary texts (e.g. K 686, dated 994). The identical formula to that introducing the bounds has not been found elsewhere, but two charters dated 1001 and 1015 are very similar (K 706, 1310), and *confini(i)s* occurs in charters dated 997 (K 698) and 1035 (K 1322). The identical dating clause appears in K 626 (980), and very similar ones in K 1301 (1005), K 1304 (1007); see also K 655 (986). Finally, the phrase introducing the witness list is of standard form (CS 1125, K 624, 629, 648, 650, 652 etc.); *libenti animo* occurs in K 647, and *frater clitonum* in K 643.

AUTHENTICITY

It will be seen that as with many other diplomas of Æthelred's reign, the text echoes phrases found in charters of his predecessors throughout the previous century. Sometimes, commoner passages are reproduced precisely; in other cases only the general sense of the earlier formulas has been preserved, with occasional elements from the vocabulary; quite a substantial proportion of the Burton charter's formulas are unique. It is as if whoever composed this text was given a number of exemplars, and a free hand to construct the diploma from them as he wished. As a result, the diplomatic has little to offer in the assessment of authenticity, nor can it be utilized to establish the issuing scriptorium; for pointers in this direction, we have to resort to the unsupported evidence of palaeography, and the witness list. It seems likely that this is an authentic charter, composed probably at Burton (because of the similarity of the hand with that of Bu XXVII), and ratified perhaps during a royal visit to the Danelaw in the early part of 1009, unrecorded elsewhere. It is interesting that the charters Bu XXXI–XXXIV, issued within five years of each other, have practically no points of contact in their formulas.

HISTORY

Professor K. Cameron noted in 1959 that those parts of Derbyshire lying to the north of the River Trent and to the west of the River Derwent probably formed part of Mercia before the Danish settlement (PN *Derbyshire*, p. xxix). The charter now under consideration is one of the best surviving pre-Conquest texts for illustrating the organization and assessment within the Danelaw of a principal estate and its satellites. In the table on p. 227, the assessments of Weston and its dependencies in 1009 and in 1066 are compared. There has been some elaboration during the half-century, but the basic structure of the assessment is the same, and one cannot doubt that the *manentes* in the charter, as also the carucates of DB, represent the Danish assessments in ploughlands. It is noteworthy that Smalley and Kidsley were assessed together in 1066, as in 1009. Most of Morcar's holdings listed in the charter are shown to have descended to Earl Ælfgar, presumably as part of the estates of the Mercian earldom. Others descended to Leofric and Leofnoth, who held TRE several other properties that had been left to Morcar in the will of Wulfric Spot (No. 39).

BOUNDS

The bounds of the 8 *manentes* at Weston-on-Trent must embrace a larger area than the present parish, for the eastern limits are placed at the River Derwent. Aston, Shardlow, and Great Wilne must therefore have been included within the OE boundary, and it seems probable that Chellaston also was part of the original 8 *manentes*, although this is assessed separately in DB. The River Trent formed the southern boundary. The bounds can be traced on OS $2\frac{1}{2}''$ sheets SK 32, 33, 42, 43. The perambulation proceeds in a clockwise direction:

1. from *siðriðe forda*. Possibly one should read OE *sið rið*, 'warrior's stream', but Stenton (*Papers*, p. 322 n. 1) prefers for the first element the feminine name Sithrith. The Trent is too wide and deep to be forded, so the ford must lie on a tributary. It seems probable that the OE boundary leaves the Trent at grid ref. 395273, rather to the east of the modern parish boundary of Weston, and that the Trent and Mersey canal, running north-westwards from this point, follows the original course of the *sið rið* as far as 386283, where it is joined by the upper reach of the stream. If so, the ford was probably located at 387283, where the stream is crossed by the road from Weston to Swalkestone.

2. to *mæres forda*. The boundary ford may have been at 391286, where the stream is crossed by a footpath from Weston to Glebe Farm.

3. westwards along the *rugan dic*. The rough dyke may be the ditch running north-westwards beside the footpath to Glebe Farm.

4. to *hina hoh*. OE *hi(g)na*, '(monastic) community'; *hoh* 'hill spur', the community being presumably Burton. Probably the hill at 387296, now the site of a sand pit.

5. westwards along (to) the *holan mære*. A boundary hollow? The modern bounds run westwards past Chellaston Hill to Home Lea at 378296.

1009 (Bu XXXI)		1066 (DB)			
Holding	Assessment	Holding	Assessment	Owner TRE	DB entry (VCH Derbys. 1)
Weston upon Trent	8 manentes	Weston and berewicks	10 carucates $+ 2\frac{1}{2}$ bovates	Earl Ælfgar	334a
		Aston on Trent and Shardlow (berewick)	$6\frac{1}{2}$ bovates	Earl Ælfgar	334a
		Weston	$\frac{2}{3}$ of 2 carucates	King	331b[1]
Morley	1 manens	Morley	$\frac{1}{3}$ of 2 carucates	Siward	343a, 346b[2]
Smalley and Kidsley	1 manens	Smalley and Kidsley	4 bovates	King	331b[1]
Crich	1 manens	Crich and Scochetorp (? Oakerthorpe)	4 bovates	Leofric and Leofnoth	349ab
Ingleby	1 manens	Ingleby	$1\frac{1}{6}$ carucates	antecessor of Ralf son of Hubert[3]	350ab
		Ingleby (sokeland of Repton)	3 bovates	Earl Ælfgar	332a
		Ingleby (sokeland of Foremark)	3 bovates	Ulchel	352b
		Ingleby (member of Stanton by Bridge)	$\frac{2}{3}$ bovate	—	355b

(Assessments for Ingleby and the three further Ingleby entries are braced together as 2 carucates.)

[1] Entry in margin of the DB text.   [2] Duplicate entries in DB.
[3] The only antecessors of Ralf elsewhere in Derbyshire were Leofric and Leofnoth, either independently or jointly.

6. to *ceoleardes beorge*. Cēolh(e)ard gave his name to Chellaston. *beorge* here perhaps means barrow rather than hill. Possibly at 374307, north-west of Chellaston.

7. to *mæres dic*. At this point the boundary becomes easier to ascertain. The modern bounds join a dyke at 396310, to the south of Thulston Field Farm.

8. to *pulfeardes þorn*. Striking eastwards along the dyke to 412312, where the modern bounds cross the road from Aston to Thulston. Wulfheard's thorn bush may have been here.

9. to the *grenan dic*. A dyke is joined at 423310, west of Shardlow.

10. along the ditch to a pit. Eastwards along the ditch to a point south of Ambaston Grange, at 436316. I have been unable to locate the pit.

11. to *deorpentan*. The bounds join the River Derwent at a weir, west of Church Wilne, at 443317.

12. to the *myðan*. OE *gemȳðe*, 'meeting of streams'. The confluence of the Rivers Derwent and Trent at Derwent Mouth, 459309.

13. up along *treontan* back to *siðriðe ford*. Upstream along the River Trent to the starting-point.

XXXII. King Æthelred II to his thegn Elemod. 2 'cassatæ' at Hallam, Derbyshire.
A.D. 1011

Carta Æþelredi Regis de Burhalim. anno d[omin]i.M⁰.xi⁰.

Smme[1] vereq[ue] bonitatis deum solum. substantia sim-plu[m]. p[er]sonis t[ri]plu[m]꞉ constare nemini ratione vigentiu[m] hesitandu[m] est. qui sue incircu[m]sc[ri]pte dinamia[2] maiestatis circu[m]sc[ri]pta queque q[ua]si pugillo c[on]tinet chirali꞉[3] cunctaq[ue] que su[n]t ei[us] bonitate bona su[n]t꞉ no[n] tame[n] c[on]dita p[er] se꞉ set quia a sum[m]o bono essendi cep[er]ant formam꞉ bona su[n]t. Q[ua]m ob causam ei[us]dem sum[m]e bonitatis bona p[er]pet-ualit[er] seq[ui]dem p[er]manenda. viuati mentis intenc[i]one iugit[er] appetenda su[n]t꞉ quib[us] quippe adeptis꞉ nichil

---

[1] for *Summe*, without abbreviation mark (A *Sunne*).

[2] for *dynamia* (A *diuamia*).

[3] *chirali* = 'manual', from the Greek Χείρ = 'hand'.

desiderabilius excellenti[us]ve requiri quibit. Hinc eteni[m]
ego Eþelredus tocius rector archosq[ue] Brẏttannie꞉ regalis
potentie dignitatib[us] dei dapsilitate inpensima[1] fauente
p[re]ditus opum largitione caducaru[m] t[ra]nsitoriar[umq[ue] ꞉
bona haut caduca hautq[ue] defectiua adipisci om[n]i modo
exoptans int[er] cetera bonoru[m] studia largiendor[um]
quib[us] me minime deficientis agalhasmata[2] regni adepturu[m]
esse spero꞉ terre p[ar]tic[u]lam q[ua]ndam duas videl[ice]t
cassatas Elemod ministro g[ra]tissimo libens hilarisq[ue]
imp[ar]tior꞉ ob ip[s]ius siq[ui]dem indefessi obseq[ui]a fam-
ulat[us]. Que q[ui]dem t[er]ra agnoscitis pat[ri]e accolis
Burhhalim nu[n]cupatur꞉ Eandem deniq[ue] t[er]ram q[ua]mdiu
spiramine att[ra]hendo u[e]l emittendo frui valeat. toci[us][3]
alicuus[4] conflictus securus possideat. dumq[ue] se viuacis[5]
alitum[6] flaminis amissum ire p[er]spexerit꞉ arbitriu[m] ei
liberum assistat cui successor[um] eius. alieno scil[ice]t u[e]l
p[ro]pinquo eandem t[er]ram subigat possidendam. Mat[ro]næ
aute[m] sup[ra]sc[ri]pte tam naturales q[ua]m legittimas villas
m[ichi] iure decretario assignatas minist[ro] p[re]memorato
Elemodo viginti [et] uni[us] librar[um] appensib[us] aureis
m[ihi] concessis alacriter condonaui. Itaq[ue] hoc n[ost]re
largitionis donu[m] in ip[s]ius arbit[ri]o tuta semp[er] valletur
lib[er]tate cu[m] cunctis ad ip[s]am rite p[er]tine[n]tib[us]
t[er]ram. campis videl[ice]t Et cet[er]a.[7] Trib[us] causis
exceptis [et] c[etera].[8] Sit [er]g[o][9] t[er]re isti[us] libertas
vndiq[ue] solida [et] munita.[10] Etanti q[ui]oris u[e]l futuoris
libri q[uo]cu[m]q[ue] m[odo] p[ro]lati n[u]llo m[odo] c[on]-
t[ra]d[i]c[i]oni subiaceat. set magis om[n]ib[us] hostib[us]
deuictis p[ro]p[ri]e potestatis ditione floreat. Istis t[er]minib[us]
p[re]d[ic]ta t[er]ra circu[m]girata est [et] c[etera].[11] M°. xi°.[12]

---

[1] for *inpensissima*, as suggested in A.
[2] Presumably a cognate of Medieval Latin *agalma*, 'statue, image'.
[3] A *totius*.   [4] for *alicuius* (A *alitnus*).
[5] for *viuans*, as the reading in A.   [6] for *halitum*, as suggested in A.
[7] The rest of the immunity clause is omitted.
[8] The rest of the clause excepting the three common burdens is omitted.
[9] *Sic*, for *igitur*.   [10] for *imunita* (A *inunita*).
[11] The bounds are omitted in the MS.
[12] The dating clause is abbreviated.

✠ Ego Æþelred rex toci[us] brittanice telluris h[a]nc lib[er]tatem confirmaui.

✠ Ego Ælfheag[us] dorab[ernensis][1] ecc[lesie] Arch[iepiscopus] c[on]signaui.

✠ Ego Þustan[us][2] ebor[acensis] ecc[lesie] Archiep[iscopu]s consensi.

✠ Ego Ælfgẏuu collaterana ei[us]de[m] reg[is] hoc m[ihi] placere p[ro]fessa sum.

✠ Ego Æþelstan[us] clẏto. confirmaui.

✠ Ego Eadmu[n]d. clẏto. consignaui.

✠ Ego Eadred clẏto. corroboraui.

✠ Ego Eadpig clẏto. coniuui.[3]

✠ Ego Eadpeard clẏto. consolidaui.

✠ Ego Ælfhun ep[iscopu]s conquieui.

✠ Ego Æþelpold ep[iscopu]s coniugaui.[4]

✠ Ego[5] Lẏuingc ep[iscopu]s co[m]muneraui.

✠ Ego Æþelric ep[iscopu]s consensi.

✠ Ego Ælfpold ep[iscopu]s conclaui.

✠ Ego Aþulf ep[iscopu]s confixi.

✠ Ego Godpine ep[iscopu]s confirmaui.

✠ Ego Eadnoð ep[iscopu]s coadunaui.

✠ Ego Ælfmær ep[iscopu]s consolidaui.

Et cet[er]i Abb[at]es sex. Duces iiij or. [et] Ministri. viginti [et] tres.[6]

TEXT

National Library of Wales, Aberystwyth, Peniarth MS. 390 (cited here as the Peniarth Cartulary), ff. 182ᵛ–183ʳ (old numbering pp. 364–5), dated 1240–64. This omits the bounds, parts of the immunity and exemption clauses, all the dating clause apart from the year of grace, and all the witness list after the bishops. There is also at least one sentence missing from the body of the charter.

EDITIONS

A. Barlow, EC pp. 328–9, with comments. The chrismon prefacing

[1] for dorob[ernensis].　　[2] for Þulstanus. A corrects this silently.
[3] A coninni.　　[4] A coniungaui.
[5] The second column of witnesses begins here.
[6] In this line, ceteri, iiii or, and viginti et tres are scored through.

the cartulary text is not reproduced. Abbreviations are extended silently.

B. In this edition, abbreviations are extended between square brackets; the cartulary punctuation is unchanged. The cartulary rubric is reproduced.

DATE AND WITNESSES

The surviving portion of the witness list is compatible with the date. The sees represented are Canterbury, York, London, Winchester, Wells, Sherborne, Crediton, Hereford, Rochester, Dorchester, and Selsey. See the notes to Bu xxxiv for Archbishop Ælfheah's signature.

CHRISMON

The cartulary copyist has drawn a chrismon with a capital 'A' joined to the left edge of the 'P'. As far as I know, this occurs in only one other contemporary text, K 736, which is an Evesham charter relating to an estate at Newnham, Northants., dated 1021 × 1023 (see No. 19). There seems little doubt, therefore, that the exemplar before the cartulary copyist was in a hand contemporaneous with the date claimed for the charter.

FORMULAS

Barlow, EC p. 328 points out that there are omissions in the text, which has an unrelated reference to an 'above-mentioned woman', who appears to have lost her estates to Æthelred II. He concludes 'some very difficult Latin has not been successfully transmitted'. While the general structure of the charter is consistent with its date, much of the phraseology is unique. Occasional stock phrases occur, such as *rex tocius brittanice* (as in K 711 etc.) and *tribus causis exceptis* (K 1299 etc.), and the passage introducing the boundary clause (CS 735, K 1282 etc.). Unusual words include *chirali* and *agalhasmata*.

AUTHENTICITY

This appears to be a garbled and incomplete text of an authentic charter of Æthelred II, compiled in some provincial scriptorium, probably Burton.

XXXIII. King Æthelred II to his thegn Morcar. 5 hides at 'Ufre'. a.d. 1011

Carta Æðelredi regis de Ufra. anno d[omi]ni M⁰. xi⁰.

D[omi]no n[ost]ro Ih[es]u Chr[ist]o cum patre [et] flamine sacro om[n]is essentie machinam. genuino naturalis potentie gubernante moderamine om[n]is   1 usie creatura que in p[ri]ncipio formata formoseq[ue] condita. videlicet phebea lampas. cinthia firmame[n]to-q[ue] celi affixa v[e]l errantia sidera. terrena q[uoque] animalia seu maritima siue aerea. necno[n] herbaru[m] v[e]l leguminu[m] atque v[ir]gultor[um] ab origine qua esse cep[er]u[n]t indice sibi nature statuta co[n]ditoris no[n] sunt t[ra]nsgressa p[re]-cepta. set usq[ue] defectum sui ea seruantia p[er]mane[n]t. Set heu p[ro]h dolor inp[ro]uida fragilitas hominu[m] om[n]ib[us] creaturis p[re]latior p[ro]pt[er] p[re]uaricac[i]o[n]em corruens in cecitatem caliginose mortis p[ri]mam inmortalitatis stolam lugubrit[er] amisit. Idcirco meritam i[n]currit int[er]² om[n]e genus humanu[m]. regnu[m]q[ue] post regnu[m] mobilit[er] uadit [et] p[er]nicit[er] recedit. Qua de re ego Eþelred diuina arridente gr[ati]a rex cu[m] archana cordis indagatione p[er]hennem gratulac[i]o[n]em [et] tutissimu[m] fulcimentu[m] cum peculiari donac[i]o[n]e q[ua]m arcitenens hilarit[er] suis deuotis datur[us] est insup[er] [et] vitam et[er]nam. Aliq[ua]n-tulam ruris p[ar]ticulam cu[m] consensu optimatu[m] meor[um] id est. v. mansas ubi a rurigenis æt ufre apellatur meo fideli minist[ro] morcare satis deuote inpendere curaui. ita ut ab om[n]i mu[n]diali censu p[er]petualit[er] ditali munificac[i]o[n]e libera collocetur. nisi ab expedic[i]one sicut ab antiq[ui]s constitutu[m] est. Int[er] agmina s[an]c[t]or[um] et[er]nalit[er] in celi galaxia exultantiu[m] et[er]ne beatitudinis repperia t[ri]pudia qui n[ost]re donac[i]oni co[n]sentiri animu[m] impulerit. Si q[ui]s u[ero] no[n] exhorruerit machinari c[ontra] n[ost]r[u]m decretu[m] sciat se casurum in p[ro]fundum

---

¹ Space in MS.

² *Sic.* The text is suspect here. If extended to *int[eritum]*, this does not go with *meritam.*

auernalis orci baratrum. Anno d[omi]nice incarn[ationis] millesimo. xi⁰. Hiis t[estibus] consentientib[us].¹

✠ Ego Æþelred rex Anglor[um] hoc donatiuu[m] dando sub astipulac[i]o[n]e m[u]ltor[um] firmaui.

✠ Ego Æþelstan regis fili[us] c[on]sensi.

✠ Ego Eadmund frat[er] ei[us]de[m] subsc[ri]psi.

✠ Ego Eadred t[er]cia p[ro]les regia adq[ui]eui.

✠ Ego Ælfheh archiep[iscopu]s corroboraui.

✠ Ego Þulfstan[us] archiep[iscopu]s annui.

✠ Ego Adulf pontifex adnotaui.

✠ Ego Godwine antistes no[n] renui.

✠ Ego brihtpold ep[iscopu]s no[n] abnui.

✠ Ego Eadnod p[re]sul co[n]solidaui.

✠ Ego Ælfhun ep[iscopu]s co[n]f[ir]maui.

✠ Ego Æþelric pontif[ex]. co[n]sensi.

✠ Ego Æþelsig ep[iscopu]s conq[ui]eui.

✠ Ego Ælfpald Ep[i]s[copus] [con]'.²

✠ Ego Godpine Ep[iscopu]s [con]'.²

✠ Ego Ælfgær Ep[iscopu]s [con]'.²

✠ Ego Ælfstan Ep[iscopu]s [con]'.²

✠ Ego Germanus Abbas.

Et cet[er]i Abb[at]es septem. Et ceteri Duces. quatuor. [et] Ministri. xxx. ta.³

TEXT

National Library of Wales, Aberystwyth, Peniarth MS. 390 (cited here as the Peniarth Cartulary), f. 183ʳᵛ (old numbering pp. 365–6), dated 1240–64. This omits the bounds, part of the dating clause, part of the phrase introducing the witness list, and the names of the abbots, ealdormen, and thegns witnessing.

EDITION

The charter is hitherto unpublished. This edition retains the spelling and punctuation of the cartulary version. Abbreviations are extended between square brackets. The cartulary rubric is reproduced

1 This clause appears to be abbreviated. The bounds are omitted.

2 These abbreviations are too short for extension.

3 Partly scored through.

DATE AND WITNESSES

The surviving portion of the witness list is compatible with the date. The sees represented are Canterbury, York, Rochester, Ramsbury, Dorchester, London, Sherborne (followed by the name of the *chorepiscopus*, Æthelsige), Crediton, Lichfield, and Elmham. The last bishop to witness is named Ælfstan, and there is some difficulty attending his identification. Lyfing of Wells had an alternative name Ælfstan, but when present he usually witnesses much higher in the list at this period. Moreover the contemporary charter Bu xxxi, which is witnessed by Lyfing in his correct position, is also witnessed by an Ælfstan after Ælfgar of Elmham. It seems probable that, just as Æthelsige was *chorepiscopus* in the diocese of Sherborne, so Ælfstan was *chorepiscopus* in the diocese of Elmham. After the bishops, Germanus appears as abbot (of Cholsey), but the names of the seven other abbots who witnessed the text lying before the cartulary copyist are not given. This charter, like Bu xxxii, appears to have been issued some time before 29 September, when the Danes captured Archbishop Ælfheah of Canterbury. Morcar the recipient is probably the same thegn as in Bu xxxi.

CHRISMON

The Peniarth Cartulary copyist prefaced his text with a unique chrismon, almost certainly copied from his exemplar. It resembles that of Bu xxxi, but with rather more elaborate decoration at the intersection of the cross on the 'P'. The decoration of the chrismon of the original K 744, dated 1031, is rather similar, as is that of the obverse dies of the quatrefoil issue initiating the run of the coins of Cnut.

LOCATION

Probably Littleover and Mickleover in Derbyshire, where the abbey had interests at the time of DB and subsequently.

FORMULAS

For the most part, these are unique.

AUTHENTICITY

This looks like an authentic charter of Æthelred II, probably drawn up at Burton.

XXXIV. King Æthelred II to Abbot Wulfgeat.
1½ hides at Wetmore, Staffordshire.
A.D. 1012

Carta Æþelredi regis de Withmere. Anno ab Incarn[atione]
d[omi]ni. M⁰. xii. Ind[ictione]. x.[1]

Uniu[er]sor[um] conditor [et] creator d[omi]n[u]s n[oste]r
Ih[esu]s Chr[istu]s seruili forma semetip[su]m p[ro] n[ost]ra
redempc[i]o[n]e circu[m]tegens. [et] int[er] ho[m]i[n]es deus
homoq[ue] ver[us] conu[er]sat[us] cu[n]ctos fideles salutarib[us]
instruit docume[n]tis [et][2] ad celestia gaudia toto mentis
conamine (q[ua]mtoci[us] p[ro]p[er]em[us] talit[er] om[n]ib[us] p[ro]-
clamat dicens Thesaurizate[3] uob[is] thesauros in celo [et] cet[era]).[4]
Hinc co[m]punctus ego Æþelred rex Anglorum ([et]) cu[m] substantia[5] (m[ih]i ab ip[so] d[omi]no ubertim donata celestia mercari
cupio:[6])[7] cuidam meo fideli abbati W[u]lfgeto cognominato quandam
t[er]re p[ar]tic[u]lam dedi ei in loco quem solicole vicini[8] Withmere[9]
appellant. id est unu[m] mansem [et] dimidiu[m] p[ro] amabili
obedientia ei[us]q[ue] placabili pecunia qua[m] m[ich]i in sue
deuoc[i]o[n]is obseq[ui]o detulit. id est. lxx.ᵗᵃ libras in auro
[et] argento. ideo ei libent[er] inpendo ad monasteriu[m] suu[m]
q[uo]d no[m]i[n]atur s[an]c[t]i benedicti om[n]iumq[ue] s[an]c[t]-
or[um] quod est in villula Bẏrtuniens[is][10] situm ad usum dei seruor[um]
eidem loco famulantiu[m] inp[er]petuu[m] co[n]firmo hereditate[11]
Quatin[us] victum vestitutu[m]q[ue] atq[ue] om[n]em utilitate[m] eis

---

[1] This is the rubric in B. In A the rubric is *Carta de villa de Withm[er]e.*

[2] *Sic*, for *ut*, as in Bu xxx, p. 211.   [3] Matt. vi. 20.

[4] For the completion of the text, see No. xxx. B omits this passage,
inserting *et cetera ut supra in precedenti folio* (referring to No. xxx).

[5] Both versions of No. xxx have *cum consubstancia* here, omitting *et*. B also
omits *et*, showing that he was copying his transcript of No. xxx at this
point, rather than the charter that lay before him.

[6] No. xxx has *cupiens.*

[7] B omits this passage, inserting *et etera ut supra.*

[8] No. xxx has *vicini.* B has *vicine.*

[9] B *þithmere.*   [10] B *Byrtoniensis.*

[11] So in A and B, and therefore in their exemplar. Both versions of No.
xxx, however, have *in perpetuo confirmo hereditatem.*

administ[ra]ndum q[ua]mdiu hui[us] volubilis orbis vergit[ur] rota. Si aut[em] temp[or]e co[n]tigerit aliq[uo][1] *que[m]piam ho[m]i[n]em (alique[m])*[2] *antiq[ui]ore[m] libru[m] cont[ra] isti[us] libri lib[er]tatem p[ro]ducere: p[ro] nich[i]lo co[m]putat[ur].*[3] *Isto p[er] om[n]ia in sua stabilitate p[er]mane[n]te atq[ue] vigente. Sit aut[em] hec p[re]sc[ri]pta tellus ab om[n]ib[us] libera secularib[us] negociis cu[m] om[n]ib[us] ad illam rite p[er]tinentib[us]. in campis. (pascuis. p[ra]tis. siluis. aquaru[m]q[ue] cursib[us]) trib[us] (tantu[m] reb[us])*[4] *exceptis (que legalit[er] seruantur hacten[us]. id est expedic[i]one pontis arcisue consctruct[i]one.)*[5] *Si q[ui]s (aut[em])*[6] *q[uo]d no[n] optam[us] (hoc n[ost]re munificentie donu[m] p[er]u[er]tere conamine stolido studuerit. collegio p[ri]uat[us] p[er]petue felicitatis eru[m]pna[m] hauriat atrocissime calamitatis mortis. nisi ante t[er]minu[m] p[re]su[m]ptione[m] h[an]c tem[er]aria[m] legali satisfact[i]one eme[n]dare studuerit.)*[7] *Hiis*[8] *metis rus hoc giratur.*

✠ þis sýnt þa land gemære to þithmere. Ærst of trente þær þa ðeofes hangað on middan bere fordes holme. of ðan holme to ge riht to þan lepe butan fif lan be heonan of þan landan to þan sice. of þan sýce to þan mære þorne uspeardan forstun of þan þorne to an æcer: of an æcere in þone hæge. of ðan hæge: in þæm broce. and long broces: ꝥ cume on þone dic: on ansýðelege. norð æfter dice ꝥ cume on ceolfes crofte. on þone þe ioerneð fram eansýðelege æfter stræte to þan stubbe. of þan stubbe: on þone dic. æfter dic ꝥ on stræte ꝥ ýruð bi ebrocan. of ðan stræte on þone dic. of þan dic: on geriht on þone sich þe ýruð be chese pælle hýlle. ꝝ hunger hýlle. æfter sýche on geriht on þe ellen ꝥ stundað on pihtmere mære ant stretones. of þan ellen: on þone forð æfte sýce þe scoet of þan forðe on trentan up æfter trente ꝥ cum þær þe þeofes hengað. ✠ ant pýlltunes landes æcer ant mæd land: healf in to þihtmere healf in to roluestune.)

Acta est (aut[em])[9] *hec mea donatio anno incarnac[i]o[n]e*

---

[1] So in A and B, and therefore in their exemplar. Both versions of No. xxx, however, have *si autem contigerit tempore aliquo.*

[2] B omits *aliquem.*

[3] *Sic,* for *computetur.* The same slip occurs in No. xxx.

[4] B omits *tantum rebus.*   [5] Omitted in B, which substitutes *et cetera.*

[6] B omits *autem.*

[7] Omitted in B, which substitutes *et cetera ut supra* (referring to No. xxx).

[8] B *Istis.*   [9] Omitted in B.

(d[omi]ni n[ost]ri Ih[es]u Chr[ist]i). Mᵒ. xiiᵒ. *Indictione* (vero).[1]
x.ᵐ *Hii testes* adera[n]t (qui ha[n]c consc[ri]pseru[n]t [et]
c[on]senseru[n]t [et] cum signo s[an]c[t]e[2] crucis Chr[ist]i
corroborauerunt [et] firmauerunt.)[3]

✠ *Ego Æþelred rex anglor[um]* h[a]nc (meam donac[i]o[n]em
    consensi. [et] scrib[er]e iussi [et] manuu[m] in-
    p[re]ssione signaui.)[4]

✠ *Ego Æþelstan fili[us] regis.*

✠ *Ego Ælfheah Archiep[iscopu]s* co[m]*posui.*

✠ *Ego Þulfstan Archiep[iscopu]s* consignaui.[5]

✠ *Ego Leofing ep[iscopu]s* conclusi.

✠ *Ego Ælfhun ep[iscopu]s* consensi.

✠ *Ego*[6] *Æþelric ep[iscopu]s* condixi.

✠ *Ego Æþelþold ep[iscopu]s* confirmaui.

✠ *Ego Godþine ep[iscopu]s* assensi.

✠ *Ego*[7] *Ælfgar ep[iscopu]s* adquieui.

✠ *Ego Æscpẏ ep[iscopu]s* corroboraui.

✠ *Ego Sigegar ep[iscopu]s* addonaui.

Et cet[er]i abb[at]es[8] q[ui]nque. Duces. v. [et] Ministri qui[n]-
q[ue].

TEXTS

A. BM Loan MS. 30 (cited here as the Anglesey Cartulary), ff. 10v–
11r (cf. Davis No. 91), dated 1230–41. This omits most of the
witness list.

B. National Library of Wales, Aberystwyth, Peniarth MS. 390
(cited here as the Peniarth Cartulary), f. 183v (old numbering
p. 366), dated c. 1240–64. This abbreviates some clauses in the
text, and omits the bounds, but has a more complete witness list
than A.

---

[1] Omitted in B.

[2] Inserted after initial omission.

[3] Omitted in B, which substitutes *et cetera ut supra*.

[4] Omitted in B, which substitutes *et cetera*.

[5] A ends here, with *et alii q[ua]mplures Ep[iscop]i Abb[at]es. Duces. [et]
ministri.* The remainder of the witness list is supplied from B.

[6] The second column of witnesses begins here.

[7] The third column of witnesses begins here.

[8] *Et ceteri abbates* scored through.

1. S. Shaw, *The History and Antiquities of Staffordshire*, London, 2 vols., 1798–1801, I, pp. 19–20, from MS. A.

2. This edition is from MS. A, collated with MS. B. The last part of the witness list is supplied by B. Those parts of the text appearing also in Bu xxx are printed in italic. Portions surviving only in MS. A are enclosed between curved brackets. Abbreviations are extended between square brackets.

TRANSLATION

Bridgeman pp. 124–5.

FORMULAS

The whole charter, including the chrismon, is modelled on Bu xxx, relating to Rolleston, which lies almost adjacent to Wetmore, with only the village of Stretton between them. We may be sure that the copying occurred from xxx to xxxiv, rather than in the reverse direction, because the witness list of the former is compatible with its date, whereas with the Wetmore charter this is not so (see below). In three places the copyist has attempted (unsuccessfully) to improve on his exemplar (*cum substantia* in the exemplar is rendered *cum consubstancia*; similarly, *in perpetuo confirmo hereditatem* is copied as *in perpetuo confirmo hereditate*; again, *si autem contigerit tempore aliquo* is written as *si autem tempore contigerit aliquo*). Further reasons for supposing the Wetmore text to be derivative are discussed below.

DATE AND WITNESSES

As with the rest of the charter (excluding the bounds), the witness list is a modification of the text of Bu xxx. The copyist suppressed the names of four of the aethelings witnessing Bu xxx, but he has repeated not only the order of precedence of the bishops, but also the verbs (*conclusi, consensi, condixi*, etc.) concluding their signatures. By retaining the name of Archbishop Ælfheah he has produced an anachronism, for Ælfheah was in captivity during 1012 (the date claimed for the charter) up to the time of his death. Furthermore, the copyist has added to the list of bishops the names of Æscwig (the bishop of Dorchester who died in 1002) and Sigegar (the bishop of Wells who died in 996 or 997). Comparison with the Peniarth Cartulary entry of Bu xxx shows that in all probability the copyist of the Wetmore charter suppressed the names of five abbots in his exemplar, and 'promoted' two of the *ministri* to *duces*. However, he supplied the right indiction for the year of grace assigned to the charter.

HISTORY AND AUTHENTICITY

Wetmore is not one of the estates mentioned in the Burton foundation charter (No. 40); evidently it was acquired by the abbey some time between 1004 and 1066. By the charter now under discussion, King Æthelred II is made to grant to Abbot Wulfgeat of Burton $1\frac{1}{2}$ hides at Wetmore in return for 70 pounds in gold and silver. The transaction is dated 1012, but it has been shown already that the text is copied from an earlier Burton charter, and the witness list is anachronistic. It is rather suspicious, too, that the hidation of Wetmore in the charter is the same as Wetmore's assessment in DB and in the twelfth-century Burton Abbey surveys, for it is known that the demesne of estates acquired by the abbey was relieved of its assessment (pp. 177, 206). Although the DB hidation included Wetmore's appendages, probably at Horninglow and Anslow (VCH *Staffs* IV, p. 43 n. 50), the charter bounds can be shown to embrace Wetmore only. I am inclined to the opinion that the abbey may have been asked to produce before the Domesday commissioners written evidence of title to its estates. Most of its property is listed in its foundation charter (No. 40) or in Wulfric Spot's will (No. 39), but not so Wetmore, so a separate charter had to be constructed, modelled on the Rolleston charter already preserved in the abbey archives. The forger may have copied the boundary clause from an earlier charter, considerably antedating Domesday. The fact that *pylltunes landes* (evidently a berewick) was divided equally between Rolleston and Wetmore shows that there was a strong tenurial link between these two estates.

BOUNDS

Wetmore village was situated on the bank of the River Trent only a mile to the north of Burton Abbey itself, and some of the $1\frac{1}{2}$ hides said to have been conveyed in this charter have been built over by the suburbs of Burton on Trent. It is clear from DB that the estate then included Anslow and Horninglow (VCH *Staffs* IV, p. 43 n. 50), but the charter boundary is confined to the limits of Wetmore itself. The perambulation, which proceeds in a clockwise direction, can be followed on OS $2\frac{1}{2}''$ sheet SK 22:

1. First from *trente* where the thieves hang in the middle of *bere fordes holme*. OE *bereford* was a common description of fords carrying trackways along which barley was transported. The *holme* or water-meadow lay north of the present Trent Bridge, grid ref. 256233. One wonders just how old the brewing industry is at Burton. Shaw

(*Staffs*) says that the site was still called Gallows flat in his day, whence Gallows Lane.

2. straight on to the *lewe, buton fif lan be heonan*. Reading OE *hleo* 'defence', and *land* 'acre strip', this passage may mean 'straight on to a point five strips short of the stockade (defending Burton)'. About 248235.

3. from the *land* to the *syce*. The present borough boundary runs along a marshland stream, which the perambulation joins at about 237220.

4. up the ridge to the boundary thorn. Leaving the stream at 223224, and striking north-west up the steep wooded slope south of Sinai Park. Perhaps the boundary thorn was near 220229, an area still known as The Thorns. Here the present boundary turns sharply eastwards, running along the bottom of the ridge.

5. to an *aecer*, then along a *haege* to a brook. Along a field boundary to join a stream at 224235.

6. along the brook to a dyke. The dyke is the Shobnall Dingle, reached at 224237.

7. at *ansyðeleage*. Anslow, see Stenton (*Papers*, p. 321 n. 5); the name recurs in the Rolleston bounds (p. 217). Probably the Anslow bounds were joined at 215245, north of Henhurst Wood.

8. north by the dyke to *ceolfes croft*. Reading OE *celf* 'a calf', this would be a cattle enclosure or pound at about 219258 where the bounds take a sharp turn eastwards.

9. alongside the grove to the *straete*. Joining the A50 from Burton on Trent to Tutbury at 230267.

10. to a tree stump then along a dyke to the street. The bounds take several turns here, returning to the street at 234264.

11. by a brook and dyke to the stream running from *chese welle hylle* and *hunger hylle*. 'Cheese well' does not sound a very likely translation. Possibly from OE *cicc, welle*, 'a stream with a bend in it' (cf. *cheesebroke*, a lost stream name in Dagenham, Essex. JEPN 2, 1970, p. 41). The hill may be the promontory north-east of Outwoods Barn. *hunger hylle* (probably from OE *hongra*, 'a wood on a hillside') would then be the modern Beam Hill, and the bounds would join the streams running from these hills at 236255.

12. along the stream to the elm tree that stands on the boundary of Wetmore and Stretton. The bounds run east along the stream to meet the Stretton boundary at 243257.

13. to the ford. Crossing Ryknild Street at 253250.

14. along the stream to the River Trent. The stream runs south of Wetmore Hall Farm to join the Trent at 258248.

15. up the Trent to where the thieves hang. Back to the starting-point.

The bounds conclude with a statement that *pylltunes land*, arable strips and meadow, belongs half to Wetmore and half to Rolleston. It is possible that this is a berewick, to be identified with Pillaton Hall in Penkridge, a Burton property; this however lies a long way from Wetmore and Rolleston.

XXXV. King Æthelred II to his man Theodulf. 5 'Cassatæ' at 'Burtune'.

A.D. 1012

Carta Æþelredi Regis de Burtone ab Incarn[atione] d[omi]ni. Ann[o] Millesimo. xij.

In no[m]i[n]e d[omi]ni n[ost]ri Ih[es]u Chr[ist]i. Om[n]ia que hic humanis c[on]siderantur obtutib[us] tam p[re]-t[er]ita q[ua]m etia[m] p[re]sentia n[ec]n[on] futura festinando iugiter de die in diem sine ulla dilatione declina[n]t ad ruina[m] rapidissimoq[ue] cursu annor[um] cu[m] mensib[us] temporalia siq[ui]dem temp[or]a fugitiuis incessant[er] horis p[ro]perant ad finem. Quap[ro]pt[er] dispensante d[omi]no om[n]ia regnor[um] terre regna ego Æþelredus Anglor[um] videlicet rex sollicita mente cogitando p[er]scrutaui p[ro]futuru[m] ac nece[ssariu]m esse cu[m] hiis t[ra]nsitoriis ac minime mansuris diuiciis p[er]petua atq[ue] iugiter p[er]seu[er]antia celor[um] p[re]mia adq[ui]rerem. Idcirco tali memoria instructus atq[ue] meor[um] utiq[ue] antecessoru[m] roborat[us] exemplis dabo meo fideli homini þeodulfo aliq[ua]m t[er]re p[ar]tem id est. v. cassatos in loco qui uulgari co[n]suetudine dicitur æt burtune. cu[m] om[n]ib[us] ad se rite p[er]tine[n]tib[us] p[ra]tis campis t[er]ris pascuis siluis. liberaboq[ue] illam sup[ra]d[i]c[t]am t[er]ram ab om[n]i seruitute regali p[re]ter expedic[i]one [et] arcis instructione pontisve. Ita ut habeat [et] possideat [et] post obitum eius cuicu[m]q[ue] uolu[er]it in p[er]petua[m] here-ditatem derelinquat. Hiis metis [et] c[etera].[1] Si quis h[uius]

---

[1] The bounds are omitted in the MS.

cupiditatis sp[irit]u inlectus frangere u[el] irrita face[re]
temptau[er]it h[uius] p[ri]uilegii testimonia: sciat se sep[ar]a-
tum a p[ar]ticipac[i]one s[an]c[t]or[um]. Si q[ui]s u[ero] augere
voluerit: augeat deus p[ar]tem illi[us] in iudic[i]o in resur-
rect[i]o[n]e iustor[um]. Sc[ri]pta est h[ec] [et] c[etera].[1]
Mill[esimo]. xij. Hiis t[estibus].[2]

                                              ✠

✠ Ego Æþelred rex h[a]nc mea[m] donac[i]o[n]em hoc
    signo crucis Chr[ist]i c[on]f[ir]maui.

✠ Ego Æþelstan fili[us] regis.

✠ Ego Eadmund fr[ater] p[re]d[i]c[t]i clitonis adiuui.

✠ Ego Eadred donu[m] regis co[n]f[ir]maui.

✠ Ego Þulfstan Archiep[iscopu]s corroboraui.

✠ Ego Godpine po[n]tifex.

✠ Ego Adulf ep[iscopu]s hilaris.

✠ Ego[3] Ælfhun ep[iscopu]s no[n] renui.

✠ Ego Æþelpold pontifex solidaui.

✠ Ego Bẏrhtpold Ep[iscopu]s muniui.

✠ Ego Ædnoð presul c[on]firmaui.

✠ Ego Æþelsige Ep[iscopu]s assensum p[re]bui.

✠ Ego[4] Leofing presul.

✠ Ego Ælfgar Ep[iscopu]s c[on].[5]

✠ Ego Godpine ep[iscopu]s.

✠ Ego bruhtpold ep[iscopu]s.

Et cet[er]i Abb[at]es vj. Duces iiij or. [et] Ministri xvj.[6]

TEXT

National Library of Wales, Aberystwyth, Peniarth MS. 390 (cited
here as the Peniarth Cartulary), ff. 183ᵛ–184ʳ (old numbering pp.
366–7), dated c. 1240–64. This omits the bounds, parts of the dating
clause and of the phrase introducing the witness list, and the names
of the abbots, ealdormen, and thegns witnessing. The text is prefaced
by a chrismon of contemporary form, identical with that of No.
XXXIV.

[1] This clause is abbreviated.   [2] This clause is abbreviated.
[3] The second column of witnesses begins here.
[4] The remaining witnesses are written across the page. It may be that in
the charter before the copyist, the third column of witnesses began here.
[5] This word is too heavily abbreviated for extension.
[6] This sentence is partly scored through.

EDITION

The charter is hitherto unpublished. This edition retains the punctuation of the cartulary version. Abbreviations are extended between square brackets. The cartulary rubric is reproduced.

DATE AND WITNESSES

The surviving portion of the witness list is strictly compatible with the date. The archbishop of Canterbury, who does not witness, was either dead or held captive by the Danes at the time the charter was issued. The sees represented, in order of appearance, are York, Rochester, Hereford, London, Winchester, Ramsbury, Dorchester, Sherborne, Wells, Elmham, Lichfield, and Cornwall. This is the earliest appearance of Burhwold of Cornwall in the lists, and the last appearance of Æthelwold II of Winchester. The whole list is close to that of K 719, dated after 13 February but before August 1012; these two charters may have been drawn up on the same occasion. In both witness lists, Godwine of Rochester is given an unusually high place, presumably because of the vacancy at Canterbury. The charter reinforces the evidence of K 719 that Æthulf survived at Hereford until 1012.

LOCATION

It is difficult to believe that this could be Burton on Trent, where the abbey was already well established by 1012. Barton under Needwood, Staffs (DB *Beretone*) is a possibility, from late confusion between OE *burh tūn* and *bere tūn*. TRE this estate had been in the possession of Earl Ælfgar, with an assessment of 3 hides (Staffs DB No. 21). Perhaps the most likely identification is with Burton Hastings in Warwickshire, and this could well be the *Burhtun* of Wulfric Spot's will (No. 39). In the absence of a boundary clause, however, any such identification is fraught with danger.

FORMULAS

These are unremarkable. They do not come from any tenth- or early eleventh-century formulary represented by surviving texts, but give the impression that the scribe composed his charter by picking and choosing individual passages from a number of exemplars lying before him. As is so often the case with this type of charter, the proem is unique. Although incomplete, sufficient of the text survives to show that the dating clause and the clause introducing the witness list followed a form commonly encountered in Æthelred II's diplomas (e.g. K 621, 687). The cross above the king's subscription is noteworthy.

AUTHENTICITY

This looks like a typical royal diploma from late in the reign of Æthelred II, drawn up probably in the scriptorium of some provincial abbey. There is nothing in the surviving text to suggest that the charter was other than authentic.

XXXVI. King Æthelred II to his thegn Morcar. 2 mansæ at Eckington, Derbyshire. A.D. 1012

Carta Æþelredi regis de Egentona. Anno d[omi]ni M⁰. xij.

✠ *Flebilia fortiter detestanda totillantis seculi piacula diris obscene horrendeq[ue] mortalitatis circu[m]septa latratib[us]. no[n] nos p[at]ria indepte¹ pacis securos, set q[ua]si fetide corruptele in voragine[m] casuros p[ro]vocando ammone[n]t ut ea toto me[n]tis conamine cu[m] casib[us] suis no[n] solum despiciendo s[et] etiam uelud fastidiosam melancolie nausiam abhomina[n]do fugiam[us] tendentes ad illud euu[a]ng[e]licum. Date² [et] dabit[ur] uobi[s]. Qua de re infima q[uas]i p[er]ipsema quisq[ui]liaru[m] abiciens sup[er]na ad instar p[re]ciosor[um] moniliu[m] eligens. animu[m] sempit[er]nis in gaudiis figens. ad* nanciscendam³ *melliflue dulcedinis misericordiam. p[er]frue[n]damq[ue] infinite leticie iocu[n]ditatem: ego Æþelredus rex Angloru[m] p[er] om[n]ipat[ra]ntis dext[er]am que Chr[istu]s est tocius brita[n]nie regniolio⁴ sublimat[us] q[ua]nda[m] telluris p[ar]tic[u]lam meo fideli ministro* Morcero, *id est* duas mansas *in illo loco qui⁵* solicole æt Ecgintune *vocitant* libent[er] *tribuo. Ut ille eam sine iugo honerosi vectigalis cu[m] p[ra]tis pascuis. siluis. riuulis. om[n]ib[us]q[ue] ad eam vtilitatib[us] rite p[er]tine[n]tib[us] libenter ac et[er]nalit[er] q[ua]m[diu] verberanti ocelloru[m] co[n]uolatu, auraq[ue] spirabili potiat[us] habeat. Et post generale[m] qui om[n]ibus cert[us] incert[us]q[ue] homunciis⁶ constat*

---

¹ *adepte* written above line (wrongly).   ² 1 Luke vi. 38.
³ CS 677 has *adipiscendam*.   ⁴ *Sic*, for *regni solio*.
⁵ *Sic*, for *quem*.   ⁶ *Recte*, homunculis as in CS 677.

t[ra]nsitum. Cuicu[m]q[ue] successionis heredi uoluerit condonando[1]
derelinquat. [et] p[er]petualit[er] contradat. *Predictu[m] siquidem*
rus.[2] *hiis t[er]minis circu[m]cincta* patescit. [et] c[etera]. *Si* hoc
quod fieri no[n] optam[us] *aliq[ui]s tipho* sup[er]cilii turgens
h[a]nc mee donac[i]o[n]is *breuicula[m] elidere* aut *infringe[re]*
conauerit, *sciat se* ultima contionis *die classica clangente*
archang[e]li salpice. tumulis *sponte dehiscentib[us] somata diu*
fessa relinque[n]tib[us]. om[n]ib[us] pauefactis creaturis *cum Iuda*
melius non nato.[3] impiisq[ue] cont[ra] Chr[istu]m confligenti-
b[us] iudeis. *quia* no[n] dictus *p[ro]ditor a satoris pio sato filius*
p[er]ditionis[4] *dicitur. et[er]na.* dampnat[i]one *edacib[us] in[n]umer-*
abiliu[m] tormentor[um] flam[m]is p[er]ituru[m]. H[uiu]s *namq[ue]*
a deo inspirante atq[ue]. inuente volu[n]tatis scedula. Anno d[omi]ni
inc[arnationis] M⁰. xij⁰. *Epis[copis].* abb[at]ib[us]. *Ducib[us]*
pat[ri]e p[ro]curatorib[us] regia dapsilitate ouantib[us] p[er]sc[ri]pta
est. *Cui[us] [etia]m inco[n]cusse* ſ[ir]mitatis *auctoritas hiis testib[us]*
roborata co[n]stat. q[uo]r[um] no[m]i[n]a subt[us] *caracterib[us]*
depicta annotantur.

✠ *Ego* Æþelred[us] singularis p[ri]vilegii ierarchia p[re]dit[us]
     rex h[uius] *indiculi fulcimentu[m] cu[m] signo s[an]c[t]e*
     semp[er]q[ue] *amande crucis corroboraui et* subsc[ri]psi.

✠ *Ego* Æþelstan[us] Cliton c[on]sensu[m] p[re]bui figens
     Crucem.

✠ *Ego* Eadmu[n]d illi[us] sup[ra]d[i]c[t]i regis filius *consensi*
     [et] subsc[ri]psi.

✠ *Ego* Þulfstan[us] Ebor[acensis] *ecc[lesie] Archiep[iscopu]s*
     c[on]s[ensi].

Et cet[er]i epi[scopi]꞉ x. Abb[at]es꞉ vij. Duces꞉ iiij.ᵒʳ [et]
Ministri꞉ xvij.

TEXT

National Library of Wales, Aberystwyth, Peniarth MS. 390 (cited
here as the Peniarth Cartulary), f. 184ʳ (old numbering p. 367),
dated c. 1240–64. According to the cartulary copyist, the charter
was prefaced by a cross. There is no boundary clause in the surviving
text, and the witness list is abbreviated.

---

[1] CS 677 has *imperpetuum*.   [2] CS 677 has *tellus*.
[3] Matt. xxvi. 24.   [4] John xvii. 12.

EDITION

The charter is hitherto unpublished. In this edition, abbreviations are extended between square brackets, and the cartulary punctuation is retained. Formulas shared with CS 677 are placed in italic. The rubric heading the text was supplied by the cartulary copyist.

HISTORY

DB shows that TRE part of Eckington was a berewick of the royal estate at Newbold (VCH *Derbys.* I, p. 329a); the remainder, comprising four carucates, was in the hands of Leofnoth (*ibid.*, p. 348ab), to whom had descended most of the property left to Morcar by Wulfric Spot (cf. W p. 155). It seems likely therefore that half of these four carucates is represented by the estate at Eckington left to Morcar in Wulfric's will (No. 39), and the other half is the estate granted to Morcar by King Æthelred by the present charter, Bu XXXVI.

FORMULAS

These are of considerable interest, for they reveal that almost the whole charter, including the small cross prefacing the text, is modelled on an exemplar from Athelstan's reign, one of a series issued between 23 March 931 and 26 January 933. The group is discussed by Mr Eric John in OB pp. 49–50; the surviving examples comprise CS 674–7, 689, 691–2, and 694–6. In this edition of Bu XXXVI, I have placed in italic those parts of the text that are identical with CS 677, a contemporary diploma dated 12 November 931. Most of the words and phrases in the Burton charter that are not paralleled in CS 677 are to be found in other diplomas of the group. Thus *verberanti ocellorum*, *non optamus*, *creaturis*, *innumerabilium*, all occur in CS 674, dated 23 March 931; *verberanti ocellorum convolatu*, *auraque spirabili . . .*, *tipho supercili turgens*, *impiisque Judeis Christum*, all appear in CS 689, dated 30 August 932; *libenter* and *nanciscendam* occur in CS 695, dated 26 January 933, and *vectigalium* and *nanciscendam* in CS 694. Unlike the rest of the series, this last charter is not dated precisely, and there are anomalies in the witness list (cf. H. P. R. Finberg, *West-Country Historical Studies*, 1969, pp. 53–4). However, the occurrence of the word *vectigalium* in both CS 694 and Bu XXXVI, and not elsewhere, is strong evidence that CS 694 is based on an authentic diploma of the period.

The phrase *singularis priuilegii ierarchia* following the king's royal title in the witness list of Bu XXXVI must also have been derived from the same exemplar of Athelstan's reign, for it is found only in

CS 689, 701–3, dated 930 × 934. (K 1322 and 1324 utilize the same title). As one might expect, however, it is more difficult to identify the source of the remaining diplomatic in the surviving portion of the witness list. *Consensum prebui figens crucem* first makes its appearance in a small group of charters of the period 949 × 951 (CS 877, 879, 888, 892); later it recurs only in two great confirmation charters of the early reform period (CS 1046 for Abingdon, dated 959, and CS 1304 for Wilton, dated 974), and in a solitary early diploma of Æthelred II (K 629, dated 981). Finally, although *eiusdem regis filius* was common in charters dated 1004 × 1008 (K 711, 714, 1301, 1303, 1305 etc.), the exact phrase *illius supradicti regis filius* has not been found elsewhere.

WITNESSES

The witness list is considerably abbreviated, but sufficient names survive to show that like other charters issued in 1012 (K 719, 1307, Bu xxxv), this was witnessed during a vacancy at Canterbury.

AUTHENTICITY

It seems probable that this was an authentic charter, drawn up for Morcar by a scribe who utilized for his exemplar a diploma issued by King Athelstan in the period 931 × 933. It is clear that the scribe of this Burton charter must have followed his exemplar very closely; the small amount of variant material is insufficient to allow one to assign the charter with confidence to any particular scriptorium. It could have been composed by a chancery scribe, or by someone working in the Burton scriptorium. An Ely diploma of 1008 was based similarly on a text from Athelstan's reign (K 725).

XXXVII. King Edward the Confessor to his 'comes' Tofig. 2 'territoria' in 'Berghe'.

A.D. 1048

Carta S[an]c[t]i Eadwardi Regis [et] conf[essoris]. pat[ro]ni Westm[onasterii]. de Berghe. Anno d[omi]ni M⁰. xlviij⁰.

Adstipulatione siq[ui]dem sacri spermatis herilis promulgando intonat buccina mestiferam trem[en]di examinis ẏmeram p[re]peti[1] fore subreptione occursuram glomeratis terrigenu[m] univ[er]salis ubi astabit cuneus ac cuncti- tonantis almifluo altithroni[2] clangente diathemate ac in diecula palatinis raptim collegio addicti co[n]tub[er]nialib[us] luci comi nasciscu[n]tur poli ciuilia acta quor[um] lanx trutinando fore p[ro]bat faustissima quor[um]q[ue] eneruit studia p[ro]bis actionib[us] extant classia imp[er]petua ceu cleronomi multabu[n]tur erumpna. ac p[ro] talione infanda gehennalis stẏogie[3] sine meta hauient infernalia. Quap[ro]p[ter] ego Eadpeard toci[us] albionis basileos mee donationis arte libere fruens q[ua]ndam telluris p[ar]tic[u]lam. ij. videl[ice]t t[er]ritoria in loco qui ab incolis Berghe cognominat[ur] cuidam m[ichi] fideli Comiti Touig[4] uocitamine in p[er]petuam hereditatem donant[er][5] concedo. Ut h[ab]eat ac possideat q[ua]mdiu vitali calore arctus caluerint. [et] p[ost] uite sue t[er]minu[m] cuicu[m]q[ue] sibi libuerit sine aliquo scrupulo in hereditariam lib[er]tatem concedat. Tellus aut[em] p[re]d[i]c- [tu]m[6] sit cu[m] om[n]ib[us] ad eandem rite p[er]tine[n]tib[us]. campis, pascuis. siluis. aquar[um] riuulis ab om[n]i mu[n]diali obstaculo liberu[m]. tantu[m] expedic[i]o[n]e. po[n]tis arcisue restaurac[i]o[n]e exceptis. Quod si quispia[m] h[a]nc n[ost]re donac[i]o[n]is lib[er]tatem inuidie face turgens eu[er]tere

---

[1] *Sic*, for *perpeti*.

[2] A reads *alterithroni* and corrects to *altithroni*, but this latter form is the correct reading; the mark above the first 't' in the MS. is in fact part of a gloss.

[3] for *stẏcgie*.

[4] A reads *Touig'*, but what was thought to be an abbreviation mark is in fact a stroke representing the dot of the 'i'.

[5] for *donata*.   [6] *Sic*.

conatus fuerit: cum Pilato [et] Iuda scariothen. caẏpha
q[uoque] eor[um]q[ue] co[m]manipularib[us] et[er]nalit[er] ac
herontica combustione trudatur. nisi ante mortis articulum
satisfactione penituerit congrua q[uo]d n[ostr]e donac[i]o[n]is
p[re]sumpsit violare q[uo]d absit statuta. Hiis nempe metis rus
antescriptum circu[m]cingitur. [et] c[etera].[1]

Acta est aut[em] h[ec] mea donac[i]o anno ab incarn[atione]
d[omi]ni n[ost]ri Ih[es]u Chr[ist]i. M⁰. xlviij. Ind[ictione]. ij a.

Hiis testib[us] consentientib[us] quor[um] no[m]i[n]a hic
inferius karraxantur.

✠ Ego Eadpeard rex Anglor[um] c[um] t[ri]umpho s[an]c[t]e
   Crucis hoc donu[m] Inmobile corroboraui.
✠ Ego Exi[2] Archiep[iscopu]s regie roborator donationis
   agẏe t[ri]umphale crucis signac[u]l[u]m depinxi.
✠ Ego Ælfric Archiep[iscopu]s triumphale tropheum agẏe
   crucis Impressi.[3]
✠ Ego Æðelstan ep[iscopu]s co[n]solidaui.
✠ Ego Eadnoð ep[iscopu]s consu[m]maui.
✠ Ego Stigand[4] ep[iscopu]s confeci.
✠ Ego Aldred ep[iscopu]s adq[ui]eui.
✠ Ego Duduc ep[iscopu]s subsc[ri]psi.
✠ Ego Rodbeard ep[iscopu]s c[on]sensu[m] p[re]bui.
✠ Ego Ægelpeard Abb[a]s
✠ Ego Þulfric Abb[a]s
✠ Ego Ælfpine Abb[a]s
✠ Ego[5] Leofstan. Abb[a]s
✠ Ego Leofsig. Abb[a]s
✠ Ego Earnpig. Abb[a]s
✠ Ego Ospig. Abb[a]s
✠ Ego Godpine. Dux
✠ Ego Leofric. Dux

[1] The boundary clause is omitted in the surviving text.
[2] A reads Ea[ds]i, but 'Exi' was a normal spelling for 'Eadsige' at this
period.
[3] A reads suppressi, but this is not supported in the MS.
[4] A reads Stigandus, but there is no mark of abbreviation after 'd' in the
MS.
[5] The second column of witnesses begins here.

✠ Ego Sipard Dux
✠ Ego Harold Dux
✠ Ego Beorn. Dux.
✠ Ego[1] Leofpine Minister.
✠ Ego Tostig Min[ister]
✠ Ego Ælfstan Min[ister]
✠ Ego Ælfgar Min[ister]
✠ Ego Odda. Min[ister]
✠ Ego Ordgar. Min[ister]
✠ Ego Ordulf Min[ister]
✠ Ego Brihtric Min[ister]
✠ Ego Ælfpine. Min[ister]

TEXT

National Library of Wales, Aberystwyth, Peniarth MS. 390 (cited here as the Peniarth Cartulary), f. 184ᵛ (old numbering p. 368), dated c. 1240–64. According to the cartulary copyist, the charter was prefaced by a chrismon. There is no boundary clause in the surviving text, but the text appears otherwise to be intact. It was glossed by a later scribe, but in several places the gloss is now illegible.

EDITIONS

A. Barlow, EC pp. 332–3, with comments. The chrismon prefacing the Peniarth Cartulary text is not reproduced. Abbreviations are extended slightly. Readings of the gloss are attempted.

B. In this edition, abbreviations are extended between square brackets; the cartulary punctuation is unchanged. The cartulary rubric is reproduced. No attempt has been made to give readings of the gloss, as it does not appear that the glossator had anything useful to contribute to the text.

CHRISMON

The chrismon prefacing the Peniarth Cartulary text of this charter is similar to those first developed in 961–2 (see notes to No. 107 in the hand-list). However the type continued in sporadic use throughout the eleventh century (e.g. K 770 dated 1044), and was also utilized by twelfth-century forgers (e.g. CS 1050).

---

[1] The third column of witnesses begins here.

DATE AND WITNESSES

The year of grace is given as 1048, but the indiction corresponds with 1049. There is no way of telling for certain which is the correct figure, but 1048 is perhaps the more likely. The witness list is fully compatible with either year. Sees represented are Canterbury, York, Hereford, Dorchester, Winchester, Worcester, Wells, and London. Abbeys represented are Glastonbury, St Augustine's, Ramsey, Bury St Edmunds, Ely, Peterborough, and Thorney. The earls are from Wessex, Mercia, Northumbria, and the East and Middle Angles. The witnessing thegns are identifiable in several cases; they are correct for the period.

IDENTITY OF THE ESTATE AND ITS RECIPIENT

Comes at this period could be a title held by a very powerful thegn; it was not restricted exclusively to earls. It is difficult to think who else named Tofig could be addressed in this way on this occasion, other than Tofig 'the Proud', the founder of Waltham Abbey and grandfather of Esgar the Staller, one of the principal royal officials of Edward the Confessor. The Waltham chronicler was exaggerating, no doubt, when he described Tofig as 'the first man in the kingdom after the king', but the phrase does indicate how he might come to be addressed as *Comes*. Esgar's estates, and those of his grandfather Tofig, were centred on East Anglia, and the fact that the abbots of all five of the great fenland houses witnessed this charter as a group is probably significant. It is true that Æthelmær the diocesan bishop (of Elmham) did not witness, but he is absent from the witness lists of all the Confessor's authentic royal diplomas, and it is apparent that his see was represented in the lists by his brother, the great pluralist Stigand, after the latter's election to Winchester in 1047. The assessment of the estate at *Berghe* in *territoria* is strongly suggestive that it lay within the carucated Danelaw, for hides were never described by this Latin term. The charter is separated sharply by date from the rest of the Burton series, and there is no need to assume that the estate conveyed lay anywhere near Burton Abbey; the likely situation is East Anglia, and it seems very probable that the *Berghe* of this charter was in fact part of Bergh Apton in Norfolk. There is extant the text of a will, dated 1042 × 1043, by which Ælfric *Modercope* left part of this estate to Ely, naming Tofig the Proud as one of his executors (W XXVII). The remainder of the estate was left to Ely at a later date, some time before 1058, by the will of the thegn Edwin (W XXXII; ECEE p. 83), and I suggest that it is this portion

of Bergh Apton which had been granted to Tofig by the Confessor
in 1048–9.

FORMULAS

These are unremarkable, individual phrases being drawn from
texts of all periods back to the charters of Athelstan. Characteristic
of the age are the references to the Styx, the river of Hades of
classical mythology, and to Pilate and Judas Iscariot (ECEE p. 89;
K 761, 766, 771, 776, 792, 801). In the witness list, *consummaui* is
not very common, but it occurs in K 769.

AUTHENTICITY

On the face of it, this is a routine text from the Confessor's reign.
If *Berghe* is correctly located, one would suspect that Tofig's charter
was drawn up at Ely. Unfortunately, we have only the Confessor's
privilege to Ely with which to compare it (K 907; LE pp. 161–3);
the two charters are concerned with vastly different situations, and
it is not really surprising that they have no points of contact in their
diplomatic. Barlow remarks that the charter to Tofig 'has some
obviously unauthentic features', which he does not discuss in detail
(Barlow, EC p. 88 n. 2). I cannot detect them. The only questionable
element that I can find is the indiction, and this could easily arise
from a transcriber's error. Here and there the text has suffered in
transmission, but this is only to be expected. Until it is proved
otherwise, this charter is best regarded as an authentic diploma of
Edward the Confessor, drawn up probably in the scriptorium of one
of the greater abbeys north of the Thames, perhaps Ely. The boundary
clause has been lost; otherwise the text is intact.

CHAPTER XII

BIOGRAPHICAL NOTES
ON THE BURTON CHARTERS

I N THE following section, brief biographical sketches are
supplied for all the persons whose names appear in the
Burton charters listed on pp. 167–71. The roman numerals
following each name refer to the Burton charter in which it
appears.

Ælfgar   XXVIIa, XXX–XXXI, XXXIII–XXXV
  Bishop of Elmham 1001 × Christmas 1021.
  He was a priest at Christ Church, Canterbury, and became
Archbishop Dunstan's private chaplain and confessor. In 988 he had a
vision of Dunstan's death and reception into heaven (*Memorials of St
Dunstan*, pp. 64, 120–3, 317–19). Ælfstan, his predecessor at
Elmham, last witnessed in 1001 (K 705). Ælfgar witnessed K 706,
dated 1001, as bishop of the East Angles (i.e. Elmham), and regularly
thereafter until July 1012 (S 904(1), K 1295; Bu XXVIII; LE II, c. 58,
K 714, 1303–5, Bu XXX–XXXI, XXXIII–XXXV; K 719, 1307). He
witnessed also K 727 dated 1018, but this is a doubtful charter; his
successor Bishop Ælfwine witnessed K 729 dated 1019, another
doubtful charter (cf. Chaplais, *Exeter*, pp. 20, 23), and the authentic
K 734, dated 23 June 1022. Ælfgar was the second of three successive
bishops of Elmham having close connections with Ely Abbey, and it
seems probable that he retired there some time between July 1012
(K 1307) and 18 October 1016, the date of the battle of *Assandun*
(LE p. 144 n. 7). Ælfwine, who succeeded eventually to the
bishopric, appears to have been appointed as *chorepiscopus* in the
diocese late in the reign of Æthelred II (*ibid.*), but Ælfgar retained
the title until his death. At Ely he was remembered as a benefactor
(LE p. xxxviii), and the ASC obit calls him 'the almsgiver'. The
date of Bishop Ælfgar's death is of importance because of its connection with the foundation of Bury St Edmund's Abbey (ECEE p. 64),
and because of its bearing on the commencement of the year in the

Anglo-Saxon Chronicle for this period. The obit is entered under the year 1021 in the 'D' text of the Chronicle, and the same year is given in Florence of Worcester and the *Liber Eliensis*. The Chronicle, however, says he died at dawn on Christmas Day (*on Christes mæsse uhtan*), and since this portion of the Chronicle is thought to begin the year on Christmas Day, Dr Blake would argue that his death occurred on 25 Dec. 1020, rather than 25 Dec. 1021 (LE p. 143 n. 1). Examination of the full context of the Chronicle entry, however, makes this view difficult to defend, for Ælfgar's death is recorded immediately after the banishment of Earl Turkil at Martinmas in the same year, i.e. 11 Nov. 1021. An early Ely kalendar, moreover, commemorated the death on 24 December, and since Ælfgar died at Ely, this could well be more accurate than the Chronicle itself (cf. 'The day of Byrhtnoth's death and other obits from a twelfth-century Ely kalendar', *Leeds Studies in English*, No. VI (1937), pp. 15–17). The weight of the evidence, therefore, definitely favours Christmas 1021. Perhaps *uhtan* in the Chronicle could mean the eve of Christmas, rather than the dawn of Christmas Day. On *uhte* see E. G. Stanley, *Anglia* LXXIII (1955), pp. 434–5.

Ælfgar, bishop of Lichfield, *see* Wulfgar.

Ælfgar, thegn   XII, XIV
   Witnesses 951 × 962.

Careful sifting of charter evidence allows the identification of this witness with the kinsman of King Edgar who died in Devon in 926, and was buried at Wilton (ASC A). No thegn of this name is to be found in witness lists of the period 947 x 950, and Bu XII represents his first appearance, in 951. His name recurs in 952 (CS 895), 953 × 955 (CS 902), and in 955 (CS 917). In 956 he witnessed no less than 26 charters of which the texts have survived, and on a number of occasions he headed the list of thegns, e.g. Bu XIV, CS 924, 935, 938, 964–5, 975, 986, 1183. At other times he was usually in the top five, and only once fell below eighth (CS 981). That Ælfgar lived in Wessex is apparent from the fact that from soon after May 957 (cf. CS 999) until 1 Oct. 959, during which the kingdom was divided between Eadwig and his brother Edgar, Ælfgar witnessed only the former's charters (CS 1022 and 1047 can be set aside as spurious). Once Edgar acceded to the whole kingdom, however, Ælfgar when present almost invariably headed the thegns in the witness lists of royal charters (CS 1073 is an exception) until 962. In that year he witnessed three charters of which the texts have survived (CS 1082,

1092, 1095), but he failed to witness several others (CS 1083, 1093–4, 1096), and from the Chronicle entry we may assume that he was dead or dying when these charters were drawn up. No thegn named Ælfgar witnessed for several years after 962 (CS 1103 is a forgery). An Athelney charter of King Eadwig dated 959 calls Ælfgar '*amicus regis*' (ECW p. 140). In CS 1074 Ælfgar was given the honorific title of 'consul', and it is probable that he was also the Ælfgar 'consul' who appears in CS 667, a spurious charter utilizing an authentic witness list of the time of King Eadred. In CS 1035 Ælfgar is called the king's '*propinquus*', and this supports his identification with the man referred to in the Chronicle entry of 962. CS 1035 reveals also that Ælfgar had a younger brother Brihtferth (q.v.), and it is instructive to observe that their names appear adjacent to each other throughout the witness lists; in charters of the tenth and eleventh centuries this happened commonly with brothers (e.g. Ælfhere and Ælfheah before they became ealdormen). The thegn Ælfgar who received land at Camel, Somerset, in 939 × 946 (ECW 455), and Wokefield, Berks., in 946 × 951 (CS 888) cannot be identified with certainty with the thegn considered here.

Ælfgar, thegn   xxviiia
   Witnesses 989 × 1014, and 1002 × 1008.
   The two men here discussed witnessed seventh and eleventh of the 17 thegns in Bu xxviiia, dated 1004. It is not possible to identify them with certainty. Neither of them is the Ælfgar who was the recipient of Ebbesbourne and Wylye, Wilts. (K 655, 664), and who witnessed high in the lists of the period 976 × 990; but the seventh thegn witnessing Bu xxviii may be the Ælfgar of Honiton, Devon, who witnessed in 989 (EHD I, p. 533). He continued to witness, low down on the lists, from 994 (K 687) until at least 1014 (K 1309). A second Ælfgar appears in Bu xxviiia, in K 1296, and in K 1303–5 (dated 1002–8). Three Ælfgars witnessed K 1303 and 1305 (dated 1007–8).

Ælfgar, thegn   xxxvii
   Witnesses 1048.
   The name is too common to permit of firm identification (cf. Oleson p. 117), but it is probable that the Ælfgar who witnessed Bu xxxvii (1048) was the brother of Ordgar of Devon (q.v.), and a descendant of Ordulf, the founder of Tavistock Abbey, and uncle of Æthelred II. Professor Finberg suggests that he is the Ælfgar the Tall who held Tavistock property in 1066 (*Lucerna*, pp. 195, 200).

Ælfgifu, queen   XXXII
   Witnesses 1011.
   For a full biography, see A. Campbell, *Encomium Emmæ Reginæ*, R. Hist. Soc., Camden 3rd series, LXXII, 1949, pp. xl–l.

Ælfheah   XXVI–XXVIIIa, XXIX–XXXIV
   Priest and monk of Glastonbury, abbot of Deerhurst 968 × 975–9; abbot of Bath 975–9 × 984; (II) bishop of Winchester 984 × 1006; archbishop of Canterbury 1006 × 12 April 1012.
   It appears likely that the Ælfheah who witnessed from 968 to 974 as abbot was in fact the Ælfheah who became archbishop of Canterbury (CS 1220, 1257, 1302, 1268, 1282, 1303–4), and that although later sources describe him as only a monk of Deerhurst, he was in fact abbot. William of Malmesbury says that he had been a monk and priest of Glastonbury (AD p. 92). Some time during the antimonastic reaction in the reign of King Edward the Martyr, Deerhurst Abbey was suppressed, and Ælfheah was translated to Bath, where he became abbot after Æscwig's elevation to the see of Dorchester (q.v.). It is clear that he was shaken by the suppression of Deerhurst, and at Bath he lived as a recluse, in a cell apart from the rest of the community (*Memorials of St Dunstan*, pp. 116, 217, 312; *Vita Elphegi*). During his tenure of Bath, Ælfheah figures in a story in the *Vita Oswaldi* concerning the death of his friend, Foldbriht of Pershore (HCY I, pp. 439ff). In sharp contradistinction to his activities while at Deerhurst, Ælfheah witnessed only one surviving charter as abbot of Bath (CS 1278, dated 982). As soon as Ælfheah was appointed to Winchester, his successor Ælfhere at Bath commenced to represent the abbey at court again, being one of only four abbots witnessing in 985 (K 1283, 648, 650). As bishop and then archbishop, Ælfheah appears regularly in the witness lists from 985 to September 1011, when he was taken prisoner by the Danes. He remained in their hands until his martyrdom, and so could not have witnessed Bu XXXIV in 1012. See further, Ashdown, *English and Norse Documents*, p. 296; Freeman NC (3rd ed.) I, pp. 673–7; KBL p. 28. Osbern's *Vita Elphegi* was printed by Wharton in *Anglia Sacra* II, pp. 122–47.

Ælfheah, bishop   XVIII
   Witnesses 958.
   There is no other evidence for the existence at this date of a bishop named Ælfheah, and the witness list of Bu XVIII has been tampered with.

Ælfheah   XXIV–XXVII

Bishop of Lichfield 975 × June 1002–4.

His predecessor Wynsige (q.v.) witnessed CS 1312 dated 975. Ælfheah first witnessed CS 1314, also dated 975. Subsequently he witnessed the following, in chronological order: K 621, 624, 626, 629, 633, 1279, 1281, 641, Bu xxiv, K 654, Bu xxv, K 712–13 (dated 990), K 684, 687–8, 1289, S 1380, K 696, 1291–2, EHD I, p. 534, Bu xxvi–xxvii, K 698, Crawf 8, K 700, 703, 706–7, Crispin p. 168, K 1295–6. This last charter was witnessed as archbishop by Wulfstan, who did not succeed to York until some time after June 1002. Ælfheah's successor Godwine (q.v.) witnessed K 709 and Bu xxviiia, both dated 1004. No other biographical material survives for Ælfheah.

Ælfheah the Bald   II, X, XII

Monk of Glastonbury, (I) bishop of Winchester 934 × 12 March 951.

He first witnessed as 'priest and monk' CS 641 dated 925, cf. SBW p. 33. His dates as bishop are given in ASC, but see O'D II, pp. 111–12. His nickname *calvus* (preserved by Florence of Worcester) derived probably from his tonsure, then rare in England. He was a relative of Dunstan (q.v.) whom he tonsured together with Æthelwold (q.v.), so initiating the movement for the English Benedictine reform. See further, OB p. 156; Bullough p. 477.

Ælfheah   XXIII

Ealdorman of Wessex 959 × 971.

He was the younger brother of Ealdorman Ælfhere of Mercia (q.v.), and the son of Ealdorman Ealhhelm (q.v.). Ælfheah was one of the king's discthegns; unlike his brother, he did not accompany King Edgar to Mercia in 957. He remained in Wessex with King Eadwig, who just before his death gave Ælfheah an ealdordom comprising Hampshire, Wiltshire, and Sussex, a position he retained after King Edgar's accession to the whole kingdom. There is as yet no adequate biography of Ælfheah, but see W pp. 121–2; R pp. 338–9.

Ælfheah, thegn   XII, XVII

Witnesses 951 × 956.

It does not seem possible to identify with any certainty the Ælfheah who received *Northtune* from King Eadred in 951 (Bu XII); it is not even certain that the thegn Ælfheah who witnessed this charter was the same person as the recipient of the estate. It seems unlikely that he was the thegn who became ealdorman of Wessex (q.v.), for no estate named *Northtune* is mentioned in Ealdorman Ælfheah's will. For thegns named Ælfheah at this period, see R pp. 338–9.

Ælfheah, thegn   XXXI
     Witnesses 1009.
     Nothing more is known of the two thegns named Ælfheah who witnessed Bu XXXI.

Ælfhelm   XXVIIIa, XXIX
     Bishop of Dorchester 1002 × 1007–11.
     His predecessor Æscwig (q.v.) witnessed K 1297 and 1295, both dated 1002, but this latter charter was witnessed also by Ælfhelm, who may therefore have been appointed *chorepiscopus* in the diocese just before Æscwig's death. Probably Ælfhelm had succeeded by the time he witnessed K 1296, dated some time after June 1002. He witnessed Bu XXVIIIa, K 714, 1301, and finally Bu XXIX, dated 1007. His successor Eadnoth I (q.v.) witnessed as abbot two charters of that year, and he did not witness surviving texts as a bishop until 1011. No biographical material survives for Ælfhelm.

Ælfhelm   XXVIIIa, XXVIIIb
     Ealdorman of Deira 993 × 1006.
     The brother of Wulfric Spot (q.v.), he is called *Norðanhumbrensium Provinciarum dux* in K 698, and *dux Transhumbranæ gentis* in S 1380 (994), but since Waltheof witnessed as *dux* in 994 (K 687), it is probable that Ælfhelm's ealdordom was confined to the southern half of Northumbria. From his brother Wulfric he received extensive territories in Wirral and between the Rivers Ribble and Mersey, and also lands in Staffordshire, and the large formerly royal estate of Conisbrough in Yorkshire. He possessed estates in Northamptonshire, which he gave to Peterborough Abbey (No. 14). His attestations as thegn up to the year 990 cannot be distinguished from those of other thegns named Ælfhelm (see below). After 990, however, only one surviving charter of the reign of Æthelred II is witnessed by a thegn of this name (K 688). Since K 672 which claims to be dated 990 is spurious (its witness list is of the period 1002 × 1005), the earliest surviving charter witnessed by Ælfhelm as ealdorman is K 684, dated 993. He seems, therefore, to have succeeded Thored after the latter's failure against the Danes in 992 (cf. D. Whitelock in Clemoes, p. 80). From that date until 999 he witnessed usually as third of the ealdormen, and thereafter as second. He was murdered in 1006,

possibly by order of King Æthelred II (ASC and Fl Wig). His daughter Ælfgifu of Northampton became the concubine of King Cnut and the mother of King Harold Harefoot. It appears that she was allowed to inherit the bulk of Ælfhelm's Northamptonshire estates, but his lands in Staffordshire and south Lancashire fell into the king's hands (W p. 154). His Yorkshire properties may have descended to his successor as earl of Northumbria, for eventually Conisbrough came into the possession of Peterborough Abbey, probably from this source (ECEE p. 246).

Ælfhelm   xxvıııb
    Kinsman of Wulfric Spot 1004.
    Probably the recipient of Palterton, Derbyshire (Bu xxvıııb), should not be identified with Ealdorman Ælfhelm (q.v.). Nothing more is known of him.

Ælfhelm, thegn   XXI, XXIII
    Witnesses 966 × 968.
    He was the recipient of Parwich, Derbyshire. It is possible, but unlikely, that this was the Ælfhelm who became ealdorman of Deira (q.v.). One cannot distinguish satisfactorily between the various thegns named Ælfhelm who attest charters of the second half of the tenth century. The Ælfhelm who received Parwich may have been identical with the Ælfhelm who received Witney in Oxfordshire in 969 (CS 1230), but the Ælfhelm who received Wratting, Cambridgeshire, in 974 was undoubtedly Ælfhelm Polga, an important thegn of the eastern Danelaw who died in 989 (W xiii; ECEE pp. 28, 31, 44; *Proc. Camb. Antiq. Soc.* lvi–lvii, 1964, pp. 61–7). EHD i, p. 533 refers to an important synod at London, which can be dated 989 × 990 from other persons present. An Ælfhelm headed the thegns witnessing an act of this synod, which was witnessed also by Ælfhelm Polga; since the latter died on 31 Oct. 989, the synod must have been held earlier in that year.

Ælfhere   XXXI
    Abbot of Bath 984 × c. 1009.
    He succeeded as abbot to Ælfheah (q.v.), who was consecrated bishop on 19 Oct. 984, and enthroned at Winchester on 28 Oct. 984 (ASC). His abbey is identified in K 684, 698, and he must be the abbot of that name who received an estate in Somerset (W xxi), and who carried the king's seal to a Berkshire moot in 990 × 992 (R lxvi). He witnessed some charters as *Æl(f)uere*, but the *Æluere* of K 657 was probably Abbot Ælfweard of Glastonbury (q.v.), since

the witness list of this charter is otherwise identical with that of K 658, in which Ælfweard's name appears (all the abbots are 'promoted' to *duces* in this charter). Abbot Ælfhere witnessed the following charters: K 648, 650, 1283, 673, 712–13 (dated 990), 684, 686 (wrongly called *Ælfred*), 687, 1289, 696; EHD I, p. 534; OS Facs III, 35; K 706–7, 1295, 1297, 1301, 1303–4, Bu XXXII. As suggested by Professor Whitelock (W p. 174), the Abbot Ælfhere who witnessed the following charters of the period 1018 × 1031 may have been a different person: K 728 (a doubtful charter with an apparently authentic witness list), 729–30, 734, 739, 743–4; LH pp. 374–6. As with many other foundations, there is a long gap in the history of Bath Abbey in the first half of the eleventh century.

Ælfhere   XIV, XVII, XXIII
　　Ealdorman of Mercia 956 × 983.
　　He was the son of Ealdorman Ealhhelm (q.v.), and the elder brother of Ælfheah, ealdorman of Wessex (q.v.), of the discthegn Ælfwine (q.v.), of the thegn Edgar (q.v.), and of the thegn Ælfweard (Chron E, p. 78). Although his brother Ælfheah may have been witnessing charters for some time previously, it is remarkable that Ælfhere's name does not appear among the *ministri* until CS 906, dated 955. He then witnesses CS 917, a charter dated after 23 Nov. 955, as Ælfhere *ex parentela regis*, *minister*, and his brother's name follows immediately afterwards as Ælfheah *frater eius*, *minister*. Early in 956, the two brothers witnessed CS 958 and 963 in adjacent places among the thegns. Ælfhere was created ealdorman by King Eadwig before 13 Feb. 956 (CS 919); but after the revolt of the ætheling Edgar in 957, Ælfhere ceased to witness King Eadwig's charters; subsequently he subscribed only to those of Edgar as king of Mercia: CS 1036–7, 1040, 1042, 1044, 1052. Ælfheah, by contrast, continued to witness King Eadwig's charters until the latter's death: CS 992, 998, 1004, 1032–4, 1045–6. After King Edgar's accession to the whole kingdom in 959, the two brothers began to witness next to each other again; e.g. CS 1051, 1053, 1055, Muchelney 3, S 704. Ælfhere continued to subscribe until his death in 983, when he was succeeded in the Mercian ealdormanry by his brother-in-law, Ælfric Cild. Ælfhere was the most powerful ealdorman of his day, and is remembered chiefly for his leadership after King Edgar's death of a lay reaction against the ever-increasing landed interests of the newly revived monasteries. His precise objectives in this famous quarrel are still a matter for debate, but modern opinion has softened somewhat the harsh strictures of the early monastic chroniclers.

Certainly the account in the Evesham Chronicle of his alleged despoliation of that house does not stand the test of independent enquiry (see under Abbot Frithugar). Ælfhere's son Eadric is described as *major regiæ domus* in Chron Abingd I, p. 357, where he is said to have 'purchased' the abbey of Abingdon for his brother Eadwine, who was abbot 984 × 990. A full-scale investigation of Ælfhere's career is badly needed. See also under King Eadwig, where the relationship of his family to that monarch is discussed. See further, J. Fisher in *Camb. Hist. Journ.*, x, pt III, pp. 234–50; OB pp. 158, 179, 221–2; R p. 319; W p. 124; Plummer II, p. 164.

Ælfhun   xxvIIIa, XXIX–XXXV

Abbot of Milton, Dorset, 974 × 1002–4, bishop of London c. 1002–4 × 1015.

Cyneweard (q.v.), his predecessor at Milton, succeeded to the bishopric of Wells some time after 15 May 974 (CS 1303–4). Ælfhun first witnessed as abbot CS 1315, dated 975 (name misspelt *Ælfhim*). He witnessed, also as abbot, K 633, 1278, EHD I, p. 533, K 712–13, 684, S 1380 (misspelt *Ælfwine*), and K 1289; these charters are dated 982 to 995. His abbey is identified in K 684; although one of the first to be reformed, it was not an important house, and usually Ælfhun witnessed low down on the list of abbots. The abbey is not represented on a list of fourteen houses whose abbots witnessed in 997 (K 698), and a similar list of fourteen in 1002 (K 1295). It seems very probable that it was Abbot Ælfhun of Milton who was elevated to the see of London in 1002 or later; his predecessor Wulfstan of London (q.v.) was not appointed to York until after July in that year. Ælfhun first witnessed as bishop two charters dated 1004, Bu xxvIIIa and K 709; the latter was witnessed on 7 December. Ælfhun witnessed also as bishop the following charters, in chronological order: K 714, 1301, Bu xxIX, K 1303–5, Bu xxx–xxxI, K 1306 (misspelt *Ælfin*), Bu xxxII–xxxV, W xxII (this last being impossible to date precisely). In sharp contradistinction to his predecessors, Ælfhun witnessed usually low down in the lists of the bishops. Most of his diocese was under Viking control during the greater part of his episcopate. Late in 1013 he accompanied Queen Ælfgifu and her sons to exile in Normandy (ASC E). Florence of Worcester says he acted as *magister* to the aethelings. King Æthelred II followed soon after, and England then acknowledged the sovereignty of Swegn, king of Denmark. On 3 Feb. 1014, however, Swegn died at Gainsborough and was buried at York, where the inhabitants had accepted already Swegn's second son Cnut as their king. A fortnight later at York, Archbishop Wulfstan II consecrated Ælfwig (probably the abbot of Westminster) as bishop of London (ASC D). It has been assumed in the past that Ælfhun had died, or at least that he never returned to England from exile. This is disproved by his witnessing, as bishop of London, K 1310, an authentic charter of King Æthelred dated 1015. It follows that Wulfstan had consecrated Ælfwig without Æthelred's approval (he was indeed still in exile), and that when Æthelred returned from Normandy, he brought Ælfhun with him, and gave him back possession of his diocese. After King Cnut's accession we hear no more of Ælfhun, whose fate is unknown. Ælfwig does not appear again in charters until 1022 (K 734, which he witnessed as bishop), but few diplomas survive from the early years of Cnut's reign. See further, KBL p. 56.

Ælfmær   xxviiia, xxxii

Monk of Glastonbury, abbot of Tavistock c. 994 × 1009, bishop of Selsey 1009 × 1032.

The abbey was founded in 981, and Ælfmær is the first abbot whose name has come down to us. William of Malmesbury says he had been a monk at Glastonbury (AD 1, p. 94). His house was of insufficient importance to be represented on two very long lists surviving for 993 and 997 (K 684, 698), and the earliest reference to Ælfmær as abbot of Tavistock is dated 994 (H. P. R. Finberg, *Tavistock Abbey*, 2nd ed., 1969, pp. 2–3). It seems probable that he witnessed Bu xxviii (1004), K 714 (1005), K 1304 (1007), and K 1305 (1008), in each case low down on the list. The Abbot Ælfmær who witnessed K 643 (1006 × 1009), and headed the abbots in the witness lists of OS Facs iii, 39 (1018) and K 737 (1023) is, however, more likely to have been from St Augustine's, Canterbury (for this Ælfmær, see Goscelin's *Vita Wlsini* p. 82; Barlow p. 223 n. 5; KBL p. 35). It is very probable that Ælfmær of Tavistock became bishop of Selsey in 1009. As bishop, he witnessed the following charters dated 1011 to 1023: Bu xxxii; K 719, 1307; OS Facs iii, 39; LH pp. 324–6; K 736, 734, 737, 739. A namesake (probably the abbot of St Augustine's) was appointed bishop of Sherborne some time in the period 1023 × 1027, but the length of his tenure is unknown (H p. 548); the earliest date recorded for his successor is 1031 (K 744). It would seem impossible, therefore, to determine whether the Bishop Ælfmær who witnessed the following charters dated 1024 × 1031 came from Selsey or Sherborne: K 741, 743; OS Facs ii, Exeter xi. The Ælfmær who witnessed K 744 must, however, have been from Selsey. See also KBL pp. 71–2.

Ælfmær, thegn   xxviiia
     Witnesses 1004.
     He was the last of 21 thegns to witness Bu xxviiia, and is perhaps
to be identified with the thegn Ælfmær who witnessed K 714 (1005)
and K 719 (1012). The thegn Ælfmær who witnessed K 684 (993)
and OS Facs iii, 35 (997) was perhaps another person.

Ælfnoth, thegn   XVII
     Witnesses 956.
     Two Ælfnoths appear in 959 among the 70 thegns witnessing CS
1046 (see OB p. 188 for authenticity), being in the 3rd and 50th
places respectively. Perhaps it is permissible to identify the witness of
Bu xvii with the senior of these (given the title 'custos' in CS 1046),
and to suggest that he was the thegn who witnessed in the period
949 × 959 charters CS 882, 887, 892, 895, 899–900, 903, 908, 931,
977, and 1022; the junior Ælfnoth was possibly the thegn who
witnessed in the period 956 × 959 charters CS 966, 1028, 1043, and
1044.

Ælfric   xxvi–xxviiib
     Monk of Abingdon, abbot of St Albans c. 970 × 991–3; (II) bishop
of Ramsbury 991–3 × 1005, archbishop of Canterbury 21 April
995 × 16 Nov. 1005.
     Ælfric appears to have been preceded as abbot at St Albans by
Ealdred, who witnessed 959 × 970 (CS 1047; R xlv; S 766; CS 1228,
1266; cf. KBL p. 226); the date of Ælfric's appointment is uncertain.
The Ælfric who witnessed a large number of charters from 959 to 968
(CS 1030 to 1224–7) was no doubt abbot of St Augustine's; unfortunately the date of his death is unknown (it is given as 971 in a late
St Augustine's source, but this is unreliable). At our present state of
knowledge, it is uncertain whether the Abbot Ælfric who witnessed
the following charters dated 969 × 973 was from St Albans or St
Augustine's: CS 1229–30, 1233, 1257, 1266, 1268–9, 1282, 1302,
1309. (Abbot Ælfric I of Malmesbury (q.v.) does not appear to have
witnessed any royal diplomas.) The Abbot Ælfric who witnessed CS
1303–4 dated 974, however, was probably from St Albans, for these
two charters were witnessed also by Ælfnoth, who had succeeded
to St Augustine's. The probability is that the Ælfric who headed the
abbots witnessing K 1312–13, 1315–16, all dated 975, and K 624
(980), was the abbot of St Albans, but although he retained this
office until at least 991 (see below), he witnessed only two more
surviving charters during this period (K 712–13, dated 990). Ælfric

succeeded to the bishopric of Ramsbury some appreciable time after 13 Feb. 990, for his predecessor at Ramsbury was translated to Canterbury after the death of Archbishop Æthelgar on that date. Ælfric was still an abbot when he attended St Oswald's consecration of the rebuilt abbey church at Ramsey on 8 Nov. 991 (Chron Rams pp. 93, 95–6). Ælfric was succeeded at St Albans by his brother Leofric (KBL p. 65). The precise date of his appointment to Ramsbury is uncertain; the earliest surviving charter witnessed by him as bishop is dated 993; he went on to witness as bishop K 684 (which confirms that he had been a monk at Abingdon); S 1380; K 686–7, 689–91, 1289. He was elected archbishop of Canterbury at Amesbury on 21 April 995, and witnessed K 688 and K 692 before his consecration at Christchurch. He witnessed the following charters as archbishop: K 696; Bu XXVI–XXVII; K 698 (misspelt *Æðelfric*); K 700, 703, 705–6, 1295–7, 1299, 709, 711; Bu XXVIIIab; K 714, 1301. There can be no doubt that Ælfric continued to hold his former see of Ramsbury in plurality, throughout almost the whole of his tenure of the archbishopric. Ramsbury is not represented in the witness lists during this period, but although ASC E, F *s.a.* 1006 records the appointment of his successor at Ramsbury (Brihtwold, q.v.) as well as at Canterbury (Ælfheah, q.v.) upon Ælfric's death, it seems that Brihtwold had been appointed a little earlier, possibly in 1002; perhaps he acted as *chorepiscopus* until Ælfric died. In his will, Ælfric left ships to the people of both his dioceses. According to K 715, Ælfric was responsible for the ejection of canons and installation of monks at Christchurch. The surviving text of this charter was entered in a gospel book at Canterbury within the lifetime of some of those who must have witnessed the events that it describes, and it seems probable that the charter is wholly authentic, apart from some late tampering with the dating clause. The story is corroborated, and considerably embroidered, in the annal for 995 in ASC F. While Ælfric was at Canterbury, the first life of Dunstan was dedicated to him. For his will and biography, see W pp. 160–1; R pp. 380, 405; Barlow pp. 94 n. 4, 103; KBL p. 65; *Gesta abbatum monasterii S. Albani* I, pp. 23–4.

Ælfric   XXIV

(I) Abbot of Malmesbury c. 971 × 977, bishop of Crediton 977 × 985–7.

As abbot of Malmesbury, Ælfric was addressed in two charters dated 974 (CS 1300–1, on which see OB pp. 58, 280). His election to Crediton is recorded by William of Malmesbury (*Gesta Pontificum*

p. 406). At Crediton, his predecessor Bishop Sideman died 30 April 977 (ASC B, C). Ælfric succeeded in the same year, according to Florence of Worcester. He witnessed as bishop the following charters: K 621, 624, 626, 629 (name misspelt *Æðelric* in K), K 632–3, 636, 638, 1279; Bu xxiv; K 641, 1281, 648, 650, 1283. This last charter is dated 985. His successor Bishop Ælfwold II (q.v.) first witnessed in 987 (Bu xxv).

Ælfric   II, VIII, IX, X

Bishop of Hereford c. 940 × 951.

His dates are difficult to establish from witness lists. The position is confused by past assumptions that there was a contemporary bishop of the same name who held the see of Ramsbury. The outside possible dates for the alleged Bishop Ælfric of Ramsbury are 942 × 950, so that the Bishop Ælfric witnessing earlier and later charters should be assigned to Hereford. But the Bishop Ælfric who witnesses from 942 onwards is found to occupy the same position in the witness lists as the Bishop Ælfric who witnesses charters of the period 940 × 941; it seems reasonable to assume, therefore, that the same Bishop Ælfric witnesses throughout the period 940 × 951. In fact, there is no trustworthy evidence for the existence of any other bishop named Ælfric during these years. Comparison of episcopal lists for Ramsbury shows that the Ælfric appearing as the third bishop in the LVH list, between Oda and Oswulf, has been misplaced; he should have been entered between Sigeric and Brihtwold. The error is given added credence by the appearance of two bishops named Ælfric in Bu x, dated 949; but this charter is discredited on pp. 92–3 above, and should be dismissed from the argument. Ælfric was preceded at Hereford by Bishop Tidhelm, who last witnessed in 934, at Frome on 16 December (CS 705), and at Dorchester on 21 December (CS 716); I cannot follow Miss O'Donovan in assigning the ecclesiastical witnesses of this charter to the year 937: O'D I, p. 36. The Wulfhelm who is entered between Tidhelm and Ælfric in episcopal lists may have been Tidhelm's *chorepiscopus*; probably he became bishop of Wells (q.v.). It is not known when Ælfric succeeded Tidhelm, but his signatures cover the period 940 × 951. His successor Æthulf (q.v.) first witnessed in 955 (CS 905). In this discussion CS 670 and Bu II are disregarded, being unreliable. In 942 Ælfric was granted 100 hides at Blewbury, Berks. (CS 801), and in 944 he received 30 hides at Badby, Northants. (CS 792).

Ælfric Puttoc ('the kite')   XXXVII
    Archbishop of York 1023 × 22 Jan. 1051.

    Florence of Worcester says he was formerly dean (*præpositus*) of Winchester. In 1026 he went to Rome, where he received the pallium from Pope John XIX on 12 November (ASC *s.a.*). A supporter of King Harthacnut, he was given Worcester to hold in plurality with York for a while in 1040–1, but this was discontinued after a revolt by the men of Worcester against royal taxation (ASC *s.a.*). His nickname may derive from this event. He died at Southwell and was buried at Peterborough (SD II, p. 166), to which house he left costly vestments and altar furnishings. He gave also some vestments to Ramsey (Chron Rams p. 199); these gifts suggest that Ælfric, like his predecessor at York, was a man from the eastern Danelaw. See further, Barlow pp. 72–3: Cooper pp. 14–18.

Ælfric   XXVI, XXVII, XXVIIIa, XXXI
    Ealdorman of Hampshire 982 × 1016.

    There is little one can add to Miss Robertson's competent biographical summary (R pp. 373–4). Ælfric succeeded Æthelmær (q.v.) as ealdorman of Hampshire in 982 (LH pp. 217–27 is witnessed by Ælfric. K 638 is a forgery modelled on K 636, which is authentic). He is described as *Wentaniensium Prouinciarum dux* in 997 (K 698), and probably his ealdordom comprised Wiltshire as well as Hampshire, since he was leading an army drawn from both shires in 1003 (ASC C). He was 'one of those whom the king trusted most' (ASC F, *s.a.* 992), but was remembered as a coward who deserted on two occasions when battles with the Danes were imminent (ASC C, *s.a.* 992, 1003). In October 994 he was responsible, together with Archbishop Sigeric and Ealdorman Æthelweard, for coming to terms with a Danish army led by Olaf Tryggvason (the provisions of the treaty fit in more closely with the events recorded in ASC for 994 than for 991, and the defence of the latter date suggested in Stenton p. 272 n. 1, and repeated in EHD I, p. 401, is unconvincing). Until the battle of Maldon in 991, Ælfric usually witnessed last among the ealdormen, but thereafter he was second only to Æthelweard, ealdorman of the Western Shires (q.v.). Æthelweard ceased to witness in 998, and subsequently Ælfric headed the witness lists, although Æthelweard is thought to have survived until c. 1002 (R p. 387). After the chaotic events of 1010 × 1012, Ælfric was displaced from the top of the witness lists by Eadric Streona, ealdorman of Mercia (q.v.). He was killed at the battle of *Assandun* on 18 Oct. 1016; he must then have been an old man by the standards of the time. Ælfric was addressed in a charter of King Æthelred II dated c. 984 (K 642); in 988 he granted South Heighton in Sussex to Bishop Æthelgar (q.v.) in exchange for Lambourne, Berks. (LH pp. 238–42). He witnessed most of the surviving charters of Æthelred II.

Ælfric, thegn   IV
    Witnesses 926.
    There are insufficient charters of this period to allow of safe identification.

Ælfric, thegn   XII
    Witnesses 951.
    This thegn cannot be identified with safety. He witnesses lower than the Ælfric who appears among the *ministri* in charters of 948–9, and no thegns of this name occur in the lists between this solitary reference in Bu XII, dated 951, and CS 917, dated 23 Nov. × 31 Dec. 955.

Ælfric, thegn   XVII
    Witnesses 956.
    Thegns of this name occur commonly in witness lists of charters of 956–8. Three witness CS 982. Probably one of them was created ealdorman of Kent and Sussex in 957 (CS 1005); he witnesses as ealdorman in 958 (CS 1022, 1028, 1033–4).

Ælfsige   XXVIIIa, XXXI
    ?Abbot of Chertsey 998 × 1007–?
    The allocation to their respective houses of the various abbots witnessing under the name of Ælfsige forms one of the most difficult exercises in charter criticism for the period of Æthelred II's reign. The following notes relating to Chertsey, Ely, New Minster, and Peterborough lay no claim to being definitive, but it is hoped that they carry a stage further the task of analysis. There is no clear evidence for the succession at Chertsey after Lyfing (q.v.) last witnessed in 998 (K 700), but an Abingdon charter dated 999, having every appearance of authenticity, is witnessed by two abbots named Ælfsige, and the copyist of the best surviving text (who had the original charter before him), has added by the first name *ceās*, and by the second name *elig* (K 703). How much credence should be assigned to these entries must remain a matter of opinion, but *elig* stands clearly for Ely, and it is difficult to suggest any other satisfactory expansion of *ceās* than *ceortesege*, for Chertsey. There is nothing in the known history of the house to prevent the supposition that between 998 and 1007 – and possibly for a good deal longer – Chertsey was

ruled by an abbot Ælfsige, who could have been responsible for most of the appearances of this name in the charters of the period. Chertsey was an important house; its abbot witnessed fourth of fourteen in 997 (CS 698), and it is hard to believe that it is unrepresented in the witness lists from 998 onwards. Three abbots named Ælfsige witnessed high in the list of the contemporary Crawf No. 11, dated 1007. Two may have come from Ely and Peterborough respectively (see below); it could well be that the third was from Chertsey. For this reason I have assigned, provisionally, to this house the senior of the two Ælfsiges witnessing Bu xxvIIIa and xxxi.

Ælfsige   xxvIIIa, xxxi
   Abbot of Ely c. 998 × c. 1016.
   Abbot Brihtnoth of Ely (q.v.) last witnesses in 996, and the first definite appearance of his successor Ælfsige is in K 703, dated 999 (see above). It seems probable that he was the second of the two abbots Ælfsige witnessing a number of charters in the period 1004 × 1012 (Bu xxvIIIa; K 1303; Crawf 11; K 1305; Bu xxxi; K 719). The length of his tenure of office is unknown.

Ælfsige   xxvi, xxvii
   Abbot of New Minster 988 × 1004.
   He is identified in CS 684 dated 993, where he witnesses second of 19 abbots, and in CS 698 dated 997, where he witnesses third of 14 abbots. He issued a lease dated 995 × 997 (R lxx). His predecessor Æthelgar (q.v.) was created bishop of Selsey in 980, but continued to hold his office as abbot in plurality, and Ælfsige does not begin to witness until 988 (K 663). He also witnessed K 713, dated 990, and a large number of charters, in a high position in the lists, until 1004 when he was succeeded by Brihtwold (q.v.).

Ælfsige
   Abbot of Peterborough c. 1007 × 1042.
   This abbot did not witness any Burton charters, but his biography is included here to differentiate him from others bearing the same name. He may have been one of the three abbots Ælfsige witnessing Crawf 11 (1007). In 1013 he accompanied Queen Ælfgifu to Normandy (ASC C, D, E). It is difficult to identify him in the charters. See also HC pp. 48–65, KBL pp. 59–60.

Ælfsige, bishop 949
   Bu x is discredited on pp. 92–3 above, and is therefore not available as evidence for the existence of a bishop Ælfsige at this date.

Ælfsige   XIII, XIV, XV, XVII
    (I) bishop of Winchester 951 × 958, archbishop of Canterbury
958.
    His predecessor at Winchester died on 21 March 951, and he
succeeded at Canterbury on 2 June 958. He does not witness any
surviving charters as archbishop, and this makes it appear likely that
he died late in 958, rather than in 959 as is usually accepted. See
further, W IV; OB pp. 192–3.

Ælfsige   XXXIII
    (II) bishop of Winchester 1011 × 1032.
    See Barlow, EC p. 30 n. 3. King Cnut tried, but failed, to replace
him (Barlow p. 72 n. 2).

Ælfsige, thegn   (XI), XII, XVII
    Witnesses 951, 956.
    Thegns of this name witness consistently from 930 onwards; it
was perhaps the most common personal name of the period, and no
less than four thegns named Ælfsige witnessed a charter dated 956
(CS 963). In view of this, it is hazardous to try to identify the in-
dividuals with this name witnessing among the thegns in the Burton
charters.

Ælfstan, archbishop of Canterbury, *see under* Lyfing.

Ælfstan, bishop   XXXI, XXXIII
    Witnesses 1009, 1011.
    See p. 234 above, where it is suggested that he might have been a
chorepiscopus at Elmham.

Ælfstan   XXI–XXIV
    Bishop of London 964 × 995–6.
    It is necessary to differentiate Ælfstan carefully from his con-
temporaries and namesakes at Rochester (q.v.) and Ramsbury
(q.v.). His antecedents are unknown. Dunstan (q.v.) appears to have
kept the see of London in his own hands from the time of his
elevation to Canterbury in 960 until early in 964, and the Bishop
Ælfstan who witnesses charters of this period was from Rochester.
Ælfstan of London first appears in CS 1134–5, two charters dated 964.
He witnesses high up in the lists from the outset, often in a place
second only to the archbishops, and he subscribes nearly every
surviving royal diploma from this year until his death. One cannot

avoid linking Ælfstan's abrupt appearance at London with the launching of the monastic reform movement in 964 (OB pp. 162–3), but there is no evidence that he pursued at St Paul's a policy similar to that of Æthelwold at Winchester or Oswald at Worcester, of replacing the clerks of the *familia* by a body of monks. For this reason, I am inclined to the view that he was a protégé of Dunstan, who maintained the rule of secular clergy at Christ Church. A passage in the Liber Eliensis shows the canons of St Paul's admitting a member to their confraternity, provided the applicant endowed them with an estate in his possession (LE II, c. 31), and it is probable that some of the 'shoelands' used for the endowment of the prebends of St Paul's originated during Ælfstan's episcopate (*Journal of the English Place-Name Society* IV (1971–2), pp. 6–11). Ælfstan appears to have received charge of the abbey of Evesham from King Æthelred II after the banishment of Bishop Æthelsige II of Sherborne (q.v.); he kept it for five years until his death, and the abbey seems to have been run by seculars during this period. During his rule, no major abbeys were founded within Ælfstan's diocese, in significant contrast to the developments in the fenland, within the adjacent see of Dorchester. An important innovation during Ælfstan's career was the organization of diocesan estates to provide crews for manning warships used to protect the country against Danish raids (LT pp. 119–22). In 992 we find Ælfstan appointed by King Æthelred II to be one of the leaders of the sea-*fyrd* from London and East Anglia (ASC C), and there is extant a list, dating from the last years of his episcopate or the early years of his successor, giving the arrangements for manning the ship provided by St Paul's (ECEss, 1st edn, II, p. 29). Ælfstan last witnesses a number of charters dated 995 (K 688–90, 692, 1289). His successor Wulfstan (q.v.) was consecrated in the following year (ASC F).

Ælfstan

Monk of Abingdon, abbot of Glastonbury 964 × 970, bishop of Ramsbury 970 × 981.

Ælfstan of Ramsbury does not witness any Burton charters, but his biography is considered here in order to differentiate him from his namesake at London (q.v.). A pupil of Bishop Æthelwold (q.v.) at Abingdon, he is the subject of a story by Ælfric, Æthelwold's biographer, who says he later became an abbot, and subsequently bishop of Ramsbury (EHD I, pp. 834–5). His abbacy is identified as Glastonbury by Florence of Worcester (*s.a.* 970). He witnessed the following charters as abbot: CS 1135, 1143 (964); CS 1169, 1171–2

(965); CS 1176, 1190–1 (966); CS 1199, 1200 (967); CS 1216–17, 1219, Dugdale II, pp. 323–4 (968); CS 1229, 1230 (969); CS 1257, 1260, 1266, 1268–9 (970). At Ramsbury he succeeded Osulf (q.v.), who last witnessed in 970. Ælfstan was present as bishop at the translation of the relics of St Swithun at Winchester on 15 July 971 (E. S. Ducket, *St Dunstan*, 1955, p. 124). He witnessed occasional charters as bishop from 973 to 981, always in a much lower position than his namesakes at London and Rochester: CS 1309 (972 × 15 May 974); CS 1292 (973); CS 1301, 1303 (974); K 1275 (978); K 629 (981). According to two doubtful texts preserved at Abingdon, in 975 × 978 he was granted 12 hides at Kingston Bagpuize, Berks., which he gave to his former abbey of Abingdon (K 1276–7), where he was buried (ASC *s.a.* 981). See also KBL p. 50.

Ælfstan

Monk of Winchester, bishop of Rochester c. 961 × 995.

Ælfstan of Rochester does not witness any Burton charters, but his biography is considered here in order to enable him to be differentiated from Bishop Ælfstan of London (q.v.). He was a monk of Winchester before being appointed bishop (R. R. Darlington, EHR LI (1936), pp. 385–428). Tenth-century bishops of London nearly always witness high in the lists, usually directly after the archbishops and the bishop of Winchester. London in the early part of this period seems to have been kept in the hands of Dunstan (q.v.), and there is good reason to believe that the Bishop Ælfstan who witnesses at or near the bottom of the lists of bishops in a few charters from 961 to 963 was from Rochester, and not from London as has previously been accepted: CS 1066–7, 1072–3, 1079–80, 1319 (961); CS 1083 (962); CS 1101 (963). CS 1134 is a charter dated 964, in which (for the first time) both Ælfstans appear, with their sees identified in the witness list. Ælfstan of London subscribes directly after the archbishops, and Ælfstan of Rochester appears in his usual place, second from bottom of the episcopal list. CS 1184 is another charter, dated 972, in which the sees are named and appear in a similar order of precedence, an order maintained as late as 993 (K 684) and 995 (K 691). From this evidence it is clear that the second of the two bishops named Ælfstan witnessing the following charters is always from Rochester: CS 1143 (964); CS 1164 (965); CS 1176, 1189–91 (966); CS 1145 (968 × 972); CS 1257, 1269 (970); CS 1268 (972); CS 1295, 1297 (973); CS 1307 (973–4); CS 1314–15 (975); K 622 (979); K 624 (980); K 632–3 (982); K 639, 1279–80 (983); K 641, 1281–2 (984); K 673 (990).

For a list of charters witnessed by all three bishops named Ælfstan (London, Rochester, and Ramsbury), see under Ælfstan of Ramsbury. Ælfstan of Rochester does not witness any charters of the years 985 to 988 inclusive, and this absence must be related in some way to the entry in ASC C *s.a.* 986, which records that King Æthelred II laid waste the diocese of Rochester. Ælfstan of Rochester last witnesses K 689–91, all dated 995. His successor Godwine I (q.v.) received an estate from King Æthelred later that year (K 688).

Ælfstan, thegn   XXXVII
    Witnesses 1048.
    A thegn of this name witnesses the following charters: K 774–5, OS Facs II, Exeter 12 (1044); K 776, 778–81 (1045); K 792–3 (1050).

Ælfthryth, queen c. 940 × 12 Nov. 1002   XXI, XXVI, XXVII
    She was the daughter of Ordgar, who became ealdorman of Devon soon after Ælfthryth married King Edgar. Her brother Ordulf (q.v.) was founder of Tavistock Abbey. She married (1) Æthelwold, ealdorman of East Anglia 956 × 962, (2) in 964, Edgar, king of Mercia, East Anglia, and Northumbria 957 × 959, king of England Oct. 959 × 11 May 975, by whom she had two sons: Edmund, died 970–1, and Æthelred, born 968–9, king of England 19 April 978 × 23 April 1016. She brought up the aetheling Athelstan, son of King Æthelred II by his first wife Ælfgifu (W xx). Ælfthryth is remembered chiefly as a key figure in the Benedictine monastic reform movement, an interest acquired, no doubt, from her first husband, who was the elder brother of Æthelwine 'Dei amicus', the lay patron of Ramsey Abbey. Before marrying King Edgar, she was instrumental in persuading him to allow Bishop Æthelwold to purchase 10 hides at Stoke near Ipswich, which Æthelwold used subsequently to endow his foundation at Ely (LE p. 111 n. 11; see also the endorsement to the Stoke charter, CS 1269). Her interest in Ely seems to have been stimulated by Queen Eadgifu (q.v.), who willed her 5 hides at Holland, Essex (not far from Stoke), which subsequently she gave to Ely (LE p. 105; I assume that the Ælfthryth of this passage was in fact the person who became Edgar's queen). Her interest was maintained in later years; she visited Ely with her son Æthelred during the reign of Edward the Martyr, and subsequently, when Æthelred became king, she continued to support the abbey (LE p. 146). On her status as Edgar's queen, see Asser p. 202; *Encom.Emmæ*, pp. 63–4; Richardson and Sayles p. 401. A twelfth-

century writer, who appears to be reliable on this matter, contrasts her position with that of Edgar's first wife, Æthelflæd; Ælfthryth had been both crowned and consecrated queen, whereas Æthelflæd had been crowned only (*Memorials of St Dunstan*, p. 423). After her marriage, Ælfthryth was given general responsibility for the newly reformed nunneries (EHD I, p. 848; *Regularis Concordia*, c. 3). She obtained from Bishop Æthelwold an OE translation of the Rule of St Benedict, written for the use of nuns (LE p. 111; Ker p. 195), in return for which Edgar granted Æthelwold an estate at Sudbourne in Suffolk, for the endowment of Ely. Together with King Edgar, Ælfthryth also endowed Ely with land at Marsworth, Bucks. (LE p. 116), which had been left to King Edgar by the will of Ælfgifu, the sister of Ealdorman Æthelweard (W VIII). In c. 1002 she was left an estate at Woodham, Essex, by Ælfflæd, the widow of Ealdorman Brihtnoth, for the endowment of the nunnery at Barking (W xv). Ælfthryth herself founded nunneries at Wherwell, Hants. (on property that had been left to New Minster by Kings Eadred and Eadwig, Ha XXI; ECW 87; K 707), and at Amesbury, Wilts. (an estate left by King Alfred to his younger son Æthelweard, from whom it descended via Kings Athelstan and Eadred to Queen Eadgifu, Ha XII; CS 691–2; Ha XXI; ECW pp. 103–4). She possessed an estate at Cholsey, Berks., the site of one of the newly founded monasteries (EHD I, p. 532; Chron Rams p. 110; CS 698). Another estate, at Buckland Newton, Dorset, given to her in 966 (CS 1177), was used for the endowment of Glastonbury. In 968 she interceded with King Edgar for renewal of the freedom of Taunton, an endowment of the Old Minster at Winchester (R XLV; H 108; ECW pp. 221–3, 229–30). Her interest in the Winchester monasteries is further illustrated by her presence in the same year as witness to an agreement drawn up between the three houses (R XLIX), and she witnessed also the great New Minster charter of 966 (OB p. 275). In about 971 she interceded with King Edgar for the refoundation of Peterborough (HC p. 28). Her paramount interest in the reform movement is perhaps best brought out by a passage in Byrhtferth's *Vita Oswaldi*, in which he relates that while Edgar was feasting with the bishops and nobles at his coronation, his consort Ælfthryth, gorgeously attired, was presiding over the abbots and abbesses at a similar banquet (I accept John's interpretation of this account, in OB pp. 285–6, in preference to that of Richardson and Sayles p. 401). Outside these interests, Ælfthryth was doubtless a very influential person in secular affairs of state. A thegn willed her thirty mancuses of gold and a stallion, for her advocacy with the king that his will should stand (W XI); similarly, Ælfgifu the sister of Ealdorman Æthelweard left her a necklace and an amulet of gold weighing together 10 mancuses, and a drinking cup (W XVIII); Ealdorman Ælfheah also willed her an estate, no doubt for a similar reason (W IX). Her support was sought in lawsuits (R LXVI). In addition to her landed interests in Wessex and East Anglia, mentioned already, she received estates in Kent and Berks. (R LXIII; CS 1143), and she held Rutland as her dower (Gaimar, *L'Estoire des Engles*, I, 4134; cf. VCH *Rutland*, pp. 132, 135, 166). Ælfthryth was deeply involved in the power struggle for the succession that followed King Edgar's death. She fostered the claims of her own son Æthelred against those of Edward, Edgar's son by a former union. In this she was supported by Ealdorman Ælfhere of Mercia (q.v.), her opponents being the English episcopate, headed by Dunstan (q.v.) and supported by Ealdorman Æthelwine of East Anglia (q.v.). After the death of Edward the Martyr (q.v.), the two factions were reconciled (Fisher pp. 255 ff.), but the monastic party never forgave her, and later chroniclers accused her of murdering Ealdorman Æthelwold her first husband, and Abbot Brihtnoth of Ely, and of responsibility for the death of her stepson. Modern writers are in general agreement that she was innocent of these crimes (W p. 123; H p. 551; Stenton p. 368; C. E. Wright, *The Cultivation of Saga in Anglo-Saxon England*, Edinburgh, 1939, pp. 146–53, 157–71). Undoubtedly she became the subject of a considerable amount of saga during the Confessor's reign, not all of it laudatory. According to Goscelin's *Vita S. Wulfhilde*, for example, she secured the expulsion of Abbess Wulfhild from Barking, an act for which she subsequently did penance (M. Esposito, 'La Vie de Sainte Wulfhilde par Goscelin de Canterbery', *Analecta Bollandiana* XXXII (1913), pp. 10–36). Ælfthryth died on 17 Nov. 1002, according to an entry in the Wherwell Cartulary (Egerton MS. 2104, fo. 43). King Æthelred gave lands to Wherwell for her soul (K 707).

Ælfweard   XXVI–XXVIIIa
    Abbot of Glastonbury 979–87 × 1009.
    Ælfweard's predecessor at Glastonbury appears to have been Sigegar (q.v.) who is last found in the charters as abbot in 979, and who first witnesses as bishop of Wells in the same year. Ælfweard does not appear as abbot in surviving texts until 987, but he may in fact have been appointed to Glastonbury soon after Sigegar's promotion to Wells. Ælfweard's name appears last on the list of the four abbots witnessing his first two charters, but habitually thereafter he heads the lists of the abbots, with very few exceptions (K 712–13;

Bu XXVI–XXVII; K 1301). His abbey is identified in K 684 and K 698. He last witnesses in 1009, and his successor Brihtred (q.v.) first witnesses later in the same year. Ælfweard subscribed to the following charters: K 657–8 (987); K 665 (988); K 673, 712–13 (990); K 684 (993); K 687 (994); K 692, 1289, Muchelney 4 (995); K 696, 1292, EHD I, p. 534, Bu XXVI–XXVII (996); K 698, OS Facs III, 35 (997); K 700, Crawf 8 (998); K 703 (999); K 706 (1001); K 707, 715, 1295, 1297, Crispin p. 168 (1002); K 672 (1002 × 1005); Bu XXVIIIA (1004); K 714, 1301 (1005); K 1303–4 (1007); K 1305 (1008); K 1306 (1009). See also KBL p. 51.

Ælfwig   XVII

The king's butler, witnesses 956 × 961.

He first appears low down among the *ministri* witnessing the following charters dated 956: CS 927, 932, 960, 984, 934, 914, 982, 983, 948. In 957 he witnessed CS 988, 997, 1001, 992, 1004, 1005. In 958 he witnessed (sometimes higher in the lists) CS 1302, 1022, 1027, 1028, 1033, 1034, 902. In 959 he witnessed CS 1305 as *regis pincerna*, also CS 1045 and CS 1046. All these charters were issued by King Eadwig, so that Ælfwig was probably a West Saxon thegn. After Eadwig's death, Ælfwig witnessed a few charters of King Edgar dated 960–1, usually much lower on the list than in King Eadwig's reign (CS 1055, 1058, 1077, 1079).

Ælfwine   XXXVI

Abbot of Ramsey 1043 × 1081.

Oleson, pp. 119–20, distinguishes between three abbots named Ælfwine: one of Buckfast, early in the Confessor's reign, about whom little is known; the second of New Minster 1032 × 24 Nov. 1057 (witnessed K 746; R LXXXV; OS Facs II, Exeter 12; cf. R p. 437, H p. 551, LVH p. xxxi); the third of Ramsey, whom Oleson considers the most important, because he was an intimate of the Confessor. Oleson lists the charters that he considers Ælfwine of Ramsey to have witnessed during the Confessor's reign. Ælfwine was the son of an Essex priest named Eadbriht (*Memorials of St Edmund*, I, p. 41). He became prior of Ramsey, and was elected abbot by the monks, with the king's consent, after the murder of his predecessor Æthelstan on 29 Sept. 1043 (Chron Rams pp. 155–6). Various local transactions concerning the abbey, undertaken by Abbot Ælfwine in his early years, are entered in Chron Rams pp. 161–70. One of these entries shows that Ælfwine had already gained the king's confidence, and he was employed by King Edward on several continental missions. He was one of the English churchmen who attended the Council of Rheims on 30 Oct. 1049, bringing back with him a bull of Pope Leo IX in favour of his abbey (ASC; Chron Rams p. 171). Some time before 1053 he was sent on a mission to Saxony, in return for which King Edward granted the abbey an estate at Broughton, Hunts. (H p. 472). He also went to Denmark (DB I, 208 ai). In 1062–5, while on a mission to Rome, he obtained a second bull for Ramsey, this time from Pope Alexander II (Chron Rams p. 176). He contracted an illness on this visit which caused him to give up the charge of all external business, and Æthelsige, *alias* Ælfsige, abbot of St Augustine's, was appointed by the king to have the care of Ramsey; a modern writer, reviewing Ælfwine's career, says 'he wore himself out in the king's service' (Chron Rams p. 177; Barlow p. 137; for the career of Æthelsige, see Freeman, NC IV, pp. 749–52; KBL pp. 35–6, 62; R. W. Southern in *Medieval and Renaissance Studies*, IV, London, 1958, pp. 194 ff.). In 1066 Ælfwine had a vision of King Edward, encouraging King Harold to engage Harald Hardrada and Earl Tostig at Stamford Bridge; Ælfwine intercepted the king on his march to the battle, to tell him his vision (Chron Rams p. 179; Osbert of Clare, *Vita Edwardi*, c. xxvi, ed. Marc Bloc in *Analecta Bollandiana*, XL (1923), p. 114). In 1072, while Æthelsige was out of the country, Ælfwine witnessed a charter as abbot of Ramsey (WM II, p. 351). His death is entered under the year 1081 in the Ramsey Annals (EHR LXXV (1970), pp. 34, 44); the date (which is an important limiting date for the inquest at Kentford, attended by his successor, cf. LE p. 427) is confirmed in the Ramsey Chronicle, which gives his accession as 1043 and notes that he was abbot for 38 years (Chron Rams p. 156). See also Barlow, *passim*; KBL pp. 61–2.

Ælfwine *alias* Ælla   III, IV
    Bishop of Lichfield 904–c. 916 × 935–41.
    The succession at Lichfield in the late ninth century is difficult to reconstruct. According to Florence of Worcester, Ælfwine's predecessor was named Tunbeorht, but the date 928 given by Florence for Ælfwine's succession is demonstrably wrong. The last recorded charter witnessed by Tunbeorht is CS 492 (18 April 857). Charters then give the following evidence for the succession: Wulfsige CS 503, 535 (862); CS 513–14 (866); Eadbeorht CS 524 (869); CS 540–1 (875); Wulfred CS 551 (883); CS 552 (884); CS 547 (887); CS 557 (888); CS 561 (889); Eadferth Bu 1 (900); Wigmund CS 596, 607 (900); CS 603 (903); CS 605, 1338, 607

(904). There follows a break until 9 Sept. 915, when Ælfwine appears as witness to CS 632. Florence of Worcester records that Ælfwine had a second name, Ælla, and he witnesses in this fashion CS 641 (925); CS 659, Bu IV (926); CS 739 (931-4); CS 704 (934); CS 707 (935). He witnesses as Ælfwine the following charters: Bu III (925); CS 663 (928); CS 665-6 (929); CS 669 (930); CS 674, 677, 680, 683 (931); CS 689, 691-2 (932); CS 695-6 (933); CS 702-3, 705, 1344 (934); ECStP J. 10 (935). After 935 there is a reduction in the number of sees represented in the witness lists of the royal diplomas of Athelstan and his successor; the only regular witnesses are from Canterbury, London, Winchester, Ramsbury, Wells, Rochester, and Worcester, in that order, with an occasional appearance of Hereford and Selsey. The absence of representatives from the Danelaw is quite extraordinary, and makes one wonder if Athelstan's hold over the north in his later years was as firm as the chroniclers would have us believe. Wulfgar (q.v.), Ælfwine's successor at Lichfield, first appears in 941 (CS 765).

Ælfwine, discthegn   XXIII
    Witnesses 956 × 970.
    He was a Berkshire thegn, who was given 3 hides at Barkham by King Eadred in 952 (CS 895), 15 hides at Milton by King Eadwig in 956 (CS 935), and 10 hides at Boxford by King Edgar in 968 (CS 1227). All these charters were preserved at Abingdon. Probably he is the thegn of that name who received 8 hides at Stourton, Wilts., from King Eadwig, which he used to endow Glastonbury (ECW 288); possibly he is the Ælfwine who gave 25 hides at Grittleton, Wilts., to Glastonbury during the reign of Edgar, in fulfilment of the wish of his predecessor, Wulfric (CS 750; ECW pp. 85-6); almost certainly he is the Ælfwine who received 10 hides at Highclere, Hants., from King Edgar in 959, soon after King Eadwig's death (CS 1051). It will be shown below that he was the brother of Ealdorman Ælfhere of Mercia (q.v.) and Ealdorman Ælfheah of Hampshire (q.v.); the family is known to have had connections with Abingdon and Glastonbury. The Ælfwine who received 10 hides at Yaxley and 5 hides at Farcet, Hunts., from King Eadwig in 956 (ECEE p. 159), however, was probably a different person, since these estates were in the possession of other landholders before the death of the Ælfwine whose biography we are considering here (ECEE p. 163). Ælfwine first appears low down on the witness lists of charters issued by King Eadwig towards the middle of 956 (CS 971, 949, 985, 970, 943, 984, 925, 934, 914, 942, 945, 946, 982, 983, 1009, 927, 930, 1029). Of

these, he appears in CS 930 and 970 next to his brother Ælfheah, and in CS 983 next to his brother Eadric (q.v.). In 957 Ælfwine witnessed a number of King Eadwig's charters issued before the revolt of the aetheling Edgar (CS 988, 997, 1001, 999), but only two charters of Eadwig after Edgar's revolt (CS 992, 998). He did not witness any surviving charters of King Eadwig issued in 958 or 959, and there is presumptive evidence that he crossed the Thames in the summer of 957, to become the principal official of Edgar's immediate entourage. He witnessed the following charters issued by Edgar as king of the Mercians, as head of the thegns in every case except one: CS 1036, 1040, 1042, 1043, 1044 (958); CS 1052 (959). After King Edgar's accession to the whole of England on 1 Oct. 959, Ælfwine regularly witnessed second only to the West Saxon brothers Ælfgar (q.v.) and Brihtferth (q.v.), who were the king's kinsmen; when these were absent, Ælfwine headed the thegns at court (CS 1054, 1073, 1118–19, 1142, 1164–5, 1190, 1268). In view of his importance in the witness lists, he should be identified with the Ælfwine, brother of Ealdorman Ælfhere of Mercia, who witnesses an undated endorsement by King Edgar of CS 562, a charter issued by Swithwulf, bishop of Rochester, in 889. Four of the thegns witnessing this endorsement appear in witness list of CS 1212, a Kentish charter dated 968. Altogether, Ælfwine witnessed 64 charters of Edgar, the texts of which have survived. He last appears in CS 1268, dated 970, where he headed the thegns witnessing. A second thegn named Ælfwine witnessed a few of these charters (CS 1055, 1123, 1190–1, 1200, 1230, 1266), and it is probable that this is the man who witnessed low down on the lists of the following charters: CS 1269, 1046 (970); CS 1282, 1309 (972).

Ælfwine, the king's writer 984   XXIV

He was the recipient by Bu xxiv of lands in Oxfordshire. It does not seem safe to identify him with other thegns named Ælfwine who appear in charters of this period (K 629; LH p. 228; K 641, 1281, 686; OS Facs III, 35).

Ælfwine, thegn   XXXI

Witnesses 1009.

Thegns named Ælfwine occur sporadically in the charters of Æthelred II and Cnut, but there is no convincing evidence to identify them with the Ælfwine of Bu xxxi.

Ælfwine, thegn   XXXVII

Witnesses 1048.

Oleson p. 120 has notes on two thegns named Ælfwine at this period, but safe identification with the Ælfwine of Bu xxxvii is not possible.

Ælfwold   xiii, ? xxi

Monk of Glastonbury, (I) bishop of Crediton 953 × 972.

His predecessor Æthelgar last witnesses in 953 (CS 899), and Ælfwold first witnesses CS 900, dated the same year. These charters support the date 953 given for his appointment by Florence of Worcester, who had evidently an accurately dated list of the bishops of Crediton. Florence says that Ælfwold's appointment was made on Dunstan's advice, and this is borne out by a Glastonbury tradition that he was a monk of that house (E. S. Duckett, *St Dunstan*, 1955, p. 91). It is noteworthy that he witnessed the important late 'Dunstan A' charter CS 937 as *didasculus* = 'teacher', his name being followed by that of Dunstan, who is given the title *dogmatista* = 'upholder of doctrine'. Ælfwold last witnesses two charters dated 972 (CS 1282, 1309). These are also witnessed by Abbot Sideman of Exeter, who succeeded Ælfwold at Crediton and first witnesses as bishop CS 1295, dated before 15 May 973, and CS 1201, also dated 973. In 964 or earlier, another Ælfwold was appointed bishop of Sherborne (q.v.), and from then until Ælfwold I of Crediton's death in 972, although the great majority of surviving charters are witnessed by only one bishop named Ælfwold, it is not possible to identify his see with certainty (in the majority of cases, probably it was Sherborne). There is however a small group of charters of this period that are witnessed by two bishops named Ælfwold, and in this group it is evident (from CS 1134 and 1282, where the sees are identified) that the bishop Ælfwold witnessing higher on the lists was from Sherborne, and his namesake lower down the lists was from Crediton. The charters of this group are as follows: CS 1134, 1143 (964); CS 1176, 1189 (966); CS 1221–6 (986); CS 1257, 1266, 1269 (970); CS 1282, 1309 (972).

Ælfwold   xxv, xxvii, xxxi–xxxiii

(II) bishop of Crediton 985–7 × 1011–15.

It is assumed here that only one bishop of this name held the see of Crediton during the period under review; there is no supporting evidence for the two successive bishops named Ælfwold appearing in Florence of Worcester's list. Bishop Ælfric of Crediton last witnesses three charters of 985 (K 648, 650, 1283). His successor Ælfwold II first witnesses Bu xxv dated 987. His see is identified in the following charters: K 665, 684, 688, 698, 706, 709, 1289, 1292, Bu XXVII, Bu XXXI. He last witnesses two charters dated 1011 (Bu XXXII–XXXIII). His successor Eadnoth first appears unequivocally in 1015 (K 1310, where his see is identified). The Bishop Eadnoth who witnesses earlier charters may be from Dorchester, 1008 × 1016 (q.v.). Ælfwold II of Crediton witnesses the following charters: Bu XXV (987); K 665 (988); EHD I, p. 543 (989–90); K 712 (990); K 684 (993); K 686–7, Duignan (994); K 688, 1289 (995); K 1211–12, Bu XXVII, EHD I, p. 534 (996); K 698, OS Facs III, 35 (997); K 700, Crawf 8 (998); K 703 (999); K 706 (1001); K 707, 1295, 1297, EHD I, p. 540 (1002); K 709 (1004); K 714, 1301 (1005); K 1303 (1007); K 1305 (1008); Bu XXXI (1009); Bu XXXII–XXXIII (1011). He was granted land at Sandford, Devon, by King Æthelred II in 997 (OS Facs III, 35); on this, see Finberg, 1969, pp. 42–3. His will is preserved (Crawf 10; EHD I, pp. 536–7; cf. Barlow pp. 212–13).

Ælfwold   ? XXI, XXII

Abbot of ? Glastonbury 959 × 964, (I) bishop of Sherborne 964 × 978.

Bishop Wulfsige II of Sherborne (q.v.) last witnesses CS 1032, dated 958, some time before 2 June. According to Florence of Worcester, he died that year and was succeeded by a certain Brihthelm. I think it likely that this was in fact Bishop Brihthelm of Selsey (q.v.), who held the two sees in plurality until the early autumn of 959, when (some time before King Eadwig's death on 10 October), he became also bishop of Winchester. The see of Sherborne appears to have been retained by Brihthelm until his death in 963, and Ælfwold I of Sherborne does not witness unequivocally as bishop until CS 1134, 1143, both dated 964. Another bishop named Ælfwold also witnesses these two charters; he was from Crediton, and I have listed under Ælfwold I of Crediton the charters witnessed by both bishops. From 972 onwards, after the death of Ælfwold of Crediton, the sole Ælfwold witnessing as bishop was from Sherborne. He last witnesses K 1275, dated 978, and his successor Æthelsige I (q.v.) first witnesses K 621, dated 979. This agrees with the date 978 for Ælfwold's death given in both ASC and Fl Wig, who says he was buried at Sherborne. It seems to me probable that Bishop Ælfwold I of Sherborne is to be identified with the Abbot Ælfwold who witnesses 959 × 964, whose house was probably Glastonbury (CS 1030, 1045–6, 1120, 1124, 1079 – where he is 'promoted' to bishop, as is also Abbot Æthelwold of Abingdon; Muchelney 3). KLB p. 56 would assign this Abbot Ælfwold to

Muchelney; I cannot accept this, however, for there is no real evidence that this comparatively undistinguished house was re-established so early; nor can I believe it likely that Glastonbury would be completely unrepresented in the witness lists of this period. A second Abbot Ælfwold, witnessing 980 × 1002, was from Winchcombe (reading *wincł* for *winđ* in K 684, see KBL pp. 78–9).

Ælfwold (IV)

Ealdorman of Wessex 925 × 938.

He may be the thegn of this name who witnesses high among the *ministri* CS 620–8, dated 909. From 925 to 934 he appears as second in the lists of the six to eight ealdormen who regularly witness King Athelstan's charters. After the death of Ealdorman Osferth, Ælfwold headed the ealdormen in the witness lists until his own disappearance in 938. It is possible to allocate all of King Athelstan's ealdormen to particular ealdordoms, and that of Ælfwold comprised Wessex, excluding the Western Provinces; it excluded also Sussex, Surrey, Kent, and possibly Berkshire, all of which were within Osferth's ealdordom. Ælfwold was succeeded as ealdorman of Wessex by Ælfhere in 939 (CS 742). Ælfwold witnesses the following charters as ealdorman: CS 641 (4 Sept. 925); CS 658–9 (926); CS 663–4 (16 April 928); CS 665–6 (929); CS 669 (3 April 930); CS 1343 (29 April 930); CS 675 (20 June 931); CS 676 (15 July 931); CS 677 (12 Nov. 931); CS 689 (30 Aug. 932); CS 691–2 (29 Dec. 932); CS 635 (11 Jan. 933); CS 695–6 (26 Jan. 933); CS 702 (28 May 934); CS 703, 1344 (7 June 934); CS 705 (16 Dec. 934); CS 716–18 (21 Dec. 934); CS 714, Athelney 97 (937); CS 729–31 (938). The Ealdorman Ælfwold who witnessed the following charters was another person: CS 603 (903); CS 604, 607, 612–13 (904).

Ælla, *see* Ælfwine

Æscwig XXI, XXXIII–XXXVI

Monk of Winchester, abbot of Bath 959–63 × 975–9; bishop of Dorchester 975–9 × 1002.

The secular minster which evolved from the early nunnery at Bath was staffed in 944 by a group of clerks from St Bertins in Flanders (OB p. 157; Robinson pp. 61–4). From that time onwards, it was certainly ruled by a titular abbot, for the abbot's holding there is referred to incidentally in the last line of the boundary clause of a charter dated 946, which appears to be authentic (CS 814). The church of Bath received substantial additions to its land endowments in the mid-tenth century (CS 670, with lay and ecclesiastical witnesses from King Edmund's reign; CS 927, 936, 973, 1001, 1009, 1073). In the West Country it ranked second only to Glastonbury, and it received the earliest attention of the Benedictine reformers. There is some evidence for the establishment of a scriptorium there, under Dunstan's tutelage, as early as 956 (CS 1009). It is possible that about this time a monk of Bath, contemplating from his abbey gate the stones of the deserted Roman city, composed the beautiful poem known as 'The Ruin', now preserved in The Exeter Book. In 956-7 Bath was ruled by the priest Wulfgar (CS 927, 1001). CS 1030, an important charter dated some time before 1 Oct. 959, is witnessed by four abbots: Ælfric of St Augustine's, Ælfwold probably from Glastonbury, Æthelwold of Abingdon, and Clement probably from Bath. CS 1120, 1124, issued together before 29 Nov. 963, are witnessed by the same abbots, except that Æscwig has replaced Clement. From then onwards, Æscwig witnessed usually as first or second of the abbots. He had been a monk at Winchester, presumably under Ælfheah I, who may have tonsured others besides Dunstan and Æthelwold (LVH p. 23). He is addressed in two charters of King Edgar, CS 1164 (965) and CS 1257 (970); and in 973 Edgar was crowned at Bath during Æscwig's abbacy (ASC C, D; CS 1304). He witnessed the following charters as abbot: S 728 Muchelney 3, CS 1135, 1143, 1145 (964); CS 1169, 1171-2 (965); Bu xxi, CS 1176, 1189-91 (966); CS 1199-200 (967); CS 1213, 1216-17, 1219, 1221-2, 1224-7, ECW 108 (968); CS 1229-30, 1234 (969); Cs 1257, 1260, 1266, 1268-9 (970); CS 1302 (968 x 970); CS 1270 (971); CS 1201, 1309, 1286 (972); CS 1303-5 (974); CS 1312, 1315-16 (975); K 1277 (975-8). There can be little doubt that he is to be identified with the Æscwig who was appointed to Dorchester, but no firm date can be offered for his translation. He first witnessed as bishop K 621 dated 979. By 990 he witnessed high on the lists, a position he retained until his last appearance in K 1297, dated 1002. In addition to charters appearing in K, Æscwig witnessed as bishop the following: LH pp. 217-227 (982); LH pp. 238-42, GC iii, p. 704 (988); EHD i, p. 554 (989-90, 996); S 1380 (994); Muchelney 4 (995). In 992, when already elderly, he was chosen to lead the sea-fyrd against the Danes (ASC). In 995 he leased Monks Risborough, Bucks., from Christ Church, Canterbury, in return for money which was used to buy off a Danish raid; later, he gave the estate back to Canterbury (K 689, 690). In the pages of the Liber Eliensis and the Ramsey Chronicle he can be watched attending his duties as diocesan bishop; he presided at a shire-moot at Wittlesford,

Cambs., and was present at the dedication of the abbey churches at Ramsey and St Neots; he decreed the expulsion of unruly monks from Ramsey, and witnessed a will at Ely, to which house he bequeathed a stole and a finely embroidered red purple chasuble. See further, KBL p. 28.

Æthelflæd, lady of the Mercians c. 887 × 12 June 918   I

She was the daughter of Alfred the Great and sister of Edward the Elder; in c. 887 she married Ealdorman Æthelred of Mercia, and she was herself the sole ruler of the Mercians for seven years after her husband's death. She witnessed CS 547 (887), CS 557 (888), CS 561 (889), Ha xiv (896), and CS 603 (903). Together with her husband, she issued Ha xiii (c. 887 × 899) and CS 587 (901); by herself she issued Bu i (900) and CS 632 (9 Sept. 916). See further, F. T. Wainwright, 'Æthelflæd, Lady of the Mercians', in Clemoes, pp. 53–69.

Æthelflæd of Damerham, queen 944–6 × 975–91   VIII

She was the daughter of Ealdorman Ælfgar of Essex, the second wife of King Edmund, and subsequently the wife of Ealdorman Athelstan 'Rota' of S.E. Mercia (q.v.), whom she survived. Her sister Ælfflæd married Ealdorman Brihtnoth of Essex (q.v.). King Edmund granted her 100 hides at Damerham, Wilts. She witnessed Bu viii as 'consilarius' (sic), and was a benefactress to Ely (LE pp. 136–7), Christ Church, Glastonbury, and a number of major churches in Essex and Suffolk (Barking, Bury St Edmunds, West Mersea, Stoke by Nayland, and Hadleigh). Her will survives, W xiv.

Æthelgar   II, VIII, X–XII

Bishop of Crediton 934 × 953.

His see is identified by Florence of Worcester. His predecessor Eadulf (q.v.) died on 9 Nov. 934. Æthelgar first witnessed CS 705, dated 16 Dec. 934. He last witnessed CS 899, dated 953. (On the date, see O'D p. 37). A number of manumissions entered in the Bodmin Gospels for 'King Eadred and Bishop Æthelgar' show that Æthelgar's bishopric still included Cornwall; the Bishop Conan appointed to Cornwall by King Athelstan must therefore have been Æthelgar's chorepiscopus (Lucerna, p. 113). Florence of Worcester, who records that Æthelgar was buried at Crediton, wrongly states that he was bishop for 21 years.

Æthelgar   XXI, XXII, XXIV, XXV

Monk of Glastonbury and Abingdon, abbot of New Minster

964 × 988, bishop of Selsey 2 May 980 × 988, archbishop of Canterbury June 988 × 13 Feb. 990.

The son of Æthelflæd (LVH p. 58), and one of a distinguished group of pupils of Dunstan at Glastonbury (W. Malmes. *De Antiq. Glas. Eccles.*, ed. Gale, p. 325), he became a disciple of Bishop Æthelwold (Chron Abingd II, p. 261, and hence HC p. 46), who appointed him as first abbot of the reformed house at New Minster in 964 (ASC A). He built a tower and two chapels there (LH pp. 9–10), and took part in the settlement of the boundaries of the abbey's Winchester property (R XLIX). He witnessed as abbot a transaction by which the reversion was granted of a Somerset estate to the Old Minster, in the presence of the communities of Glastonbury and the three Winchester foundations (W VII). He presided over the translation of the relics of St Swithun (E. S. Duckett, *St Dunstan*, p. 124). He was consecrated Bishop of Selsey on 2 May 980 (ASC C, confirmed by charters; the date 977 in LVH is wrong), and elevated to Canterbury in June 988 (ASC F). He died on 13 Feb. 990 (LVH p. 270), and was buried in the cathedral church (HC p. 59). Selsey was a poorly endowed bishopric, and it is evident that Æthelgar was allowed to keep the abbacy of New Minster in plurality until his appointment to Canterbury (LVH p. xxviii). No doubt his Winchester connections enabled him to do some caretaking for Bishop Æthelwold (q.v.) while the latter was busy consolidating the reformist position after the anti-monastic reaction that followed the death of King Edgar. He was in attendance at Æthelwold's deathbed. It seems probable that he surrendered New Minster upon his appointment to Canterbury. In 983 Æthelgar was granted a meadow in Winchester (LH pp. 228–31), and at Easter 988, just before his appointment to Canterbury, King Æthelred confirmed to him 7 hides at South Heighton, Sussex, which Æthelgar had received from Ealdorman Ælfric of Hampshire (q.v.), in exchange for land at Lambourne, Berks. (LH pp. 238–42). Æthelgar witnessed many charters in his career, including the 'golden' foundation charter of New Minster in 966 (CS 1190). Usually he witnessed last of the abbots until 969, but gradually thereafter he assumed greater precedence; in 972 he witnessed fourth of thirteen abbots (CS 1282). Once appointed to Selsey, his usual place was high on the lists, witnessing after the bishops of London and Winchester (e.g. K 629, 665). This high position suggests that he was already a candidate for primacy. He witnessed as archbishop only one charter of which the text survives (K 663, dated 988). See further, KBL pp. 80–1.

Æthelgar, thegn XXXI

Witnesses 1009.

Although he appears high in the witness list of Bu XXXI, I have been unable to trace any other reference to Æthelgar.

Æthelgeard, thegn XII, XVI

Witnesses 932 × 958.

He was one of the most powerful West Saxon thegns of the period. His interests were centred on Winchester, where he held property (CS 758, 786; cf. ECW 58, 61), and he left land to New Minster for the souls of himself and his wife; it seems likely that they were buried there, and that he is the Æthelgeard *preng* (? prince) whose name appears in a list of benefactors to the house (LVH p. 22; cf. W VI). Nine charters survive in the *Codex Wintoniensis* and the Hyde Abbey Register (formerly New Minster), by which successive kings from Athelstan to Eadwig grant him over 100 hides in the Thames Valley and in East Hampshire (CS 689, 758, 765, 786, 810, 830, 864, 976, 988); in addition, he received an estate in the Isle of Wight, which probably he gave to Evesham (CS 1025). Towards the end of his career, Æthelgeard rose to third in the hierarchy of thegns in constant attendance upon the king; some of his charters show evidence of this special service to the royal family (e.g. the dispositive clauses of CS 758, 830); he knew King Eadred in his childhood (CS 810), and King Eadwig described him as his *karus* (CS 944). Æthelgeard remained true to King Eadwig after Edgar's revolt in 957; subsequently he witnessed several of Eadwig's charters, but none of Edgar's. The last charter he witnessed (of which the text has survived) is CS 1032, before 2 June 958. See further, CW pp. 15–17.

Æthelm, thegn XXII

Witnesses ? 959 × 968.

Æthelm is an uncommon name at this period, and probably the witness of Bu XXIII (968), a Mercian charter, is to be identified with the thegn Æthelm who witnessed low down on the lists two Abingdon texts, and charters relating to lands in Somerset and Shropshire: CS 1046–7 (959); CS 1074 (961); CS 1119 (963). The Æthelm who held on lease 2½ hides at Elmstree, Gloucestershire, from Worcester in 962 may be the same person (R XXXIV).

Æthelmær

Ealdorman of Wessex 977 × 982.

Æthelmær did not witness any Burton Abbey charters, but his

career is summarized here so that he may be distinguished from other persons of the same name. Æthelmær began to witness as a thegn in 972; previously, no thegn of this name appears in the charters after 957. He witnessed as a thegn CS 1282 (972); CS 1303 (974); CS 1312 (975), being the fourth in order of precedence in this last charter. There is no record of the succession in the West Saxon ealdordom after the death of Ælfheah (q.v.) in 970, and it seems probable that Ælfheah's brother Ealdorman Ælfhere of Mercia (q.v.) administered Wessex until the death of King Edgar in 975. Æthelmær first witnessed as ealdorman in 977, and continued to witness low down on the list until his death in 982 (ASC, Fl Wig); he appears in the following charters: K 611 (977); K 621 (979); K 624, 626 (980); K 629 (981); K 632, 1278 (982). Æthelmær's will survives (W x), and shows that he left a wife and two sons; he was buried at New Minster, to which house he was a benefactor (LVH pp. 21, 54). The date 982 given in ASC for Æthelmær's death is confirmed by the appearance of Ælfric, his successor in the West Saxon ealdordom, as witness to two charters of that year (K 633, LH p. 217). K 638, a charter dated 983 purporting to grant land at Clyffe Pipard, Wilts., to Æthelmær, is in fact a forgery modelled on the authentic K 636, a charter with identical formulary and witnesses by which the same estate was granted to Æthelmær's son Æthelwine, who also figures in K 692. It is noteworthy that K 636 is witnessed by Ælfric (q.v.), Æthelmær's successor.

Æthelmær 'the Fat'   XXVI–XXVIIIa, XXXI
    Ealdorman of the Western Shires c. 1002 × 1014.
    He witnessed 983 × 1004, nearly always as first of the thegns from 994 onwards; in the OE text of K 715 he witnessed as *mines hlafordes discðen*, but occasionally he is referred to as ealdorman, particularly towards the end of his life. This rather casual and equivocal attitude to the rank of ealdorman is evidenced also in the career of his contemporary, Ulfketel 'Snilling' (q.v.), who held all the authority of ealdorman in East Anglia without receiving the rank and title. Æthelmær was the founder of monasteries at Cerne and Eynsham, and patron of Ælfric the Homilist. The ealdordom passed from his father through Æthelmær to his son. See further, W pp. 144–5, R pp. 386–7; H p. 555.

Æthelmær, thegn   XIV
    Witnessed 955 × 957.
    No thegn of this name witnessed surviving charters of the period

949 × 954 or 958 × 971, and the Æthelmær who witnessed Bu xiv
appears elsewhere only as a witness to charters of King Eadwig of the
period 955 x 957, where he is usually between second and sixth of the
thegns subscribing. These charters are: CS 917 (955); CS 938, 935,
970, 969, 971, 985, 941, 949–50, 973, 982, 945–6, 957, 1009,
964–5, 967, 978, 930, and 1184 (956); CS 988, 1001 (957). It is
just possible that he is the Æthelmær '*præses*' who received 20 hides
at Chetwood and Hillesden, Bucks., from King Eadred in 949
(CS 883).

Æthelmær, thegn   XXVI–XXVIIIa
  Witnesses 994 × 1005.
  Two thegns named Æthelmær witnessed Bu xxvi–xxviiia. Of
these, the first became ealdorman of the Western Shires (q.v.); the
second is named as the son of Æthelwold (q.v.) in K 703 (999), and
witnessed 994 × 1005, see R p. 386.

Æthelmund   V, XII, XIV
  Ealdorman of N.W. Mercia 940 × 965.
  Uhtred, ealdorman of N.W. Mercia, last witnesses CS 716–18
dated 21 Dec. 934. For the rest of Athelstan's reign no Mercian
ealdorman witnesses the royal diplomas that have survived. The
reasons for this are obscure, but it is noteworthy that the northern
dioceses are also unrepresented in the witness lists of this period,
and it may be that Athelstan's last years witnessed a considerable
diminution in his power. Edmund succeeded in October 939, and
early in the following year he appointed three ealdormen: Æthelwold,
son of Athelstan 'Half King' (q.v.) to Kent (with Sussex and Surrey),
Ealhhelm to Central Mercia, and Æthelmund to N.W. Mercia.
Later in 940 another Athelstan was appointed to S.E. Mercia.
Æthelmund witnessed regularly the charters of King Edmund and
King Eadred, usually as fifth or sixth of the ealdormen until 952,
after which he witnessed in second place; for the rest of King
Eadred's reign he was the only Mercian ealdorman witnessing, and
he appears to have had control of those parts of Mercia not administered by Athelstan 'Half King' of East Anglia. Eadwig succeeded
in November 955; immediately he appointed a third Athelstan,
nicknamed 'Rota' (q.v.), to the vacant S.E. Mercian ealdordom,
and Æthelmund dropped to fifth or sixth place in the lists of ealdormen subscribing to the royal diplomas. Æthelmund ceased to witness
the surviving charters of King Eadwig after Christmas 956 (CS 1029),
and in 958 he began to witness the charters of King Edgar. While

Edgar's kingdom was confined to the north of the Thames, Æthelmund witnessed as second of the *duces*; but after Edgar acceded to the whole of England, Æthelmund dropped to a lower position, and witnessed from fourth to seventh among the ealdormen. He last witnessed CS 1165, dated 965. A thegn named Æthelmund witnessed from 928 to 940 (CS 663 to CS 753, 758, 762), and as no thegn of this name witnessed thereafter, it is probable that this was the person who became ealdorman in 940. It seems, therefore, that Æthelmund was at least 55 when he died, and few ealdormen of the period survived to a greater age.

Æthelnoth, thegn 956   XVII
   Various thegns named Æthelnoth appear as witnesses to charters and as recipients of grants in the period 931 × 978, but it is hazardous to try to identify any of them with the Æthelnoth who was granted land at Darlaston, near Stone, Staffordshire, by King Eadwig in 956 (Bu XVII). The estate descended to Wulfric Spot (q.v.).

Æthelred II, king   XXIV–XXVIIIa, XXIX–XXXVI
   March 978 × autumn 1013, and 3 Feb. 1014 × 23 April 1016.
   The second son of King Edgar by his second wife Ælfthryth, Æthelræd 'unræd' was born in 968 or 969. His elder brother Edmund died a year or two later, and Æthelred inherited the English crown when only ten or eleven years old, after the murder of his half-brother Edward the Martyr. He married first Ælfgifu, in *c.* 987, by whom he had six sons and four or five daughters; and secondly, in the spring of 1002, Emma, daughter of Richard I, duke of Normandy, by whom he had two more sons. Whatever else Æthelred may be blamed for, he cannot be reproached for failing to secure the succession, as far as this lay in his power. He named his sons after his royal ancestors, from Alfred the Great onwards. He was succeeded by his third son, Edmund Ironside, and twenty-six years later by his seventh son, Edward the Confessor. There is no adequate biography of King Æthelred 'unræd'; the best account so far is in Barlow, EC, *passim*.

Æthelric   XXVII, XXVIIIa, XXIX–XXXIV
   Abbot of Athelney c. 993 × c. 1002; bishop of Sherborne 1001–2 1012.
   Æthelric, the first recorded abbot of the newly reformed abbey of Athelney, witnessed K 684 (993), where his abbey is identified. He did not witness many of King Æthelred's charters, but appears in

S 1380 (994); Bu XXVII (996); K 698, OS Facs III, 35 (997). Abbot
Ælfric, his successor, first appears in K 707 (1002). It is a reasonable
supposition that Æthelric was appointed to the see of Sherborne,
where a bishop of that name began to witness in 1002; his predecessor
Wulfsige III (q.v.) last witnessed in 1001 (K 706). Æthelric witnessed
as bishop the following charters: OS Facs III, 36 (11 July 1002);
Crispin p. 168, K 707, 1295, 1297 (1002); K 715 (with an authentic
witness list of 1002); Bu XXVIIIa (1004); K 709 (misspelt *Æthelbriht*)
(1004); K 714, 1301 (1005); K 1303, Bu XXIX (1007); K 1305, Bu
XXX (1008); K 1306, Bu XXXI (1009); Bu XXXII, XXXIII (1011); Bu
XXXIV, R LXXIV (1009 × 1012). Of these, Bu XXXI, XXXIII, and R
LXXIV are witnessed by a Bishop Æthelsige (q.v.), who appears just
below Æthelric in the lists. It is evident that this was Æthelric's
successor to the see – he first witnesses alone in 1012 (K 719, Bu
XXXV); he may have been appointed as *chorepiscopus* a few years
before he succeeded. During Æthelric's episcopacy, Sherborne was
heavily taxed to meet the cost of opposing the Danes, and Æthelric
had to sell some of the properties of the see (H no. 63; K 1309).
According to Goscelin, *Vita Wulfsini* p. 81, Æthelric died in 1016;
this is quite possible, as he may have retired from the see, because of
illness, some time before his death (but see Barlow pp. 222–3, n. 6
for a different view). See also KBL p. 26.

Æthelric, thegn   XXVI–XXVIIIa, XXXI
    Witnesses 987 × 1013.
    He witnessed the following charters: K 657–8 (987); EHD I p.
534 (989); K 687, S 1380 (994); K 688, 692 (995); Bu XXVI (984
for 996); K 1292, Bu XXVII, EHD I, p. 534 (996); OS Facs III, 35,
K 698 (997); K 700 (998); K 703 (999); K 1294 (1000); K 705–6
(1001); K 707, 715, 1295, Crispin p. 168, EHD I, p. 540 (1002);
Bu XXVIIIa (1004); K 1301, 672, 714 (1005); K 1303–4 (1007); K
1305 (1008); Bu XXXI (1009); Thorney x (1013). The Æthelric who
was second of the thegns witnessing K 663 (988) is probably an
error for Æthelsige (q.v.). Æthelric begins to witness high on the
lists in 995 (K 688), and from 999 onwards he is usually in the top
seven. He may be the Æthelric who received 17 hides at Harwell,
Berks., from King Æthelred in 985 (K 648). In the OE text of K 715
he is distinguished as Æthelric *ealda*.

Æthelric, thegn   XXVIIIb, XXXI
    Witnesses 1004, 1009
    The Æthelric who received Wibtoft, Warwicks., and Tong, Salop

in 1004 (Bu xxviiib) may be the Æthelric who witnessed last of 28 thegns Bu xxxi (1009).

Æthelsige   XXIV, XXV

(I) bishop of Sherborne 978 × 990–3.

Little is known about him. He first witnessed K 621 (979), and last witnessed K 672–3 (990). His predecessor Ælfwold I (q.v.) died in 978, and his successor Wulfsige III (q.v.) first witnessed in 993 (K 684). In 988 Bishop Æthelsige received a curtilage in Winchester (GC iii, p. 704). He is said to have been given charge of the abbey of Evesham by King Æthelred II, but to have incurred the wrath of the king, and to have been banished (Chron E p. 80).

Æthelsige   XXXI, XXXIII, XXXV

(II) bishop of Sherborne 1012 × 1014–31.

Æthelsige II witnessed as bishop three charters of the period 1009 × 1012, immediately beneath the signatures of Bishop Æthelric of Sherborne (q.v.); it seems likely that he was a *chorepiscopus* in the diocese at this period. The need for such an appointment would not have been due to the size or the resources of the see, but it is conceivable that Bishop Æthelric was partially incapacitated. After his accession to Sherborne, Æthelsige witnessed K 719, Bu xxxiii (1012), K 1309 (1014). According to lists in Fl Wig and LVH, Æthelsige II was followed by Brihtwine, Ælfmær, and Brihtwine again (for Ælfmær, see H p. 548, and F. Barlow, *The Life of Edward the Confessor* 1962, p. li, n. 1). Unfortunately it is not possible to supply any firm dates for this succession until 1031, when K 744, an original charter, was witnessed by two bishops named *Byrhtwig* and *Byrhtwine*, the former being from Wells and the latter from Sherborne.

Æthelsige   XII, XIV, XVII

Ealdorman of Wessex c. 951 × 958.

A thegn Æthelsige witnessed the following charters of the period 945 × 949: CS 808, 810, 813–14, 818, 821, 830, 834, 864–6, 868, 870, 877, 888. His position varied between bottom and fifth of the thegns witnessing. No lists survive for 950. Ealdorman Æthelsige first witnessed Bu xii, one of four charters of 951 with adequate lists. He did not witness the solitary surviving charter of 952 (CS 895), or the two of 953 (CS 899, 900), but very few ealdormen – only two or three – witnessed at this period. He witnessed CS 903, 905, 887 (955), and nearly all of King Eadwig's charters to the end of 958. After Edgar's revolt in 957, he subscribed second only to Ealdorman

Edmund of the Western Provinces. In spite of his importance at this period, no biographical material survives. (The thegn Æthelsige who witnessed CS 900 dated 953 is a mistake for Ælfsige, see CS 899.)

Æthelsige, thegn 987   XXV

He was the recipient of *Æsce* in 987 (Bu xxv). A thegn of this name witnessed a Hyde charter of 988 (LH pp. 238–42), K 684 dated 994, and BM Stowe charter No. 34, dated 997. It is uncertain if all these references are to the same man.

Æthelsige, *pedisequus*   XXIII

Witnesses 958 × 987.

He was the third son of Athelstan 'Half King' (q.v.), the brother of Æthelwine 'Dei amicus' (q.v.), and *camerarius* to King Edgar. He died on 13 October 987. See further, Hart 1973, pp. 132–3.

Æthelweard   XXXVII

Abbot of Glastonbury 1023 × 9 Nov. 1053.

His predecessor Brihtwine or Brightwig was appointed to Wells by 1023 (ASC D); he witnessed K 739 both as bishop and as abbot, and Æthelweard also witnessed this charter (dated 1023) as abbot. It seems likely that the charter was witnessed at the meeting at which Brihtwine's appointment was made. Æthelweard's death is recorded in ASC D, where his abbey is identified (it is also identified in OS Facs II, Exeter 12). He witnessed the following charters: K 793, 1324, 741, 743–4; OS Facs II, Exeter 11; K 746, 1318, 1322; OS Facs III, 42; K 769, 762–3, 767, 774; OS Facs II, Exeter 12; K 776, 781; Bu xxxvii; K 787, 791–3. The last charter witnessed, K 796 (1052), contains spurious material, and is untrustworthy. His obit is recorded in AD I, p. 87.

Æthelweard   XXVI, XXVII

Ealdorman of the Western Shires 973 × c. 1002.

See *The Chronicle of Æthelweard*, ed. A. Campbell, pp. xii–xvi for his biography.

Æthelweard, thegn   XXVI, XXVII

Witnesses 977 × 998.

A thegn of this name received from King Æthelred in 990 (K 673) 15 hides at Wooton St Laurence, Hants., together with a meadow at Basingstoke, a mill at *Hinesclifæ*, and nine messuages in Tanner Street, Winchester (now Lower Brook Street). It was probably he who witnessed the following charters: K 611 (977); K 629 (981); K

636, 639 (983); K 641 (984); K 654 (986); K 658 (987); K 687, S 1380 (994); K 688, 692 (995); K 696, Bu xxvi–xxvii, EHD i, p. 534 (996); K 698 (997); K 700 (998).

Æthelweard, thegn   xxviiia
   Witnesses 1002 × 1019.
   He may be identified with the Æthelweard who was the son-in-law of Æthelmær 'the Fat' (q.v.), ealdorman of the Western Shires 1002 × 1014, and is mentioned in 1005 in the foundation charter of Eynsham (K 714). He is thought to have succeeded to his father-in-law's ealdordom, and to have been expelled by King Cnut in 1020 (R. Flower, *The Exeter Book of Old English Poetry*, pp. 85–9). He witnessed the following charters as thegn: K 1296 (1002); K 709, Bu xxviiia (1004); K 1301, 672, 714 (1005); K 1303 (1007); K 1305 (1008); K 1307, 719 (1012); K 1309 (1014); K 1310 (1015); LH pp. 324–6 (1019).

Æthelwine 'Dei amicus'   xxiii
   Ealdorman of East Anglia 962 × 992.
   The son of Athelstan 'Half King' (q.v.), and founder of Ramsey Abbey, he died on 24 April 992. For his biography, see Hart 1973, pp. 133–8.

Æthelwine, thegn   xxxi
   Witnesses 1002 × 1013.
   He witnessed the following charters, usually low in the lists: K 707, 1296 (1002); K 709 (1004); K 1301, 672, 714 (1005); K 1303–4 (1007); K 1305 (1008); Bu xxxi (1009); K 1307, 719 (1012); Thorney x (1013).

Æthelwold   viii
   Bishop of Dorchester 934–43 × 949.
   He witnessed as last of the bishops the following charters of the period 943 × 949: CS 812, 808, 815, 883, Bu viii. Formerly he has been assigned to Lindsey or Elmham, but the will of Theodred (q.v.) shows that the see of Elmham was held by the bishop of London at this period, and it seems likely that Lindsey was included within the diocese of Dorchester. The location of Æthelwold's see is revealed in a charter dated 948, by which land beside Wallingford, on the River Thames, was conveyed with rights within and without the borough, *ealswa Æþelpold bisceop ær hæfde*, the phrase quoted being a later insertion (CS 864; cf. CW p. 17, n. 3). The only Bishop

Æthelwold known at this period is the one now under consideration; he could not have been the shire bishop of Berkshire because this office was held by Cynesige (q.v.) at this time (both Cynesige and Æthelwold witnessed CS 812); his diocese must therefore have been north of the Thames, and this locates it at Dorchester. Since writing this, I have found that Professor Whitelock, from different considerations, has reached the same conclusion (*The Will of Æthelgifu* p. 44; see also O'D I, p. 38). The Bishop Wynsige (q.v.) who witnessed 925 × 934 was probably Æthelwold's predecessor at Dorchester; his successor Oscytel (q.v.) succeeded in 949, and first witnessed in 951 (CS 890–1).

Æthelwold   XX–XXIII
   Monk of Glastonbury, abbot of Abingdon c. 953 × 963, (I) bishop of Winchester 29 Nov. 963 × 8 August 984.
   The son of a powerful Winchester thegn, Æthelwold was born c. 910. As a boy he attended King Athelstan's court, and was sent by the king to the monk Ælfheah for education. In 934 Ælfheah became bishop of Winchester (q.v.) and a year or two later he ordained Dunstan (q.v.) and Æthelwold on the same day. Soon after King Athelstan's death, his successor King Edmund appointed Dunstan to be abbot at Glastonbury, and Æthelwold followed him there to become a monk of the newly reformed foundation. He stayed there for perhaps 13 years until 953, when at about the age of 43 he was appointed by King Eadred to be the first abbot of the refounded monastery at Abingdon. When King Eadwig succeeded two years later, Dunstan fell into disfavour and was exiled, but Æthelwold was left in charge of Abingdon, where he had been made responsible for the education and upbringing of the aetheling Edgar, who became King of Mercia in 957 and of all England upon Eadwig's death in 959. It seems that after Mercia's defection to Edgar in 957, Abingdon remained an outpost of Eadwig's sovereignty on the bank of the Thames, for in the closing months of Eadwig's reign Æthelwold began to witness royal diplomas as abbot (CS 1030, 1045). After Edgar's accession this custom continued, and until he succeeded Brihthelm (q.v.) as bishop of Winchester on 29 Nov. 963, Æthelwold was the only abbot regularly witnessing King Edgar's charters; it is clear that he had great influence over his pupil, and he seems to have gained control of the royal chancery, as all royal diplomas were issued from Abingdon at this period. Upon Æthelwold's appointment to Winchester, he launched the Benedictine reform in England, expelling the clerks from the Old and New Minsters, and replacing

them by monks. Later he planted or refounded further monasteries, including the great fenland group of Ely (970), Peterborough (971), Thorney (973), and Crowland (probably 974). For part of their endowment, Æthelwold recovered from the royal fisc estates that had belonged to Mercian monasteries in the pre-Viking era. Examples include Oundle in Northamptonshire (R XL), Breedon in Leicester-shire (Bu XXII), and Barrow-on-Humber in Lincolnshire (CS 1270). Records of Æthelwold's estate-building activities survive in the archives of Peterborough, Thorney, Ely, and Abingdon. In return for one of the estates used for the endowment of Ely, Æthelwold made an English translation of the Rule of St Benedict for the use of nuns; in the same year (970) he compiled the *Regularis Concordia*, and he was responsible also for a vernacular account of the early years of the reform movement in England (EHD I, pp. 846–9). The *Vita Oswaldi* names Æthelwold as King Edgar's principal counsellor, and his position is illustrated by the fact that every surviving authentic royal diploma issued between Æthelwold's accession to Winchester and his death bears his attestation. He appears to have controlled the chancery throughout Edgar's reign. He introduced the use of caroline minuscule for royal landbooks, and established a standard form of writing in the vernacular. Two early lives of Æthelwold survive (EHD I, pp. 831–2; cf. D. J. Fisher, 'The Early Biographers of St Æthelwold', EHR LXVII (1952), pp. 381–4), but there is no adequate modern biography. The best accounts so far are by J. Armitage Robinson (Robinson pp. 104–22), E. S. Duckett (*St. Dunstan of Canterbury*, 1955, pp. 111–36), and Eric John (OB pp. 154–63). For his obits, see KLB p. 23.

Æthelwold   XXIX–XXXII, XXXIV–XXXV
(II) bishop of Winchester 1006–7 × 1012.
Very little is known about him. Ælfheah II (q.v.) was translated from Winchester to Canterbury after 15 Nov. 1005, and was succeeded at Winchester by Kenulf, abbot of Peterborough (q.v.) who died in 1006 (ASC E). Æthelwold II first witnessed in 1012 (K 719, Bu XXXIV–XXXV). In a later charter of that year, Winchester is not represented in the witness list (K 1307). Æthelwold's successor at Winchester, Ælfsige II, is first mentioned as bishop late in 1012 (W XX, dated by Barlow EC p. 30, n. 3).

Æthelwold   XIV, XVII
Ealdorman of East Anglia 956 × 962.
He succeeded his father Athelstan 'Half King' (q.v.) as ealdorman

of East Anglia in 956. His wife Ælfthryth (q.v.) was the daughter of Ordgar, who became ealdorman of the Western Shires; after Æthelwold's death in 962, she married King Edgar (q.v.). Æthelwold was succeeded as ealdorman of East Anglia by his brother Æthelwine 'Dei amicus' (q.v.). See further, Hart 1973, pp. 128–29.

Æthelwold 'the Stout', thegn   xxviiia
    Witnesses 986 × 1008.
    Two thegns named Æthelwold witness King Æthelred's charters. The first appears in K 654 (986); K 658 (987); EHD I, p. 533 (989); K 687 (994); K 703 (999); K 1295–6 (1002); Bu xxviiia (1004); K 1301, 714 (1005); K 1303–4 (1007), and K 1305 (1008). In charters of the period 999 x 1005 he usually witnesses immediately below a thegn called Æthelmær (q.v.), and in K 703 Æthelmær is described as the son of Æthelwold. He is probably to be identified with the Æthelwold 'the Stout' of EHD I, p. 533, and with the Æthelwold who received 10 hides at Manningford Abbots, Wilts., from King Æthelred in 987 (LH pp. 231–6), which he willed to his wife, with reversion to the New Minster at Winchester (W xii). His importance is suggested by the fact that Æthelwold appears second or third among the thegns in the last three charters he witnesses.

Æthelwold, thegn   xxxi
    Witnesses 1005 × 1012.
    He subscribes to K 714 (1005); K 1304 (1007); Bu xxxi (1009); and K 719 (1012), and is to be distinguished from Æthelwold 'the Stout' (q.v.) by his lower position in the witness lists.

Æthelwulf, see Æthulf.

Æthulf   xvii, xix
    Bishop of Elmham 951–5 × 966–70.
    Theodred, bishop of London (q.v.) held the diocese of East Anglia (Elmham) before his death in 951–3. The date of Æthulf's appointment to the see is unknown; the text of his profession to Archbishop Oda survives, but it is undated (CS 918). Æthulf's signature first occurs as bishop in CS 905, a charter of King Eadwig issued late in 955; thereafter he witnessed the majority of King Eadwig's charters in 956–7. Subsequently he supported King Edgar, witnessing all his surviving charters as king of the Mercians in

the period 958–9 (CS 1042, 1040, 1036–7, 1043–4, 1023, 1052). He continued to witness King Edgar's charters after Eadwig's death, and his name appears frequently in the lists of the period 959 × 966, the last charter witnessed being CS 1190. His see is identified as Elmham in CS 918, his profession to Archbishop Oda (which should be assigned to 951 × 955), and also in CS 1112 and 1134, issued in 963 and 964 respectively. After 966 there is a gap in the attestations of the bishops of Elmham until 970, when Ælfric appears (CS 1266), and then again until 974 when bishop Theodred II of Elmham appears (CS 1303; he witnesses also CS 1201 dated 974 × 975, and CS 1314 dated 975). In the past, it has been thought mistakenly that the Bishop Æthulf who witnessed many of the charters issued in 955 × 966 was from Hereford (see below). The charter S 728, ostensibly dated 964, and witnessed by Æthulf as bishop of Hereford and Theodred as bishop of Elmham is, however, spurious.

Æthulf   XXIV, XXVII, XXIX, XXXI–XXXIII, XXXV
    Bishop of Hereford 970–1 × Feb.–July 1012.

It now seems probable that the Wulfric who witnessed as bishop charters issued in the period 958 × 970 was in fact from Dorchester (q.v.), rather than Hereford (CS 1040, 1073, 1119, 1135, 1164, 1211, 1229, 1234). However, no bishop named Æthulf witnessed surviving charters issued between 966 (CS 1190) and 971 (CS 1270), and it is clear that the Æthulf witnessing up to 966 was from Elmham (q.v.), while the Æthulf who figures in a long list of charters from 971 (CS 1270) to 1012 (K 719, Bu xxxv) was from Hereford. His see is identified in a number of charters issued during the period 993 × 1001 (K 684, 688, 692, 705–6, 1289, 1292, S 1380, Bu xxvii). Æthulf's position in the witness lists gradually rises through the years from last to second or third of the bishops, and for this reason it seems probable that there was only one bishop of Hereford of this name during the period 971 to 1012. He last witnesses K 719 dated after 13 Feb. 1012, and Bu xxxv issued in the same year. His successor Athelstan first witnesses K 1307 dated July 1012. The statement in R lxxxiii that Bishop Athelstan was at Hereford before Archbishop Ælfheah's capture by the Danes in September 1011 is evidently mistaken; this was written some twelve years later, and the memory of the writer (or his informant) must have been at fault.

Alchelme, *see* Alhhelm.

Aldhun, *see* Ealdhun.

Alfred VIII, XI

Bishop of Sherborne 933–4 × 943, bishop of Selsey 940 × 953.

Alfred first witnesses CS 702 dated 28 May 934, and his subscriptions occur regularly until CS 899–900, dated 953. From 931 to 940 the see of Selsey was held by Wulfhun, and from 943 onwards the see of Sherborne was held by Wulfsige II (q.v.); it seems that Alfred held both sees in plurality between 940 and 943. In 939 Alfred was granted 5 hides at Orchard, Dorset, within the diocese of Sherborne (CS 744), and in 945 he was granted land belonging to his bishopric, together with 4 hides at Bracklesham and 2 at Thorney, Sussex, presumably to supplement his poor endowment at Selsey (CS 807). See further under Brihthelm, bishop of Selsey, and Wulfsige II, bishop of Sherborne. A second Bishop Alfred who witnesses low down on the lists of three charters in 934 (CS 702–3, 705) and possibly one in 935 (CS 707) may be from Lindsey or Elmham; probably he is to be identified with the Bishop Alfred who witnesses the Mercian charter CS 632, dated 915–16.

Alfred, thegn (IV), XII, XIV, XVII

Witnesses 926 × 959.

The witness list of Bu IV is incomplete, but probably it was identical with that of CS 659, issued on the same occasion. Two thegns named Alfred witness this charter, in second and eighth positions respectively. Of these the senior cannot be traced in the lists of later charters, but the junior is probably (but not certainly) the thegn Alfred who continued to subscribe until the death of King Eadwig in 959, by which time his position in the lists was sometimes as high as third of the thegns witnessing. His adherence to King Eadwig after Edgar's revolt locates him south of the Thames, and he may be identified with the *optimas* named Alfred who received land in Dorset from Eadwig in 956 (CS 959). The Alfred who was granted lands in Somerset between 939 and 955 may have been the same person (ECW 454, 463–4), but he is to be distinguished from the thegn Alfred who held lands in Hants. and Wilts. which he bequeathed to New Minster c. 933 (R pp. 309–10).

Alhhelm, ealdorman c. 883 × c. 900 I

Alchelme, the recipient of *Stantun* (? Stanton, Derbyshire) in 900 (Bu I), was probably the man of that name who is last of four Mercian ealdormen witnessing a charter dated 883 (CS 557). His position in the list enables us to identify him with the Alhhelm who witnessed as last of the ealdormen Mercian charters issued in 884 (CS 552) and

896 (CS 574), and a Mercian memorandum of the same period, the precise date of which is doubtful (CS 537. ECWM 270. Finberg dates this 883 × 911. Eadnoth and Alfred, who witness this memorandum as '*duces*' after Alhhelm, are clearly the Eadnoth and Alfred who witness CS 574 after Alhhelm, as '*mass preostes*'. They appear together as witnesses to CS 557, but without titles). It seems likely that Ealdorman Alhhelm was the '*princeps huius patriæ, Alchelmus nomine*', who is recorded in the Evesham Chronicle as taking possession of the landed properties of that house (Chron E p. 77, where the event is wrongly assigned to the reign of King Edmund).

Ascytel, thegn   XXXI
    Witnesses 1009.
Two thegns named Ascytel and Asketel witness Bu XXXI, but the name does not recur in the witness lists of King Æthelred's charters. It is a northern form of Oscytel, and later in the century appears as Askil.

Athelstan, ætheling   XXVI–XXVIIIa, XXX–XXXVI
    c. 988 × c. 1015.
He was the eldest son of King Æthelred II by his first wife Ælfgifu. Besides the Burton charters, he witnesses the following: K 684, 697, 703, 1294, 705–6, 1295, 1297, 707, 1296, 709, 714, 1301, 1303–6, 1308. He had three younger brothers in 993, and probably he was born c. 988. He died c. 1015. See W xx for his will and biography.

Athelstan   XXXVII
    Bishop of Hereford c. July 1012 × 10 Feb. 1056.
His predecessor Æthulf (q.v.) witnessed a charter of 1012 (K 719, dated after 13 February), and Athelstan first witnessed K 1307 dated July 1012. Subsequently he figured in or witnessed the following charters: R LXXXIII (1012 × 1023); R LXXVIII (1016 × 1035); K 1313 (1017); K 736 (1021–3); R LXXVI, LXXXII (1023); K 749, 752 (1033); K 760 (1038); K 762–4 (1042); K 769 (1042–4); K 767 (1043); K 771, 774–5, 796 (1044); K 776, 778, 780 (1045); K 784 (1046); Bu XXXVII (1048). During his episcopacy, he rebuilt the cathedral church at Hereford, but it was devastated four months before his death; he was, however, buried there. Athelstan, who was well remembered in his diocese, was blind for 13 years before his death, and Tremerin, bishop of St Davids, acted as his coadjutor (ASC C, D, 1055–6, elaborated by Fl Wig). See further, Barlow p. 217.

Athelstan, 'Half King' XII
Ealdorman of East Anglia 932 × 956.

Athelstan was the second of four sons of Æthelfrith, one of the three sub-ealdormen of Mercia during the closing years of the ninth century. All four sons became ealdormen. Athelstan's ealdordom embraced the whole of the eastern Danelaw from the Thames to the Welland, bounded to the south-west by Watling Street and to the north-west by the territory of the Five Boroughs. In addition, towards the end of his career he was responsible for the overall supervision of English Mercia, and for many years he was virtually the regent; he fostered the aetheling Edgar. Athelstan 'Half King' was closely associated with the founders of the English Benedictine reform movement. He was one of the earliest benefactors to the reformed monastery at Abingdon, and in 956 he retired to become a monk at Glastonbury, to which house he gave all his extensive possessions in the West Country. The important charter CS 937, issued late in 956 and witnessed by Dunstan but not by Athelstan, suggests that the 'Half King' retired to Glastonbury before Dunstan was banished; indeed, it is not unlikely that Athelstan's arrival at Glastonbury contributed to the reasons for Dunstan's banishment. Athelstan married soon after receiving the East Anglian ealdordom. By his wife Ælfwynn he had four sons: Æthelwold (q.v.), Ælfwold, Æthelsige, and Æthelwine 'Dei amicus' (q.v.). Of these, the first and fourth succeeded him as ealdormen of East Anglia, and Æthelsige became King Edgar's chamberlain. See further Hart 1973, pp. 115–44.

Athelstan 'Rota' XIV, XVII, XXIII
Ealdorman of S.E. Mercia 955 × 970.

It is necessary to distinguish carefully between the three ealdormen named Athelstan who witness charters in the mid-tenth century. Athelstan 'Half King' of East Anglia (q.v.) began to witness as ealdorman in 932. In 940-1 he appears usually as third, in 942 as second, and from 943 until midsummer 956 as first of the ealdormen subscribing. A second ealdorman named Athelstan began to witness towards the end of 940 (CS 757). By 944 he took third place in the witness lists, a position he retained until his last signature in 949 (CS 875). Always he appeared below the Half King in the witness lists, and it is very probable that his ealdordom lay in S.E. Mercia. From early in 949 to the end of 955, only one ealdorman named Athelstan witnessed; this was the Half King (CS 883, 879, 880, 894, 892, 891, 895, 899, 900, 908, 903, 905, and 887, in chronological order). A third ealdorman named Athelstan began to witness at the beginning of King Eadwig's reign, usually in third position until the Half King's retirement. In CS 917, dated 23 November to 31 December 955, the first charter he witnessed, he is given the nickname 'Rota' (? 'the Red') to differentiate him from the Half King. After the Half King's retirement, Athelstan 'Rota' jumped to first place among the ealdormen witnessing King Eadwig's charters; this group comprises, in rough chronological order, CS 965, 978, 956, 948, 1009, 930, and 927 (all issued in the autumn of 956), CS 1029 (with an authentic witness list dated Christmas 956), CS 988, 997, 999, 1001, 1003, and 994 (all dated 957). After the revolt of the ætheling Edgar in the summer of 957, Ealdorman Athelstan 'Rota' ceased to subscribe to King Eadwig's charters, but in 958 he began to witness those issued by Edgar as King of Mercia. Until Edgar's accession to the whole kingdom of England in 959, Athelstan 'Rota' usually witnessed in second place among the ealdormen; thereafter until 965 he witnessed in third place. In 966 he witnessed fourth, and from 967 to 970 his position varied between fourth and first. The last surviving charter witnessed by Athelstan 'Rota' is CS 1268. He may have been the son of the Ealdorman Athelstan who witnessed from 940 to 949, and who probably held the same ealdordom. He married Æthelflæd of Damerham (q.v.), the widow of King Edmund.

Athelstan, king of England 924 × 939   II, III, IV
    The eldest son of King Edward the Elder, and his only known child by Ecgwynn, he was born c. 894 (WM I, p. 145; Asser p. 184 n. 4), acceded between 18 July and 24 Dec. 924, was crowned at Kingston-on-Thames on 4 Sept. 925, and died a bachelor in Oct. 939. There is no adequate biography; the best accounts to date are in Robinson pp. 25–80, and Stenton pp. 335–52.

Athelstan, thegn 949   X
    He was the alleged recipient of Eatun by CS 885. Since this charter is of very doubtful authenticity, it is not possible to attempt a biographical account of Athelstan.

Athulf, see Æthulf.

Beorhthelm, see Brihthelm.

Beorn Estrithson, earl 1045 × 1049   XXXVII
    He was the son of Jarl Ulf, and younger brother of King Swegn of

Denmark, nephew of King Cnut and of Earl Godwine, and cousin of Earls Harold and Swegn. Surprisingly little is known of him. His earldom included Hertfordshire (H nos. 78–9), and may have included the whole of Middle Anglia (Freeman, NC II, pp. 557 ff). His treacherous murder at Dartmouth by his cousin Earl Swegn is recorded in ASC (C, D, E) s.a. 1049; see also Barlow, EC, pp. 99–103. He was buried beside King Cnut at Winchester. He witnessed as earl K 778, 781 (1045); K 784 (1046); Bu XXXVII (1048); K 787 (1049).

Beornheah   IV
    Bishop of Selsey 909 × 929–June 931
    Beornheah was one of the seven bishops consecrated on the same day at Canterbury by Archbishop Plegmund (CS 614–15; Crawf 7; EHD I, pp. 822–3). He witnessed CS 641 (4 Sept 925); Bu IV (926; the correct spelling in the MS is *Beornneah*); CS 659 (926); CS 665–6 (spurious charters based on a text from the reign of King Eadred, with an authentic witness list of the period 929 × 29 May 931 grafted on to it). His successor Wulfhun first witnessed CS 675, dated 20 June 931.

Berhtferth, Birhtferth, *see* Brihtferth.

Brihtferth, thegn   XI, XII, XIV
    Witnesses 949 × 970.
    He was the younger brother of the West Saxon thegn Ælfgar (q.v.), and hence a kinsman of King Edgar (CS 1035). In his early appearances in the charters, Brihtferth often witnessed alone (CS 879, 882–3, 892–3, 889, 900, 903), but in a charter of 951 his name appears next below that of Ælfgar (Bu XII), and from 955 until the death of King Eadwig in 959 he witnessed habitually in this position. In the closing years of Eadwig's reign Ælfgar usually witnessed first of the thegns, a position he retained after Edgar's accession until he died in 962. During Eadwig's reign Brihtferth witnessed next to his brother, but in the early years of Edgar's reign a thegn named Ælfwine (q.v.) sometimes witnessed second to Ælfgar, with Brihtferth in third place. After Ælfgar's death, however, these positions were reversed, and from 962 to 970 Brihtferth headed the list of thegns, with Ælfwine next to him. The last surviving charters witnessed by Brihtferth are CS 1260 and CS 1266. Together with his brother Ælfgar, he is given the title *consul* in CS 1074, dated 961.

Brihthelm   XXVI, XXVII
    Abbot of Exeter 990–3 × c. 1003.
    Leofric, his predecessor, last witnesses in 990 (K 673). Brihthelm
first witnesses K 684 dated 993, and last witnesses K 698 dated 997.
His abbey is identified in both these charters. He witnesses also
Bu xxvi, xxvii; K 686–7; S 1380; Muchelney 4; K 692, 1289, 1292;
W xvi (2). The name of his successor is unknown; Brihthelm may,
in fact, have held the abbey until it was sacked by the Danes in 1003
(EHD i, p. 217).

Brihthelm   XIII, XIV, XVII
    Bishop of London c. 953 × summer 957.
    Bishop Theodred I of London (q.v.) last witnessed in 951, and he
was followed in the see by Bishop Wulfstan I (W p. 99). The earliest
surviving charters witnessed by Bishop Brihthelm of London are
CS 899, 900, issued on the same date in 953. No texts have survived
of charters issued in 954. From 955 onwards the bishop named
Brihthelm who witnessed the following charters held the see of
London: CS 903, 905, 908, 917, R xxx, Bu xiii (955); CS 919, 920
(a doubtful text), 924–6, 930, 932, 942–3, 945–6, 948, 952–3, 955,
957–62, 964–5, 967, 970, 973, 975–7, 979, 981–3, 985–6, Bu xiv
(956); CS 1009 (956 × 957); CS 987–8, 997, 1001, 1003, 1029
(all issued in 957, before 9 May). In all of these charters, only one
bishop named Brihthelm appears in the witness lists; but towards the
end of 956 and carrying on into the early months of 957, a group of
charters witnessed by two bishops named Brihthelm were issued by
King Eadwig. In this group, the senior bishop was from London and
the junior from Wells (q.v.); this can be stated with confidence
because CS 966 issued on 29 November 956 identifies the see of the
senior Brihthelm as London. The following charters belong to this
series: CS 927, 934, 966, 974; Bu xvii (956); CS 994, 999 (957).
All the charters of this group were witnessed by Edgar as King
Eadwig's brother. In addition, King Eadwig granted 10 hides at
Orsett, Essex, to Brihthelm early in 957, which remained the
property of his see until the Norman Conquest (ECStP p. 6; ECEss
No. 14). No more is heard of Bishop Brihthelm of London after the
revolt of Edgar in the summer of 957; Edgar gained control of
London and made Dunstan (q.v.) bishop there, and what became of
Brihthelm is unknown. Perhaps he died before Dunstan's appointment. Sufficient charter evidence survives to show that he was not
the man of that name who became bishop of Wells (q.v.), nor the
other Brihthelm who became bishop of Selsey (q.v.).

Brihthelm   XIX, XX

   Bishop of Selsey c. 957 × 963; ? bishop of Sherborne 958 × 963;
? bishop of Winchester 959 × 963.

   There is some doubt as to the succession at Selsey after Alfred,
who witnessed in 953 (CS 898–900). If a charter attributed to
Brihthelm is to be believed, the temporalities of the see, amounting
to 74 hides of land including Selsey itself, were illegally occupied by
one Ælfsige *contra decretum sanctorum patrum Niceni consilii*. Towards
the end of 956 restoration appears to have been made to Brihthelm by
King Eadwig (CS 930; this charter has late interpolations, but an
authentic basis); early in the following year the settlement was
confirmed by charter, in return for 100 mancuses of gold (CS 997).
One assumes that Ælfsige had claimed the see as bishop, presumably
before Eadwig's accession in November 955. It looks as if he might
have held it in plurality with some other bishopric. The neighbouring
diocese of Winchester was held by an Ælfsige at this time, but since
he was promoted by King Eadwig to Canterbury, he can hardly have
been the usurper at Selsey whom Brihthelm's charter castigates so
severely; besides, he witnesses the charter. Perhaps a more likely
identification of the usurper is with Wulfsige II of Sherborne; to
accept this would involve the supposition that the name 'Ælfsige' in
CS 997 is an error for Wulfsige; certainly there are other corruptions
in the witness list. Wulfsige was preceded at Sherborne by Alfred
(q.v.), who appears to have transferred to Selsey by 943, so we have
here an earlier link between the two sees, which could have formed
the basis of a claim by Wulfsige to both of them. Now Wulfsige is
said by Florence of Worcester (who was following at this point the
first life of Dunstan, by the priest 'B', see SBW p. 64) to have been
succeeded in his bishopric of Sherborne by one Brihthelm, 'a mild,
modest, humble, and benevolent man'; this tallies with the gap in
charter attestations from Sherborne from the death of Wulfsige in
958 to the appearance of Bishop Ælfwold I (q.v.) in charters of 964
(CS 1134, 1143). It seems reasonable to postulate that Wulfsige II
was replaced by Brihthelm at Selsey in 957 and at Sherborne in the
following year. If this was indeed the case, then one can produce
charter evidence to support a further suggestion that Brihthelm
succeeded also to Winchester late in 959 (but before the death of
King Eadwig on 1 October), and that he then held Selsey, Sherborne,
and Winchester in plurality until just before his death in 963. It is
evident from its hidage that Selsey was a poorly endowed bishopric,
and there are ample precedents from other dioceses for pluralism
at this period. Whether or not this chain of purely circumstantial

evidence can be accepted, it is evident that the junior of the two Brihthelms witnessing the following charters was bishop of Selsey: CS 992, 998, 1005 (957); CS 902, 1027–8, 1032–3 (958); CS 1035, 1046 (959). Bishop Brihthelm of Winchester witnessed two charters of the same date later in 959 (CS 1045; ECW 483), and a third charter still later that year (CS 1051). From then onwards he witnessed the following: CS 1053, 1055–6, 1058 (960); CS 1066–8, 1071–5, 1077, 1079–80 (961); Bu XIX, CS 1082–3, 1085, 1092–6 (962); Bu XX, CS 1101, 1103, 1114, 1116, 1118, 1120–1, 1124 (963). From CS 1101, a contemporary charter dated 963, it appears that Ealdhelm had succeeded to Selsey before the death of Brihthelm of Winchester, so if Brihthelm had held both sees, he surrendered Selsey before his death. Brihthelm of Winchester was a kinsman of King Edgar, who granted him $7\frac{1}{2}$ hides at Easton, Hants. in 961 (CS 1076). In the same year Brihthelm issued a lease of a Winchester property (R XXXIII). His successor at Winchester was ordained on 29 November 963 (ASC). See also SBW pp. 62–4.

Brihthelm   XVII, XXI
　　Bishop of Wells 956 × 15 May 974; archbishop of Canterbury 959 (resigned).
　　Possibly he was the deacon named Brihthelm who witnessed CS 917, dated 23 Nov. × 31 Dec. 955. In 956, while still only a priest, he was granted land at Sunningwell, Berks. (CS 971); subsequently, after he became bishop of Wells, he exchanged this for 17 hides at Curbridge, Oxon, which was owned by Abingdon Abbey (R XXXI). The Eynsham foundation charter, K 714, reveals that Brihthelm bequeathed 20 hides at Esher, Surrey, to his kinsman Æthelweard, ealdorman of the Western Shires (q.v.). Brihthelm was also related to the royal house, and in 956 King Eadwig gave him a further 5 hides at Stowe Nine Churches, Northants. (CS 986); at the time of this grant Brihthelm was still only bishop-elect; subsequently he gave the estate to Abingdon (Chron Abingd I, p. 234). All these transactions suggest that Brihthelm's early connections were in the Thames Valley. A charter issued mid–956 is witnessed by Bishop Brihthelm of London and by another Brihthelm, who is given the precedence but not the title of bishop in the witness list (CS 970); probably this second signatory was the Brihthelm who was appointed soon afterwards to Wells. Later in 956 he witnessed as bishop CS 927, 934, 966, 974, and Bu XVII; and early in 957, CS 994 and 999. All these charters were witnessed by two bishops named Brihthelm, the senior from London (q.v.) and the junior from Wells. After

Edgar's revolt in the summer of 957, the composition of the witness lists of King Eadwig's charters underwent a radical change, for he lost control of London and his support was confined to Wessex, Sussex, and Kent. From this time onwards, his charters were normally witnessed by the bishop of Selsey, who had not witnessed his earlier charters. The bishop of Selsey was also called Brihthelm (q.v.), so that the two bishops of that name witnessing King Eadwig's charters from mid-957 onwards held the sees of Wells and Selsey. The following charters belong to this group: CS 992, 998, 1005 (957); CS 902, 1022, 1027–8, 1032–3 (958); CS 1035, 1046 (959). In addition, a few charters of this period were witnessed by only one bishop named Brihthelm, who was probably from Wells: CS 1002 (957, before Edgar's revolt – his low position on the list shows that this was not the bishop of London); CS 995, 1004 (957, after Edgar's revolt); CS 1026, 1034 (958). Towards the end of Eadwig's reign, Brihthelm was given the precedence of an archbishop. This is first evidenced in CS 1035, dated 958 but in the fourth year of Eadwig's reign, and therefore probably a charter of 959. CS 1030 is a similar charter, dated unequivocally 959. Probably these two charters were issued after 17 May, for Brihthelm is not given this precedence in CS 1046, issued on that date. Some time later, Brihthelm of Wells was appointed to Canterbury by King Eadwig, and Brihthelm of Selsey was given the see of Winchester; in these new capacities they witness together CS 1045 and ECW 483, charters issued on the same date (for they have identical witness lists), some time in the period 17 May × 1 October 959. (See further, SBW pp. 65–7 and O'D II, p. 106, which discusses the identity of the Bishop Brihthelm who was appointed to Canterbury). It is noteworthy that Brihthelm witnesses these two charters as 'bishop' of Canterbury, rather than 'archbishop'. After Eadwig's death, his brother Edgar became king of all England. He left Brihthelm of Winchester in possession of that see, which he continued to hold in plurality with Selsey (q.v.), but Brihthelm of Canterbury was relieved of his office as archbishop on account of being 'too gentle', and returned to his see of Wells; Dunstan was ordained in his place on 21 October 959 (*Mem. St Dunstan*, p. xci). From this time onwards Brihthelm of Wells witnesses lower down on the lists of charters than his namesake at Winchester. The following charters of this period are witnessed by both bishops: CS 1051 (959); CS 1056 (960); CS 1072–4 (961); CS 1094 (962); CS 1101, 1116, 1118, 1121 (963). Brihthelm of Winchester died some time before 29 November 963, and thenceforth the only Bishop Brihthelm witnessing is from Wells: CS 1112,

1119 (963); Muchelney 3, CS 1142 (964); Bu xxi, CS 1190–1 (966); CS 1197–8 (967); CS 1217, 1220 – a list which looks genuine; Dugd ii, pp. 323–4 (968); CS 1302 (968 x 970); CS 1230–1 (969); CS 1265–6, 1268 (970); CS 1282, 1285 (972); CS 1292, 1295 (973); CS 1301 (974). His death is dated 15 May by William of Malmesbury (*De Antiq. Glast.*, Gale *Script XV*, p. 325), no doubt from an episcopal list. Florence of Worcester gives the year as 973, but CS 1301 shows that Brihthelm survived until 974 (the attestation *Byrhthelm geminique Athelwoldi* is unique; evidently the second name is an error for Ælfwold, the two bishops Ælfwold of Sherborne and Ælfwold of Crediton being intended). That Brihthelm died in 974 is supported by the evidence of CS 1305 and Bu xxii, which show that Cyneweard (q.v.), his successor at Wells, was still abbot of Milton early in that year. Cyneweard witnessed CS 1303, later in 974, as bishop. According to Florence, Brihthelm was buried at Wells. See also SBW pp. 62–7.

Brihthelm, thegn 940   ii

According to Bu ii, he received an estate called *Eatun*; but this charter is a late fabrication, and safe identification of the recipient is not possible.

Brihtnoth   xvii, xxiii

Ealdorman of Essex 956 × 991.

The best biographical account is that by Professor E. V. Gordon, *The Battle of Maldon*, 2nd edn., 1949, pp. 15–21. He may be the royal *præses* named Brihtnoth who persuaded King Eadwig to endow Worcester late in 956 (CS 937), but he does not witness charters before his appointment as ealdorman. Afterwards, in addition to those appearing in CS, he witnesses the following charters: Muchelney 3 (964); EHD i, pp. 552–3 (977); LH pp. 217–27 (982); LH pp. 231–6 (987); LH pp. 238–42 (988); EHD i, p. 353 (989).

Brihtnoth   xxvi, xxvii

Monk of Abingdon, prior of Old Minster, Winchester c. 964 × 970; abbot of Ely 970 × 5 May 996–9.

Ely was refounded in 970 (LE pp. liii, 74 n. 3) and Brihtnoth was its first abbot. He is described as a pupil of Æthelwold, so presumably he had been a monk at Abingdon (Ælfric, *Vita Æthelwoldi* c. 17; cf. EHD i, p. 836). He was prior of the Old Minster (LE p. 74); presumably he was instituted by Æthelwold after the clerks had been evicted there. His activities in building up the Ely endowment are recorded in some detail in LE *passim*. In 991 he attended the consecration of the newly rebuilt church at Ramsey (Chron Rams pp. 93, 95–6). According to LE p. 146, he and his successors at Ely regularly performed the duties of *cancellarii* in the king's court for four months each year, commencing 2 February. He last witnessed in 996, and his successor Ælfsige can first be identified with certainty in K 703, a charter of 999. Charters witnessed by Brihtnoth form a patchy series, comprising CS 1257, 1269 (970); 1282 (972); K 624 (980); K 633, 1278 (982); R p. 131 (989); K 713 (990); K 684 (993); Duignan (994); K 689, 1289 (995); Bu xxvi, xxvii, EHD i, p. 534; K 1292 (996). For his obit, see KBL p. 44.

Brihtred   XXXI
    Abbot of Glastonbury 1009 × 1015–19.
    His predecessor Ælfweard (q.v.) last witnessed in 1009, and Brihtred first witnessed later in the same year. He last witnessed in 1015. His successor Brihtwig first appears in an authentic charter in 1019 (K 730; he also witnessed K 728 and K 729, but these are doubtful texts). Brihtred witnessed the following charters: Bu xxxi (1009); Th x, K 1308 (1013); K 1309 (1014); K 1310 (1015). According to AD i, pp. 87, 101, his dates were 1000 × 1016, but clearly the earlier of these is wrong, so the later date must remain doubtful.

Brihtric, thegn   XXXVII
    Witnesses 1042 × 1065.
    Brihtric was a common name, but although two thegns bearing it witness high on the list of K 764 (1042), most of the signatures of thegns named Brihtric in charters of the Confessor appear to relate to one man, who is usually in the fifth place 1044–5, second c. 1050, and the first of the thegns witnessing from about 1060 onwards. In K 791 the name is misspelt 'Rymhtricus'. In 1059 he is described as 'nobilis' (ECDC 1053); in 1061 as 'consilarius' (K 811); and in 1062 as 'princeps' (K 813, the Waltham charter, which abounds in honorific titles, but contains much authentic material). In a Worcester lease of 1051–5 he is described as 'Ælfgares sunu' (R cxi), and this enables us to identify him as the man of that name appearing in the Gloucestershire Domesday as a landholder TRE (DB fo. 166b); he held lands also in Dorset, Devon, and Worcestershire. See further, Freeman, NC iv, pp. 761–4 for a legend about him circulated by the Anglo-Norman chroniclers.

Brihtsige　　　　　　　　　　　　　　　　　　　　　　　　　　XIII
　　Bishop of Rochester 946–9 × 955–61.
　　Burhric, bishop of Rochester (q.v.), first appears in 28 May 934 (CS 702) and witnesses fairly regularly until 946 (CS 813). Ælfstan, bishop of Rochester (q.v.) first witnesses in 961 (CS 1066–7, 1072–3, 1078–80, 1319), and last witnesses in 995 (K 691). A bishop named Brihtsige witnesses low down on the lists CS 880 (949), CS 892 (951), CS 909, 911 (955), and unless he is a suffragan (and this is unlikely) the only see he can represent is Rochester. It is noteworthy that the first of these four charters concerns a Kentish estate, the second may have been drawn up by an Abingdon scribe, and the third and fourth are from the Danelaw series drawn up by Glastonbury scribes (DC pp. 125–32). It would appear that from the death of Burhric c. 946–9 to the accession of Ælfstan c. 961, the scribes of chancery charters habitually omitted the names of the bishops of Rochester from the witness lists. Possibly they considered that the diocese was adequately represented by the archbishops of Canterbury.

Brihtwold　　　　　　　　　　　　　　　　　　　　　　　　　xxviiia
　　Abbot of New Minster, Winchester 1004 × 17 March 1012.
　　LVH gives his dates as 995 × 1008, but the chronology of this source is most unreliable for the abbots. Brihtwold's successor Brihtmær first witnesses in 1012 (K 719), and the abbot Brihtwold who witnesses from 1004 to 1012 is probably from New Minster (K 710, 1301, 714, 1303–7, in that order). A second abbot named Brihtwold, who witnessed K 1303, is probably from Malmesbury; he makes an earlier solitary appearance in 997 (OS Facs III, 35). For the former Brihtwold's obit, see KBL p. 81.

Brihtwold　　　　　　　　　　　　　　　XXIX, XXXI, XXXIII, XXXV
　　Monk of Glastonbury, bishop of Ramsbury ?1002–5 × 22 April 1045.
　　According to William of Malmesbury, Brihtwold was a monk and abbot of Glastonbury. After his election to Ramsbury he continued to favour Glastonbury as a patron, and when he died on 22 April 1045 he was buried there (Gesta Pontificum p. 182; AD I, pp. 94–6). There is, however, some difficulty in accepting this. Ælfweard, abbot of Glastonbury (q.v.) first witnesses in 987 and continues in the lists up to 1009, being succeeded by Brihtred (q.v.) in that year. Sigegar (q.v.) last witnesses as abbot (of Glastonbury) in 975, and it is possible therefore that Brihtwold was abbot there some time during the period 975 × 987. If so, he was a very old man when he died;

moreover, no abbot named Brihtwold witnesses between these dates. It does not seem possible to accept William of Malmesbury's statement *in toto*; he may be confusing Brihtwold with Brihtred. Brihtwold may well have been a monk at Glastonbury, but in the absence of charter evidence it would be hazardous to assume that he held a major abbacy before his appointment to Ramsbury, which was certainly not later than 1005 (R p. 405; K 714). Brihtwold's appointment is recorded in ASC E, F *s.a.* 1006, after the entry of Archbishop Ælfric's death; but he seems to have taken office earlier than this. It could well be that *Brihtred* in the corrupt witness list of K 707 is an error for Brihtwold; if so, he was appointed to Ramsbury by 1002. During his retirement at Glastonbury in 1042, Brihtwold had a famous vision concerning Edward the Confessor (Barlow, EC pp. 59–60).

Brihtwold, thegn XXVI, XXVII
    Witnesses 980 × 999.
    He witnesses the following charters: K 624, 629 (980); K 632 (982); K 635, 1279 (983); K 641, 1281 (984); K 655 (986); K 658 (987); K 663–4 (988); K 684 (993); K 686–7 (994); K 688, 692 (995); Bu XXVI, XXVII, EHD I, p. 534 (996); K 698, OS Facs III, 35 (997); K 700 (998); K 703 (999). Usually he is well up in the lists, often lying third among the thegns towards the end of his career. On two occasions he heads the thegns witnessing. No biographical information survives.

Bruhtwold, *see* Burhwold.

Bryhthelm, *see* Brihthelm.

Burhric II
    Bishop of Rochester 933–4 × 946–9.
    He witnessed regularly from 934 to 946, but nothing else is known about him. According to CS 779 he was granted land in West Malling, Kent, by King Edmund, but this charter seems to be a late fabrication. The formulas are abnormal, and the witness list is hopelessly jumbled and anachronistic. Among the signatories, several of the thegns do not witness any charters of King Edmund, nor does his wife Ælfgifu; Ealdorman Osferth died in 934 and Ealdorman Edmund was not appointed until 949.

Burhwold XXXV
    Bishop of Cornwall c. 1002 × 1027.
    There is much confusion about him by both ancient and modern

writers, occasioned partly by the fact that his name resembles that of Brihtwold, his contemporary at Ramsbury (q.v.), and partly from failure to differentiate between *Coruinensis* (for Ramsbury) and *Cornubiensis* (for Cornwall) in the charters (e.g. R p. 409 wrongly assigns to Cornwall the Brihtwold who witnesses R LXXXII and K 1324). Generally speaking, the Brihtwold who witnesses 1005 × 1045 was from Ramsbury, but some charters are witnessed by a second bishop with a similar name, who must be assigned to Cornwall. Thus K 729 (1019) is witnessed by two bishops named 'Brihtwolf' (*sic*), the first being presumably Brihtwold of Ramsbury, and the second Burhwold of Cornwall. Similarly in Bu XXXV (1012), Bishop 'Byrhtwold' is from Ramsbury, and probably Bishop 'Bruhtwold' at the bottom of the list represents Burhwold of Cornwall. The 'Buruðwoldus' of K 723 (a rather doubtful Evesham text dated 1016, with a slightly earlier witness list), and 'Buruhwold' of K 730 (1019) are also, presumably, for Burhwold of Cornwall. He witnesses correctly as *Burhwold* in K 728 (1018, but unfortunately not authentic), and again in K 981, p. 312, a manumission dated *c.* 1002 at St Petroc's, Bodmin, in which he appears in company with Ealdorman Æthelweard (q.v.) and Abbot Germanus (q.v.).

Byrhtferth, *see* Brihtferth.

Byrhtnoth, *see* Brihtnoth.

Byrhtwold, *see* Brihtwold.

Byrnric, thegn   XVII
    Witnesses 956–7.
    He witnesses low down on the lists Bu XVII, CS 927, 1029 (956); CS 988, 994, 1001 (957), but no earlier or later charters. King Eadwig gave him 6 hides at Langford, Wilts., and 5 hides at Polhampton, Hants., on the same date in 956 (CS 934, 974).

Cenwald   II, V, VI, VIII, XI–XIII, XV, XVII, XVIII
    Bishop of Worcester 929 × 28 June 957 or 958.
    Wilfrith (q.v.), Cenwald's predecessor at Worcester, last witnesses in 928 (CS 663), and Cenwald first appears as bishop in CS 655, a grant to Worcester by King Athelstan which may be dated 929 × 29 May 931, but contains some spurious elements. Florence of Worcester, whose chronology is usually good for his own see, gives the date 929 for both Wilfrith's death and Cenwald's succession. Soon after his appointment as bishop Cenwald was sent

by King Athelstan on a mission to Germany, possibly in connection with the marriage of Athelstan's daughter Edith to Otto, son of Henry the Fowler. Early in October 929 he visited the Swiss monasteries of St Gall, Reichenau, and Pfäfers, where he left presents from King Athelstan, and sought in return their prayers for the king; his name was recorded in their confraternity books (Stubbs, *Memorials of St Dunstan*, pp. xci, 60; SBW pp. 60–1). It is possible that Athelstan's diplomas to Worcester, though ill-recorded in CS 665–6, represent genuine gifts by the king in return for Cenwald's continental mission. Florence of Worcester notes that Cenwald was a monk, and of deep humility. He may have been tonsured during his German mission; if so, he was the second of the English bishops to accept the monastic vows since the eighth century. He witnessed as *monachus* three notable charters in the 'Dunstan A' Danelaw series, dated 949, 955, and 956 (CS 883; R xxx; CS 937), but he could not have been cloistered, for there were then no abbeys in England in which the monastic rule was enforced. From 929 to 957 Cenwald witnessed many royal diplomas, the last being CS 999 dated 9 May 957, and CS 1042 dated 958. He also appears in Bu xviii dated 958, but this witness list is unreliable, see p. 78 above. Florence of Worcester records Cenwald's death in 957, and William of Malmesbury supplies 28 June for his obit (*De antiq. Glas. eccles.*, ed. Gale, p. 325). CS 1042 appears to be a wholly authentic text (although it does have a duplication of two names in the witness list), and it seems reasonable to prefer its evidence to that of Florence concerning the date of Cenwald's death. Dunstan is said to have been given the sees of Worcester and London by King Edgar upon his return from exile, but in fact he witnesses CS 1052 as bishop of London and the presumption is that he received London first, then Worcester after Cenwald's death. When Dunstan was elevated to Canterbury in 959, he appears to have continued to hold both Worcester and London, surrendering the former to Oswald in 961 and the latter to Ælfstan in 964.

Cenwulf, *see* Kenulf.

Ceolstan, thegn (IV)
    Witnesses 926.
    His only occurrence is in CS 657–8.

Cynath III
    Abbot of Evesham c. 916 × 925.
    Surviving evidence favours Cynath's assignation to Evesham rather

than Abingdon (Stenton, *Abingdon*, pp. 33–4, would argue conversely). The Evesham Chronicle records an Abbot Cynath contemporary with King Athelstan (Robinson p. 36 et seq.). Probably
he was the deacon Cynað or Cinað who witnesses Worcestershire
charters of 904 (CS 608–9). As abbot he appears as witness to two
Mercian charters of 916 and 925 (CS 632, Bu III), and a Kentish
charter, also of 925 (CS 641). The witness list of Bu III is confined to
people from Mercia. Cynath may have accompanied Cenwald (q.v.)
on his mission to Germany in 929 (Robinson p. 39). The Dumbleton
charter, claiming to be dated 930, by which Cynath receives as
abbot of Abingdon land from King Athelstan, is an obvious forgery,
being supplied with a witness list of the time of King Eadred, and it
seems likely that Cynath's name has been substituted or interpolated
in an effort to render the charter more plausible (CS 667–8).

Cyneferth   IV
    Bishop of Rochester 909–26 × 933–4.
    His predecessor Ceolmund last witnesses in 909, and his successor
Burhric first witnesses on 26 May 934. Cyneferth witnesses the
following charters: Bu IV, CS 659 (926); CS 663 (928); CS 669
(930); CS 675 (20 June 931); CS 677 (12 Nov. 931); CS 692
(24 Dec. 932); CS 635 (11 Jan. 933); CS 695 (26 Jan. 933).

Cynesige   V, (VI), VIII, XI, XIII
    Bishop of Berkshire c. 928 × c. 946, bishop of Lichfield c. 946 ×
964.
    The early group of charters witnessed by Cynesige are also
witnessed by the bishops of Lichfield, and his location at this period
is revealed by CS 687, an anomalous text assigned to 927 × 928 by
Stenton (*Abingdon*, pp. 34–5). As Stubbs surmised, he must have
been a *chorepiscopus* in the diocese of Ramsbury, acting as shire-bishop
in Berkshire (*Memorials of St Dunstan*, p. lxxxviii). Perhaps this policy
reflected the ancient control of Berkshire by the Mercians. The exact
date at which Cynesige was given the diocese of Lichfield cannot be
ascertained, but his predecessor Wulfgar (q.v.) last witnesses CS 815
(946), and it is probable that Bu VIII is witnessed by Cynesige as
bishop of Lichfield. The last datable charter he witnesses is CS 1112
(after 29 Nov. 963), and his successor Wynsige witnesses CS 1134
(964). Cynesige was a kinsman of Dunstan, and went with him to
reprimand King Eadwig for his scandalous behaviour at his coronation
banquet (EHD I, p. 829). Afterwards he rarely witnessed Eadwig's
charters, but from 957 to 959 he regularly witnessed the charters of

Edgar, king of Mercia. He witnesses the following charters (ignoring CS 667, which has a witness list of the time of King Eadred): CS 674–5, 677 (931); CS 689 (932); CS 701–3, 705 (934); CS 716 (31 Dec. 934); Bu v (942); CS 812 (942 × 946); Bu viii, CS 880, 882–3 (949); Bu xi (951); CS 899–900 (953); Bu xiii, CS 903, 905, 908, 917, R xxx (955); CS 921, 923–4, 941, 949 (956); CS 999 (957); CS 1023 (957 x 958); CS 1063–7, 1042–4 (958); CS 1052 (959); CS 1056 (960); CS 1073, 1079 (961); CS 1093 (962); CS 1112, 1119, 1121 (963).

Cyneweard   XXII
  Monk of Glastonbury, abbot of Milton 964 × 974, bishop of Wells 974 (after 15 May) × 28 June 975.
  He must have been at Glastonbury in 956 or earlier, for he was a pupil of Dunstan (LVH pp. 94, 162 n. 16). The first abbot of the reformed house at Milton after the expulsion of the clerks there and their replacement by monks, he was one of the three abbots whose appointment by King Edgar is recorded in ASC (A) *s.a.* 964. He first appears in CS 1135, dated 28 Dec. 964, as last of the six abbots witnessing. Subsequently he witnessed the following charters, usually as sixth of the abbots, but towards the end of the period as third: CS 1176 (966); CS 1199 (967); CS 1216, 1220, ECW 108 (968); CS 1229–30, 1234 (970); CS 1257, 1266, 1302, 1268–9 (971); CS 1202, 1309 (972); Bu xxii, CS 1304–5 (974). Bu xxii cannot be earlier than 974, because it is also witnessed by Frithugar (q.v.), abbot of Evesham, whose predecessor Osweard witnesses CS 1303, an original of 974. Cyneweard and Osweard witness together as abbots CS 1304, which must therefore have been issued before CS 1303. Cyneweard's succession to Wells is recorded by Fl Wig *s.a.* 974, and could not have occurred before 15 May, when Brihthelm (q.v.), his predecessor there, died. He witnessed CS 1303 (974) as bishop, and his death is recorded as ten days before that of King Edgar, *s.a.* 975, by ASC C, where he is described as 'a famous man, good from his innate virtue'. He was buried at Wells. His successor at Milton was Abbot Ælfhun (q.v.), who first witnesses CS 1315 (975). At Wells he was succeeded by Abbot Sigegar (q.v.). See also SBW pp. 47–8; KBL p. 56.

Daniel   XIV
  Monk of Glastonbury, bishop of Cornwall 953–5 × 8 Oct. 959–62.
  He witnessed the following charters of King Eadwig: CS 917 (23 Nov. × 31 Dec. 955); CS 919 (13 Feb. 956); CS 920 (956 –

where he is wrongly given the title *Wintoniensis*); Bu xiv, CS 926–7, 930, 935, 938, 942, 945–6, 949, 957, 964–71, 973, 977, 982–5 (956); CS 1009 (956 × 957); CS 987, 992, 998–9, 1001 (957); CS 1022, 1027–8, 1034–5 (958); CS 1046 (17 May 959); CS 1030, 1045, ECW 483 (959, before 1 Oct.). No other Cornish bishop witnessed between June 934 (CS 703) and Feb. 963 (CS 1118), and Finberg (*Lucerna*, pp. 112–13) has shown that during most of the tenth century Cornwall was served by *chorepiscopi* only, in subjection to Crediton. Daniel is referred to as bishop of Cornwall in a letter of Dunstan to King Æthelred II, which states that he was consecrated by order of King Eadred (Crawf 7; SBW pp. 27–8; EHD I, pp. 822–3). O'Donovan has recently pointed out that this letter also implies that Daniel did not take office until after the death of Æthelgar of Crediton in 953 (O'D I, p. 37). He witnessed a manumission of King Eadwig at Exeter (ECDC 31). William of Malmesbury says he was a monk of Glastonbury, and gives his obit as 8 Oct., but wrongly assigns his death to 956 (AD I, p. 93).

Duduc XXXVII

Bishop of Wells 11 June 1033 × 18 Jan. 1060.

A Saxon or Lotharingian (Fl Wig I, pp. 218, 237), Duduc became one of King Cnut's priests (K 1318), and was given minsters at Congresbury and Banwell in Somerset (Barlow p. 156). He was one of the first royal priests to receive a bishopric, being appointed to Wells in 1033. A cultured man, he bequeathed to his see estates, books, and ecclesiastical ornaments, but as a bishop he was ineffectual (Barlow p. 75). In 1049 he attended a synod at Rheims (ASC E, *s.a.* 1046). He died in 1060 (ASC D). He was addressed in a writ of 1033 × 1035 (H no. 53), and witnessed the following charters: K 760 (1038); K 762–4, 1332 (1042); K 767 (1043); R xcviii (1043 × 1044); K 770–2, 774–6 (1044); K 778–81 (1045); K 784 (1046); Bu xxxvii (1048); OS Facs II, Exeter 12, K 787 (1049); K 791–3 (1050); K 807 (1051 × 1060); K 800 (1054); OS Facs II, Exeter 14 (1059).

Dunstan XI, XV, XIX–XXIV

Abbot of Glastonbury 940 × 956, bishop of Worcester and London, 957 × 959, archbishop of Canterbury 959 × 19 May 988.

Dunstan was born c. 909 at Baltonsborough, Somerset. He was related to the royal family, and was a kinsman of Cynesige, bishop of Lichfield, and of Ælfheah who became bishop of Winchester, and a nephew of Athelm who became archbishop of Canterbury. Dunstan was educated at Glastonbury, and subsequently (under his uncle) at Canterbury, and was then ordained priest at Winchester by Ælfheah, on the same day as his friend Æthelwold (q.v.). King Edmund appointed him abbot of Glastonbury in 940, but he was banished in 956 by King Eadwig, and retired to the monastery of St Peter's at Ghent. In 957 he was recalled by Eadwig's brother Edgar, who had just been made king of Mercia. He was consecrated by Archbishop Oda of Canterbury, and given the vacant sees of London and (later) Worcester. He witnessed CS 1052, dated 959, as bishop of London. After Edgar succeeded to the kingdom of all England later that year, he appointed Dunstan archbishop of Canterbury. Probably he held the sees of Worcester and London also, in plurality until 961 and 964. He died on 19 May 988. He is remembered as the leader of the Benedictine reform movement in England. Two pre-Conquest lives of Dunstan were edited by Bishop Stubbs in the Rolls Series. See also Robinson, *passim*; EHD I, pp. 826–31; DC pp. 125–32; ASE II, pp. 182–3.

Eadferth, bishop ? 900   I

He is otherwise unknown. The succession of the Mercian bishoprics is so uncertain for this period, that he could have held the see of Dorchester, or Lichfield, or Hereford. Of these, Lichfield is perhaps the most likely, as the land conveyed in Bu 1 was in this diocese.

Eadgifu, queen c. 900 × c. 966   XII, XIII

She was the daughter of Ealdorman Sighelm of Kent, and c. 919 became the third wife of King Edward the Elder. Usually she witnesses the charters of her sons, Kings Edmund and Eadred, and occasionally those of her grandsons, Kings Eadwig and Edgar. King Eadred left her estates in Kent, Surrey, and Sussex. All her property was confiscated during the reign of King Eadwig, but it was restored to her by King Edgar. Queen Eadgifu was a notable supporter of the Benedictine reform, and influential in the refounding of Abingdon (Chron Abingd I, p. 130; II, p. 257) and Ely (ECEE p. 41). For a list of charters witnessed by her, see *Encom. Emmæ*, pp. 62–4. She last witnesses CS 1190, the New Minster foundation charter of 966. See also Ha xxi, xxiii; R p. 313; LE *passim*; OB pp. 193, 274; SBW p. 61. A more extensive review of her place in the reform movement will appear in my *Danelaw Studies*, forthcoming.

Eadhelm   XI

Abbot of St Augustine's, Canterbury c. 949 × 952.

His house is identified in R xxxii, an undated Kentish will (the date 958 allotted to this in R p. 315 has no early authority; probably it derives from the date of the death of Archbishop Oda, one of the signatories). He witnessed as abbot CS 880, a Kentish charter dated 949, and (together with Dunstan) two companion pieces ECEE No. v and Bu xi, both dated 951. He was killed at Thetford in Norfolk in 952; King Eadred ordered the borough there to be ravaged in compensation (ASC D *s.a.*).

Eadnoth   XXXI–XXXIII, XXXV

Monk of Worcester, abbot of Ramsey 993–7 × 1008; (I) bishop of Dorchester 1008 × 18 Oct. 1016.

The Ramsey Chronicle (p. 110) claims that Eadnoth was elected abbot of Ramsey immediately after the death of Bishop Oswald of Worcester (on 29 Feb. 992), but this tradition is contradicted by the evidence of K 684, dated 993, which shows that Germanus (q.v.) was then abbot of Ramsey (another charter, K 672, cannot be cited as evidence of Eadnoth's earlier election, for the witness list of this doubtful text is to be assigned for the most part to 1002 × 1005). The earliest surviving charter witnessed by Eadnoth is K 705, dated 1001; but Germanus witnessed K 698, dated 997, as abbot of Cholsey, and it seems probable that Eadnoth had been appointed to Ramsey by this date; the transfer of Germanus to Cholsey by Æthelred II is recorded in Chron Rams p. 110. Eadnoth witnessed as abbot the following charters: K 705 (1001); K 1295, 1297 (1002); K 672, 714, 1301 (1005); K 1303–4, Crawf 11 (1007). Ælfhelm (q.v.), Eadnoth's predecessor at Dorchester, witnessed Bu xxix dated 1007, and the date 1008 given for Eadnoth's appointment to Dorchester in a late Ramsey source is probably reliable (Chron Rams p. 339; the date 1006 assigned by the editor on p. 115 is contradicted by charter evidence). The earliest surviving charters witnessed by Eadnoth as bishop are two dated 1011 (Bu xxxii, xxxiii). It seems likely that the Bishop Eadnoth who witnessed charters of the period 1011 × 1016 was from Dorchester rather than from Crediton, with the exception of K 1310, where the see is identified as Crediton. That Germanus and Eadnoth remained closely associated may be deduced from the frequency with which they witness together (K 714, 1295, 1297, 1301, 1303–4). Eadnoth founded daughter cells of Ramsey at St Ives (Hunts.) and Chatteris (Cambs.) (CAS lvi–lvii, pp. 61–7), and a house of canons at Stowe St Mary (Lincs.) in subjection to the bishopric of Dorchester (R pp. 465–6). He was killed at *Assandun*. See further, LE p. 140 n. 5.

Eadnoth   XXXVII

Monk of Ramsey, (II) bishop of Dorchester Dec. 1034 × 19 Sept. 1049.

He was related to Bishop Eadnoth I of Dorchester (q.v.). Stubbs, *Regesta* p. 33, gives 8 December for the obit of his predecessor Æthelric. For his appearance in the witness lists, see Oleson p. 123. Bu xxxvii is the last surviving charter he witnesses. See further, Chron Rams *passim*, and CAS lvi–lvii, p. 61 n. 4, p. 63 n. 7, p. 64, and pedigree facing p. 66.

Eadred   xxviiia

Abbot of Milton 1002–4 × c. 1016.

Ælfhun (q.v.), his predecessor, did not leave Milton until at least 1002. In addition to Bu xxviii and K 710, both dated 1004, Eadred witnessed K 723, a doubtful charter dated 1016, on which see ECWM p. 67, and *Encom. Emmæ* p. 64 n. 2. His house is identified in a late mortuary roll, see KBL p. 56.

Eadred   XXVI, XXVII, XXX–XXXIII, XXXV

Ætheling c. 992 × 1012.

He was the fourth son of King Æthelred II by his first wife Ælfgifu. In addition to the Burton charters, he witnessed the following: K 684, 697, 703, 1294, 706, 1295, 707, 710, 714, 1301, 1303, 1305–6, all of which are authentic. He could not have been more than a year or two old when he first 'witnessed' in 993; he last witnessed in 1012, and is likely to have died in that year, as he did not witness Bu xxxvii, or K 1308–10.

Eadred, King   VIII–XIII, XVIII

May 946 × 23 Nov. 955.

The second son of King Edward the Elder by his third wife Eadgifu (q.v.), Eadred was born c. 924 and crowned at Kingston-on-Thames on 16 August 946. He suffered from chronic ill health, and died a bachelor. His will survives (Ha xxi; EHD i, pp. 511–12). For his reign, see Stenton pp. 355–9.

Eadric Streona   XXXI

Ealdorman of Mercia 1007 × 25 Dec. 1017.

The most powerful ealdorman of his day, but remembered as a traitor. Leofwine, ealdorman of the Hwicce (q.v.), was probably subordinate to him. There is no adequate modern biography, but see ECWM p. 254; Freeman, NC i, pp. 654–8, 720–2; Plummer ii, pp. 196, 200–1; R p. 393.

Eadric, thegn 925   III

The recipient of *Hwitantune* (? Whittington, Staffs., near Lichfield), he is difficult to identify; it is doubtful if he was the youngest brother of Athelstan 'Half-King'. See Hart, 1973, p. 120.

Eadric, thegn 956 × 961   XVII

He does not appear in the witness lists until after the accession of King Eadwig, but very quickly thereafter he became one of the most influential thegns in the south, witnessing high in the lists and receiving from King Eadwig very large estates, amounting (in the surviving charters) in all to 133 hides, at Welford, Padworth, Lecklampstead, Longworth, and Drayton, all in Berks., at Pirford in Surrey, and at East Meon, Steep, Langrish, and Froxfield, in Hants. (CS 955, 963, 982, 984, 996, 1028). He remained true to King Eadwig after Edgar's revolt in 957, but continued to witness, as third or fourth among the thegns, after Edgar's accession in 959. King Edgar gave him 5 hides at *Hamstede* (CS 1075, unlocated, but cf. CS 789, 996) in 961, but he witnessed only one other charter in that year (CS 1076), and afterwards disappeared from the lists. Moreover, CS 1319 shows that by 961 one of his estates was already in someone else's hands. An OE charter dated 956 × 957 shows that Eadric was the brother of Ælfheah (q.v.), who became ealdorman of Hampshire (R XXXI).

Eadric, thegn 997 × 1017   XXVIIIa

A thegn of this name witnesses the following charters: OS Facs III, 35 (997); K 705–6 (1001); Crispin p. 168, K 707, 1295–6 (1002); K 762 (1002 × 1005); Bu XXVIIIa (1004); K 714, 1301 (1005); K 1303 (1007); K 1305 (1008); K 1313 (1017). K 1296 and K 1305 are both witnessed by two thegns named Eadric, and K 1303 and K 1305 are witnessed in addition by Ealdorman Eadric Streona (q.v.).

Eadsige   XXXVII

Priest, chaplain to King Cnut, monk at Christ Church, bishop at St Martin's, Canterbury 1035 × 1038, archbishop of Canterbury 1038 × 1044; 1048 × 29 Oct. 1050.

H p. 559; W pp. 190–1; Barlow pp. 58, 108–9. He resigned in 1044 because of ill-health, but resumed his duties in 1048. For his charters, see Oleson pp. 46, 123; for his Kentish estates while a priest, see R LXXXVI. Eadsige still controlled the endowment of the see during the period of his retirement, as is shown by the con-

temporary deed R ci, dated 25 Dec. 1045 (Harmer p. 51) × 1047
(death of Bishop Ælfwine, one of the signatories). He held Kent as an
earl during his tenure of the archbishopric (Barlow, EC, p. 115 n. 2).

Eadulf   IV
   Bishop of Crediton 909 × 9 Nov. 934.
   The Leofric Missal names Eadulf as the first bishop appointed to
the newly created see of Crediton in 909, upon the dismemberment
of the old diocese of Sherborne. He witnesses from 926 (CS 658–9)
to 7 June 934 (CS 703); the next surviving charter, dated 16 Dec.
934 (CS 705) is witnessed by his successor Æthelgar (q.v.), and this
agrees with Eadulf's obit, recorded on 9 November in the kalendar
of the Leofric Missal. Bishop Eadulf figures in two charters, CS 694
and CS 1343, concerning which there has been considerable recent
debate as to their authenticity. The arguments are summarized in
Chaplais 1966, pp. 10–12, and H. P. R. Finberg, *West-Country
Historical Studies*, 1969, pp. 29–69.

Eadulf, thegn   IV
   Witnesses 926 × 931.
   He witnesses Bu iv, CS 659, 674, 677, but is otherwise unknown.

Eadwig, ætheling c. 997 c. 1017   XXX, XXXII
   He was the fifth son of King Æthelred II by his first wife Ælfgifu.
In addition to the Burton charters XXXI, XXXIII, he witnessed the
following: K 697, 1294, 706, 1295, 1297, 707, 710, 714, 1301,
1303, 1305, 1306, 1308, 1309, all of which are authentic. Probably
he was born in 997, for he does not witness earlier charters (K 684,
Bu XXVI, XXVII), and it seems that the names of Æthelred's æthelings
were added to the witness lists of royal charters as soon as they were
born. His eldest brother Athelstan left him a silver-hilted sword
(W xx). After the death of Edmund Ironside (q.v.), Eadwig was the
eldest surviving son of King Æthelred, and he was exiled by King
Cnut in 1017. According to ASC, Cnut had him killed, but William of
Malmesbury says that after long wandering, he returned secretly to
England, fell sick, and was buried at Tavistock (Freeman, NC I,
p. 700; Finberg, *Lucerna*, p. 188).

Eadwig, king of England   XIII–XVIII
   23 Nov. 955 × 1 Oct. 959.
   It is probable that Eadwig, the elder of the two sons of King
Edmund and Queen Ælfgifu, was born in 940. His mother died in or

before 944, and his father two years later. Eadwig appears then to have been separated from his baby brother Edgar, and fostered by the Berkshire thegn Ælric, who is otherwise unknown (CS 949). Æthelgeard (q.v.), another thegn with landed interests in Berkshire, also knew Eadwig in his boyhood (CS 810). Among his kinsmen were the five sons of Ealdorman Ealhhelm (q.v.), all of whom must have known him as an ætheling; four of them, led by Ælfhere, became very influential in the early months of Eadwig's reign, and all four received land in Berkshire. Later in his boyhood, Eadwig may have been educated by Abbot Æthelwold at Abingdon, as was his brother Edgar (q.v.). Their uncle, King Eadred, a bachelor who suffered from chronic illness, brought the two æthelings Eadwig and Edgar into court towards the end of his reign, and in 955 they began to witness royal diplomas (CS 905, 909; Bu XIII). Upon Eadred's death on 23 November in that year, Eadwig succeeded to the kingdom of England, being separately chosen by the West Saxons and the Mercians (*Vita S. Dunstani auctore 'B'*, c. 21); soon afterwards, he was crowned at Kingston-on-Thames on the border between the two kingdoms (Fl Wig). Eadwig was well thought of by the common people, being nicknamed 'All-Fair' because of his beauty (Æthelweard, p. 55), but he began his reign inauspiciously by a major confrontation with the monastic reform party, headed by Dunstan (then abbot of Glastonbury, q.v.), during his coronation banquet. Dunstan and his friends disapproved of Eadwig's fascination with a noblewoman named Æthelgifu, and with her daugher Ælfgifu, whom subsequently he seems to have married (CS 972). Later, the area of disagreement widened, and led to events which were to shake the foundations of the Old English monarchy. Within a few months of his accession Eadwig brought about a radical upheaval in the composition of his court. Undoubtedly his first (but not his sole) objective was to break the growing power of the small but influential group of highly placed persons, both lay and ecclesiastical, who were dedicated to the cause of the Benedictine revival of English monasticism. Since the monks, later in the century, held a virtual monopoly of literary activity (the Chronicle of Æthelweard is an important exception), one now has access only to heavily biassed accounts of Eadwig's reign (Robinson, pp. 161–2), and full allowance must be made for this when assessing his character and objectives. To some extent, a more balanced view can be achieved by drawing on the evidence of charters, which show that far from being opposed to such quasi-monastic institutions as existed in England at the commencement of his reign, Eadwig was a generous supporter of them. His surviving charters record endowments of Abingdon (CS 919, 981, 1002, 1046; Stenton, *Abingdon* p. 49, went sadly astray here), Bath (CS 927, 936, 1001, 1009), Glastonbury (CS 920, 933), Malmesbury (CS 921), New Minster (CS 1000, 1045), Worcester (CS 937), and the nunneries of Shaftesbury (CS 970) and Wilton (CS 917); in addition, he entrusted Ely to Archbishop Oda (CS 999, 1347). A few of these texts may contain spurious elements, but the overwhelming weight of their united evidence can leave little room for doubt that Eadwig was not ill-disposed towards the very lax concept of monasticism current in England at the time of his accession. Indeed, in this respect the attitude of Eadwig and his advisers was conservative; the radicals were the reforming party, who sought to destroy the enjoyment of these monastic endowments by clerks who, according to the custom of the times, were treating them as their personal possessions. In pursuit, it can be held, of his anti-reformist policy, Eadwig confiscated the extensive estates of his grandmother, Queen Eadgifu (q.v.), and banished Dunstan to the continent. Cynesige, bishop of Lichfield (q.v.), a relative and supporter of Dunstan and a regular attendant upon King Eadred, appeared only rarely before the new king's presence (as shown by the scarcity of his attestations to Eadwig's royal diplomas). The most powerful lay figure in the monastic movement was Athelstan 'Half King' (q.v.), who up to the time of Eadwig's accession was virtually the regent, with direct personal control of most of England north of the Thames, including Mercia and East Anglia. Eadwig appears to have set about a skilful and sustained attack upon the Half-King's position. Within a month of his accession, he appointed another Athelstan, nicknamed 'Rota' (q.v.) to the long-vacant ealdordom of south-east Mercia. Later, Athelstan 'Rota' married Eadwig's stepmother, Æthelflæd of Damerham (q.v.). In January or February 956 Eadwig created his kinsman Ælfhere (q.v.) ealdorman of central Mercia, so filling another post that appears to have been kept vacant during the concluding years of the Half-King's rule. By the late summer of 956 the Half-King's position had become untenable, and he retired to accept the tonsure at Glastonbury. Before doing so, however, he managed to secure the succession of his son Æthelwold (q.v.) to the East Anglian ealdordom; later in the year this was followed by the elevation of Brihtnoth (q.v.) to the ealdordom of Essex. By his attack on the Half-King, Eadwig appears to have alienated the support of the whole of England north of the Thames, and much of his own province of Wessex. In an attempt to retain the loyalty of the northern archbishopric, he endowed the see with the very substantial soke of

Southwell (CS 1029, 1348). In Mercia and East Anglia, he relied –
unwisely as events were to prove – on the support of his four newly
appointed ealdormen. In Wessex, he pursued a wild and irresponsible
policy of packing his council with new men, whose loyalty had been
purchased by large-scale hand-outs of the West Saxon royal demesne
(OB pp. 157–8, 190–1). The biographer of St Dunstan describes
him as 'losing the shrewd and wise who disapproved of his folly, and
eagerly annexing men of his own kin' (*Vita S. Dunstani auctore 'B'*,
c. 24). Clearly this passage refers not only to his banishment of
Dunstan, but also to his replacement of the influence of the Half-
King's family by that of Ealdorman Ælfhere and his brothers. These
measures secured Eadwig some support in Wessex, but he failed
utterly to establish his position north of the Thames. In the summer
of 957 his brother Edgar, a boy of fourteen, broke away and with the
encouragement of local bishops and ealdormen (most of the latter
having owed their positions to Eadwig) set himself up as king of
Mercia, East Anglia, and Northumbria. The Thames became the
dividing line between the two kingdoms; in particular, the whole
of Berkshire, including the abbey of Abingdon, remained under
Eadwig's control. The importance to Eadwig of retaining this
frontier district is perhaps illustrated by his booking to thegns (some
of them no doubt friends of his boyhood) over 160 hides within
the county, comprising seven per cent of its total hidation, in the
single year 956 – and this figure is derived only from charters of
which the texts have survived, without taking into account the large
number of charters of that year which must be presumed lost (OB
p. 42); several more Berkshire estates were booked to thegns in 957
and 958. In addition, in spite of his quarrels with the monastic
reform party, he found it expedient to augment the endowment of
Abingdon, largely with Berkshire properties (OB pp. 190–1). A
further concession came early in 958, when he yielded to pressure
from Oda, archbishop of Canterbury, and put away his wife Ælfgifu,
who had caused so much offence at his coronation (ASC D). The
remarkable feature of this period is the way in which the two brothers
Eadwig and Edgar each ruled their respective share of the kingdom,
without coming to blows. Edgar's charters at this time rarely claim
for him more than the kingdom of Mercia and (rather vaguely)
'other nations' (CS 1042), or (more precisely) Mercia and
Northumbria and 'the Britons', meaning presumably Cumbria (CS
1040); the two charters CS 1043–4 in which he is called 'Rex
Anglorum' are copying earlier formulas. In sharp contrast, Eadwig
continued regularly to claim sovereignty over the whole of England

after Edgar's revolt, just as if nothing had happened; in spite of this, however, he never attempted to assert his authority north of the Thames, so presumably some *de facto* agreement was reached between the two sides. It is even possible that Eadwig was made to approve from the outset, however reluctantly, Edgar's assumption of rulership over the Mercian kingdom. There is no evidence of any deep-seated rivalry between the top lay and ecclesiastical figures of Wessex and Mercia at this period; Mercian bishops maintained their subordination to Canterbury, and families such as that of Ealdorman Ælfhere, with landed interests on both sides of the Thames, appear to have remained united in spite of individual members owning loyalty to different monarchs. Nevertheless, with one king aged only seventeen and the other but fourteen, it must have seemed very questionable at the time how long stability could be maintained, before either internal or external stresses brought the truce to an end. In the event the matter was never put to the test, for on 1 October 959 King Eadwig died, very conveniently, at Frome. He was buried at New Minster, and his brother Edgar succeeded to the whole kingdom.

Eadwig, thegn 956   XIV
    In 956 King Eadwig granted him 8 hides at Braunston, Northants. (Bu XIV). Nothing else is known of him.

Ealdgyth   XXVIIIb
    Wife of Morcar, 1004.
    Her husband was the thegn of the Seven Boroughs who was killed in 1015 (q.v.). Wulfric Spot, founder of Burton Abbey, left her by will an estate at Austrey in Warwickshire (Bu XXVIIIb). Probably her daughter was related to Wulfric (W p. 153), but whether through her mother or her father does not appear.

Ealdhun   XXXI
    Bishop of Chester-le-Street 990 × 995, bishop of Durham 995 × 1018.
    Apart from his solitary appearance as witness to a Burton charter dated 1009 (Bu XXXI), all of our information concerning Ealdhun comes from the *Historia Dunelmensis Ecclesie* printed in SD, and from the tract *De obsessione Dunelmi* (see pp. 143–50). He succeeded Ælfsige as bishop of Chester-le-Street in 990. Because of the unrest caused by Danish attacks, he left in 995 with a small group of followers, carrying the relics of St Cuthbert, and after wandering as far as Ripon finally settled at Durham. There a small wattle church

was erected to house the relics, which attracted many pilgrims and a considerable landed endowment. Work was began on a grand new church, known as the White Church, which was erected on the rock at Durham. Building took three years, and with the help of Uhtred, son of Earl Waltheof, a substantial number of men drawn from the countryside between the Tees and the Coquet were employed on it. The relics of St Cuthbert were translated to the new church on 4 September 998, under Ealdhun's supervision. Some time before 1006 Ealdhun gave his daughter Ecgfrida in marriage to Uhtred. As part of the settlement, Uhtred received the lease of considerable territories in County Durham belonging to the bishopric. Later, he and his subordinates, Æthelred and Northman, were leased another large portion of the newly acquired endowment of the see, comprising lands in the East Riding, most of which were lost to the church permanently. Nevertheless, Ealdhun was well remembered at Durham, where he died in 1018 (on the date, see Stenton p. 412 n. 2; Janet Cooper, 'The dates of the bishops of Durham in the eleventh century', *Durham University Journal*, N.S., XXIX (1968), pp. 132–3; H. S. Offler 'Hexham and the *Historia Regum*', *Transactions of the Architectural and Archaeological Society of Durham and Northumberland*, II (1970), pp. 51–62, n. 46. See also Offler p. 10.

Ealdred   VIII, XIII

Bishop of Chester-le-Street 944 × 968.

His dates are established by Florence of Worcester (*s.a.* 944, 968) and in Symeon of Durham (RS I, pp. 77–8; II, p. 130), but very little is known of him. King Eadred visited the relics of St Cuthbert at Chester-le-Street after his invasion of Northumbria in 948 (SD I, pp. 77–8), and in the following year Bishop Ealdred witnessed three of his charters (Bu VIII, CS 882 – where his name is printed mistakenly as *Ælbred*, and CS 883). Eadred then lost control in the North, and it was not until he regained the ascendancy there that Bishop Ealdred again witnessed one of his charters (Bu XIII, dated 955). Ealdred witnessed also three charters of King Edgar in 958–9, while his sovereignty was recognized only in Mercia and the North (CS 1042, 1044, 1052); but once Edgar became the sole king, the York suffragans ceased to witness his charters.

Ealdred   XXVII

Bishop of Cornwall 983–90 × c. 1002.

It seems likely that he was the abbot who witnessed K 633 (982)

and K 636 (983), but his house is unknown (it may have been Tavistock). The Cornish bishops rarely witnessed authentic OE charters, and their precise dates are therefore difficult to establish. Ealdred's predecessor Wulfsige witnessed in 980 (K 624) and in 981 (K 629; see H. P. R. Finberg, *Tavistock Abbey*, pp. 278–83 for a better text). Ealdred first witnessed as bishop R LXIII, a charter dated 988 × 12 Feb. 990. He witnessed also in 993 (K 684), in 994 (K 686; Duignan), and in 996 (K 1291, Bu XXVII). Until Ealdred's time, the Cornish bishops were merely *chorepiscopi* under the bishop of Crediton, but in 994 King Æthelred II gave the bishopric full diocesan jurisdiction (Finberg, *Lucerna*, p. 113). Ealdred appears under the guise of *Æthelred* in 1001 (K 706, an otherwise reliable charter with a number of misspellings – *Alfstan* for Ælfheah of Winchester, *Ælphech* for Ælfheah of Lichfield, *Liefwine* for Lyfing of Wells, and *Alwoto* for Ælfweard of Crediton). Finally, he witnessed two charters dated 1002 (K 1295, 1297). His successor Burhwold (q.v.) first witnessed a datable text in 1012 (Bu XXXVI). He witnessed also a manumission at St Petroc's which cannot be dated precisely, but is unlikely to have occurred much later than 1002 (K 981, p. 312).

Ealdred   XXXVII
    Monk at Winchester, abbot of Tavistock 1027 × 1046, bishop of Worcester 1046 × 1062, bishop of Hereford 1056 × Christmas 1060, archbishop of York Christmas 1060 × 11 Sept. 1069.
    He may have been Lyfing's coadjutor during the latter's last years at Tavistock. The best biographical account is by Cooper, pp. 23–9; see also H. P. R. Finberg, *Devon and Cornwall Notes and Queries*, XXII (1943), p. 159; R p. 456; H p. 554; Oleson p. 124; Barlow pp. 86–7, 99, 103, 198–9, 208–10, 215–18; R. R. Darlington, EHR XLVIII (1933), pp. 3 n. 2, 4 n. 2; KBL p. 72.

Ealdred, thegn   XII
    Witnesses 951 × 955.
    He witnessed low down on the lists three charters dated 951, 952, and 955 (Bu XII, CS 895, 906). In view of the large number of charters not witnessed by a thegn of this name in the intervening years, it is probable that the individuals named Ealdred who witnessed in 943 (CS 779) and from 958 onwards (CS 1027 etc.) were different persons.

Ealdulf   XXVI, XXVII
    Abbot of Peterborough c. 980 × 992, bishop of Worcester 992 × 1002, archbishop of York c. 995 × 6 May 1002.

The claim in ASC E that Peterborough Abbey was refounded in 963 is unsupported elsewhere, and may well be untrue; it was preceded in point of time by Ely (*Vita Æthelwoldi* c. 17), which was not founded until 970, and the earliest acceptable date for the existence of Peterborough is CS 1270, dated 971. Even then its founder Bishop Æthelwold may not have installed an abbot from the outset, preferring rather to keep the abbacy in his own hands, as he did for Thorney, and as did Bishop Oswald for his foundation at Ramsey. It is noteworthy that Ealdulf witnessed as abbot only three charters of which the texts have survived, namely K 633 dated 982 (this has a very doubtful witness list, with numerous errors; the list of thegns must be assigned to a date at least four years later than the date claimed in the dating clause), and K 712–13, dated 990, which he witnessed as fourth of thirteen abbots (he witnessed another, now lost, dated 989, see EHD 1, p. 533). Although we have good independent evidence that Ealdulf was appointed abbot before Bishop Æthelwold's death in 984 (R XL), it is doubtful if the event occurred a very long while previously. A record survives of the transactions involved in building up Peterborough's landed endowment (R XL). It falls into three parts: (a) transactions negotiated by Bishop Æthelwold, (b) those negotiated by Bishop Æthelwold and Abbot Ealdulf jointly, and (c) those negotiated by Ealdulf alone. All three sections may be allocated to the period c. 980 × 985, after the intervention of the thegn Ælfwold had secured the restoration of the community's rights at Peterborough, Oundle, and Kettering (LE pp. xii–xiii). There is no evidence to support Professor Knowles's assertion that Ealdulf had been a monk at Abingdon (*Monastic Order in England*, p. 50 n. 5); this would seem to derive from a mistranslation of Ælfric's *Vita Æthelwoldi*. Hugh Candidus (pp. 29–31), a late but usually reliable chronicler of the house, tells a story that deserves better attention than has been given it in the past. Ealdulf, he says, was the chancellor (*cancellarius*) to King Edgar, and he and his wife suffocated their only son accidentally one night, while they were drunk (evidently by lying on him in bed, a well-known hazard with drunken parents). Ealdulf confessed to Bishop Æthelwold his godfather, who persuaded him in penance to meet the cost of restoring the derelict abbey of Peterborough. Later, he was tonsured there by Æthelwold in King Edgar's presence; what became of Ealdulf's wife is not related. If Ealdulf had indeed been Edgar's chancellor, we might perhaps expect to find his name occurring in the witness lists of some of his royal diplomas; in fact we do encounter an Eadulf witnessing seventh of the eight thegns subscribing to a

Wilton diploma of 972 (CS 1285, which has, however, an anachronism in the witness list, see W p. 121). Of much greater significance is the recurrence of the name as the last of the signatories of CS 1301, a Malmesbury charter dated 974 which Professor Whitelock has pronounced to be spurious (Sawyer p. 254). She offers no evidence in support of her opinion, which must be questioned. Mr E. John thought a companion charter, CS 1300 (also condemned by Professor Whitelock, *op, cit.*) to be a genuine text (OB pp. 58, 280). Certainly both charters are highly individualistic, and are unlikely to have been written by a chancery scribe, but they might well have been written at Malmesbury at that time. The witness list of CS 1301 could only have been constructed by a contemporary writer, who knew that bishops named Ælfwold held the adjacent sees of Crediton and Sherborne (he calls them *gemini Athelwoldi episcopi*), and that Ealdorman Æthelweard (q.v.) had a brother named Ælfweard. Apart from the ealdormen, the lay witnesses are confined to Wulfstan (doubtless of Dalham, q.v.) and Eadulf, and this alone suggests that the latter held some high official position, close to the king. It seems very likely that he was the man who became abbot of Peterborough. (The spelling *Eadulf* is normally found for *Ealdulf* in post-Conquest texts, and both CS 1285 and CS 1301 survive only in post-Conquest copies). The implications of the term *cancellarius* are discussed elsewhere (p. 37), but setting this problem on one side, Hugh's story has much to commend it as a plausible explanation of how Æthelwold acquired so rich an endowment for his foundation. It is entirely likely that Æthelwold would be the godfather of a high official at Edgar's court. Early Peterborough records emphasize the important part played by Ealdulf in acquiring property for his abbey (R xxxix, xl). On 8 Nov. 991 he attended the consecration by Archbishop Oswald (q.v.) of York of the rebuilt abbey church at Ramsey (Chron Rams, pp. 93, 95–6). When Oswald died nearly four months later (SD), Ealdulf was appointed his successor (ASC C). The see of Worcester was commonly held in plurality with York at this period, but charters show that although Ealdulf inherited Worcester straight away (he witnessed as bishop low down on the lists of K 684 (993), K 687 (994), and K 1289 (995)), his election to York was not followed by consecration to the archbishopric until after 12 April 995 at the earliest (he witnessed K 688 and K 692 as bishop *electus*, but issued a lease as archbishop in 996 (K 695)). Thereafter he witnessed as archbishop regularly until his death on 6 May 1002 (Fl Wig). His charters of this period include Dugd vi, pp. 1443–6 (994 – this has a doubtful witness list and may be discounted here); K 696, 1291–2, EHD I, p. 534 (996); K 698 (997); Crawf 8, K 700–1 (998); K 703 (999); K 705–6 (1001); K 707 (1002). While he was bishop of Worcester, and after the death of Bishop Ælfstan of London (q.v.), Ealdulf was given charge of Evesham Abbey; but upon his establishment at York, he appointed Ælfric to the abbacy, so reinstituting regular observance there after a break of 20 years.

Ealhhelm   (XI), XII
   Ealdorman of Central Mercia 940 × 951.

   His name is not common; in the period 930 × 951, of 69 charters in which the name appears, only two have the name Ealhhelm duplicated in the lay section of the witness lists (CS 677 and 765). It is very likely, therefore, that all the other appearances relate to the same individual. He occurs first in CS 669, dated 3 April 930, as the sixteenth of twenty thegns witnessing, and he remains roughly in this position throughout Athelstan's reign (CS 669, 671 dated c. 939, 675, 677, 682 dated c. 939, 689, 694, 702, 714, 730, 734, 741–3 – these last four charters have virtually identical lists). CS 670 is a doubtful charter dated 937 × 939 which is best ignored in this review. In 940 King Edmund succeeded at the age of 18, and soon afterwards his counsellors promoted three thegns to the rank of ealdorman: Æthelmund (q.v.), Æthelwold, and Ealhhelm. Some of the charters of 940, therefore, can be divided chronologically into two groups: those witnessed by Ealhhelm as a thegn (CS 753, 758, and 763 – the two last were probably witnessed on the same occasion), and those he witnessed as ealdorman (CS 748, 757, 761, 763). From then until 951, Ealhhelm witnessed regularly, usually fourth or fifth of six or seven ealdormen (CS 765, 769–70, 774–5, 777–8, 780, 782, 784, 786–9, 791–2, 795–6, 798, 801–2, 808, 810 – doubtful, 812 – dated 942 × 946, 814–15, 818, 820–1, 824, 830–4, 860, 864–866, 868–71, 875, 877–8, 882–3, 888 – dated 949). The two last charters witnessed, Bu XII and CS 892, are both dated 951. Outside the charters, Ealhhelm's name appears in a famous passage in the poem on the Battle of Maldon, in which his grandson Ælfwine refers to him as a distinguished ancestor. It seems reasonable to accept Professor E. V. Gordon's interpretation of this passage (*The Battle of Maldon*, 1954 reprint, pp. 83–4), from which he deduces that Ealhhelm was ealdorman of Mercia, father of Ealdorman Ælfhere of Mercia (q.v.) and of Ealdorman Ælfheah of Hampshire (q.v.), and father-in-law of Ælfric Cild, successor to Ælfhere in the Mercian ealdordom. The names and careers of three other sons are known:

Ælfwine (q.v.), Eadric (q.v.), and Ælfweard (Chron E. p. 78). If this pedigree is correct, Ealhhelm was closely related to the English royal house. There are grounds for believing that his sons were close friends of the ætheling Eadwig (q.v.), who became king in 956.

Eanulf, discthegn XXIII

Witnesses 958 × 975.

He witnessed CS 1042, 1046, 1073–4, 1077, 1079, 1112, 1118, 1121, 1135, 1143, 1164, 1198–1200, 1216–17, 1229 and 1234 (identical lists), 1230–1, 1257, 1266, 1268–70, 1282, 1285, 1145 (dated 972), 1309 (dated 972–3), 1292, 1303–5, and 1316. This is not a very common name; it does not appear at all, for instance, in the witness lists of the period 941 × 957. It is probable, therefore, that with one exception (CS 1199 dated 967, witnessed by two men of this name) all the charters of the period 958 × 975 in which the name Eanulf is to be found, refer to the same man. Eanulf's dates are confined strictly to the reign of King Edgar, and it is clear that he stood high in the king's favour from the outset. He was a Mercian thegn, one of the first to support Edgar after his revolt from the rule of his brother Eadwig. He first appears in CS 1036, by which King Edgar granted him 14 hides in Ducklington, Oxfordshire. The charter is dated 958, while Edgar's kingdom was still confined to the north of the Thames. Two years later, Eanulf was granted 11 hides at Perranzabuloe and Ladock in Cornwall (CS 1056). Usually Eanulf's name appears high in the witness lists; as early as 958 he was third of 11 thegns (CS 1042); he heads the lists in 968–9 and again in 974 (CS 1219, 1230, 1304), and he is second of 41 thegns witnessing in 970, and of 20 in 971 (CS 1266, 1270). He is called *discthegn* in 968 (Bu XXII) and in 971 (CS 1270). His last appearance is in 975 (CS 1316), one of Edgar's last charters.

Earnwig XXXVII

Abbot of Peterborough 1042 × 26 May 1052.

Described as 'a very good and gentle man', 'of marvellous sanctity and simplicity', he resigned the abbacy while in good health, and survived a further eight years (ASC E *s.a.* 1041, 1052; HC p. 65). He witnessed K 797 (1044) and Bu XXXVII (1048). For his obit, see KBL p. 60.

Eathhelm, *see* Æthelm.

Edgar, ætheling 1001 × c. 1010 XXX

The sixth and last son of King Æthelred II by his first wife Ælfgifu, he witnessed the following charters: K 706, 1295, 707, 710, 714, 1301, 1303, 1305, all of which are authentic. Probably he was born in 1001, for he does not witness earlier charters (particularly K 697, 1294), and it seems that the names of Æthelred's æthelings were added to the witness lists of royal charters as soon as they were born. Edgar last witnesses in 1008, and his omission from Bu XXXII suggests that he was dead by 1011.

Edgar   III, IV
Bishop of Hereford 888–c. 900 × 930–1.

His predecessor Cynemund witnessed as *electus* CS 557 (888); thereafter Hereford is unrepresented in the lists until Edgar first appears in Ha XVI (c. 900). He witnessed CS 596–7, 598 (misspelt *Cudgar*), 603, 607, all dated 901 × 904; he then disappears until 925, partly because of a reduction in the number of sees represented in the diplomas of Edward the Elder, and partly because of a gap in the run of charters in the later years of Edward's reign. From 925 to 3 April 930 he witnessed CS 642, 658–9, 663–4, 665–6, 669. His successor Tidhelm first witnessed CS 677 dated 12 Nov. 931. According to the lists in Fl Wig, Tidhelm was succeeded at Hereford by Wulfhelm, but I think this is an error. The Wulfhelm who witnessed the following charters of the period 20 June 931 × 21 Dec. 934 was probably a *chorepiscopus* in the diocese of Wells: CS 675, 635, 695–6, 702, 703, 705, 716–18. CS 716–18 is witnessed by a second Wulfhelm, but from his position in the list it is apparent that his name is an error for Wulfhun of Selsey. Wulfhelm (q.v.) succeeded as bishop of Wells after the death of Ælfheah in 937; he first witnessed as diocesan bishop CS 729–31, dated 938.

Edgar   XIII–XXIII
King of Mercia summer 957 × Oct. 959, king of England 1 Oct. 959 × 8 July 975.

Born in 943, he was the younger son of King Edmund and Queen Ælfgifu. His mother died in 943 or 944 (perhaps at Edgar's birth), and his father was killed in May 946. As an infant, Edgar was separated from his elder brother Eadwig, and fostered by Ælfwyn, wife of Ealdorman Athelstan 'Half-King'. He knew Abbot Dunstan of Glastonbury in his childhood; later he was educated by Abbot Æthelwold of Abingdon. In the closing months of the reign of his bachelor uncle Eadred, he came to court and began to witness charters. Upon the accession of his brother Eadwig in November 955, Edgar appears to have stayed with him for about 20 months, then crossed the Thames and set himself up as king of Mercia, East Anglia, and Northumbria. It is possible, however, that Edgar was appointed under-king in Mercia soon after Eadwig's succession, for he is entitled *regulus* in the witness list to the important Worcester charter CS 937, drawn up late in 956. When Eadwig died on 1 Oct. 959, Edgar became king of all England. His reign was free from pressures brought about by Danish attacks, and he brought the Welsh and Scottish kings under his supremacy. His most notable achievement was the inauguration of the Benedictine reform movement, led by his childhood mentors Dunstan and Æthelwold, with his foster-brother Æthelwine 'Dei amicus' as its chief lay patron. The primary objective secured by the reform was a spiritual and intellectual revival on a national scale, but there were widespread material repercussions, including a revolutionary change in land tenure and private jurisdiction, brought about by the endowment of many new and refounded monasteries. Edgar also reformed the coinage, and issued two law codes which were models for the laws drawn up by his successors. Edgar married (1) Æthelflæd 'Eneda', daughter of Ordmaer, who was probably a Hertfordshire thegn with estates centred on Hatfield; (2) in 964, Ælfthryth, the daughter of Ordgar who became ealdorman of Devon, and widow of his foster-brother Æthelwold, ealdorman of East Anglia. By Æthelflæd he had a son Edward (q.v.), who succeeded him as king of England. By Wulfthryth, a concubine, he had a daughter Eadgyth, who became a nun at Wilton. By his second wife Ælfthryth he had two sons; Edmund (who died in 970 or 971) and Æthelred, who succeeded after Edward. Edgar was crowned at Bath on 11 May 973, and died on 8 July 975. He was buried, very appropriately, at Glastonbury. There is no adequate modern biography, but reference may be made to Stenton pp. 361–6, EHD I, pp. 46–8, and OB *passim*.

Edmund   XI, XII, XIV
    Ealdorman of the Western Shires 949 × 963.
    No information survives about him outside the witness lists of royal diplomas, but one suspects that he was an important figure in mid-tenth-century politics, and the main buttress of the lay support for King Eadwig after Edgar's revolt. As H. M. Chadwick first suggested (*Anglo-Saxon Institutions*, p. 176), his ealdordom lay in the Western Shires. His predecessor Wulfgar last witnessed in 948 (CS 865, 871), and Edmund began to witness in 949 (CS 877, 888, 879, 880; his name appears also in CS 814 dated 946, but here it is a misspelling for Æthelmund). From then onwards he witnessed

practically every surviving royal diploma (except those of Edgar as king of Mercia) until 959, and then sporadically until 963, in which year he witnessed CS 1118, 1103, 1116–17, 1121, 1125, 1112. His successor Ordgar (q.v.) first witnessed in 964 (CS 1142). That Edmund's ealdordom lay south of the Thames is established by his appearance in King Eadwig's charters, and not those of his brother Edgar, during the period 957 × 959. At this time the Wessex ealdordom was held first by Æthelsige (q.v.) and then by Ælfheah (q.v.). The only other ealdorman witnessing King Eadwig's charters was Ælfric, who was appointed in 957 to the resuscitated ealdordom of Kent and Sussex, and disappeared from the lists in the following year (CS 1005, 1022, 1028, 1033–4). Edmund heads the ealdormen witnessing four charters issued in 949 and 951 (CS 877, 880, 892, 891), but thereafter he takes second place to Athelstan 'Half-King'. During the period 952 to mid-955, the only ealdormen witnessing were Athelstan, Edmund, and Æthelmund of N.W. Mercia (q.v.). Mercia and Wessex were then subdivided to form a number of fresh ealdordoms, but until the summer or early autumn of 956, Edmund yielded precedence only to the Half-King. After the latter's retirement, Athelstan 'Rota', ealdorman of S.E. Mercia (q.v.) headed the lists, with Edmund still in second place. In mid-957, Athelstan 'Rota' joined King Edgar in Mercia, and for the rest of Eadwig's reign Edmund headed the ealdormen witnessing charters issued south of the Thames. After Edgar's accession to the whole of England, Edmund was immediately relegated to fifth place among the ealdormen (CS 1051), a position he maintained with little variation until he ceased to witness in 963.

Edmund

V–VII

King of England Oct. 939 × 26 May 946.

The elder son of King Edward the Elder by his third wife Eadgifu, he was born in 921 and succeeded in October 939, upon the death of his half-brother Athelstan. In the following year he lost control of the northern Danelaw to Anlaf Guthfrithson, but in 942 he recovered the Five Boroughs, and later brought York and Cumbria under his control. These events were celebrated in a famous poem in the ASC (s.a. 942), and by his royal title in charters issued for the Danelaw (DC pp. 125–32). For the whole of his reign Edmund was strongly under the influence of his mother Eadgifu and of Athelstan 'Half-King' (q.v.), who formed the power behind the throne. He married first Ælfgifu, who died in 943 or 944, then Æthelflæd of Damerham, the daughter of Ealdorman Ælfgar of Essex. By Ælfgifu he had two sons, Eadwig and Edgar, both of whom succeeded to the English crown.

Edmund Ironside   XXVII, XXVIIIa, XXX–XXXIII, XXXV, XXXVI
King of England April 1016 × 30 Nov. 1016.

He was the third son of King Æthelred II by his first wife Ælfgifu. In addition to the Burton charters, he witnessed the following as ætheling: K 684, 697, 1294, 705–6, 1295, 1297, 707, 714, 1301, 1303, 1305–6, 1308–10; all of these are authentic. He had a younger brother Eadred (q.v.) by 993, but is unlikely to have been born before 990. He is referred to in the will of his elder brother Athelstan (q.v.), after whose death he became the heir to the English crown. In the late summer of 1015 he revolted against his father, and married the widow of Sigeferth (q.v.), a prominent thegn of the confederation of East Midland townships known as the Seven Boroughs. By her he had two sons, Eadward and Edmund. He moved to the Peterborough area (probably Peterborough was one of the Seven Boroughs) and issued from there two charters couched in the phraseology of solemn royal diplomas (K 726; CS 809; cf. ECEE pp. 200–3). In April 1016, upon his father's death, Edmund was chosen king in London. Subsequently he fought an unsuccessful battle against Cnut at *Assandun* in Essex. He died on 30 November that year, at Ross-on-Wye (ECWM p. 145). There is no adequate modern biography.

Edward the Confessor   XXXII, XXXVII
King of England June 1042 × 4 Jan. 1066.

He was the seventh son of King Æthelred II, the first by his second wife Emma. Probably he was born in 1005 (in which year he witnesses K 714 and K 1301), for he does not witness earlier charters. After his father's death, Edward spent many years in exile on the continent, and there is reason to believe that he was at Rouen when he succeeded to the English crown in June 1042 (ECEE p. 252). He died on 4 or 5 Jan. 1066, see H pp. 559–60. For his biography, see F. Barlow, *Edward the Confessor*, London, 1970.

Edward the Elder   IV
King of England 26 Oct. 899 × 17 July 924.

The second child and first son of King Alfred by his wife Ealhswith, he is remembered chiefly for his reconquest of the Danelaw, and his establishment of an overlordship over the rest of northern England and of Wales. Even so, his importance has been underestimated, partly through lack of charter evidence for his reign. There is reason to believe that he was responsible for a reorganization of the West Saxon diocesan system, and for fundamental changes in the hidation of Wessex and Mercia, involving the shiring of Mercia and Middle Anglia, and the creation of a hundredal system. For his children, see *Handbook of British Chronology*, R. Hist. *Soc.*, 2nd edn., 1961, p. 25. There is no adequate modern biography; the best account to date is in Stenton, pp. 315–42.

Edward the Martyr   XXI
  King of England July 975 × 18 March 979.
  The eldest son of King Edgar, and his only issue by his first wife Æthelflæd, Edward was born c. 962; his mother died soon afterwards, possibly at his birth. He attests CS 1190, the great foundation charter of New Minster, beneath his younger step-brother Edmund, and there is good reason to believe that he was regarded as of questionable legitimacy. (Finberg, *Tavistock Abbey*, p. 279; OB pp. 274–5). Bu XXI is the only other surviving charter witnessed by Edward as ætheling. Brihtferth, the author of the *Vita Oswaldi*, gives Edward a black reputation; he is said to have been violent in speech and action, inspiring terror among his retinue, and his youngest step-brother Æthelred (q.v.) is considered to have been more gentle (EHD I, p. 841; OB pp. 290–1). Stenton (p. 367) accepts Brihtferth's assessment. It must be remembered however that Brihtferth was a heavily biased witness, for he was a monk of Ramsey, the house endowed by Æthelwine 'Dei amicus' (q.v.), whose brother's widow Ælfthryth became the second wife of King Edgar. Ælfthryth (q.v.) was a strong supporter of monasticism, whereas Edward's reign was marked by a considerable lay reaction against the growing landed possessions of the monks. It is only to be expected, therefore, that Brihtferth, reviewing the period some thirty years later, should have compared Edward's character unfavourably with that of Ælfthryth's son Æthelred. Edward's succession was contested, and he was murdered less than three years afterwards, while still in his youth. The few surviving diplomas issued during his reign all relate to land in Wessex, and it is doubtful how far his authority was maintained in Mercia and the Danelaw. It is noteworthy that in the region of the Five Boroughs (particularly at Stamford and Lincoln) his coinage was executed to a much lower standard than that of his father (M. Dolley, *Anglo-Saxon Pennies*, London, 1964, p. 26). See further, J. Fisher in *Camb. Hist. Journ.* X, pt. III, pp. 234–50, and Christine Fell, *Edward King and Martyr*, Leeds Texts and Monographs, New Series No. 3, 1971.

Egberht, ætheling c. 989 × c. 1006   XXVI–XXVIIIa
  He was the second son of King Æthelred II by his first wife
Ælfgifu. In addition to the Burton charters, he witnessed the
following as ætheling: K 684, 697, 706, 1295, 707, 714, 1301; all
of these are authentic. He had two younger brothers (Edmund and
Eadred, q.v.) by 993, and probably he was born c. 989. He last
witnessed in 1005, and his omission from the witness lists of
subsequent charters of King Æthelred (particularly K 1303–4, dated
1007) suggests that he died soon afterwards.

Elemod, thegn   XXXII
  Witnesses 1011.
  He was the recipient of Hallam, Derbyshire, by Bu XXXII, but
nothing else is known of him. The name is uncommon, but it was
borne by a contemporary moneyer. M. Dolley (*Anglo-Saxon Pennies*,
London, 1964, p. 13) points out that *Ele-* appears to be a common
dialect form of *Æthel-* in the north-west – particularly at Chester – at
this period.

Fræna, thegn   XXVIIIa
  Witnesses 970 × 1004.
  This prominent Danelaw thegn first appears as a witness to two
Ely charters dated 970 (CS 1266, 1269), and to a Peterborough
charter dated 971 (CS 1270). Presumably he is the Fræna of
Rockingham, Northants., a large royal estate, who acted as a surety
for the purchase of estates for Peterborough Abbey (R pp. 78, 80,
82), and who gave to the abbey Langton in Leicestershire (HC p. 70).
He witnessed two wills concerning the eastern counties, W XVI (2)
dated c. 997, and W XXII dated c. 1004. Probably he is the man of
that name who deserted the English cause in an encounter with the
Vikings on the Humber in 993 (ASC *s.a.*). In addition to the charters
already quoted, Fræna witnessed K 624 (980); K 654 (986); K 687
(994); K 688–92 (995); EHD I, p. 534 (996); K 698 (997); K 700
(998); K 705 (1001); K 1295, 1297 (1002); Bu XXVIIIa (1004).

Freothegar, *see* Frithugar.

Frithugar   XXII
  Monk of Glastonbury and Abingdon, abbot of Evesham 974.
  According to the Evesham Chronicle, the abbey and its lands were
seized by Ealdorman Ælfhere in 976, and later given by him to a
monk named Freodegar, who became abbot, but afterwards gave the
abbey to a certain powerful man named Godwine, in exchange for

Towcester, Northants. (Chron E pp. 78–9; R p. 404). It may be presumed that Freodegar was the monk of that name who, according to Ælfric's *Vita Æthelwoldi* c. 7, followed Æthelwold from Glastonbury to Abingdon in about 955. Charters, however, do not bear out the story in the Evesham Chronicle, for they show Abbot Osweard of Evesham witnessing from 970 to 974 (CS 1257, 1269, 1282, 1303–4), then an abbot Frithugar witnessing Bu xxII, a perfectly respectable charter of King Edgar, issued later in 974. The name is sufficiently uncommon for it to be virtually certain that this was the abbot of Evesham; and since the anti-monastic reaction did not get under way until after the death of King Edgar in 975, Ealdorman Ælfhere could not have given the abbey to Frithugar. Unfortunately it is not possible to test the next statement in the Evesham Chronicle against charter evidence, for the only Abbot Godwine we know of at this period witnessed from 970 to 983 (CS 1257, 1302, 1269, 1282, 1309, 1303, 1304, 1316; K 621, 624, 632–3, 1279). His house has not been identified, but certainly it was not Evesham, for five of these charters were witnessed also by Abbot Osweard. Ealdorman Ælfhere had a son named Godwine (W ix) and one is tempted to speculate that it is he who figures in the Evesham story. The charters do not supply unequivocal evidence of another abbot of Evesham until Ælfric witnesses K 698 dated 997, so the chronology of the house remains in doubt. According to the Evesham Chronicle, p. 80, it was given by King Æthelred II first to Bishop Æthelsige (presumably Æthelsige I of Sherborne, q.v.), then to Bishop Æthelstan (presumably Ælfstan of London, 964 × 995–6, q.v.), and finally to Ealdulf, bishop of Worcester 992 × 1002 (q.v.). Previously, Bishop Osulf of Ramsbury (950 × 970, q.v.) is said to have held the abbey property for a while (Chron E p. 77). The descent of the temporalities of the abbey may therefore be reconstructed, very tentatively, as follows: Bishop Osulf, some time before 970; Abbot Osweard, 970 × 974; Abbot Frithugar, 974 × c. 975; Godwine, c. 975 × c. 978; Bishop Æthelsige, c. 978 × c. 990–3; Bishop Ælfstan, c. 990–993 × c. 995–6; Bishop Ealdulf, c. 995–6 × c. 996; Abbot Ælfric, c. 996 × c. 1002.

Frithugist, thegn 1009   XXXI

A man of this name witnessed CS 1266, an Ely charter dated 970, and two Frithugists witnessed CS 1270, a Peterborough charter dated 971. One of these was probably a Lincolnshire landowner who was a benefactor to Peterborough (ECEE p. 244), but since his sons were of age in 980, he is unlikely to have been the Frithugist who witnessed K 714 (1005) and Bu XXXI (1009). A thegn of this name appears as a traitor to the English cause in an encounter with the Vikings at the mouth of the Humber (ASC E *s.a.* 993).

Germanus   XXVIIIa, XXXI, XXXIII

Priest at Winchester, monk of Fleury, prior successively of Westbury-on-Trym c. 961 × c. 968, and Ramsey c. 968 × c. 969, abbot successively of Winchcombe c. 970 × 975, Ramsey c. 975 × 993-7, and Cholsey 993-7 × c. 1013.

The following account depends chiefly on Ramsey material embodied in the *Vita S. Oswaldi* (HCY I, pp. 399-475) and in Chron Rams. There was some editorial distortion in both these works, but the main succession of events can be followed without much difficulty (see also R p. 374). A priest at Winchester, Germanus followed Oswald to the monastery of Fleury-sur-Loire some time in the period 950 × 958, and evidently was tonsured there. In 961 or soon afterwards he was recalled by Oswald (then bishop of Worcester, q.v.) to become prior at Westbury-on-Trym near Bristol. Oswald, however, feared that his small foundation might suffer at the hands of his successors to the see of Worcester, so in about 968 he founded the abbey of Ramsey and transferred the Westbury community there. Germanus was given charge of the spiritual affairs of the house, and Eadnoth (who was to succeed him eventually as abbot, q.v.) was made responsible for administering the abbey's endowment. About a year later, however, Germanus was made abbot of Oswald's newly founded monastery at Winchcombe, only to be ejected with his monks in 975, during the anti-monastic reaction which followed the death of King Edgar. He retired to Fleury, but later in the same year was recalled once more by Oswald, and again placed in spiritual charge of Ramsey. It is not clear at what date he assumed the full office of abbot there. Later the chronicles of the house said he never was fully installed during Oswald's lifetime, but this is belied by his appearance as abbot witnessing a charter dated 988-9, before Oswald's death He witnessed a further charter, dated 993, as abbot of Ramsey, and another dated 997 as abbot of Cholsey, to which house he had been transferred by King Æthelred II; but the precise date of his transfer is unknown. He continued to keep contact with Ramsey; in April 1002 he officiated there at the interment of the body of St Ivo. Although a late record states that Cholsey was destroyed by the Danes in 1006, and nothing further is heard of the house, Germanus continued to witness as abbot until 1013; towards the end of this period he usually headed the lists of abbots witnessing charters (K 723 dated 1016 is best discarded, as is K 729 which claims to be dated 1019, cf. Chaplais, *Exeter*, pp. 4–5, 20). It is possible that he retired to St Petroc's, Bodmin, where he witnessed manumissions in company with Ealdorman Æthelweard of the Western Provinces (q.v.) and Bishop Burhwold of Cornwall (q.v.) in 1002 or later (K 981, p. 312). He must have been of great age when he died. Germanus witnessed as follows: EHD I, p. 533 (988–9); K 684 (993); S 1380 (994, described as 'of Fleury'); K 1289 (995); EHD I, p. 534 (996); K 698 (997); K 1295, 1297 (1002); LE pp. 129–30, Bu XXVIIIa (1004); K 714, 1301 (1005); K 1303–4 (1007); K 1305 (1008); Bu XXXI (1009); Bu XXXIII (1011); K 1307 (1012); Thorney X (1013).

Godeman   xxviiia
Monk of Abingdon and Winchester, abbot of Thorney 984 × c. 1013.

Godeman started his monastic life as a pupil of Abbot Æthelwold at Abingdon (Chron Abingd II, p. 262). After Æthelwold's appointment to the see of Winchester and his ejection of the clerks from the minsters there, he brought Godeman from Abingdon to be his chaplain. Godeman's name is one of the earliest recorded in LVH (p. 24). He may have been the artist who composed Æthelwold's famous *Benedictional*, one of the finest examples of the work of the Winchester school, written c. 963 × 984 (*The Chatsworth Benedictional*, ed. G. F. Warner and H. B. Wilson, Roxburghe Club, 1910, pp. xi, xiii, lv–lvi). Subsequently Æthelwold appointed him to be the first abbot of Thorney. Godeman's name does not figure in the Thorney foundation charter (ECEE No. VII), and according to the *Gesta Abbatum* in the Red Book of Thorney he did not take charge there until Æthelwold's death in 984. He does not witness charters as abbot until 990, but thereafter his name continues to appear sporadically in the witness lists until 1013; his abbey is identified in K 684. On 8 Nov. 991 he attended the consecration by Archbishop Oswald of the rebuilt church at Ramsey (Chron Rams pp. 93, 95–6). The date of his death is unknown; he must have survived until at least the age of 70. His successor as abbot of Thorney was Leofsige, who does not witness charters before his elevation to the see of Worcester in 1016 (Fl Wig). Godeman witnessed the following charters: K 712–13 (soon after 13 Feb. 990); K 684 (993); K 707 (1002); Bu XXVIIIa (1004); K 714, 1301 (1005); Crawf 11 (1007); K 1307 (1012); Thorney X (1013). See further, F. Wormald, *The Benedictional of St Æthelwold*, 1959, pp. 9–10; KBL p. 74.

Godwine   XXVIIIa, XXXI, XXXIII–XXXV
 Abbot of ?Athelney 997 × 1002, bishop of Lichfield 1002–4 ×
1019–26.
 It seems probable that the later bishop of Lichfield was the abbot
who witnessed the following charters of the period 997 × 1002: OS
Facs III, 35 (997); K 701 (998); K 706 (1001); K 1295, 1297,
Crispin p. 168 (1002). His house is not yet identified for certain, but
probably it was Athelney. It seems likely that the Abbot Godwine
who witnessed from 970 to 983 was another person; his house
remains unidentified. At Lichfield, Godwine's predecessor Ælfheah
(q.v.) last witnessed several charters dated 1002 (K 1295–6; Crispin
p. 168; K 707). Godwine first witnessed as bishop K 709 and Bu
XXVIIIa, both dated 1004. In the former charter, his see is identified;
the latter of the two is witnessed by two bishops named Godwine,
the second being from Rochester (q.v.). Godwine of Lichfield then
witnessed the following charters: K 714, 1303 (1007); K 1308
(1008); Bu XXXI (1009); Bu XXXIII (1011); K 719, Bu XXXV (1012).
After this date it is difficult to disentangle his signatures from those of
his namesake at Rochester, but it is probable that the Godwine who
witnessed the local Worcester charter K 1313 (1019) was from
Lichfield. His successor Leofgar appears only in a short undated
notification (K 803); Brihtmær, the next bishop, witnessed first in
1026 (K 743), but even this charter is suspect. Godwine's dates are,
therefore, impossible to establish as closely as one would like for
this important see.

Godwine I   XXVI–XXVIIIa, XXIX–XXXV
 Bishop of Rochester 995 × 1046–58.
 It is probable that there were two successive bishops named
Godwine at Rochester during this period, but it seems quite im-
possible to establish the date of the succession. Ælfstan (q.v.) last
witnessed as bishop (of Rochester) K 689–91, all dated 995. Godwine I
of Rochester received an estate at Wouldham and Littlebrook, Kent,
from King Æthelred later that year (K 688). Godwine figures also in
a law memorandum dated 995 × 1005 relating to Snodland, Kent,
(R LXIX), and in 1012 he received from King Æthelred an estate at
Hilton and Fenstanton in Huntingdonshire (K 719). The signatures of
Godwine end in 1046 (K 784); the succession of Siweard to the see
in 1058 is reported in ASC.

Godwine   XXXVII
 Earl of Wessex 1018 × 15 April 1053.
 His father's name was Wulfnoth, so it seems that Godwine was an

Englishman (see further L. W. Barlow, 'The Antecedents of Earl Godwine of Wessex' in *The New England Historical and Genealogical Register*, CXI (1957), pp. 30–8). In 1018 he was raised to an earldom by Cnut (OS Facs III, 39; K 728, which is often quoted, is untrustworthy; cf. Chaplais, 1966 pp. 21–2). Two years later he was given charge of Wessex, and from then until his death he heads the lay witnesses to every surviving authentic English diploma (except K 767). Curiously, there is no adequate modern biography. Most of the materials are brought together in Freeman, NC I, pp. 719–32, 743–6, 789–90; II, pp. 547–70, 643–9, 656–60, 705–7; but one must of course allow for Freeman's bias in handling them. See also D. C. Douglas, *William the Conqueror*, London, 1964, pp. 163–71, 411–13; Barlow EC *passim*.

Godwine, thegn 996, 1004, 1009   XXVI–XXVIIIa, XXXI

Godwine was a very common name at this period, and it seems impossible to identify the thegn or thegns witnessing these Burton charters with any degree of certainty. In particular, they cannot safely be identified with the Godwine who became earl of Wessex. The following charters were witnessed by thegns named Godwine: K 705 (1001); K 1296 (1002); K 709, 710, LE pp. 129–30 (1004); Bu XXXI (1009); K 1307, 719 (1012); K 1308 (1013); K 1309 (1014); K 723 (1016).

Harold   XXXVII

Earl of East Anglia 1044–5 × 24 Sept. 1051, Sept. 1052 × April 1053; earl of Wessex April 1053 × 6 Jan. 1066; earl also of Herefordshire 1057 × 1066; king of England 6 Jan. 1066 × 14 Oct. 1066.

He was the second son of Earl Godwine of Wessex and Gytha; in 1066 he married Ealdgyth, daughter of Ælfgar, earl of Mercia. For his issue (mostly by his concubine, Eadgyth Swanneshals), see Freeman, NC IV, Appendix R. For his biography see Barlow, EC, *passim*.

Healmstan, thegn 926   IV

Probably he is not the Healmstan who figures in the letter dated 901 × 924, translated in EHD I, pp. 501–3, but it is very likely that he is to be identified with the Helmstan who witnesses as ninth of the thegns CS 703, a charter drawn up at Nottingham on 7 June 930.

Kata, thegn 1009   XXXI

This Scandinavian name does not recur elsewhere in the surviving charters of this period.

Kenulf XXVI–XXVIIIa

Abbot of Peterborough 992 × 1006, bishop of Winchester 1006.

Archbishop Oswald of York (q.v.) died on 28 Feb. 992 (*Vita S. Oswaldi* pp. 463–7). Abbot Ealdulf of Peterborough (q.v.) succeeded to the see of York, and Kenulf to the abbacy of Peterborough, both in the same year (ASC C). Ælfheah II of Winchester (q.v.) was promoted to Canterbury some time after 15 Nov. 1005. Kenulf was then appointed to Winchester, but died in 1006 (ASC D). He was well remembered at Peterborough (HC pp. 47–8). He witnessed the following charters: K 684 (993); S 1380 (994); K 1289 (995); Bu XXVI–XXVII (996); K 698 (997); K 703 (999); K 1294 (1000); K 705 (1001); K 715, 707, 1295, 1297, Crispin p. 168 (1002); Bu XXVIIIa, EHD I, p. 545 (1004); K 714, 1301 (1005).

Leofgar, abbot 1009 XXXI

This is his only recorded appearance, and I have been unable to identify his house. It is possible that he is the Leofgar who was bishop of Lichfield 1020 × 1027.

Leofric XXVI–XXVIIIa

Abbot of Muchelney c. 983 × c. 1005.

It is necessary to distinguish carefully between three abbots named Leofric witnessing charters in the period 974 × 1005. The first, from Exeter, appears in CS 1303 (974), then frequently from K 624 (980) to K 673 (990); after his first appearance, his position in the lists improves steadily from fifth to second place. He was succeeded at Exeter by Brihthelm, who first witnesses in 993 (K 684). A second Leofric witnesses as last of the abbots K 636 (983), and regularly from then onwards until K 714 (1005). His house is identified as Muchelney in K 684 (993) and in K 698 (997). Towards the end of this period he usually witnesses in about the fifth place. A third Abbot Leofric witnesses low down on the lists three charters: K 698 (997), K 1295 (1002), and K 714 (1005). In the first of these, his house is identified as St Albans, and Professor Whitelock suggests that he was the younger brother of Ælfric, who preceded him as abbot, and that Leofric became abbot when Ælfric was made bishop of Ramsbury in 990 (W pp. 160–1). Later, Ælfric became archbishop of Canterbury (q.v.), but there is no charter evidence that Leofric was promoted from St Albans. The identity of his successor at St Albans has not been established, and it is not known how long Leofric held the abbacy; he ceased to witness in 1005. It is probable that the Leofric who witnessed all three of the Burton charters

XXVI–XXVIIIa was from Muchelney. It is important to note that K 714, dated 1005, was witnessed both by Leofric of Muchelney and by Leofric of St Albans, for this charter was witnessed also by an Abbot Æthelnoth, who is presumably to be identified with the abbot of that name who witnessed K 703 (999), K 707 (1002), and K 1303 (1007). An Abbot Leofric 'also called Æthelnoth' witnessed Dugdale VI, pp. 1443–6, dated ? 995, but it will be apparent from the above discussion that he cannot be assigned to Muchelney, Exeter, or St Albans. This charter, however, contains spurious elements, and its Abbot Leofric 'also called Æthelnoth' may have been no more than a scribal error.

Leofric   XXXVII

Earl of Mercia c. 1023 × autumn 1057.

Leofric was the son of Ealdorman Leofwine (q.v.). His elder brother Northman appears to have held a subordinate post under his father, and probably this descended to Leofric after Northman had been put to death on King Cnut's orders in 1017. About 1023 Leofric inherited his father's ealdordom, and a year later he may have added to this the earldom of Earl Eglaf. Earl Leofric was remembered at Worcester as a despoiler of the abbey estates, chiefly for the benefit of his own thegns and for his brothers Godwine and Edwin (*Vita Wulfstani* p. xxiv). Subsequently, however, he restored to Evesham an estate at Hampton, Worcs. Together with his wife Godgifu, he built a church dedicated to the Holy Trinity at Bengeworth, Worcs. (Chron E pp. 84–5); in 1043 they founded Coventry Abbey (where he was to be buried), and between 1053 and 1055 they founded a priory at Stow St Mary, Lincs (ECEE p. 103). Leofric was survived by his wife, whose widespread Mercian estates are recorded in DB. He was succeeded in the Mercian earldom by his son Ælfgar, and subsequently by Ælfgar's son Edwin. See further H pp. 565–6; Freeman, NC I, Appendix CCC; II, Appendix G; Barlow, EC *passim*.

Leofsige   XXXVII

Abbot of Ely ?1029 × ?1055.

There can be no certainty as to his dates. Miss Robertson and Miss Harmer both thought his death occurred probably in 1055 (R p. 467; H p. 566), but Dr Blake thought 1044 more likely (LE pp. 412–13). The charter Bu XXXVII (1048) was not utilized in these discussions. The Abbot Leofsige witnessing this charter appears between the abbots of Ramsey and Bury St Edmunds on one side, and Peterborough and Thorney on the other, and for this reason I think it very probable that his house was Ely. His obit was kept on 5 November (KBL pp. 44–5).

Leofsige   XXVI, XXVII

Ealdorman of Essex 994 × 1002.

He witnessed as ealdorman from 994 to 1002. His ealdordom is assigned to Essex in K 698 (997), but I have suggested elsewhere (p. 344 below) that it also embraced East Anglia. His antecedents are unknown. In 1002 he arranged a truce with the Danish fleet, but later that year he was banished for killing Æfic, the king's high reeve (ASC). Subsequently, his sister Æthelflæd had her estates confiscated for aiding him after his banishment (K 719). He witnessed the following: K 686–7, Dudg v, p. 443 (994); K 688–92, K 1289, Muchelney 4 (995); K 696, 1291–2, Bu xxvi–xxvii, EHD I, p. 534 (996); K 698, OS Facs III, 35 (997); K 700–1, Crawf 8 (998); K 703 (999); K 1294 (1000); K 705–6 (1001); K 715 (1002).

Leofstan   XXXVII

Abbot of Bury St Edmunds 1044 × 15 July 1065.

He may have been dean there previously (W p. 192); certainly he had been a monk of Bury since its foundation in 1020, and before that at St Benet, Holme. See also H p. 566, and KBL p. 32.

Leofwine   XVIII

Bishop of Lindsey c. 953 × 965; bishop of Dorchester 955 × 965.

It is clear from his appearance in several charters of King Edgar dated 958, that Leofwine's see was in Mercia, and he is to be identified with the Leofwine who is listed by Florence of Worcester as governing the united diocese of 'Leicester' (meaning Dorchester) and Lindsey during the reign of King Edgar. However, it does not seem possible fully to reconcile Florence's account with our knowledge of the succession to the Mercian bishoprics at this period, as revealed in the charters. We know that Oscytel (q.v.) was bishop of Dorchester from 951 until at least 955; yet Leofwine witnessed as bishop from 953 to 955. At Lindsey we have knowledge of a Bishop Alfred, the second of that name, witnessing three diplomas of the period May–Dec. 934 (CS 702–3, 705), and a Bishop Sigefrith who first appears in 996 (Bu xxvii). Leofwine's dates span some of the gap. He witnessed the following charters, presumably as bishop of Lindsey: CS 899, 900 (953), CS 903, 908 (955). When Oscytel was elevated to York by King Eadred towards the end of 955, Leofwine appears to have received the see of Dorchester, and presumably from then until 965 he held the two sees of Dorchester and Lindsey; in this capacity, he witnessed CS 1040, 1042–4 (958); CS 1073 (961); CS 1164 (965). His successor Ælfnoth first witnessed in 974 (CS 1310–11).

Leofwine   XXVI–XXVIIIa, XXXI
    Ealdorman of Mercia c. 994 × 1021–3.
    There is considerable difficulty in tracing the tenure of the Mercian ealdordom after the banishment of Ælfric Cild in 985. I have suggested elsewhere that from this date until his death in 992, jurisdiction over Mercia was held by Ealdorman Æthelwine of East Anglia (q.v.), as had been the case with his father Athelstan 'Half-King' (q.v.) during the period 951 × 956. Ealdorman Leofwine begins to witness in 994, and from then until 998 only five ealdormen witness King Æthelred's charters. In order of seniority they are Æthelweard, Ælfric, Ælfhelm, Leofwine, and Leofsige. Now it is usual to give these ealdormen the titles assigned to them in K 698, the great charter by which Æthelred II restored the hundred of Downton to the Old Minster at Easter 997. Æthelweard is assigned to the Western Provinces, Ælfric to Hampshire, Ælfhelm to Northumbria, Leofwine to the Hwicce, and Leofsige to Essex. In the cases of Æthelweard and Ælfhelm, no modifications of these titles are necessary, but the position of the remainder calls for further comment. First it must be noted that their territorial titles are those of episcopal sees rather than ealdordoms: *Wentanensium Prouinciarum* = Winchester, *Orientalium Saxonum* = Essex = London, and *Wicciarum Prouinciarum* = Worcester, which diocese covered a good deal more than the county of Worcester. Apart from an entry in ASC *s.a.* 1003, which shows Ælfric in command of an army drawn from Hampshire and Wiltshire, we get no further help in the matter from chronicles or narrative sources. But it is quite clear from the charters that these five ealdormen shared between them jurisdiction over the whole of England; Leofsige was responsible for East Anglia as well as Essex, Ælfric for Kent, Sussex, Surrey, and Berkshire as well as Hampshire and Wiltshire, and Leofwine for the whole of Mercia, not just the territory of the Hwicce. The reason for the more restricted titles of K 698 is probably that the ealdormen were based on these parts of their wider territories; certainly Leofwine is known to have had considerable landed interests in Worcestershire; he and his three sons were remembered as despoilers of episcopal estates there (*Vita Wulfstani* p. xxiv), and he witnesses specifically Worcester texts (K 1313, 738). In 998 King Æthelred granted him

land in Warwickshire (Crawf 8). From 999 to mid-1002 the list of Æthelred's ealdormen is reduced to four, including Leofwine. From mid–1002 to 1005 Leofwine is the last of only three ealdormen regularly witnessing Æthelred's charters, and it seems likely that he continued to hold responsibility for the whole of Mercia during this period; but in 1007 Eadric Streona (q.v.) was appointed ealdorman of Mercia, and from then onwards Leofwine's ealdordom appears to have been restricted to the territory of the Hwicce and adjacent parts of Mercia. In 1014, King Æthelred granted him land in Herefordshire (ECWM pp. 143–5). When Eadric Streona died on Christmas Day 1017, his place was taken by the Scandinavian Earl Eglaf (Crawf pp. 139–42), and it is apparent from the charters that Leofwine became subordinate to him. Nevertheless, Leofwine retained sufficient influence in Mercia for his authority to be transferred upon his death to his son Leofric (q.v.). Leofwine witnessed the following charters: K 686–7, Dugd VI, p. 443 (994); K 688–92, 1289 (995); Bu XXVI–XXVII, K 1292, EHD I, p. 534 (996); K 698, OS Facs III, 35 (997); K 700, Crawf 8 (998); K 703 (999); K 1294 (1000); K 705–6 (1001); K 707, 715, 1295–7, EHD I, p. 541 (1002); K 709–10, LE pp. 129–30 (1004); K 672, 714, 1301 (1005); K 1303–4 (1007); K 1305 (1008); K 1306, Bu XXXI (1009); K 719, 1307 (1012); K 1309 (1014); K 1310 (1015); K 723 (1017); K 1313 (1017); K 729, EHD I, pp. 553–5 (1019); K 735–6 (1021–3); K 738 (1023).

Leofwine, thegn   XXVI–XXVII

    Witnesses 980 × 998.

    The thegn discussed here usually appears between fifth and eighth in the lists of thegns witnessing, and may be identified with the Leofwine, Leoftæte's son, who occurs in EHD I, p. 533. Probably he is to be identified with the Leofwine who received Wooton, Berks. from King Æthelred in 985 (K 1283), and possibly he was the Leofwine who is mentioned in a contemporary law memorandum concerning a dispute about lands in Berks. and Bucks. (R LXVI). It is also possible that he was the king's huntsman; a man of this name received lands in Wilts. and Somerset in 987 (K 658). He witnesses the following charters: K 624 (980); K 629 (981); K 639, 1280 (983); K 641, 1282 (984); EHD I, p. 533 (989); K 686 (994); K 688 (995); K 696, Bu XXVI–XXVII (996); K 700–1 (998).

Leofwine, thegn   XXVII–XXVIIIa

    Witnesses 987 × 1015.

    The thegn discussed here witnesses low in the lists for the first twenty years, but from 1007 onwards is usually in fourth or fifth place. Possibly he is to be identified with the Leofwine, Æthelwulf's son, who occurs in EHD I, p. 533. He witnesses the following: K 657–8 (987); EHD I, p. 533 (989); Bu xxvii (996); K 698 (997); K 700 (998); K 707, 715, 1296, EHD I, p. 541 (1002); K 709, Bu xxviiia (1004); K 672, 714, 1301 (1005); K 1303–4 (1007); K 1305 (1008); K 1307 (1012); K 1310 (1015).

Leofwine, thegn   xxviiia
   Witnesses 997 × 1007.
   A second thegn named Leofwine witnesses Bu xxviiia. He may be identified with the man of that name who appears low down on the lists of the following charters: K 698 (997); K 707 (1002); Bu xxviiia (1004); K 1301, 714 (1005); K 1303–4 (1007).

Leofwine, thegn   xxxvii
   Witnesses 1042 × 1048.
   The Leofwine who witnesses Bu xxxvii may be identified with the Leofwine, son of Æstan, who witnesses K 962 and who occurs in DB as a landowner in Bucks. and Notts. Possibly he is also the Leofwine, *nobilis*, who witnesses OS Facs II, Exeter 12 (1044). See further, Oleson p. 127.

Lyfing   xxviiia, xxix–xxxv
   Monk of Glastonbury, abbot of Chertsey 989 × 998, bishop of Wells 999 × 1013, archbishop of Canterbury 1013 × 12 June 1020.
   His alternative name, Ælfstan, is established by ASC D *s.a.* 1019. He witnessed a few charters as Ælfstan while bishop of Wells (K 707, 709, Crispin p. 168, Bu xxxiii), and he was addressed as Archbishop Ælfstan in a charter of 1018 (OS Facs III, 39). For some time after his appointment as archbishop Lyfing appears to have taken second place in precedence to Archbishop Wulfstan II of York (e.g. K 1310, dated 1015). His influence increased after the accession of King Cnut, who confirmed the liberties of Christ Church at Lyfing's request in 1017–20 (H no. 26), and entrusted him with an important mission to Rome (Liebermann, *Gesetze*, I, p. 273). He died in 1020 (ASC *s.a.*), on 12 June according to a Christ Church kalendar. He was re-membered as 'a very prudent man, both in matters of church and state' (ASC D *s.a.* 1019). At Chertsey, his predecessor Ordbriht (q.v.) last witnessed in 988. Lyfing witnessed as abbot K 684 (993); K 698 (997); K 700 (998); his house is identified in the first two of these charters (supplying the letters '*ce*' for the lacuna in K 684, to

give '*ceort*' for '*ceortesige*', i.e. Chertsey). At Wells, Lyfing was preceded by Ælfwine, who last witnessed in 998 (K 700–1). In addition to the Burton charters quoted above, Lyfing witnessed the following as bishop: K 703 (999); K 1294 (1000); K 705–6 (1001); K 707, K 1295–6, Crispin p. 168 (1002); K 709, 711 (1004); K 714, 1301 (1005); K 1303–4 (1007); K 1305 (1008); K 1306 (1009); K 719, 1307, R LXXIV (1012); Thorney x (1013). See also SBW pp. 49–50; KBL p. 38.

Maeglsothen 956   XV
  He received land at *Mortune* (possibly Morton, Derbyshire) from King Eadwig in 956 (Bu xv), but his name does not occur elsewhere in the charters. In the diploma lying before the cartulary copyist, the spelling was *Maeglsoþen*. The name appears as that of a moneyer at Chester in the time of King Edgar, *Maelsuðan*, *Maelsuðon*, *Melsuðan*, and represents Old Irish *Máel-suthian*, evidently in use on the Welsh border, cf. *England before the Conquest*, ed. P. Clemoes and K. Hughes, Cambridge, 1971, p. 200.

Morcar, thegn   XXVIIIab, XXXI, XXXIII, XXXVI
  Witnesses 1001 × 1013; died 1015.
  He was the son of Earngrim, brother of Sigeferth (q.v.), husband of Ealdgyth (q.v.), and closely related to Wulfric Spot (q.v.), the founder of Burton Abbey, but the precise nature of this relationship has not been determined. Wulfric left him a large block of territory in the north-east of Derbyshire and the adjacent parts of Yorkshire, and three charters in the Burton series record gifts to him by King Æthelred II of further Derbyshire estates. He was one of the most powerful thegns of the confederation of Danelaw districts known as the Seven Boroughs. Together with his brother Sigeferth, he was murdered in 1015 by Eadric Streona, ealdorman of Mercia; subsequently his estates were seized by Edmund Ironside (q.v.). He witnessed the following charters: K 705, 710, 714, 719; Thorney x. See further, W p. 155.

Oda   II, VI, VIII–XVIII
  Monk of Fleury, bishop of Ramsbury 926–7 × 942, archbishop of Canterbury February 942 × 2 June 958 or 959.
  Oda was a Dane by birth. The Ramsey tradition at the end of the tenth century was that his father, who had come to England with the Norsemen Inguar and Hubba, remained a pagan until he died. The F version of ASC supplies the date 870 for the successful battle of these two Viking leaders against King Edmund of East Anglia, which

was followed by the latter's martyrdom. We may suppose that Oda was born in the last decade of the ninth century. He left his father and home at an early age, and was brought up in the Christian household of an English thegn named Æthelhelm. We are not told where this occurred, but later records afford clear evidence of Oda's early connections with the eastern Danelaw. (D. Whitelock, 'The Conversion of the Eastern Danelaw', *Saga-Book of the Viking Society*, XII (1937–45), pp. 169–71). The next generation of his family included Archbishops Oswald (q.v.) and Oscytel (q.v.) of York, Abbot Thurcytel of Bedford and Crowland, and the wife of the prominent thegn Athelstan Mannesune (ECEE pp. 29–31), all of whom had interests in the eastern counties in general and in Cambridgeshire in particular. This connection with the eastern Danelaw was fostered by Oda throughout his life; in his last years, records show him still involved in the affairs of Cambridgeshire (Chron Rams p. 49; CS 999). Upon completion of his education, Oda was ordained priest, and made the pilgrimage to Rome. In 926–7 he was consecrated by Archbishop Wulfhelm of Canterbury, and appointed by King Athelstan, according to the *Vita Odonis*, to succeed Athelstan as bishop of the recently founded see of Ramsbury; in this capacity he first witnessed CS 660 (927), where he is mistakenly assigned to Sherborne (see O'D II, pp. 98–9). As our knowledge deepens of the reception in England of the Benedictine reform movement, the significance becomes more apparent of the parts played by the three bishops Ælfheah of Winchester (q.v.), Cenwald of Worcester (q.v.), and Oda of Ramsbury and Canterbury. All three were tonsured on the continent, but were not cloistered because there were at that time no houses in England at which they could live the regular life. Ælfheah's continental connections are unknown, but he was a monk by 925 (CS 641, wrongly dated 929 by E. John in OB p. 156). Probably Cenwald was tonsured during his visit to Swiss monasteries in 929. Oda is known to have received the tonsure at Fleury, possibly during a visit to France made in 936 (Richer's Annals, cf. EHD I, p. 316 n. 5), for the house was not reformed until c. 930. It may have been on this occasion that he visited the Swiss monastery of St Gall, where his name is recorded in the confraternity book (SBW p. 61). Athelstan's choice of ambassador for his continental mission in 936 shows that Oda was already in high standing with the king. A charter of 934, in which his name alone among the bishops appears in majuscules, is further evidence of Oda's importance at court (R xxv). His promotion to Canterbury came early in the reign of Edmund, Athelstan's successor, doubtless on the advice of Athelstan 'Half-King', ealdorman of East Anglia, who was virtually the regent at this period. One of Oda's first acts as arch-bishop was to join with Archbishop Wulfstan I of York in securing a peace between King Edmund and Olaf Sihtricson, king of York, by which Watling Street was reaffirmed to be the boundary of the Danelaw (SD II, pp. 93–4; see also M. L. R. Beavan in EHR xxxiii (1918), pp. 1–9 and n. 11. My interpretation here differs from that of Beavan, followed by Stenton p. 352; it seems to me that the Northumbrian annalist would not have invented the name of Oda, so that unless this is a late insertion, the transaction he records cannot antedate Oda's accession to Canterbury in 942. However, the matter remains unresolved, for recently Miss O'Donovan has made out a case for 941 as the year of Oda's succession. (O'D I, p. 33). Oda was associated with Wulftsan in another act of state at a council that met in London at Easter 942 (or possibly two or three years later, but 942 is the most likely date). This resulted in the promulgation of the first of King Edmund's law codes, which has a distinctly ecclesiastical flavour: bishops are to repair the churches within their dioceses, priests are to be celibate, laymen to refrain from adultery, to pay tithes, and do penance for homicide, sorcery, and perjury (Robertson, *Laws of the Kings of England*, pp. 6–7). Almost certainly this code is to be attributed to Oda's initiative, for the general approach is strikingly similar to that of his *Constitutiones*, which he addressed to bishops, priests, monks, secular clergy, and the laity; in particular, bishops are enjoined to perambulate their dioceses regularly (Spelman, *Concilia*, I, pp. 415 ff.). Oda proceeded to put these ideals into practice in his own cathedral church; he rebuilt the nave with higher walls and a new roof, and made many other structural improvements, and he brought to rest at Canterbury relics of the seventh-century saints, Ouen of Rouen and Wilfrid of York. Oda had a particular veneration for Wilfrid, no doubt because the latter had introduced Benedictine monasticism into northern England; it was at Oda's request that Frithegode, one of the Canterbury monks, wrote a metrical life of the saint, which has not survived. This same Frithegode was entrusted by Oda with the early education of his nephew Oswald. Subsequently Oswald was ordained by Oda, who purchased for him a small monastery at Winchester; later, Oswald was sent by Oda, laden with gifts, to Fleury to absorb the monastic discipline of the reform movement. His patronage of Oswald was but one of Oda's many services to the cause of Benedictine reform; it was he who led the monastic party in its protest con-cerning King Eadwig's behaviour at his coronation banquet, and who finally persuaded Eadwig to put away his wife, declaring that the union offended the laws of consanguinity. Oda's influence over Eadwig was such that he persuaded him to regularize the endowment of Abingdon, and he witnessed Eadwig's great confirmation charter to that monastery (OB pp. 190–3). Furthermore, he secured from Eadwig the grant of 40 hides at Ely in Cambridgeshire, doubtless with the intention of refounding the monastery there (Crawf 5; ECEE p. 41). Later in the same year he consecrated Dunstan as bishop, probably of London. Some time afterwards Oda became ill while at Canterbury. He sent to Fleury for his nephew Oswald, but did not survive long enough to see him; he died on 2 June 958 or 959 (on the date, see Stubbs, *Memorials of St Dunstan* p. xciv, OB p. 192, and O'D I, pp. 33–4), and was buried in his cathedral to the south side of the Altar of Christ, before the High Altar. His successor Ælfsige desecrated his grave, and it was not until a century and a half later than Anselm persuaded Eadmer to write his *Vita Odonis* (Wharton, *Anglia Sacra* II, pp. xxxiii, 78). There is however a fairly full account of Oda in Brihtferth's *Vita Oswaldi* (HCY I, pp. 410–12 etc.). He still awaits a modern biographer.

Odda
XXXVII

Witnesses as *minister* 1014 × 1045, *nobilis* 1044 × 1050, earl of the Western Provinces 1051 × 1052, earl of the Hwicce 1052 × c. 1055, then monk of Deerhurst until his death on 31 August 1056.

A kinsman of the Confessor, he is specially associated with Deerhurst (which he rebuilt, with a chapel in memory of his brother Ælfric), and with Pershore. After receiving the monastic habit at Deerhurst, he died there, but was buried at Pershore. For his biography, see R pp. 456–8, Barlow *EC*, pp. 114, and J. H. Round in VCH *Worcs.* I, pp. 258–60. For a list of charters witnessed by him, see Oleson p. 128.

Ordbriht
XXI–XXII, XXVI–XXVIIIa

Clerk of Winchester, monk of Abingdon, abbot of Chertsey 964 × 989, bishop of Selsey 989 × 1009.

His career is one of the best attested in the charters of the period. Bishop Æthelwold brought him from Winchester to be his pupil at Abingdon, then appointed him to Chertsey in 964 (Ælfric, *Vita Æthelwoldi*; ASC A). He witnessed as abbot frequently to 967. Except for two charters, there is then a gap until 980, when he witnessed K 624 as last of nine abbots. In 982 he witnessed K 633 in a similar lowly position, but later that year he was promoted

quite suddenly to be first among the abbots (K 1278), a position he
retained, with one exception (K 665), until his elevation to the see of
Selsey some time after September 988 (following the transference of
Æthelgar from Selsey to Canterbury, q.v.). He continued to witness
many charters, of which the texts of over 70 have survived, until his
death in 1009 (Fl Wig). As abbot he witnessed the following:
Muchelney f. 2v, CS 1143 (964); Bu XXI, CS 1176, 1189–91 (966);
CS 1197, 1199–1200 (967); CS 1266 (970); Bu XXII (972); K 624
(980); K 632–3, 1278 (982); LH pp. 228–31, K 636, 639–40, 1279
(983); K 1280, 1282 (984); K 648, 650, 1283 (985); K 655 (986);
K 657–8, LH pp. 231–6 (987); K 663–5, LH pp. 238–42 (988). He
appears as bishop in R LXIII (989) and R LXVI (990), and witnessed as
bishop the following charters: EHD I, p. 533 (989); K 673, 713
(990); K 684 (993); K 686, S 1380 (994); K 688–91, 1289 (995);
K 696, 1291–2, Bu XXVI–VII, EHD I, p. 534 (996); K 698, OS Facs
III, 35 (997); K 700 (998); K 703 (999); K 1294 (1000); K 705–6
(1001); K 707, 1295–7, EHD I, p. 541 (1002); K 1299 (1003);
K 711, EHD I, p. 547, Bu XXVIIIa (1004); K 714, 1301 (1005); K 715
(1006); K 1303–4 (1007); K 1305 (1008). See also KBL p. 38.

Ordgar, thegn 1031 × 1050   XXXVII
This important landowner is always given high place among the
thegns witnessing charters during the Confessor's reign; sometimes he
heads them in the witness lists. He is entitled *prefectus* in K 762 and
nobilis in K 787, OS Facs II, Exeter 12. Finberg suggests that he
was a descendant of Ordulf (q.v.), uncle of Æthelred II and founder of Tavistock Abbey (*Lucerna*, pp. 195–8). He had two brothers,
Ælfgar (q.v.) and Escbern (R CV); the former sometimes witnessed
charters with him – their two names are entered consecutively in K
770, 1322, 1332, as was the custom with brothers. He is described
as *Deuonensis* in K 939; manumissions in the Leofric Missal show that
his estates were centred on Lifton, Devon (*Lucerna*, pp. 195–6),
and by the time of the Conquest his descendants are shown in DB
to have held widely in south-west England. Many of the charters
witnessed by Ordgar concern land in the south-west; he was granted
land at Littleham near Exmouth in 1042 (K 1332). He witnessed the
following charters: OS Facs II, Exeter 11; K 744 (1031); K 1318
(1033); K 753, 1322 (1035); K 762–3, 1332 (1042); K 769 (1042 ×
1044); K 767 (1043); R CXIX (1043 × 1044); K 770–1, 774–5, OS
Facs II, Exeter 12 (1044); K 776, 778, 780–1, 783 (1045); R CV
(1045 × 1046); Bu XXXVII (1048); K 787 (1049). He was buried at
Tavistock (WM).

Ordheah, thegn   XII

   Witnesses 951.

   His only appearance is low down on the list of this Burton
charter.

Ordulf I, thegn   XXVI–XXVIIIa

   Witnesses 975 × 1005.

   He was the founder of Tavistock Abbey, and Finberg has surmised
that he was also high-reeve of the hundred of Lifton in Devon, in
which the abbey lay, and which extended over the border into
Cornwall. His father was Ordgar, ealdorman of Devon, and his
sister Ælfthryth (q.v.) became King Edgar's queen. His wife
Ælfwynn owned extensive lands on either side of the River Torridge.
Ordulf first witnesses CS 1315, a highly unusual charter composed at
Glastonbury in 975, probably before 28 June, and witnessed by
abbots and thegns from the West Country. He first appears in a royal
diploma in 980, as eighth of thirteen thegns witnessing. In 981 he was
given prominence in the foundation charter of Tavistock Abbey,
whose initial endowment he and his family provided. From then
until 994 he witnessed a number of royal diplomas, usually relating
to the West Country; his failure to witness many charters concerning
lands elsewhere suggests that he was not constantly at court during
this period; his position in the witness lists was usually about the
middle of the thegns subscribing, but varied from first (K 641) to
last (K 663). In c. 987 Æthelred II granted him land beside the River
Dart; the charter survives in a fragmentary state, but probably it
relates to Queen Dart in the hundred of Witheridge, Devon (H. P. R.
Finberg in *The Westward Expansion of Wessex*, by W. G. Hoskins,
Leicester, 1960, pp. 33–5). In 994 Ordulf appears to have been given
a position of responsibility in the immediate entourage of Æthelred
II, and from then until 1005 he subscribed regularly as second (or
occasionally as first) of the thegns witnessing royal diplomas. At this
period the first place was normally held by the thegn Æthelmær
(q.v.), who later became the founder of monasteries at Cerne and
Eynsham, and ealdorman of the Western Shires. This close connection
between Æthelmær and Ordulf is worth stressing; both were
discthegns (K 715, OE text), both were the sons of ealdormen of the
Western Shires related to the king, both had themselves interests in
Devon, both founded important West-Country abbeys, and both
were literate men who were actively interested in the intellectual
as well as the institutional aspects of the monastic reform movement.
They appear together in very similar passages in two charters of 995,

which record that they persuaded King Æthelred II to confirm the privileges of Abingdon Abbey, and to add to its endowment (K 684, 1312). Although he seems to have retired from active political life in 1005, Ordulf may have survived for several years longer. He is mentioned in the will of Ælfwold II, bishop of Crediton (q.v.). Bishop Ælfwold's will cannot be dated for certain more closely than 997 × 1015, but the likelihood is that it was composed towards the end of his life. After disposing of his heriot, Ælfwold names Ordulf as his first legatee, bequeathing to him a martyrology and a book by Hrabanus Maurus – possibly a computistical work. For Ordulf to be interested in such matters at this stage in his career, and (presumably) able to read about them, suggests to me that he may have entered a monastery – most likely Tavistock – after his retirement from public life. The date of his death is unknown, but according to the kalendar in the Leofric Missal his obit was kept on 16 December. For further biographical details about Ordulf, including an account of his endowment of Tavistock, see Finberg, *Lucerna*, pp. 189–95. He witnessed the following charters: CS 1315 (975); K 624 (980); K 633 (982); K 639, 1279 (983); K 641, 1281 (984); K 655 (986); K 657–8, LH pp. 231–6 (987); K 663–4, LH pp. 238–42 (988); K 673 (990); K 686–7 (994); K 688–9, 691–2, 1289, Muchelney 4 (995); K 996, 1292, Bu XXVI–XXVII, EHD I, p. 534 (996); K 998, OS Facs III, 35 (997); K 700–1, Crawf 8 (998); W XVI (2) (995 × 999); K 703 (999); K 1294 (1000); K 705–6 (1001); K 707, 715, 1295–7, Crispin p. 168, EHD I, p. 541 (1002); K 709–10, LE pp. 129–30 (1004); K 714, 1301 (1005).

Ordulf II, thegn   XXXVII

Witnesses 1044 × 1059.

He witnessed K 771, 774–5, 779, OS Facs II, Exeter 12 (1044); Bu XXXVII (1048); K 787 (1049); K 791 (1050); ECDE no. 103 (1059). Not all of these are fully authentic, but most relate to land in the West Country, and Olesen (p. 129) notes that the name occurs frequently in the Devon and Somerset entries of DB. See further, *Lucerna*, pp. 197–203, where Finberg identifies him as the son of Ordgar (q.v.), a descendant of the founder of Tavistock Abbey.

Orgar, *see* Osgar.

Oscytel   XI–XII, XV, XVII, XIX–XXII

Bishop of Dorchester 949 × 958, archbishop of York 956 × 1 Nov. 971.

Almost certainly a Dane, he was a kinsman of Oswald (q.v.), who succeeded him in the archbishopric, and of Thurcytel, abbot successively of Bedford and Crowland. His dates are difficult to establish precisely. Wynsige (q.v.), bishop of Dorchester, last witnessed on 21 Dec. 934 (CS 716), and after this the see is probably represented in the witness lists by a Bishop Æthelwold (q.v.), who witnessed in the period 943 × 949 (CS 812, 805, 815, 876, 883). The location of Æthelwold's see is supported by an OE insertion in CS 864, dated 948, which shows that he had interests at Wallingford on the Thames, not far from the seat of his bishopric. If Oscytel reigned as bishop for 22 years (ASC B, s.a. 971) he succeeded as bishop in 949. Oscytel began to subscribe (as last of the bishops) two Mercian charters issued in 951 (Bu XI–XII), and an unusual Berkshire diploma of 952 (CS 895). The few surviving charters issued during the next two years are not witnessed by Oscytel, but his subscriptions as bishop recommence in 955 (Bu XIII; CS 905, 909, 917; R XXX), and continue until 958 (CS 1036–7, 1040 etc.). Probably his re-appearance in the lists coincided with his appointment by King Eadred to take charge of the archbishopric of York during an illness (which proved terminal) of Wulfstan I (q.v.) (ASC s.a. 971), but the fact that usually he witnessed chancery charters as bishop suggests that his position at York was irregular during this period. It was as bishop of Dorchester that he was left a sum of money in the will of King Eadred, for distribution throughout the shires and bishoprics of Mercia. Wulfstan I of York died on 26 Dec. 955, being buried at Oundle within Oscytel's diocese. Subsequently Oscytel held the *de facto* position of archbishop of York, a situation illustrated by the alliterative Worcester diploma CS 937, dated from Cirencester late in 956, in which he is entitled *summus pontifex*; and there is no need to doubt the authenticity of CS 1029, also dated late in 956, by which King Eadwig granted Oscytel as archbishop a large estate and soke at Southwell in Nottinghamshire. In the early months of 957, however, Oscytel witnessed Eadwig's charters as only fifth of the bishops (CS 988, 997, 999, 994, 1001, 1003). After the summer of 957, Oscytel in common with other bishops and lay magnates north of the Thames became subject to Edgar as king of Mercia. He witnessed most of King Edgar's charters in 958 as first of the bishops (CS 1036–7, CS 1042–3; he is a little lower in the list of CS 1040), and it was to him as bishop that Edgar granted Sutton, another large Nottinghamshire estate, for the support of the see of York (CS 1044). According to Eadmer, *Vita Odonis* (HCY I, pp. 413 ff.), Oscytel journeyed to Rome at about this time to receive the pallium. Oswald (q.v.) is said to have accompanied him. Later in the year, his position seems to have been regularized, presumably as a result of this visit; certainly he was fully established as archbishop when Oswald went to stay with him soon after the death of Oda, archbishop of Canterbury, on 2 June 958 (q.v.). Oscytel witnessed as archbishop CS 1023 dated 958, and regularly from then onwards until his death on 1 Nov. 971. R pp. 110–13 records that Oscytel acquired lands in Northumbria by purchase and forfeiture, to increase the endowment of his see. He possessed also Beeby in Leicestershire, in the diocese of Dorchester, which he willed on his death to Bishop Æthelwold, possibly for the endowment of Peterborough. Later, this estate was bought from Æthelwold by Thurcytel, and used to endow Crowland (LE p. 96 n. 5).

Osferth   IV
    Ealdorman of Wessex 905–9 × 934.
    In the will of King Alfred, which was drawn up in 888 or earlier, Osferth was bequeathed 100 mancuses, the same sum as the ealdormen (Ha x). He witnessed as a thegn from 898 to 904, usually heading the lists (CS 576, 588, 590, 594, 603). He stood in some specially close familial relationship to Edward the Elder, for although the title *frater regis* given him in CS 611 (904) is certainly a mistake, he witnessed this charter after the king's son and before the archbishop; similarly in CS 603 (904) he witnessed before all the ealdormen. Again, he witnessed CS 624 (909), as *propinquus regis* before the ealdormen, and CS 664–5 (929) as *Osferth comes cum ducibus et ceteris optimatibus*, a phrase paralleled in later charters witnessed by Athelstan 'Half-King' *cum ceteris suffraganeis*. He first appears as ealdorman in the charters granted to Bishop Frithestan of Winchester in 909 (CS 620–1, 623, 625, 627–9), and from then onwards he nearly always headed the ealdormen witnessing. His ealdordom must have been located in Wessex, since this is the only one known to have been vacant during his period of office. He last witnessed CS 703, 1344 dated 7 June 934, and it seems probable that he died during King Athelstan's Scottish campaign that summer. He must have been over 60 when he died, a great age for a tenth-century ealdorman.

Osgar   XXI, XXII
    Monk of Glastonbury, abbot of Abingdon 28 Dec. 963 × 24 May 984.
    A disciple of Bishop Æthelwold (q.v.), Osgar was sent to Fleury for training (Ælfric, *Vita Æthelwoldi*), and succeeded Æthelwold at

Abingdon after the latter's appointment to Winchester on 29 Nov. 963 (ASC E); he was blessed as abbot on 28 December. He witnesses charters from 964 onwards, usually after the abbots of St Augustine's and Bath, but before Chertsey, New Minster, and Glastonbury. Towards the end of his abbacy Osgar often headed the abbots in the witness lists; his last appearance as abbot being in two charters of 979. He witnessed also K 626 (dated 980, before 8 May) where he is wrongly given the title of bishop. Florence of Worcester supplies our only evidence for the date of Osgar's death, which he places in 984 (Fl Wig I, pp. 140 n, 147 n). Eadwine, the next abbot of Abingdon of whom we have evidence, was appointed in 984 (ASC E) or 985 (ASC C) and died in 990 (ASC C). Osgar purchased 20 hides at Kingston Bagpuize, Berkshire, from Earl Ælfhere of Mercia in 971 × 979 (R LI). He witnessed the following charters as abbot: Muchelney f. 2d, CS 1135, 1143 (964); CS 1173 (964 × 969); CS 562 (964 × 975, endorsement); CS 1169, 1171–2 (965) Bu XXI, CS 1176, 1189–91 (966); CS 1197, 1199–200 (967); CS 1201 (967 × 972); R XLV, CS 1213, 1216–17, 1220–2, 1224–7 (968); CS 1302 (968 × 970); CS 1145 (968 × 972); CS 1229–30, 1234 (969); CS 1257, 1260, 1266, 1268–9 (970); CS 1270 (971); Bu XXII, CS 1282, 1286 (972); CS 1309 (972 × 973); CS 1307 (973 × 974); CS 1303–5 (974); CS 1312–13, 1316 (975); K 621–2 (979); K 626 (980). See also, KBL p. 23.

Osulf
XII–XV, XVII, XIX–XXI, XXIII

Bishop of Ramsbury 950 × 970.

He witnesses many charters, but very little is known of him. According to Chron E p. 77, he held the property of Evesham Abbey for a while. Fl Wig records that he was buried at Wilton.

Oswald
XXI–XXV

Monk of Fleury, bishop of Worcester 961 × 992, archbishop of York 972 × 28 Feb. 992.

A relative of Archbishops Oda (q.v.) and Oscytel (q.v.), he was one of the great leaders of the Benedictine reform in England. There is much information about him in the Ramsey Chronicle, and Brihtferth, a monk of Ramsey, wrote his life early in the eleventh century (HCY I, pp. 399–475; a new edition is badly needed). Modern biographical accounts appear in Robinson pp. 123–42, E. S. Duckett, St Dunstan, 1955, pp. 137–59, and J. Armitage Robinson, St Oswald and the Church of Worcester, Oxford, 1919.

Oswig xxxvii
Abbot of Thorney 1017–48 × 1049.

Apart from his single appearance witnessing Bu xxxviii, the only other reference is in ASC C, where his death is recorded, and his abbey identified. The dates of his predecessor Athelstan have not been established. See also KBL p. 74.

Robert of Jumièges xxxvii
Bishop of London Aug. 1044 × 1051, archbishop of Canterbury 1051 × 14 Sept. 1052.

He seems to have been one of Edward the Confessor's most unpopular Normans. For his biography, see H pp. 570–1, Barlow EC *passim*.

Scegth, owner of Palterton, Derbyshire 1004 xxviiib
Nothing more is known of him.

Sigeferth xxvii, xxviiia
Bishop of Lindsey. Witnesses 996 × 1004.

The see of Lindsey is poorly represented in the charters after the Scandinavian settlement, and it is not possible to establish the succession fully. Probably the tenth-century bishops were regarded as *chorepiscopi* or shire-bishops within the diocese of Dorchester. There is a long gap between Leofwine (q.v.), who last witnessed in 965, and Sigeferth, who first witnessed Bu xxvii in 996. Sigeferth's see is established as Lindsey in K 698 (997) and in K 706 (1001). He witnessed also K 707 (1002, but with a doubtful list), and Bu xxviiia (1004). Sigeferth appears to have been the last bishop of Lindsey; subsequently his see was merged with Dorchester.

Sigeferth, thegn xxxi
Witnesses 1005 × 1013, murdered 1015.

He was the son of Earngrim, and brother of Morcar (q.v.), with whom he was murdered by Eadric Streona in 1015. Sigeferth's estates, some of which were located in the eastern Danelaw, were then confiscated (ECEE pp. 200–1). His importance is illustrated by his high position among the thegns witnessing Æthelred's charters: K 714 (1005); Bu xxxi (1009); K 719 (1009); Thorney x (1013); K 1310 (1015).

Sigegar xxiv, xxvii, xxxiv
Monk of Winchester, abbot of Glastonbury c. 974 × 975–9, bishop of Wells 28 June 975–9 × 28 June 996–7.

One cannot establish his dates precisely. His predecessor Ælfstan (q.v.) was appointed from Glastonbury to Ramsbury in 970, and as Sigegar does not witness surviving charters until 974, it is possible that an unidentified abbot filled the gap. There is a similar lacuna in the succession at Wells, for which we have no record between the death of Cyneweard (q.v.) on 28 June 975 and Sigegar's first appearance in a charter of 979. He last witnessed in 996, and he died on 28 June either that year or the next (AD pp. 85, 87, 93, 101). His successor Ælfwine first witnessed as bishop of Wells in 997 (K 698). King Edgar is said to have granted land *at Hamme* to Sigegar while he was still an abbot, but this gift if genuine must be dated 970 × 975, and not 965 as is recorded (ECW no. 490). King Æthelred II is also said to have granted land to Sigegar during his abbacy (ECWM no. 133); if so, the gift was made soon after the king's accession. Sigegar witnessed as abbot CS 1303 (974); CS 1312, 1315 (975). He witnessed as bishop K 621 (979); K 624 (980); K 639, 1280 (983); Bu xxiv (984); K 650, 1283 (985); K 657–8 (987); K 663, 665 (988); K 673 (990); K 684, R lxiii (993); K 687, Duignan (994); K 688–91, Muchelney 4 (995); Bu xxvii (996). Sigegar entered into confraternity with the Old and New Minsters at Winchester. SBW pp. 48–9; KBL p. 50.

Sigehelm   IV
    Bishop of Sherborne. Witnesses 925 × 932.
His last recorded predecessor was Æthelbald (episcopal lists, and Fl Wig *s.a.* 918). Sigehelm witnessed the following charters: CS 641 (4 Sept. 925); CS 658–9 (926); CS 663–4 (928); CS 665–6 (929); CS 669 (930); CS 674, 677 (931); CS 689 (932); CS 691–2 (24 Dec. 932). His successor Alfred (q.v.) first witnessed CS 702 dated 28 May 934. William of Malmesbury's story that Sigehelm went to India arises from confusion with the ASC entry for 883; see D. Kirby, 'Notes on the Saxon Bishops of Sherborne', *Proc. Dorset Nat. Hist. and Arch. Soc.*, 87 (1966), p. 3.

Sigered, *see* Sired.

Sired, thegn   XXVII
    Witnesses 995 × 1005.
He witnesses as Sired or Sigered the following charters, fairly low among the thegns: K 688 (995); Bu xxvii (996); K 700 (998); K 706 (1001); K 707, 715, EHD i, p. 541 (1002); K 714, 1301 (1005). His name always follows that of a thegn called Siweard (q.v.), and he

is to be identified with the Sired of two undated OE Kentish transactions witnessed by *Siweard and Sired his broðor* (R LXII, LXIX). This relationship is also mentioned in his subscription to the OE text of K 715. His brother Siweard first appears in the charters in 989 (EHD I, 533), and is called *Sigeward on Cent* in R LXIII. Sired received 2 cassatæ at Sibertswold, Kent, from King Æthelred in 990 (K 1285). For a Kentish thegn of the same name, appearing in charters 1016 × 1023, see R p. 372.

Siward 'Digera' XXXVII

Earl of Northumbria and Huntingdon 1033 × 1055.

He married the daughter of Earl Ealdred of Northumbria; Earl Waltheof was their son, see H p. 572; Barlow EC *passim*. For a list of charters witnessed by Siward, see Oleson p. 130.

Siweard, thegn XXVII

Witnesses 989 × 1005.

This Kentish thegn was the brother of Sired (q.v.). He witnessed all the surviving charters witnessed by his brother, and the following in addition: EHD I, p. 533 (989); OS Facs III, 35 (996); LE pp. 129–30 (1004). His subscription to the OE text of K 715 is remarkable: + *Ic Siward cinges þegen æt ræde and æt rúnan ðisre spræce trywe gewitnys*. Whoever composed this list had access to contemporary information; the phrase quoted shows that Siweard held some special position of trust in the king's council; perhaps he was the king's *scriptor* or *scrinarius*, see p. 189.

Swaue, thegn XXXI

Witnesses 1009.

The name is Scandinavian. I have found no other references to him.

Stigand XXXVII

Royal priest at *Assandun* 1020; bishop of Elmham 3 April 1043 × late November 1043, and 1044 × 1047; bishop of Winchester 1047 × 1070; archbishop of Canterbury 1052 × 11 April 1070 (deposed); died 22 February 1072.

Barlow pp. 77–81; Barlow, *EC passim*; H pp. 572–3; Hart, *History Studies* I, 1968, pp. 10–11. For his charters, see Oleson pp. 130–1, to which should be added K 1324 (1023 × 1032); EHR 1918 p. 344 (1028 or later); K 1318 (1033); K 1322 (1035); Bu XXXVII (1048); OS Facs II, Exeter XIV (1059); Westminster Abbey Muniments 11, fo. 204^{rv} (1060), and references in the OE texts edited in H, R, and W.

Styr, thegn   xxviiia, xxxi
  Witnesses 988 × 1009.
  Styr, Ulf's son, witnessed a charter of 989 (EHD i, p. 533), in
addition to Bu xxviiia (1004), and xxxi (1009). He was a benefactor
to Durham in 988; his daughter Sige became the wife of Earl Uhtred
(q.v.) (SD i, pp. 83, 216).

Theodred   ii, iv, viii, x, xi
  Bishop of London 909–26 × 951–3.
  Wulfsige, bishop of London, last witnessed in 909 (CS 620, 627,
629), and was succeeded by Æthelweard and Ealhstan, of whom no
chronological details survive. It is improbable that Theodred was
appointed to London long before his first appearance as witness to
CS 658–9 in 926; before that date there is an unfortunate hiatus in
the charter evidence. From 940 onwards Theodred was second in
precedence only to the archbishops; Winchester was regarded as a
junior see to London at this period. It is also apparent that Theodred
held London jointly with the see of Elmham (East Anglia); indeed
it is possible that his appointment to Elmham antedated that to
London (ECEss, 1st edn., ii, pp. 33–4). Upon Theodred's death,
Elmham descended to Æthulf (q.v.), and London was separated from
it and given to Wulfstan I, becoming from that time onwards a less
important see than Winchester, as shown by the order of attestation
of the bishops in royal diplomas. In 942 King Edmund granted
Theodred as estate at Southery in Norfolk, which was used for the
endowment of his East Anglian see (CS 774). Theodred's will,
which must be dated 942 × 953, shows him in personal possession of
estates in Suffolk which he passed on to members of his family; it
shows too that he may have been of Teutonic extraction, and had
travelled in Italy (W 1). Theodred had a personal interest in the small
community that served the church at Bury in which rested the remains
of the martyred King Edmund of East Anglia. He punished some
thieves captured there, an act of which he repented for the rest of his
life (William of Malmesbury, *Gesta Pontificum*, p. 144; *Memorials of
St Edmund* i, pp. 20–1). He willed a number of estates to Bury, and
still more descended to the church there after Theodred had willed
them to members of his family. Probably as part of his penance,
Theodred was instrumental in persuading King Athelstan to raise
from twelve to fifteen the minimum age for punishing thieving by
death (VI Athelstan, 12.1). For charters witnessed by Theodred see
O'D ii, p. 98.

Theodulf, thegn 1012   XXXV

He received *Burhtune* from King Æthelred II in 1012. This OE name is not very common. I have not found it recorded elsewhere at this period.

Thurbrand, thegn   XXXI

Witnesses 1009.

As with many other signatories to Bu XXXII, the name is Scandinavian. It is perhaps permissible to identify him with the Thurbrand who gave a horse to the aetheling Athelstan, eldest son of King Æthelred II (W XX), since in Athelstan's will his name occurs in close association with that of Morcar, who is no doubt the same Morcar as the recipient of Bu XXXI (q.v.). It could well be that he was the Thurbrand the Hold who killed Earl Uhtred (q.v.) in 1016. Thurbrand's name does not appear elsewhere among the thegns witnessing King Æthelred's charters.

Thurferth, thegn   XXXI

Witnesses 1009.

The name is Scandinavian, and appears also among the thegns witnessing K 714 (1005). This man is probably to be distinguished from the Thurferth of Warmington, Northants., who appeared as a surety for estates bought for Peterborough Abbey (R pp. 78, 80, 82), who is alleged to have stolen estates from Ely Abbey in the time of Edward the Martyr (LE pp. 114–15), and who witnessed CS 1266, 1269 (970); CS 1270 (971); K 624 (980).

Tofig, *comes* 1048   XXXVII

He was the recipient of two *territoria* at *Berghe* from King Edward in 1048 (Bu XXXVII). On p. 251 it is suggested that he is to be identified with Tofig the Proud, the powerful thegn who was a confidant of King Cnut, and who founded Waltham Abbey. The chief difficulty in sustaining this, is that the tract describing his foundation states that he died soon after his marriage, which we know to have occurred in 1042 (ASC, *s.a.*). Moreover, he must have been at least 60 at the time of his marriage, for he was the grandfather of Esgar the Staller, one of the principal royal officials of King Edward the Confessor. Against this, no other Tofig is known at this period who could have borne the title *comes*, implying very high rank, usually (but not exclusively) reserved for earls. For Tofig the Proud, see R p. 400; Freeman, NC I, Appendix XXX.

Tostig, thegn XXXVII
 Witnesses 1048.
 Presumably he was the Tostig, *nobilis*, who witnessed OS Facs II, Exeter 12 in 1044. For other charters witnessed by thegns of this name, see Oleson p. 132.

Ufegeat, thegn 1004 XXVIIIb
 He was the son of Ealdorman Ælfhelm of Deira (q.v.), and the recipient of *Norðtune* by the will of his uncle Wulfric Spot (q.v.). In 1006 he was blinded, together with his brother Wulfheah (q.v.), on King Æthelred's orders. He does not appear in the witness lists of King Æthelred's charters, and nothing more is known of him.

Uhtred Cild, *pedisequus* 955 XIII
 He received Chesterfield in Derbyshire from King Eadred in 955 (Bu XIII). I have been unable to trace him elsewhere in the charters, but would suggest that he was the son of the Ealdorman Uhtred who is discussed below.

Uhtred IV, IX
 Ealdorman of N.W. Mercia 930 × c. 949.
 The *dux* Uhtred who was the recipient of Bakewell in Derbyshire in 949 (Bu IX) is to be identified with the *dux* of that name who witnessed CS 814 (946), the *eorl* Uhtred who witnessed CS 883 (949), and the Uhtred who witnessed CS 882 (also dated 949) without a title, but in a list that includes other untitled earls and ealdormen. He may have been the person of that name who received estates at Hope and Aston in Derbyshire in 926, while still a thegn (Bu IV), and it seems safe to identify him with the *dux* Uhtred who witnessed regularly during the period 930 × 934, and was probably the ealdorman of N.W. Mercia. A second *dux* Uhtred, who witnessed 931 × 944, should probably be assigned to Essex. See also under Uhtred Cild, above.

Uhtred XXXI
 Earl of Northumbria c. 1006 × 1016.
 Uhtred was the son of Waltheof I, earl of Northumbria north of the Tyne, and a member of the OE house of Bamburgh. He succeeded to his father's earldom towards the end of the tenth century, possibly in 995, and in 1006 he obtained the earldom of all Northumbria. He married three times; first Ecgfrida, the daughter of Bishop Ealdhun of Durham (q.v.), then Sige the daughter of the Yorkshire thegn Styr,

Ulf's son. These two marriages ended in divorce. He then married a daughter of King Æthelred II. Uhtred submitted to Swegn Forkbeard in 1013. He joined Edmund Ironside in 1016, but then submitted to King Cnut. He was murdered soon afterwards by Thurbrand the Hold. See Whitelock in *Clemoes* pp. 81–2. Uhtred witnessed the following charters: Bu xxxi, K 1306 (1009); K 719 (1012); K 1309 (1014); K 1310 (1015).

Ulf, thegn 1009 XXXI

Bu xxxi is the only surviving charter he witnessed.

Ulfketel, thegn 949 VIII

He received Sutton-on-the-Hill, Derbyshire, in 949 (Bu VIII). His name does not occur elsewhere at this period.

Ulfketel 'Snilling' of East Anglia XXVIIIa, XXXI

Witnesses 1002 × 1016.

Apart from the charters and the record of his death in ASC and in the Latin chroniclers, Ulfketel occurs only in the sagas, where he is praised for his military prowess, and his marriage is recorded to Wulfhild, the daughter of King Æthelred II. The Danes called East Anglia 'Ulfketelsland', and there is no doubt that he held effective power there, although for some reason unknown he is not given the rank of ealdorman in the charters (on this, see p. 286). He ranked first of the thegns witnessing charters from 1013 onwards. He witnessed the following: K 1297, Crispin p. 168 (1002); Bu xxviiia, LE pp. 129–30 (1004); K 1301, 672, 714 (1005); K 1303–4 (1007); K 1305 (1008); Bu xxxi (1009); K 719 (1012); K 1308 (1013); K 1309 (1014); K 723 (1016). He was killed at the battle of *Assandun*.

Ulfketel, thegn 1009 XXXI

A second Ulfketel witnessed Bu xxxi. Nothing more is known of him.

Wærferth I

Bishop of Worcester 7 June 872 × 915.

The day of his accession is supplied by Fl Wig as Sunday; evidently he was using a kalendar for 873 by mistake. Stubbs, however, assumed that Florence had mistaken the year rather than the day of the week, and assigned Wærferth's consecration to 7 June 873, the date now generally accepted. Bishops were usually, but not invariably, consecrated on Sundays; weekday consecrations included those of Tilbert, Frithubert, and Ealhmund of Hexham, Bregwine, Jaenberht, and Ceolnoth of Canterbury, Duduc of Wells, Ælfwig of London, Swithun of Winchester, Leofric of Crediton, Ceolwulf of Lindsey, and Æthelberht of York. CS 534, moreover, is a perfectly respectable lease issued by Bishop Wærferth in 872. Wærferth witnessed many charters, and issued several leases whose texts have survived; his name occurs also in the will of King Alfred, and in records of various disputes concerning Worcester estates. He was one of the Mercian scholars whose services were secured by King Alfred, and it was at his request that Wærferth translated Gregory's *Dialogues*. For Wærferth's copy of King Alfred's translation of Gregory's *Pastoral Care*, see EHD I, p. 817.

Wilfrith II　　　　　　　　　　　　　　　　　　　　　　　　III
　　Bishop of Worcester 922 × 929.
　　Little is known of him. His dates are supplied by Fl Wig. His predecessor Æthelhun last witnessed in 916 (CS 632). Wilfrith issued a lease in 922 (R XXI) and last witnessed CS 663–4 on 16 April 928. His successor Cenwald (q.v.) first witnessed CS 669, dated 3 April 930.

Winsige, *see* Wynsige.

Wither, thegn　　　　　　　　　　　　　　　　　　　　　　XXXI
　　Witnesses 1005, 1019.
　　Together with a few other thegns with Scandinavian names, he witnessed low down on the list of the foundation charter of Eynsham (K 714). Bu XXXI, the only other surviving charter witnessed by him, was almost certainly drawn up in the Danelaw. The name occurs in DB, but it is relatively uncommon in England; it is cognate with Old Icelandic 'Vidarr'. A thegn called Wither gave a sword to the ætheling Athelstan, whose will is dated 1012 (W XX).

Wulfgar　　　　　　　　　　　　　　　　　　XXVI–XXVIIIa, XXXI
　　Abbot of Abingdon 990 × 18 Sept. 1016.
　　His dates are supplied by ASC, which names his predecessor as Eadwine and his successor Æthelsige. Wulfgar was instrumental in restoring Abingdon's endowment, much of which had been alienated during his predecessor's rule. He witnessed most of the surviving

charters issued by King Æthelred II during his abbacy; usually he gave precedence in the lists only to the abbots of Glastonbury and New Minster. He figures also in R LXVI and in W XVI (2). See further, Chron Abingd I, pp. 357–8. For his obit, see KBL p. 24.

Wulfgar   V, VI, VII
   Bishop of Lichfield 935–41 × 946–9.
   After the disappearance of Ælla (q.v.) from the lists in 935, we have no knowledge of the succession at Lichfield until Wulfgar subscribes in 941 (CS 765); this may be because there was a general reduction in the number of sees represented in the diplomas of the period, but it may also reflect a waning of King Athelstan's influence in northern England in his later years. Subsequently, Wulfgar witnesses CS 771–2 (942), CS 812 (943), and CS 815 (946). His successor Cynesige first witnesses Bu VIII (949). In the continuation to the episcopal list in BM Cotton Vesp., B vi, Wulfgar is called *se gyldene*. According to Fl Wig, Wulfgar had an alternative name Ælfgar, but in fact he invariably witnesses as Wulfgar. The only two appearances of a bishop named Ælfgar in charters of this period are in CS 868 (dated 948) and in CS 769 (941). In both cases this is a spelling error for Æthelgar who was bishop of Crediton.

Wulfgar   XXIV
   Bishop of Ramsbury 981 × 985–6.
   The year of his appointment is recorded in ASC. His predecessor Ælfstan (q.v.) last witnessed K 629 (981). Wulfgar first witnessed K 633 (982), and last witnessed K 648, 1283 (985); his successor Sigeric first witnessed K 655 (986). Nothing is known of Wulfgar's career; he witnessed pretty consistently as last of the bishops the following charters, in addition to those already mentioned: K 636, 639, 1279–80, LH p. 228 (983); K 641, 1281–2, Bu XXIV (984).

Wulfgar   xxviiib
   'Cniht' of Wulfric Spot 1004.
   In Wulfric Spot's will he is the recipient of an estate at Balterley, Staffs., which had been obtained for him by his father. It is unsafe to identify him with other persons named Wulfgar at this period.

Wulfgar   IV
   Ealdorman of ? Central Mercia 926.
   He witnessed CS 658–9 (926). Ealdred, who may have been his successor, first witnessed in 930 (CS 669).

Wulfgar, thegn   XXIII
   Witnesses 958 × 969.

   A Mercian thegn who rose to prominence after Edgar's revolt from the rule of his brother King Eadwig in 957, he first witnesses CS 1040, a charter of the following year issued by Edgar as king of the Mercians. Subsequently he witnesses the following charters, usually about halfway down the lists: CS 1050 (959); CS 1053, 1055 (960); CS 1066–7, 1080, 1319 (961); CS 1093 (962); CS 1165 (965); Bu xxiii (968); CS 1145 (968 × 972); CS 1230 (969). CS 1304 (974) is unreliable. It is necessary to distinguish him carefully from the powerful West Saxon thegn Wulfgar Leofa, the recipient from King Edmund in 943–4 of lands in Wiltshire and Dorset (CS 782, 793), which were added to by King Eadwig in 958 (CS 1026, 1033). Wulfgar Leofa witnesses many charters of King Eadwig from 955 onwards, and appears at the head of the thegns in the witness list, with the honorific title 'custos', in the famous Abingdon charter of Eadwig dated 17 May 959 (CS 1046). It is instructive to compare this witness list with that of CS 1051, issued later in 959 after Eadwig's death, when Edgar had succeeded to the whole Kingdom. Edgar's charter shows that while some of the royal thegns of King Eadwig such as Ælfgar (q.v.) and Eadric (q.v.) retained their position in court, others such as Æthelgeard (q.v.), Ælfnoth (q.v.), and Wulfgar Leofa disappear from the scene, being replaced by thegns such as Eanulf (q.v.) and Wulfgar, who had supported Edgar for the two years during which his power was confined to Mercia and the North.

Wulfgeat, thegn 963   XX
   He was the recipient of Duddeston, Warwicks., and Upper Arley, Worcs., in 963 (Bu xx). His estate at Arley descended to his kinswoman Wulfrun, who used it to endow her foundation of Wolverhampton (W p. 164; ECWM pp. 111–12). Wulfgeat may have been the man of that name who witnessed as last of the thegns two Abingdon charters dated 965 (CS 1169, 1171).

Wulfgeat   XXVIIIa
   Son of Leofeca, thegn, witnesses 986 × 1005.

   He married Ælfgifu, the widow of Ælfgar, a royal reeve (presumably the Ælfgar who witnessed high among the thegns 979 × 990), who had an estate at Moredon, near Swindon, Wilts. (K 1305); Wulfgeat's own estates included Chilton in Berkshire (K 1310). Florence of Worcester says that King Æthelred II 'loved him almost

more than anyone', but that in 1006 his estates and those of his wife
were forfeited for the 'unjust judgements and arrogant deeds which
he had committed'. The forfeiture is also recorded in ASC. From 986
until his disgrace Wulfgeat witnessed almost all the surviving charters
of King Æthelred. His position in the lists of thegns rises gradually
over the years from almost bottom to near the top; in 1005 he
witnessed K 714, the great foundation charter of Eynsham, as second
of 45 thegns. He witnessed the following charters: K 655 (986);
K 657–8 (987); K 665 (988); EHD I, p. 534 (989); K 684 (993);
K 687, Duignan (994); K 688, 691–2, 1289, Muchelney 4 (995); K
696, EHD I, p. 534 (996); K 698 (997); K 700–1, Crawf 8 (998);
K 704 (999); K 1294 (1000); K 705 (1001); K 707, 1295–7, EHD I,
p. 540, Crispin p. 168 (1002); K 710 (1004); K 714, 1301 (1005).
See also W p. 164.

Wulfgeat, thegn 1009   XXXI
    He appears low down on the witness list of Bu XXXI (1009); it is
unsafe to identify him with other thegns of the same name.

Wulfheah, thegn   XXVIIIab
    Witnesses 986 × 1005.
    There can be little doubt that the thegn named Wulfheah who
witnessed in the period 986 × 1005 is to be identified with the son of
Ealdorman Ælfhelm of southern Northumbria (q.v.), who received
by the will of Wulfric Spot (q.v.) a share of the lands lying between
the rivers Ribble and Mersey, and estates at Barlaston and Marchington
in Staffordshire and Alvaston in Derbyshire. In 1006, soon after his
father had been killed by Eadric Streona (q.v.), Wulfheah was
blinded, together with his brother Ufegeat (q.v.), on the orders of
King Æthelred (ASC E, Fl Wig). Wulfheah witnessed the following
charters (from 995 onwards he was usually third or fourth in
precedence among the thegns): K 654–5 (986); K 548, LH p. 231
(987); K 663–4 (988); EHD I, p. 533 (989); K 673 (990); K 684
(993); K 687; Dugd v, p. 443 (994); K 689–92, 1289 (995); K 696,
1292, EHD I, p. 534 (996); K 698 (997); K 700, Crawf 8 (998);
K 703 (999); K 1294 (1000); K 705–6 (1001); K 707, 1295, 1297,
Crispin p. 168 (1002); K 710 (1004); K 672, 714, 1301 (1005).

Wulfhelm   II, IV
    (I) bishop of Wells 923 × 926, archbishop of Canterbury 926
(after 8 Jan.) × 12 Feb. 942.
    For his biography, see SBW pp. 40–2, 62; O'D I pp. 32–3;
II p. 107.

Wulfhelm   II, V, (VI), VIII, XI, XIII
   (II) bishop of Wells 938 × 956.
   He seems to have been *chorepiscopus* at Hereford during the period
931 × Dec. 934, when he witnessed the following charters: CS 675,
635 (dated 11 Jan. 933), 695–6, 702–3, 1344, 705. The bishop
of Hereford at this time was Tidhelm, who witnessed the last
four of these charters together with Wulfhelm, and also two earlier
charters, CS 677 (dated 931) and CS 689 (dated 932). Tidhelm and
Wulfhelm are entered in episcopal lists as successive bishops of
Hereford, but there cannot be much doubt that they were strictly
contemporaneous. It is uncertain at what date Tidhelm was succeeded
at Hereford by Ælfric (q.v.), who first witnessed in 940 (CS 716–18
are not utilized here, being unreliable). Wulfhelm could not have
succeeded to the bishopric of Wells before 937, for his predecessor
Ælfheah witnessed CS 714 in that year. In addition to those in the
Burton series, Wulfhelm witnessed the following charters of the
period 938 × 956: CS 730 (938); CS 734, 741 (939); CS 748, 753,
756, 758, 798, 801 (940); CS 767, 769–70 (941); CS 812 (942 ×
946); CS 780, 782, 784, 787–9 (943); CS 791, 795–6, 798, 801
(944); CS 803 (945); CS 814–15 (946); CS 880, 882–3 (949); CS
903, 905, R xxx (955); CS 917 (23 Nov. × 31 Dec. 955); CS 969
(956). He appears also in King Eadred's will (CS 912). Probably he
died early in 956, for he witnessed only one of the many charters
surviving for that year. His successor Brihthelm of Wells (q.v.) was
granted land at Stowe, Northants., in 956, while still bishop-elect
(CS 986). See also SBW pp. 42–3.

Wulfhelm   IV
   King's *discthegn*, witnesses 926 × 16 Dec. 934.
   He witnesses the following charters, usually as second to fourth of
the thegns: CS 654 (926); CS 663 (928); CS 665 (929); CS 669,
1343 (930); CS 692 (932); CS 635, 695 (933); CS 703, 1344, 705
(934). He may be the Wulfhelm who received from King Athelstan
an estate at *Hamanstane* in the West Country (ECW no. 644).

Wulfhelm, thegn 951, 957 × 963   XI
   Although he received from King Eadwig estates in Staffordshire
at Marchington in 951 (Bu xi) and at Little Aston and Great Barr
early in 957 (CS 987), Wulfhelm did not witness King Eadwig's
charters. He rose to prominence after Edgar's revolt later in 957,
and subscribed to most of the charters issued by Edgar as king of the
Mercians, usually as second of the thegns witnessing (CS 1023, 1040,

1043–4, 1052). He continued to witness after Edgar had succeeded to the whole of the kingdom in 959, but he had to give precedence to a number of West Saxon thegns, and dropped for a time to about the twelfth place in the witness lists (CS 1047, 1055, 1066–7, 1071, 1073, 1075–6, 1080). Gradually he rose again in seniority, until by about 962 he was one of the most important thegns in the country, witnessing usually in fourth position (CS 1082–3, 1085, 1095–6, 1101, 1116, 1120, 1123–5), but occasionally as third (CS 1094, 1113), and once in the second place (CS 1119). He ceased to witness in 963. One of Wulfhelm's estates (Marchington) descended to Wulfric Spot, and he may therefore have been one of Wulfric's ancestors.

Wulfmær, thegn 962, 972–3   XIX

Wulfmær, the recipient of Hilmarton and Littlecote in Wiltshire in 962 (Bu XIX), is perhaps identical with the Wulfmær who witnessed in 972 (CS 1282) and who received Berrow in Somerset in 973 (CS 1291).

Wulfmær, thegn   XXVII

Witnesses 984 × 997.

A thegn (or thegns) named Wulfmær witnessed K 654 (986), K 687 (994), K 692 (995), and K 698 (997). Possibly he was the Wulfmær who received a lease of Barton Stacey, Hampshire, in 995 × 997 (R LXX), and who was addressed in a writ of King Æthelred II to the thegns of Hampshire in 984 (H no. 107). A man of this name received estates in Somerset by his mother's will in 984 × 1016 (W XXI).

Wulfric I   XXVIIIa

Abbot of St Augustine's, Canterbury c. 986 × 9 October 1006.

His predecessor Sigeric (q.v.) was promoted to the see of Ramsbury, and first witnessed as bishop in 986. Wulfric was succeeded at St Augustine's by Ælfmær, but since the abbot of Tavistock at this period was also called Ælfmær (q.v.), the date of the succession at St Augustine's is difficult to establish. It is probable, however, that K 643 (1006 × 1009) was witnessed by Ælfmær of St Augustine's. Wulfric witnessed as abbot the following charters: K 684 (993); S 1380 (994); K 698, OS Facs III, 35 (997); K 707, 1295, 1297, OS Facs III, 36 (1002); Bu XXVIIIa (1004); K 714 (1005); K 715 (1006, but a doubtful text). He appears also in two undated transactions, R LXII, LXIX. For his obit, see KBL p. 35.

Wulfric II   XXXVII

Abbot of St Augustine's, Canterbury 26 Dec. 1045 × 18 April
1061.

He witnessed R CI (1045); Bu XXXVII as second of seven abbots
(1048), and K 810 (1061). In 1049 he was sent by Edward the
Confessor to Rheims, to attend a council of Pope Leo IX; he obtained
from the pope permission to rebuild St Augustine's, but changed his
mind subsequently, leaving the abbey as it was. Barlow p. 167 n. 2;
H p. 578; KBL p. 35.

Wulfric   XXIII

Bishop of Dorchester c. 958 × c. 970.

Florence of Worcester appears to have had a list of eighth- and
ninth-century bishops of Leicester, ending with one named Leofwine,
and a later list of the bishops of Dorchester, commencing with one
Ælfnoth; a bishop of this name begins to witness in 975 (CS 1314).
From charter evidence, a number of intermediate names can be
supplied, ending with Oscytel (q.v.), who is known to have held the
bishopric until 955, and probably until 958. It seems probable that
the gap between Oscytel and Ælfnoth should be filled by Wulfric,
who is known to have held a Mercian bishopric, for he witnessed a
charter of King Edgar dated 958 (CS 1040). Probably he is to be
identified with the Bishop Wulfric who was the recipient of Stanton
in Derbyshire in 968 (Bu XXIII). He witnessed the following charters,
in addition to those already mentioned: CS 1073 (961); CS 1119,
1121 (963); CS 1135 (964); CS 1164 (965); CS 1229, 1234 (969);
CS 1257, 1265–6, 1269 (970).

Wulfric 'Cufing', thegn   XII, XIV

Witnesses 940 × 957.

Charters of King Athelstan are witnessed by two thegns named
Wulfric in the period 931 × 934, but from then until 940 no thegns
of this name witness surviving charters. The important man we are
considering here then appears, at first fairly low down on the witness
lists, but usually in third place from 944 onwards. He subscribes
occasionally in the period 949 × 952 as first or second of the thegns,
but he is absent from the lists of the few later charters of King
Eadred that have survived intact. He witnessed 24 out of the 53
surviving diplomas issued by King Eadwig in 956. In the earlier
charters of the year he was consistently in second place among the
thegns, but during that summer there was a big shake-out at court,
and afterwards Wulfric witnessed lower down in the lists. He did

not witness any surviving charters issued in 957 before Edgar's revolt, and he witnessed (as first of the thegns) only one charter later in the year, after Edgar had left King Eadwig's court. He did not witness at all in 958 or 959, and it is evident that once Edgar had succeeded to the West Saxon crown, Wulfric 'Cufing' was deprived of his estates. In 960 they were restored to him (CS 1055), but he may have died soon afterwards, for he does not appear to have witnessed any more diplomas. Wulfric was one of the most important thegns of the period, with estates amounting to perhaps 200 hides in Berkshire, Hampshire, and Sussex. His nickname is preserved in the will of Bishop Ælfsige I of Winchester, who gave him Tichbourne in Hampshire (W IV). In royal charters he appears as 'minister' or 'minister and miles'; in CS 877 King Eadred called him 'mihi intimo præcordialis affectu amoris fideli', and his 'carus', and in CS 926 he is referred to as 'princeps'. Wulfric Cufing's charters were laid up at Abingdon; the texts of most of them have been preserved, and they show that he received from successive kings many Berkshire properties, including 20 hides at West Woolston in 944 (CS 796), 5 hides at Denchworth in 947 (CS 833), 10 hides at Stanmore in 948 (CS 866), 25 hides at Chievely in 951 (CS 892), 5 hides at Charlton in 956 (CS 925), and 20 hides at East Woolston, 10 hides at Boxton, and 5 hides at Denchworth (apparently a regrant), all in 958 (CS 902, 1022, 1034). In 949 he exchanged land in Cornwall for 18 hides at Welford (CS 877). In addition, he received 7 hides at Millbrook, Hants., in 956 (CS 926), and he gave land at Patching in Sussex to Christ Church, Canterbury (CS 823; the date 947 ascribed to this transaction may be that of the original charter granting land at Patching to Wulfric; it is doubtful if Christ Church received the estate before 960, see below). Nearly all these estates are mentioned, together with several others, in the deed of restitution granted by King Edgar in 960 (CS 1055). See further, Abingdon pp. 42–3.

Wulfric, thegn
   ? Brother of Dunstan, witnesses 943 × 956.

The thegn here considered does not witness any Burton charters, but it is necessary to differentiate him from other thegns named Wulfric. From 943 onwards he was the second of the two Wulfrics who regularly witnessed royal diplomas as thegns, the first being Wulfric Cufing (q.v.). By 944 this second Wulfric usually appeared fifth or sixth of the thegns witnessing; in 956 he subscribed to 13 out of 53 charters of which the texts survive, but thereafter his name disappeared from the witness lists. Wulfric was given the title 'procer' in CS 751. In 940 he was granted 25 hides at Grittleton and 30 hides at Kingston Langley, Wiltshire, and in 944 a further 20 hides at Nettleton; all three of these large estates lay close to each other (CS 750, 751, 800). In 946 he was granted 5 hides at Didlington in Chalbury, Dorset (CS 818). During the period 939 × 946 he received in addition 10 hides at Yarlington and 5 hides at Turnworth, Dorset (ECW nos. 453, 451, 589). In 947 and 948 he received two estates, each of 5 hides, at Idmiston in Wiltshire (CS 829, 867), and in 949 he was given a group of estates totalling 34 hides in the Cotswolds in Gloucestershire (CS 882); in the same year, a charter was issued renewing his possession of 20 hides at Merton in Surrey (CS 878). During the period 946 × 955 he received also 10 hides at Horton in Dorset, next to Chalbury, and land at *Cumbe*, possibly Culm Davey, Devon (ECW no. 647; S 1745). The lands involved in these transactions total over 174 hides; with the exception of Didlington (which was granted to the thegn Alfred after Wulfric's death, CS 958) and the Cotswold estates, all the transactions are recorded in Glastonbury sources, and it is evident that Wulfric's charters were laid up there. Moreover, most of the estates concerned descended to Glastonbury. Tintinhull was left by Wulfric to Glastonbury for his soul-scot; he gave also Yarlington and Turnworth to the abbey. Horton, Grittleton, and Nettleton descended first to his wife, then to his next heir, Ælfwine, who gave the estates to Glastonbury during Edgar's reign, on becoming a monk there. Idmiston was regranted by King Edgar to the nun Ælfswyth in 970; she left the estate to Glastonbury (CS 1259). In the case of the Cotswold group, these estates had been Evesham property, but in 941 that abbey had been secularized; K 723 dated 1016 shows that at least part of the property that had been granted to Wulfric in 949 descended to one Wulfric Ripa, who was buried at Glastonbury; upon its restoration to Evesham, his body was removed and thrown on unconsecrated ground. In DC p. 129 I have given reasons for identifying the thegn Wulfric, who held all these estates, with Wulfric the brother of Dunstan, first abbot of Glastonbury (q.v.), who was given charge of all the landed property of the abbey during Dunstan's abbacy.

Wulfric, the king's huntsman 956

This thegn is discussed here in order to differentiate him from other thegns named Wulfric. In 956 he received from King Eadwig small estates at Zeal and Donhead on Cranbourne Chase in Wiltshire, and a 5-hide property at Ebbesbourne nearby (CS 968, 962). The grants describe him as a 'procer' and as the king's huntsman, but there is no evidence that he witnessed any of King Eadwig's charters.

Wulfric, thegn   XVIII

? Father of Wulfric Spot witnesses c. 946 × c. 958.

He received 5 hides at Austrey in Warwickshire in 958 (Bu XVIII). In 1004 this estate was in Wulfric Spot's hands (q.v.); it seems likely that the Wulfric we are considering was his father, but possibly he was some other ancestor. He may be identified with the *pedisequus* Wulfric who received 7 hides at Warkton in Northamptonshire in 946 (CS 815); a thegn of the same name witnessed the Danelaw charter CS 883 in 949.

Wulfric Spot, thegn   XXVI, XXVII, XXVIIIab

Witnesses 972 × 1002.

Wulfric was the son of Wulfrun, the Mercian noblewoman whose capture at Tamworth by the Danes in 943 is recorded in ASC D. Half a century later, she founded a minster at Wolverhampton. Probably through his mother, Wulfric Spot was related to the English royal line. His father's name can only be conjectured (see below). His brother Ælfhelm (q.v.) was ealdorman of southern Northumbria; he was also related to Morcar (q.v.), the powerful thegn of the Seven Boroughs. The name Wulfric was a common one, and it is unsafe to assume that thegns named Wulfric witnessing charters of a date earlier than the reign of Æthelred II were in fact identical with Wulfric Spot. An estate at Austrey in Warwickshire was granted to a thegn named Wulfric by King Edgar in 958 (Bu XVIII); the property is known to have been in Wulfric Spot's possession by the time he founded Burton Abbey, but I am of the opinion that the Wulfric who received Austrey in 958 was in fact Wulfric Spot's father. It seems likely that the Wulfric who received Abbot's Bromley in 996, to hold 'as his mother held it' (Bu XXVII) was Wulfric Spot; but it is shown on p. 200 that Bu XXVI, purporting to have been issued to Wulfric in the same year, is in fact a late forgery. Wulfric Spot married Ealhswith; there is no record of her ancestry, nor of any progeny. His nickname derived, presumably, from some facial blemish. Wulfric founded the abbey of Burton-on-Trent in 1004 (K 710). In spite of a late story that he died in a battle near Ipswich in 1010, it is probable that he retired from public life soon after his abbey was founded, for although he witnessed regularly King Æthelred's charters from 980 onwards, and was usually fourth or fifth of the thegns witnessing from 995 onwards, his signatures cease abruptly in 1002 (no charter survives for 1003). See further, Bridgeman 1918, pp. 2–10, 62–8; W pp. 152–3.

Wulfric, thegn 1009 XXXI
This signature appears low down the list of one of the Burton charters (Bu XXXI). He does not occur elsewhere in surviving sources.

Wulfsige XXVII
Abbot of Westminster ? 958 × 993; (III) bishop of Sherborne 993 × 8 Jan. 1002.

If we are to believe various post-Conquest sources which corroborate each other (J. Armitage Robinson, *Flete's History of Westminster Abbey* p. 79; C. H. Talbot, 'The Life of Saint Wulsin of Sherborne by Goscelin', *Revue Bénédictine*, LXIX (1959), pp. 75–6; William of Malmesbury, *G. P.* p. 178), Wulfsige was appointed first abbot of the newly refounded monastery of Westminster in 958, by Dunstan (while bishop of London), on the instruction of King Edgar (while king of the Mercians). At that time, the house was said to have been merely a *cenobiolum* for twelve monks, which would explain why Wulfsige does not appear in the witness lists of Edgar's charters. Nevertheless, Westminster should probably be regarded as King Edgar's first monastic foundation, and Wulfsige as his first appointed abbot. See further the discussion by P. M. Korhammer in *ASE* II, pp. 184–5. The abbey's chronology cannot be illustrated satisfactorily from early sources, but it was certainly in existence by 989 (ECEE p. 31), and the earliest surviving witness list in which Wulfsige appears as abbot is dated 19 May 988 × 31 October 989 (EHD I, p. 533; the 'abbot' Wulfsige who witnesses K 664 dated 988, is an error for the thegn of that name). He reappears in 990 (K 713, to be dated before the death of Abbot Eadwine of Abingdon). According to Flete (*op. cit.*, p. 79), Wulfsige retained his office as abbot after his appointment to the see of Sherborne, a statement borne out by K 684, dated 993, which he witnessed both as bishop of Sherborne and as abbot of Westminster. Probably this very important charter was witnessed on the same occasion as Wulfsige's appointment to Sherborne, and the witness list ends with a *second* abbot of Westminster, named Ælfwig, who also witnesses as abbot S 1380 (994), K 698 (997), K 714 (1005), and K 719 (1012). Probably it was this Ælfwig who was consecrated bishop of London at York on 16 February 1014, in opposition to the wishes of King Æthelred II, who was in exile at the time (ASC D, *s.a.*). Upon Æthelred's return in the following year, the former bishop was reinstated (see under

Ælfhun, bishop of London). The Ælfwig who witnessed as bishop of London in 1022 × 1035 is not necessarily the same person. Wulfsige continued to witness as bishop until 1001 (K 706), and his successor in the see, Æthelric (q.v.), witnessed all the surviving charters of the following year. Wulfsige is said to have introduced monks both at Westminster and at Sherborne (Talbot, *op. cit.*, p. 76); he created a library at Sherborne (Stubbs, *Memorials of St Dunstan*, p. cxiii), and Ælfric of Eynsham dictated a pastoral epistle to him. He was recognized as a saint about 1012, and a post-Conquest life survives. See further, Goscelin's *Vita Wlsini* (Talbot, *op. cit.*, pp. 68–85); Barlow pp. 222–3; H p. 579; D. Kirby, 'Notes on the Saxon Bishops of Sherborne', *Proc. Dorset Nat. Hist. and Arch. Soc.*, 87 (1966), pp. 3–4; KBL p. 76.

Wulfsige   VIII, XI–XIII
    (II) bishop of Sherborne 943 × 958.
    There are doubts about the succession at Sherborne at this period. Wulfsige first witnesses as bishop in 943 (CS 783–4, 787–9, 812). His predecessor appears to have been Alfred (q.v.), who held Sherborne in plurality with Selsey between 940 and 943. Wulfsige witnessed regularly from 943 to early in 958 (CS 1032). It is possible that from 953 to 956 he held also the see of Selsey. His successor at Selsey and at Sherborne appears to have been Brihthelm (q.v.).

Wulfsige, thegn   XXIII
    Witnesses 963 × 974–5.
    A thegn named Wulfsige witnessed, low down on the lists, the following charters of King Edgar: CS 1112 (963) CS 1176, 1189 (966); CS 1221–2, 1224–5, Bu XXIII (968); CS 1230 (969); CS 1201 (974–5). Nearly all of these relate to estates in Mercia.

Wulfsige, thegn   XXXI
    Witnesses 1009.
    This Burton charter is the only surviving late diploma of King Æthelred II to be witnessed by a thegn named Wulfsige. It is very probable that he came from the Danelaw.

Wulfsige 'Maur' 942   V–VII, XXVII
    By a series of charters dated 942, this man received a large block of territory on either side of the river in the upper Trent valley (Bu V–VI). He must have been of very considerable importance, but it is hazardous to identify him with the thegn or thegns named Wulfsige who commonly witnessed charters of the period 938 × 946.

Bridgeman (p. 83) has suggested, very plausibly, that the nickname 'Maur' might represent Latin *maurus*, 'a Moor', for the common OE bye-name *seo blaca*, 'the black', meaning swarthy or black-haired (cf. Hrabanus Maurus of Fulda, Alcuin's pupil, archbishop of Mainz 847). It seems very likely that he is to be identified with the Wulfsige *the blaca* who once held Abbot's Bromley in Staffordshire (Bu xxvii). If so, he may have been an ancestor of Wulfrun, the foundress of Wolverhampton's minster, and of her son Wulfric Spot (q.v.). See further, DC p. 130.

Wulfstan   v, vi, viii–x

(1) archbishop of York 931 × 26 Dec. 955.

Wulfstan's antecedents are unknown, but throughout his career he showed a marked readiness to support various Viking ventures against the English crown. His subscriptions to royal diplomas sometimes provide a more accurate chronology for the sequence of events in Yorkshire than one can gather from the annalists for this troublesome period. His predecessor Hrothweard last witnessed CS 669, dated 3 April 930. Wulfstan first witnessed as archbishop CS 675 dated 20 June 931, and thereafter he witnessed King Athelstan's charters regularly until CS 716–18 dated 21 December 934. Later charters of King Athelstan have greatly abbreviated witness lists, in which the northern sees, including York, are unrepresented. It seems likely that from 935 onwards, Athelstan's control of the northern Danelaw was more precarious than contemporary annalists (and some modern historians) would make it appear. After his death in 939, York was occupied by Olaf Guthfrithson, king of Dublin. Archbishop Wulfstan became Olaf's supporter, travelling with him the following year on an expedition into the midlands. Olaf and Wulfstan were besieged by King Edmund at Leicester, but Wulfstan, together with Archbishop Wulfhelm of Canterbury, arranged a treaty by which Edmund surrendered to Olaf the territory of the Five Boroughs (SD ii, p. 94; Stenton pp. 352–3). In the following year Olaf died, and the kingdom of York passed into the hands of his cousin, Olaf Sihtricson. In 942 King Edmund redeemed the Five Boroughs, and for a brief period Wulfstan witnessed his charters (CS 771–2, 775, 777, 779). Rægnald, Olaf Guthfrithson's brother, was then made king of York, and no surviving charter of Edmund issued in 943 is witnessed by Wulfstan. In the summer of 944, however, Edmund regained possession of York, and from then onwards Wulfstan's signature appears regularly in Edmund's diplomas (CS 791–2, 794–5, 798 etc.). After Edmund's death, his brother Eadred secured Wulfstan's allegiance at Tanshelf in 947, but according to the chroniclers Wulfstan was quick to break his oath. This alleged treachery is not reflected immediately in the charters, which Wulfstan continued to witness until late in 949, although Eric Blood-axe had gained temporary control in York a year previously (Wulfstan witnessed all but three of the fifteen charters surviving for the years 948–9; no charters survive for 950). From 951 onwards, however, Wulfstan again ceases to witness, and it seems that he was out of contact with Eadred's court during the whole of the period during which Olaf Sihtricson, having displaced Eric from York, was reigning there for the second time. Wulfstan's subsequent career can be followed from entries in the Mercian Register (preserved in ASC D and in SD ii, pp. 126–7) which originated at York, but his subscriptions to charters show that the Register has an unsatisfactory chronology for the years 951 × 956. The entry for 952, recording Wulfstan's imprisonment by King Eadred at *Iudanbyrig* (probably Castle Gotha, Cornwall), should probably be assigned to 950 or 951; the entry for 954, recording that he was restored to his bishopric, at Dorchester, should be assigned to 953 (he witnessed the reputable CS 900 in that year); and as the chroniclers at that time dated the year from Christmas, the entry in ASC D for 957, recording his death on 16 December (*recte* 26 December) at Oundle in the diocese of Dorchester, should be amended to 956 (as in SD ii, p. 127), because the last surviving charters he witnessed are dated 955, some time after 23 November (CS 917 and CS 924[1]). Of the 52 charters issued by King Eadwig in 956 whose witness lists have survived, not one is witnessed by Wulfstan. The correct year for Wulfstan's death, 955, is recorded in the tract *de archiepiscopis Eboraci*, accessible in SD i, p. 226. An entry in ASC *s.a.* 971 suggests that Oscytel (q.v.), his eventual successor at York, was appointed to have charge of the archbishopric before the death of King Eadred; if so, it is possible that Wulfstan's terminal illness commenced some months before he died.

Wulfstan   XXVI–XXVIIIa, XXIX–XXXVI

Monk, (II) bishop of London 996 × 1002, (I) bishop of Worcester 1002 × 1017, (II) archbishop of York 1002 × 28 May 1023.

The *Liber Eliensis* says that Wulfstan was a monk, but his house is unknown (LE p. 156). He had a brother Ælfwig to whom he leased a

---

1 Taking the Abingdon cartulary texts of CS 924 as being superior to the sixteenth-century transcript at Corpus Christi College, Cambridge, for the date.

Worcester estate (K 1313), a sister who was the mother of Bishop Brihtheah of Worcester and of Æthelric, a monk of Worcester, and another sister who married Wulfric, a Worcestershire landowner (R LXXVI). In spite of these connections, it is probable that Wulfstan came from the eastern Danelaw. If, as Florence of Worcester claims, he became an abbot, then it must have been of a very minor house, for his name does not appear among the abbots witnessing charters of the period, and the succession in all the major abbeys at this time is known. Ælfstan (q.v.), Wulfstan's predecessor at London, last witnessed in 995 (K 688, 691–2, 1289); Wulfstan first witnessed in 996 (K 696, 1291–2, EHD I, p. 534, Bu XXVI), and his accession is recorded in ASC F for that year. It is interesting that although Ælfstan was given precedence in the witness lists over all other bishops, Wulfstan witnessed habitually second to the bishop of Winchester. Ealdulf (q.v.), Wulfstan's predecessor at York and Worcester, witnessed only one charter in 1002 (K 707), and he died on 6 May that year (Fl Wig). A number of charters survive for 1002 in which Wulstan continues to witness as bishop of London, but no one witnesses for York or Worcester (K 715, 1295, 1297, Crispin p. 168; EHD I, pp. 540–1); one of these is dated 11 July (EHD I, pp. 540–1). K 1296 dated 1002 is, however, witnessed by Wulfstan as archbishop, though his successor at London, Ælfhun (q.v.) does not yet witness as bishop. Although Florence of Worcester says that Wulfstan was succeeded at Worcester by Abbot Leofsige of Thorney in 1016, and a lease by Leofsige as bishop survives for that year (K 724), yet Wulfstan issued at least two leases of Worcester estates in 1017 (K 1313; ECWM 338); it is notable also that Wulfstan confirmed Leofsige's lease, and I am inclined to the view that Leofsige was appointed initially as *chorepiscopus*; it seems clear that his appointment had something to do with the accession of King Cnut. Nevertheless Wulfstan stood high in Cnut's favour; his reputation as a law-maker and homilist, established already before Cnut's accession, was enhanced thereafter. He was the author of the law codes V–IX Æthelred, I and II Cnut, and a number of private codes. His early homilies were preached as bishop of London. These and other literary activities have been discussed fully by Dr Bethurum, Professor Whitelock, and Professor Jost (below). Wulfstan died on 28 May 1023, and was buried at Ely, where he was venerated as a saint. See further, Cooper pp. 2–13; D. Whitelock, *Sermo Lupi ad Anglos*, 3rd edn., London, 1963; D. Whitelock, 'Archbishop Wulstan, Homilist and Statesman', in *Essays in Medieval History*, ed. R. W. Southern, Macmillan for R. Hist. Soc., 1968, pp. 42–60.

D. Bethurum, *The Homilies of Wulfstan*, Oxford, 1957; Carl Jost, *Wulfstan studien (Schweizer Anglistische Arbeiten 23).*

Wulfstan of Dalham   XXIII
    Thegn, witnesses 958 × 974.

It is generally assumed that Wulfstan took his title from Dalham in Suffolk, but it could well be that he came in fact from Dalham in Kent. In his early years he acted as a royal reeve, and he seems to have moved into East Anglia in order to become steward to Queen Eadgifu (q.v.), who was of Kentish extraction and retained interests there to the end of her life. As late as 973–4, Wulfstan was employed on royal business in Kent (R LIX). He first appears as a witness in CS 1040, 1044, two charters issued by Edgar in 958 as king of the Mercians. From 961 onwards he witnesses regularly, at first in ninth or tenth place among the thegns, but from 963 onwards as fourth or fifth. Towards the end of his career he was given still higher preference; he was first of the thegns witnessing CS 1198 (967), CS 1257, 1269 (970), and CS 1285 (972). In Bu XXIII, dated 968, he is entitled *discthegn*, and in CS 1301, issued in 974, he is called *prefectus*, a title of honour reserved for only the leading thegns and ealdormen. In East Anglia, Wulfstan was concerned chiefly with the estates that formed part of the early endowment of the monastery of Ely, refounded in 970; at one time or other he had possession of Stonea, Eye, and Swaffham in Cambridgeshire, Barley in Hertfordshire, Brandon, Livermere, and Woodbridge in Suffolk, and Northwold and Pulham in Norfolk, all of which became Ely property (ECEE pp. 219, 223–5, 227–9). He seems to have been intimately associated with the grant of Stapleford in Cambridgeshire to Ely in 954–5 (CS 1346), while the house was still a small minster staffed by canons. He interceded with King Edgar when there was an attempt to purchase the minster, and persuaded him to found a monastery there instead (LE p. 73). In 962 he endowed the minster at Bury St Edmunds with Palgrave in Suffolk (CS 1084). He left land at Hemingford and Wennington in Huntingdonshire by will to Ely (ECEE pp. 26–7). The *Liber Eliensis* describes him as being *a secretis regis*; elsewhere the *Liber* gives him the titles of *prepositus* and *sequipedus*. He held a court at Ely before the abbey's foundation. In 964 he was sent by King Edgar to Winchester to order the clerics there to vacate their prebends so that Bishop Æthelwold could replace them by monks (Chron Abingd II, p. 260; EHD I, p. 833).

Wulfstan Uccea, thegn
Witnesses 957 × 972.

This thegn does not witness any Burton charters, but he is considered here in order to differentiate him from Wulfstan of Dalham (q.v.). Wulfstan Uccea, the son of Ælfsige and the father of Wulfgar, owned estates at Ailsworth and Kettering in Northamptonshire, at Haddon, Yaxley, and Conington in Huntingdonshire, and at Godstone in Surrey (ECEE pp. 162–3). Probably he is to be identified with the second of the two thegns named Wulfstan who witnessed CS 1135 (964), CS 1200 (967), CS 1229, 1234 (969), CS 1257, 1269 (970), and CS 1282 (972).

Wulfstan, thegn   XXVIIIa, XXXI
Witnesses 1002 × 1009.

Two thegns named Wulfstan witnessed Bu xxxi and EHD i, p. 540. They are identified in the OE text of K 715 (1002) as *ealda* and *geonga*, and they appear in R LXII as Wulfstan of Saltwood (Kent), and 'the other' Wulfstan. The Wulfstan who witnessed Bu xxviiia was possibly the senior of the two.

Wulfweard, thegn 996   XXVII
He witnessed K 696 and Bu xxvii, both dated 996. Nothing more is known of him.

Wynsige   III, IV
Bishop of Dorchester 925 × 934–43.

He witnsesed CS 641–2 (925); CS 658–9 (926); CS 665–6 (929); CS 674–5, 677 (931); CS 682 (932); CS 702, 705, 716–18 (934; O'D i, pp. 36, 38, would assign the date 937 to CS 716). His successor was probably Æthelwold (q.v.), who began to witness in 943 (CS 812).

Wynsige   XXIII
Bishop of Lichfield 964 × 975.

His predecessor Cynesige (q.v.) last witnessed CS 1112, dated 963. Wynsige witnessed CS 1134 (964); CS 1164 (965); CS 1176, 1189–1190 (966); CS 1199–1200, 1209 (967); CS 1211, 1213, 1220–7, R XLV, Bu XXIII (968); CS 1229, 1234 (969); CS 1257, 1265–6, 1269 (970); CS 1282 (972); CS 1292 (973); CS 1304 (974); CS 1312 (975). His successor Ælfheah first witnessed CS 1314 (975). Nothing more is known of Wynsige.

Wynsige, monk 1007   XXIX
He is said to have composed and written Bu xxix. Presumably he was from Burton. Nothing more is known of him.

ADDENDA AND CORRIGENDA

THE EARLY CHARTERS OF DEVON AND CORNWALL
(Second edition, 1963)

For detailed examination of Nos. 2, 9, 17, 19, 37, 44, and 51, see H. P. R. Finberg, *West-Country Historical Studies*, Newton Abbot 1969, pp. 11–69.

p. 11, No. 26. The bounds are those of Uplyme. They are fully elucidated by Mr H. A. Fox, DA CII, 1970, pp. 35–47.

p. 8, No. 2. *For* Crawf I–III *read* Crawf I.

p. 12, No. 33. *Add to note*: DA CIII, 1971, pp. 19–24.

p. 12, No. 36. *For* Clyst St George *read* Clyst St Mary. *Add, after* PND p. 585: DA CIV, 1972, pp. 141–87.

p. 14. *After* No. 49 *add*: 49^A N.D. (c. 1010). Bounds of Creedyland. Crawf II. *West-Country Historical Studies*, pp. 44–61.

THE EARLY CHARTERS OF THE WEST MIDLANDS
(Second edition, 1972)

p. 22, l. 20. This hypothesis has been further developed by Dr C. R. Hart in *Land, Church, and People*, ed. J. Thirsk, Reading, 1970.

pp. 50, 58, 62, Nos. 83, 117, 130. *Add to note*: S. Everett in BGAS LXXX (1961), pp. 175–8.

p. 52, No. 91. *Add note*: The charter is dated 929, in the sixth year of King Athelstan. The reference to St Mary's, Worcester, is an anachronism, for all genuine early charters name the dedication as St Peter's. It was St Oswald who rededicated the cathedral to St Mary: cf. No. 317.

p. 52, No. 93. *Add to note*: Another episcopal witness, Ælfric, became bishop of Hereford in 937. The outside limits of date for the charter are therefore 937 x 939.

p. 54, No. 101. *For* abbot *read* priest.

p. 59, No. 119, and p. 69, No. 162. Saberton is in Beckford, not Dumbleton.

p. 62, No. 133. *For* 979 × 997 *read* 979. In that year Sigegar became bishop of Wells (K 621).

p. 109, No. 274. *For* 951 × 955 *read* N.D. *Before note on bounds add*: The witnesses belong to Edgar's reign. The charter should therefore be graded **.

p. 192. The confluence which forms the thirteenth landmark is taken in the text to be the junction of the Beesmoor Brook and the Isbourne, but is more likely to be the junction of a nameless rivulet with the Beesmoor Brook at 027278. 'Due east' in landmark 14 is then strictly correct.

THE EARLY CHARTERS OF WESSEX

p. 28, No. 5. *Add note*: The diplomatic is identical with that of No. 6, and the bounds with those of No. 77.

p. 30, No. 16. *Add to note*: The original or an early copy of this charter was extant at Winchester in 1643. – WCD, p. 60.

p. 37. *Add, at beginning of second paragraph in note on No. 40*: The pseudo-original of CS 620 is now in the British Museum (Harley Charter 43 C 1).

p. 39, No. 50. *Add note*: Alfred left North Stoneham to his wife, with remainder to the New Minster (see No. 52), which still held the property at Domesday. The charter is preserved in the cartulary of the New Minster, and it looks as if the words 'Familia quoque æt Stanham pastum semper conferre electissimum non pigrescat' were clumsily inserted after the estate and its obligation of feeding the poor had devolved upon the clergy.

p. 41, No. 59. *Add*: The original or an early copy was extant at Winchester in 1643. – WCD p. 64.

p. 44, No. 72. The date should be given as 956 and the charter graded as **. *For* King EADRED *read* King EADWIG. The witness list shows that Eadred's name has been substituted for that of his successor, and the note should be corrected accordingly.

p. 47, No. 86. *For* 959 *read* 957.

p. 49, No. 93. *Add note*: T. A. M. Bishop, *English Caroline Minuscule*, Oxford, 1971, gives a facsimile of this charter (pl. IX; comment, p. 9).

p. 50, No. 100. On the scribe, see Bishop, *English Caroline Minuscule*, p. xxi, n. 1.

p. 50, No. 101. Correct the date to 970.

p. 59, Nos. 139 and 140. *For* (990 × 992) *read* (990).

p. 61, No. 149. *The last paragraph of the note should read*: The witness-list includes three bishops, Brihtric, Saxulf, and Egwine. Ælfstan, bishop of Wells, signs here under that name; in some other charters he uses his alternative name Lyfing.

p. 64, No. 164. F. Barlow (*Edward the Confessor*, 1970, p. 331) considers this text to be a fabrication. He points out that the formula in the grant to the bishop (No. 163) is perfectly regular, but has been adapted here in a most irregular manner to fit an earl.

p. 69, No. 182. *For* ** *read* ***. The formulas are those of Athelstan's charters.

p. 87, No. 260. *Add*: See WAM LIX, 1964, pp. 110–15.

p. 112, No. 368. Exception has been taken to this charter on the ground that Aldhelm, the only episcopal witness, did not become bishop of Sherborne until the following year, 705, after the death of Hædde, bishop of Winchester. But CS 115 shows that the division of the West Saxon diocese had been expected for some time. It was postponed out of consideration, probably, for Hædde, who had been bishop for at least twenty-seven years. Nothing rules out the supposition that in his old age he was provided with an assistant bishop to administer the western part of his enormous diocese, and that Aldhelm acted in that capacity until Hædde's death removed the last obstacle to the formal constitution of a new see at Sherborne.

p. 123. Add between Nos. 413 and 414:

413A 865 × 871.   King ETHELRED to St Peter's, Bath. South
    Stoke. Somerset Record Soc., VII, 1893, p. 152, No. 808.
        Lost.

p. 128, No. 423, note. *For* Ethered *read* Æthelfrith, *and for* p. 43 *read* pp. 43, 371.

p. 129, No. 433. *For* 929 *read* 939.

p. 129. *Add* 433A. 924 × 939.   King ATHELSTAN to St Peter's,
    Bath. Lyncombe. Somerset Record Soc., VII (1893), p. 152,
    No. 808.   *Lost.*

p. 130, No. 435. *For* 934–939 *read* 937 × 939.

p. 133, No. 445. *The note should read*: The grantee, known as Athelstan 'Half-King', became ealdorman of East Anglia.

p. 141, No. 486. Substitute the following for the note:

Mrs Barbara Robertson, of Combe Hay Manor, has collected thirteen variants of the place-name, ranging in date from 961 to 1841. The latest forms, Yeosstes and Ewesteads, identify Evesty with two fields in Wellow having a combined area of 57 acres. Thanks to this helpful information the charter boundary can be interpreted from O.S. Sheet ST 75 as follows.

11. First from Deep Ford.

A crossing of the Cam Brook at 729596.

12. along the Cam Brook to Pyttel's Ford.

This ford was at 735596. *Pyttel* is the Old English word for a mouse-hawk, but here, as in Pittleworth (Hants) and Pickledean (Wilts), it is probably used as a man's nickname.

13. From Pyttel's Ford up along the husbandmen's boundary.
Still marked by a line of eight boundary stones.

14. to the stump of an elder-tree.
Perhaps marking the spot between the sixth and seventh stones where the parish boundary turns slightly westward.

15. From the elder-stump to the old pit.
Possibly the old quarry at 730591.

16. From the pit along the *wyrtrum* to Ramley Way.
Wyrtrum seems to mean a row of trees or stumps left standing, when woodland is being cleared, to mark a boundary. It must have been in part of what is now Underdown Wood, and Ramley Way is evidently the lane between Twinhoe Green and Upper Hayes (749591).

17. Along the way to the Bath highway.
The highway, still called Bath Hill, leads from Wellow to Combe Hay. The charter boundary runs up it from 734589.

18. Along the highway again to Deep Ford.
Back to the starting-point.

p. 142, No. 491. *For* 3½ *read* 7½. Cf. No. 487.

p. 148. *Add*: 522ᴬ 979 × 1016. King ETHELRED to St Peter's, Bath. *Grenta* in North Stoke. Somerset Rec. Soc., VII (1893), p. 152, No. 808. *Lost.*

p. 152, No. 542. *For* Hazel Farm in Compton Martin *read* Hazel Farm near Upper Littleton in Dundry (*ex inf.* Mrs F. Neale).

p. 168, No. 585. *Add to note*: Two of the ministri, Odda and Wullaf, are wrongly given as *duces*.

p. 170, No. 591. *Add to note*: Some of the landmarks recur in the bounds of Sturminster Newton, CS 1214. *Hamtune* may therefore be Hammoon. – *Namn och Bygd*, XXIII (1935), pp. 149–53.

p. 171. *Delete* No. 597. Cf. No. 466.

p. 182, No. 635. The place is probably Horton (Dorset), which adjoins Chalbury, the subject of a grant by Eadred to the same Wulfric (No. 592).

p. 182, No. 646. Mr S. C. Morland suggests Littleton Drew, Wilts., a Glastonbury estate in 1066.

p. 183, No. 654. *Add note*: This charter relates to Winterbourne Bassett: see *The Early Charters of Eastern England*, p. 253.

THE EARLY CHARTERS OF EASTERN ENGLAND

p. 25, No. 12. The date should be revised to N.D. (971 × 975).

p. 25, No. 13. The date should be revised to N.D. (971 × 984).

p. 27, No. 17. *For* Hathacnut, *read* Harthacnut.

p. 27, No. 19. The date should be revised to N.D. (979 × 984).

p. 30, No. 22. line 6. *For* Æthelwine, *read* Æthelwold.

p. 43, No. 56. lines 34 and 40. *For* West Wickham, *read* Witcham.

p. 46, No. 61. The date should be revised to N.D. (971 × 997).

p. 48, No. 67. *For* Morden *read* Steeple Morden.

p. 49, No. 70. line 12. *For* p. 401 *read* p. 407.

p. 53, No. 48. Professor Whitelock has pointed out that there is evidence both in HE and in CS 312 for an early division of East Anglia into two dioceses.

p. 54, No. 74. This charter should be regraded ***. It appears to be a late forgery, utilizing an authentic chancery text for its exemplar. The boundary clause is undoubtedly pre-Conquest, but may not antedate the foundation of Bury St Edmunds Abbey in 1021.

p. 58, No. 75. The recipient was presumably Wulfstan of Dalham.

p. 62, No. 84. The charter should be regraded *, and its date revised to 1006 for 1002. See Ker p. 239.

p. 70, between Nos. (41) and 108. *Insert*:

N.D. (1044 × 1065) †King EDWARD to his bishops, earls, and all his thegns in the shires in which St Edmund has land. Writ declaiming that Abbot Leofstan and the brethren at Edmund's Bury are to have sake and soke over all their men, within borough and without. H 11.

Bishop and Chaplais, 1957, plate I.

p. 70, between Nos. 118A and 119. *Insert*:

N.D. (1 Aug. 1065 × 5 Jan. 1066) †King EDWARD to Bishop Æthelmær and Earl Gyrth and Toli and all his thegns in Suffolk. Writ declaring that the sokes of the eight and a half hundreds are to belong to the abbey of Bury St Edmunds, just as Ælfric, Whitgar's son, administered them on behalf of the king's mother. H 24.

Bishop and Chaplais, 1957, plate II.

p. 70, No. 119. This charter should be regraded †.

p. 81, No. 123. The date should be revised to N.D. (1017 × 12 June 1020).

p. 85, No. 130. *For* Edwin *read* Eadric.

p. 102, No. 153. line 16. *For* No. 73 *read* No. 47.

p. 103, No. 155. line 33. *For* RE pp. 297–8 *read* RE pp. 397–8.

p. 108, No. 161. *For* minster *read* thegn.

p. 112, No. (15). *Insert*: *Castra* (Castor), and *Eilesuurthe* (Ailsworth).

p. 120, lines 2, 13. *For* 658 *read* 659 (cf. Kirby p. 520).

p. 120, line 21. *For* 17 January 675 *read* 27 January 675, the second year of his reign.

p. 126, under 'Authenticity', *add*: see Dr Chaplais' comments in Chaplais, 1968, pp. 330–2.

p. 144, line 18. *For* ESSEX *read* WESSEX.

p. 151, two lines from bottom. *For* triumphatem *read* triumphalem.

p. 156, line 17. *For* eternum *read* euum.

p. 159, line 27. *For* arcuisue *read* arcisue.

p. 159, line 31. *For* terminibus *read* terminis.

p. 165, No. VII. Some passages are repeated in the confirmation charter to Muchelney issued by Æthelred II (Muchelney pp. 43–5).

p. 168, line 25 (B text). *For* uterinus *read* uterinis.

p. 169, line 2 (B text). *For* Gearweardo *read* Gerweardo.

p. 169, line 11 (B text). *For* uocitata *read* uocitatur.

p. 169, line 32 (B text). *For* mancusis auri *read* auri mancusis.

p. 169, line 36 (B text). *For* episcopus *read* episcopo.

p. 170, line 2 (B text). *For* nominatur *read* nominantur.

p. 170, line 9 (B text). *For* mutauit *read* mutuauit. This correction should also be made on p. 169, line 34 and on p. 171, line 13.

p. 170, line 29 (B text). *For* supernominatus *read* supranominatus.

p. 177, lines 16, 23. *For* silver pounds *read* pounds of silver.

p. 179, line 25. *For* hides *read* mansae.

p. 180, line 11. *Insert*: For *Teoful*, a personal name, see N. K. Chadwick *et al.*, *Celt and Saxon* (1963), pp. 144–5.

p. 186, last line. *For* mercuri *read* mercari.

p. 190, line 21. *For* ealdun *read* ealden.

p. 190, line 25. *For* æcre *read* æcere.

p. 190, line 26. *For* grenewe *read* greneweye.

p. 195, line 28. *For* born c. 993 *read* born 1005.

p. 198, line 27. *For* infimis *read* infirmis.

p. 207, line 19. *For* ælfgifu *read* ælgifu.

p. 231, line 20. *Delete*: evidently during the reign of Eadwig.

p. 233, line 28. *For* Boughton *read* Boddington.

p. 247, No. 357. *For* Etheredeshythe *see* Sawyer No. 1628.

p. 272. *For* Eadulf *read* Ealdulf.

LIST OF CHARTERS
REFERRED TO IN CHAPTERS V–XI

The references are to numbers in the hand-list. For a list of Burton charters,
see pp. 167–71

Charter	No.	Charter	No.	Charter	No.
Chron Abingd I,		CS 890	85	H 96	97
pp. 434–5	74	911	105	114	95
		943	5	118	136
Chron Rams		946	53	119	118
pp. 74–5	10	951	106	121	134
pp. 76–8	12	954	86		
		978	4	HC p. 40	26
Crawf 8	66	986	6		
		987	87	K 617	63
CS 22, 22a	1	1021	54	650	89
48–9	33	1029, 1348	114	651	64
76	41	1041	121	666	65
122	43	1044, 1349	115	705	68
123	42	1052	122	710	40
127	44	1061	13	711	69
130–1	45	1092	56	724	71
148	153	1100	57	736	19
157	46	1111	58	749	133
239	48	1112, 1352	123	751	73
241	47	1113, 1353	124	771	82
414	99	1129	32	809	28
450	50	1175	107	818	117
453	49	1181	60	824	30
454	34	1211	108	916	23
533–4	51	1232	61	939	22
583	100	1234	62	964	78
642	80	1258, 1280–1	8	971	116
658	101	1283	37	1308	15
703, 1344	119	1310–1	9	1312	67
746	81	1312	88	1316	18
771	82			1356	31
772	83	Dugd VI,		R XXI	52
773	102	p. 1042 No. 1	96	XXXIX	7
792	2	pp. 1443–4	90	XL	11
815	3			XLIII	59
876	103	H 7	137	LIV	125
884	104	45	77	LX	126
885	84	46	76	LXVIII	127–8
		62	25	LXXIX	72

INDEX OF PLACES

References are to page numbers. A small raised figure after the page number, e.g. Abbots Bromley 206², signifies that the place occurs more than once on that page. Lost and unlocated place-names are given in italic. Places are assigned to counties as they existed before the boundary changes of 1974. County abbreviations are those used in the English Place-Name Society's publications. R = river.

INDEX OF PERSONS
AND CORPORATE BODIES

References are to page numbers. A small raised figure after the page number, e.g. Ælfgar earl of Mercia 227³, signifies that the personal name occurs more than once on that page. Figures in bold type refer to biographical notes on witnesses to Burton charters. Abbreviations: a = abbot, abp = archbishop, b = brother, bp = bishop, d = daughter, eald. = ealdorman, f = father, k = king, q = queen, s = son, w = wife.